D1591105

Airline Regulation in America

Airline Regulation in America

Effects and Imperfections

William A. Jordan

The Johns Hopkins Press   Baltimore and London

To
My Parents

Katie & Marion Jordan

They participated
in the first
and many subsequent
take-offs

Contents

List of Tables and Figures

TABLES

FIGURES

Preface

Until joining Western Air Lines' Research Department in early 1960, I thought that all significant commercial air transportation within the United States was regulated by the Civil Aeronautics Board (CAB). It soon became evident, however, that one of the important problems facing Western in its major California markets was the "cutthroat" competition of Pacific Southwest Airlines, a California intrastate carrier who, it turned out, was not subject to CAB regulation. The urgent press of day-to-day research and regulatory activities over the next 4½ years prevented a careful study of this problem, and during that period I failed to appreciate the opportunity the California intrastate carriers provided for analyzing the effects of CAB regulation on the nation's trunk and local service carriers.

In late 1964 I left Western to devote full time to the business economics doctoral program at the University of California, Los Angeles, and there I was soon faced with the problem of selecting a dissertation topic. My original plan was to study the economic effects of the CAB's activities by constructing a theoretical model of a nonregulated airline market structure with which to compare the actual performance of the regulated airlines. However, at some now forgotten point in the development of the proposal for such a topic, it struck me that the existence of the California intrastate carriers provided a ready-made, objective basis with which to measure the effects of CAB regulation. Thus began a 3½ year effort which resulted in the unpublished dissertation, *Economic Effects of Airline Regulation*.[1] This book is a revised and condensed version of that

[1] W. A. Jordan, *Economic Effects of Airline Regulation* (doctoral dissertation, University of California, Los Angeles, 1968). Available from University Micro-

dissertation. The analyses and conclusions of these two works are essentially the same, but the dissertation does contain more information in the appendices and in some tables, so that those desiring greater detail than provided here may find it useful to refer to the dissertation.

It happens that cartel theory underlies this study of airline regulation. In terms of objective analysis it is regrettable that unfavorable connotations are associated with the word "cartel." Despite the existence of many publicly promoted and socially approved cartels it is commonly thought that they are detrimental to the public welfare and, therefore, are undesirable. The reader is urged not to allow this ethical judgment to influence his evaluation of the findings of this book. The purpose here is not to criticize regulation or the lack of regulation; rather, it is to describe and estimate the effects of CAB regulation, and to put them into a theoretical framework which will further understanding of the U.S. airline industry. During the past few years I have often been asked whether CAB regulation was desirable or undesirable. Invariably my answer has been that such an evaluation depends upon one's viewpoint and the relevant circumstances. CAB regulation has benefited many individuals and firms, it has been detrimental to others, and still others have been both benefited and harmed by its effects at different times. It is suggested that the reader postpone adopting normative judgments until he analyzes the impact of airline regulation on his own situation and preferences.

As is the case with most research projects, the amount of work required to complete this study was not apparent at the outset. In particular, there was no indication of the large amounts of data that would have to be discovered from often obscure and remote sources. The task of information gathering was greatly aided by the generous assistance of a number of individuals who provided access to these sources. Some were old friends and former colleagues, some were strangers who became friends, some were passing acquaintances. Regardless of the personal relationship, each one has my sincere gratitude. The following is a list of those who contributed the most, but there were many others who also made significant contributions. California Public Utilities Commission: Mr. Charles J. Astrue; Miss Margaret Bartke; Mr. Sergius M. Boikan; Mr. Eugene Q. Carmody; Mr. Wilson E. Cline; Mr. Mitchell Matsumura; Mr. Eric A. Mohr; Mr. John

films, Ann Arbor, Michigan (Order No. 68-16,547), microfilm $9.35; xerographic enlargement $33.25, 739 pages.

L. Pearson; Mr. Jack Thompson. Former intrastate airline officials/ attorneys: Mr. Robert E. Fraley (Paradise); Mr. Robert P. Hubley (California Central); Mr. Lawrence A. Mudgett (Trans California); Mrs. Charles C. Sherman (California Central). Los Angeles Int'l Airport: Mr. Bert J. Lockwood; Mr. John Federle. Mercer Enterprises: Mr. D. W. Mercer. Oakland Int'l Airport: Mr. Deward D. Hext; Mr. Henry Van Brunt. Pacific Air Lines: Mr. R. E. Costello. Pacific Southwest Airlines: Mr. H. Eugene Swantz. San Francisco Int'l Airport: Mr. Emmett Smith. U.S. Civil Aeronautics Board: Mrs. Phyllis Saltry; Mr. Edward E. Whisman; unknown individuals in the Publications Section. U.S. District Court, Northern District of California: Mr. James P. Welsh. U.S. Federal Aviation Agency: Mr. Albert L. Butler. Western Air Lines: Mrs. Eunice Ruch; Mr. James L. Mitchell; Mr. Carl Anderson; Mr. Rodney Hanks. It is emphasized that none of these individuals is responsible for the analysis derived from the information they provided. In fact, it is likely that some of them will disagree with the conclusions of this book.

Professors Armen A. Alchian, George W. Hilton, and Frank E. Norton read the preliminary drafts of the dissertation and made many useful criticisms and suggestions. I have been greatly influenced by Professor Alchian's contributions to economic theory; Professor Hilton provided essential insights into the effects of regulation in general; and Professor Norton supplied measured criticism and crucial encouragement throughout this project. Also, Dr. Linda J. Kleiger provided a thoughtful sounding board during the early stages of this work and made many suggestions as it progressed.

During this study I was fortunate in having fast and cheerful secretarial assistance from Mrs. Famah Andrew, Mrs. Elizabeth Bilodeau, Mrs. Audrey Forbes, Mrs. Leona Burns, and Mrs. Donna Cyr. Most of the appendices appear as they were typed by Mrs. Cyr, and she helped in the final proofing. The dependable help of these ladies substantially advanced the completion date of this project and made many long hours pass more pleasantly. Mr. Frank Topiasz, of the Ontario Department of Highways, drew the figures in chapter 5.

A Ford Foundation Doctoral Fellowship provided financial aid for the first two years of the project and covered a portion of the expenses incurred in collecting data. The assistance of colleagues at Stanford University and York University also contributed to the completion of this study. Of course, none of these institutions nor the above individuals are responsible for the analyses and conclusions presented in the following pages.

Finally, it is time to express gratitude to my wife, Gretchen, and to Adam and Shawn. Despite their high implicit rates of time preference they sacrificed much companionship and many enjoyable experiences over the past five years. Their understanding was indispensable and is appreciated.

W. A. J.

Toronto, Ontario

Introduction

The Civil Aeronautics Act of 1938 created the Civil Aeronautics Board (CAB) and made the interstate, overseas, and, to a lesser extent, the international common-carrier airlines of the United States subject to the Board's direct economic regulation.[1] Between 1939 and 1965, the carriers holding certificates of public convenience and necessity issued by the CAB increased their overall operating revenues 65-fold, from just under $76 million to almost $5 billion. In physical terms, the 755 million revenue passenger-miles (RPM) carried in 1939 grew 91 times to just under 69 billion RPM by 1965. Even greater growth was achieved in overall revenue ton-miles, which include cargo as well as passenger traffic.[2] Obviously, the growth of the CAB-regulated airlines has been, and continues to be, outstanding.

Even though this expansion occurred while the certificated carriers operated under CAB regulation, it does not necessarily follow that the CAB had any measurable impact on the development of these airlines. After all, many other industries, regulated and nonregulated, enjoyed substantial growth during this same period; even if the CAB did appreciably influence the development of the airlines, the reciting of growth statistics does not indicate whether its influ-

---

[1] 52 Stat. 973. This act became effective on August 22, 1938. The CAB was originally named the Civil Aeronautics Authority; however, its name was changed and certain safety functions assigned to it by Presidential Reorganization Plan No. IV, April 11, 1940. See CAB, *Aeronautical Statutes and Related Material* (Washington, D.C., 1954), pp. v, vi, and 87–94.

[2] CAB, *Handbook of Airline Statistics* (1967 ed.; Washington, D.C., 1968), pp. 36, 47, and 93. (Unless otherwise specified, all references to the *Handbook of Airline Statistics* are to the 1967 edition.)

1

ence was beneficial or detrimental. It is possible that the airline industry could have expanded even more rapidly without CAB regulation.

The extent of CAB influence on the certificated carriers can best be investigated by comparing their development with that of similar airlines not regulated by the CAB.[3] It is possible for one such study to be made of the CAB-regulated interstate airlines because, starting in 1946, a number of airlines operated substantial scheduled service wholly within the state of California and thus beyond CAB jurisdiction. Aside from regulatory aspects, these California intrastate carriers were quite similar to the CAB-regulated interstate airlines, and a comparison of their development with that of the certificated carriers provides a basis for measuring the economic effects of CAB regulation.

Relative Scope of Airline Regulation

From its inception, the CAB has had regulatory power over the certificated carriers in the areas of entry, exit, service, and price. The California intrastate carriers have also been subject to some direct economic regulation, though not by the CAB. Since the airlines first began operations, certain provisions of Article XII of the California State Constitution (pertaining to transportation in general) have given the California Public Utilities Commission (PUC) jurisdiction over the prices charged for all scheduled air service within the state, whether provided by interstate or by intrastate carriers.[4] This was the only regulation applying to the California intrastate carriers before September 17, 1965; however, on that date the provisions of Assembly Bill No. 413 gave the PUC authority over the entry, exit, and service of the intrastate carriers, in addition to its existing power over the prices of all carriers.[5] Because of this increase in the regulation of intrastate carriers, this study is confined to the period from

[3] "The question of the influence of regulation can never be answered by an enumeration of the regulatory policies. . . . Whether the statutes really have an appreciable effect on actual behavior can only be determined by examining the behavior of people not subject to the statutes." G. J. Stigler, "The Economist and the State," *American Economic Review* 55, no. 1 (March 1965), p. 16.

[4] See Sections 17, 20, 21, 22, and 23 of Article XII, California State Constitution. State of California, *Public Utilities Code and Related Constitutional Provisions* (Sacramento: California Office of State Printing, 1965), pp. 13–17.

[5] State of California, *Statutes and Amendments to the Codes, 1965 Chapters*, compiled by G. H. Murphy, Legislative Counsel (Sacramento: California Office of State Printing, 1965), vol. 1, p. A-3, vol. 2, chapter 736, p. 2145.

Table 1-1

Comparison of the Economic Regulatory Power of the CAB
and the California PUC from 1946 to September 1965

| Regulatory Area | Scope of Regulatory Power | | | |
| | CAB | | California PUC | |
	Direct	Indirect	Direct	Indirect
Entry and Exit	Complete[a]	–	None[b]	Very Limited[c]
Service	Limited[d]	Great[e]	Insurance Only[f]	Limited[g]
Price	Complete[h]	–	Complete[i]	–

[a]Section 401, esp. subsections (a) and (j), 72 Stat. 754–56.

[b]Sections 17, 20, 21, 22, and 23, Article XII, California State Constitution.

[c]Derived from the PUC's power to regulate prices. The imposition of unduly low prices would discourage entry and encourage exit.

[d]Essentially applied to correcting significant deviations from established norms which, in turn, depended on technological and economic factors beyond the direct control of the CAB. Sections 102(c), 401(e)(4), 404(a) and (b), 405(b), 411, and 1002(i), 72 Stat. 740, 755, 760, 769, and 788. Also, see CAB Economic Regulation No. ER-223 (August 16, 1957), 22 F.R. 6756 (1957); and 30 CAB 1120, 1121 (1960).

[e]Derived from the CAB's power to regulate entry, exit, and prices, and to allow certificated carriers to meet to discuss matters of common interest. Sections 401(f), 414 and 1002(e), 72 Stat. 754, 770, and 789. Also, see 21 CAB 354, 361 and 370 (1955); 27 CAB 788, 794 (1958); CAB Economic Regulation No. ER-388 (September 27, 1961), 26 F.R. 9310 (1961); CAB Order No. E-20801 (May 8, 1964), 29 F.R. 6451 (1964); CAB Press Releases Nos. 49-77 (September 7, 1949), 49-95 (December 2, 1949), and 51-95 (December 6, 1951).

[f]Effective June 30, 1964. California, *Public Utilities Code and Related Constitutional Provisions*, pp. 162–64. Also, see 62 Cal. PUC 477 (1964); and 63 Cal. PUC 525 (1965).

[g]Derived from the PUC's power to regulate prices. Fare increases are evaluated by the PUC relative to the service offered under the proposed fares.

[h]Sections 1002(d), (e) and (g), 72 Stat. 789–90. Also, see Sections 403 and 404(a), 72 Stat. 758–60.

[i]Sections 20, 21, 22, and 23, Article XII, California State Constitution. Also, see 55 Cal. PUC 369, 372–79 (1957); and 57 Cal. PUC 407, 412–15 (1959).

Sources: As listed in the footnotes. Note: 72 Stat. 731 is the Federal Aviation Act of 1958, which replaced the Civil Aeronautics Act of 1938, 52 Stat. 973. The provisions of these two acts are essentially identical regarding the CAB's economic regulatory powers. R. E. Caves, *Air Transport and Its Regulators* (Cambridge, Mass.: Harvard University Press, 1962), pp. 140–91, and 232–52. S. B. Richmond, *Regulation and Competition in Air Transportation* (New York: Columbia University Press, 1961), pp. 10–20. M. M. Taylor, "Economic Regulation of Intrastate Air Carriers in California," *California Law Review* 41, no. 3 (Fall 1953), pp. 454–82, esp. p. 481.

1946, when the first intrastate carrier inaugurated service, to 1965. Table 1-1 summarizes and compares the economic regulatory powers of the CAB and the PUC for this 20-year period.

Because regulatory commissions have considerable discretion in the use of their statutory or constitutional powers, the degree of actual regulation may be less than the maximum allowed and may change over time. For example, as described in chapter 5 of this book, the PUC delayed until 1949 effective implementation of its power to regulate airline prices. Similarly, even though it had the power to regulate both price increases and decreases, in practice the PUC only controlled increases; the CAB, with comparable power, controlled decreases as well as increases. Overall, a detailed examination of the actual practices of the CAB and the PUC has shown that the California intrastate carriers operated under relatively limited regulation by the PUC, whereas the certificated carriers were extensively regulated by the CAB.[6] Thus, if these two groups of carriers operated under fairly comparable technological, economic, and operational conditions, major differences in performance between them can be attributed to the differences in economic regulation.

Hypotheses Pertaining to Economic Regulation

The following three diverse hypotheses will be selected for consideration from the large number that could be posited about the economic effects of direct regulation by commissions having discretionary powers:

(1) Regulation protects the consumer from exploitation by producers.

(2) Regulation has no significant effect on the regulated firm or industry.

(3) Regulation protects producers by helping them form a cartel to obtain monopoly benefits.

Although the first hypothesis is widely accepted, there is little evidence to support it, other than certain provisions of laws establishing regulatory commissions and statements made by various supporters of such laws. Indeed, those adopting the consumer-protection hypothesis almost invariably propose the supplementary perversion hypothesis, which says that even though the purpose of regulation is to protect the consumer, the regulated industries somehow manage

---

[6] See W. A. Jordan, *Economic Effects of Airline Regulation* (Ph.D. dissertation, University of California, Los Angeles, 1968), pp. 26–71. Of course, the certificated carriers also had to comply with the PUC's limited price regulation when operating within California.

to pervert their regulators until the commissions become supporters or servants of the "regulated" rather than protectors of the consumers.[7] In one respect the no-effect hypothesis is similar to the supplementary perversion hypothesis: if an already powerful industry is able to control its regulators, one would expect regulation to have little or no impact. There is more to it than that, however. Should the market structure of an industry be unchanged by regulation, it follows that such regulation may have little impact on the performance of the industry, regardless of who controls the regulators. This would be true if the "natural" market structure were competitive or even oligopolistic; it would also apply to a monopolistic market structure if regulation served to facilitate monopolies and cartels (as proposed in the third hypothesis).[8]

The producer-protection (cartel) hypothesis would be applicable if regulation served to convert a competitive or oligopolistic industry into a cartel, or to increase the effectiveness of an existing cartel. A comparison of the CAB-regulated airlines with the California intrastate carriers in fact provides evidence consistent with the implications of this hypothesis. Although the cartel hypothesis is applicable to the domestic airline industry (as this study will show), it does not necessarily pertain to all regulated industries.[9] Each of the above three hypotheses could conceivably apply to one or more industries, depending upon the "natural" market structure of each industry, the powers given to the regulatory commission, and its implementation of these powers.

For the purpose of this study, a cartel is defined as *a group of producers who form an agreement to act together.*[10] To many

[7] A good review of the existing literature that accepts the consumer-protection hypothesis and its associated perversion hypothesis can be found in M. H. Bernstein, *Regulating Business by Independent Commission* (Princeton, N.J.: Princeton University Press, 1955), esp. chapter 3.

[8] For evidence supporting the no-effect hypothesis, see G. J. Stigler and C. Friedland, "What Can Regulators Regulate? The Case of Electricity," *Journal of Law and Economics* 5 (October 1962), pp. 4–11, esp. 8, 9, and 11.

[9] An example of another regulated industry in which the cartel hypothesis applies is given in G. Kolko, *Railroads and Regulation, 1877–1916* (Princeton, N.J.: Princeton University Press, 1965), esp. pp. 3 and 231–39. Also, see the review of this book by G. W. Hilton, *American Economic Review* 56, no. 1 (March 1966), pp. 271–73.

[10] See G. J. Stigler, *The Theory of Price* (3d ed.; New York: The Macmillan Co., 1966), p. 230. Also, see R. Liefman, *Cartels, Concerns and Trusts* (London: Methuen & Co., 1932), p. 7. Cartels are generally considered to be socially undesirable institutions. This study, however, is not concerned with the

people, the word "cartel" produces a vision of businessmen around a board-room table calculating ways to exploit the consumer and subsequently sharing the large profits that result from this exploitation. This vision ignores, however, the innumerable personal and interfirm conflicts that may arise within a cartel. A major source of such conflicts is the transfer of profit allocation from market competition to competition through negotiation among cartel members. How much does firm "A" get, compared to firm "B" or firm "C"? Why should firm "A" receive a larger share of total industry profits than firm "B"? How much larger? The transfer of competition from markets to committees is just that—a transfer; competition itself is not eliminated.

The existence of rivalry among certificated carriers may be considered evidence by some that the CAB-regulated airlines do not comprise a cartel. It is important, however, to distinguish between the rivalry (competition) for larger shares of cartel production quotas and profits, and competition as a kind of market structure. The semantic problem is compounded because in a world of scarcity there is continual and universal competition for goods among rival individuals and organizations, regardless of the structure within which this competition occurs. Under differing market structures, only the *form* of competition changes (with resulting effects on prices, products, marketing activities, etc.). Therefore, the relevant question regarding the airlines becomes: is the form of competition (rivalry) among the regulated airlines consistent with the implications of the producer-protection (cartel) hypothesis?

The purpose of a cartel is to increase its members' profits (or overall utilities, if nonmonetary benefits are considered) over what could be achieved if the industry were not cartelized. Many problems must be solved by the cartel members before this purpose can be achieved.

(1) Agreement must be reached by the members on the prices to be charged by all. This agreement should include a structure

---

desirability or undesirability of producers agreeing to act together. A number of situations may be mentioned in which society explicitly approves of and promotes such agreements (for example, farmer marketing organizations and labor unions), and others in which disapproval is manifested (see the literature on antitrust activities). If the word "cartel" is disagreeable to the reader, he is urged to substitute a more preferred word such as "self-policing" or "cooperative." The word "cartel" is used in this study because it pertains to an established theory of producer behavior, the implications of which prove to be consistent with the evidence obtained by comparing the CAB-regulated airlines with the California intrastate carriers.

of discriminatory prices if consumers with differing price elasticities of demand can be identified and segregated at relatively low cost. Overall, these prices must yield higher average revenues (price levels) than would obtain in the absence of the cartel.

(2) Agreement must be reached among the members regarding the allocation of industry production and profits.

(3) Existing competitors must be induced (or compelled) to join the cartel, even though any *one* of them may increase its profits by staying outside the cartel, providing all other producers are members. At the same time, current members must be prevented from leaving the cartel if they plan to continue in production.

(4) Potential competitors must be kept from entering the market, or at least delayed significantly from so doing.

(5) Low-cost methods (to the industry) of detecting and punishing violations of the agreements must be found.[11]

To the extent that these and other difficult problems can be solved, a cartel will increase its profits (including monopoly rents) or decrease its losses. Human frailties and ignorance, however, persist even within a cartel, so one should not be surprised if a cartel fails to solve some of these problems with a resulting decrease in its effectiveness. Thus, when seeking evidence of cartelization, it is wise to look for tendencies as well as obvious examples, since any given cartel may be only moderately successful, or even largely unsuccessful, in achieving its goals.

Implications of the Cartel Hypothesis

If the CAB's regulation of certificated carriers facilitated the formation of an airline cartel, and if air transportation within California between 1946 and 1965 were similar to interstate air transportation (except for the much lower degree of regulation), then it would follow from cartel theory that the certificated carriers would differ from the California intrastate carriers in their economic performance. In terms of the three areas of regulation, these differences would be as follows:

---

[11] This list of problems is derived from A. A. Alchian and W. R. Allen, *University Economics* (2d ed.; Belmont, Calif.: Wadsworth Publishing Co., Inc., 1967), pp. 320–23; D. Dewey, *Monopoly in Economics and Law* (Chicago: Rand McNally & Co., 1959), pp. 18–24; and Stigler, *Theory of Price*, pp. 230–36.

(1) Entry and Exit
   (a) entry of new firms would be effectively limited
   (b) relatively fewer airlines would exist at any given time
   (c) exit would be controlled and the market shares of de-
       parting carriers would be reallocated or transferred to one
       or more of the remaining carriers
(2) Price
   (a) higher price levels (average revenues) would be achieved
   (b) a more varied price structure would exist, with greater
       use of price discrimination
(3) Service
   (a) relatively lower quantities of output would be produced
       as a result of the higher price levels (effective price dis-
       crimination, it should be noted, would partially offset the
       effects of higher price levels on the quantity of output)
   (b) a higher quality of service would be maintained (given
       that the CAB controlled service quality less completely
       than it controlled prices).

Higher price levels and effective price discrimination, combined
with limited entry and lower rates of output, should serve to increase
profits for cartel members over what they could achieve under other
market structures. It does not follow, however, that the profits of
the CAB-regulated airlines should have been relatively greater than
those of the California intrastate carriers. First, there is the matter of
costs. The costs of establishing, policing, and enforcing cartel agreements yield an upward shift in industry cost curves. Also, unless a
cartel assigns production quotas to its members so as to equate their
marginal costs, the industry's average cost of producing at any rate of
output will be higher than necessary.[12] Of course, such increases in
costs decrease the industry's profits for any given level of revenues.
Second, market structure plays an important role in determining
relative profits. If the airline market structure within California
between 1946 and 1965 were competitive, or even oligopolistic, one
would expect the intrastate carriers' profits to have been lower than
the system-wide profits of the cartelized, certificated carriers. If, on
the other hand, the California market structure for some period were
essentially a cartel with an oligopolistic fringe, the profits of the
intrastate carriers (comprising the fringe) could have been relatively
higher than those of the CAB-regulated airlines, since such a situation
would give the intrastate carriers a more elastic demand schedule
than the certificated carriers, and thus the ability to increase total

[12] Dewey, *Monopoly in Economics and Law*, p. 16.

revenues substantially by charging prices somewhat lower than those adopted by the certificated carriers.

Implications of the consumer-protection and no-effect hypotheses provide additional perspectives on the cartel hypothesis. For example, if CAB regulation had no significant effect on the certificated carriers during this period, one would expect to find no differences in the price levels or structures in regulated interstate air transportation and air transportation in California. A similarity in interstate and intrastate fares could also be predicted under the consumer-protection hypothesis if (as was the case) a large amount of service were provided within California by the regulated airlines and if low fares were set by the CAB to benefit consumers. In such a situation, competitive forces would have required the intrastate carriers to match the low fares of the certificated carriers, and the CAB would have effectively controlled the fares of both carrier groups.

The same general situation would apply to entry and exit. If CAB regulation had no economic effect, the relative number of airlines within California should have been comparable to the number of certificated carriers, allowing for the much greater traffic volume of the interstate markets. If regulation did serve to protect the consumer, and if one assumes that without it "unethical" airlines could have entered and survived, or even driven out "ethical" airlines ("Gresham's Law"), then regulation could be expected to have had an impact by eliminating or barring such airlines. If this were an effect of regulation, however, "ethical" airlines should still have been allowed to enter the ranks of the certificated carriers, and existing carriers whose policies served to exploit consumers would have been forced out by the CAB, or their managements would have been changed through regulatory action. Finally, if entry regulation is *necessary* to prevent the existence of "unethical" airlines, one would expect to find that such airlines operated in California, where entry was not controlled.

The findings of this study prove to be consistent with the implications drawn from the cartel hypothesis and inconsistent with the implications of the other two hypotheses. Thus, they provide evidence that CAB regulation of the certificated carriers did facilitate their organizing and operating as a cartel.[13]

---

[13] Still other evidence of the existence of a cartel is the effective enforcement of industry agreements. This book provides some examples of such enforcement in the airline industry, largely through the use of the CAB's regulatory powers. Since, however, a recent study has been devoted to this subject, it need not be emphasized here; see L. J. Kleiger, *Maximization of Industry Profits: The Case*

Similarities Between the Carrier Groups

In 1965 the California intrastate carriers accounted for 1.1 percent of total common-carrier, scheduled revenue passenger-miles flown in large aircraft (ranging from DC-3's to four-engine jets) within the contiguous 48 states, and 2.2 percent of the total scheduled domestic passenger originations.[14] In 1965 one of the intrastate carriers, Pacific Southwest Airlines, carried more passengers than any other carrier in each of the three largest California markets. These were extremely important markets in the overall domestic airline route structure, ranking first, ninth, and twenty-third in passenger volume among all domestic U.S. city-pair markets.[15] The ability of certain intrastate carriers to survive and even dominate such markets makes it clear that, within their limited geographic area, they were large-scale operators and that their service during the period studied was significant, relative even to that of the nation-wide operations of the certificated carriers. Indeed, the two intrastate airlines in operation throughout 1965 carried more RPM within California than *all* of the certificated domestic airlines carried within the 48 states in 1938.[16]

Technological conditions were essentially the same for all U.S. airlines from 1946 through 1965. Airports, air traffic control, and airways have generally been provided by federal or local governments and have been used jointly by all types of carriers. Suitable personnel, maintenance facilities, communications, marketing services, etc., have been widely available within the United States to any who care to utilize them at existing prices. Most important, substantial numbers of large commercial aircraft were available from aircraft manufacturers (located mainly in Southern California), and many commercial aircraft could be bought second-hand from the federal government, airlines, and other owners throughout the postwar

---

of United States Air Transportation (Ph.D. dissertation, University of California, Los Angeles, 1967).

[14] Calculated from data presented in Appendices 2 and 3 of this book and from data given in CAB, *Handbook of Airline Statistics*, pp. 47 and 78.

[15] These rankings were obtained by combining on-line origin and destination passenger data published in the following sources: CAB, *Competition Among Domestic Air Carriers* (1965 ed.; Washington, D.C.: Air Transport Association of America, 1966); and PUC, *Intrastate Passengers of Scheduled Air Carriers*, Report No. 1511 (Quarters ended March 31, June 30, September 30, and December 31, 1965; San Francisco, n.d., mimeographed).

[16] The domestic airlines carried 476 million RPM in 1938, compared with 596 million RPM carried by the California intrastate carriers in 1965; CAB, *Handbook of Airline Statistics*, p. 47; and Appendix 3 of this book.

years. During a substantial part of the period studied, identical aircraft types were operated by both the certificated and the intrastate carriers.

Differences did exist between the general economic and demographic conditions in California and in other parts of the country. Above average increases in population and economic development have occurred in California since World War II. The differences in these growth rates, however, do not appear to be large enough to affect significantly a comparison of California intrastate airlines with the certificated airlines. Indeed, the large growth rate of air transportation in all parts of the country probably is sufficient to "swamp" any effect of differences in economic growth.

The greatest differences between these carrier groups are to be found in operational factors—for example, in distance. The fact is that the cities comprising the longest nonstop market within California (San Diego and San Francisco) are only 449 statute miles apart.[17] In contrast, the domestic nonstop markets of the certificated carriers range up to 2,700 miles. Nevertheless, from 1949 through 1965 the average on-line passenger trip length for the certificated trunk carriers ranged from 469 to 701 miles, compared with a range of 316 to 339 miles for the California intrastate carriers, and 182 to 214 miles for the certificated local service carriers. During the same period, the average stage length for trunk carrier flights (one or more flights being required for a passenger trip) ranged from 191 to 411 miles, whereas that for the local service carriers varied from 62 to 106 miles.[18] Comparable average stage length data are not available for the intrastate carriers, but in August 1965, their average scheduled (as opposed to actual) flight stage length was 282 miles.[19] Thus, the average distances for the certificated trunk carriers' on-line passenger trips and flight stage lengths differed much less from those of the California intrastate carriers than the distance differences existing between their longest nonstop markets. Furthermore, the local service carriers' average on-line passenger trip and stage length distances were less than those of the intrastate carriers; therefore, by comparing the intrastate carriers with both classes of certificated carriers, differences due to distance may be partially accounted for.

[17] See Appendix 13 of this book.

[18] CAB, *Handbook of Airline Statistics*, pp. 83, 84, and 399. See also Appendix 2 of this book.

[19] Pacific Southwest Airlines, Flight Schedule (effective August 6, 1965); and Mercer Enterprises, Cal. PUC Application No. 48157 (filed December 28, 1965), p. 2.

Wherever differences in operational factors do seem to have a significant impact, an attempt will be made to indicate how these differences might affect the comparisons between the carrier groups.

Although the certificated and California intrastate carriers did not operate under identical conditions, the similarities were substantial and the carrier groups were sufficiently comparable to permit the conclusion that differences between them were due to differences in regulation. This is especially true when the relationship between carrier performance and regulation proves to be quite direct and when differences between carrier groups are very large—so large, in fact, that they really cannot be explained away simply by pointing to certain differences in technological, economic, or operational conditions.

Preview of Chapters

The following chapters compare the CAB-regulated airlines with the California intrastate carriers in terms of entry and exit, number of carriers in existence, service quality, prices, market shares, resource utilization, and profits. Entry and exit are treated in chapter 2; estimates are also made in that chapter about the effect of CAB regulation on the number of airlines operating at any given time. Chapter 3 examines service quality and describes how carrier rivalry influences this aspect of airline operations when price rivalry is limited. In addition, the relative safety performances of the carriers are compared in this chapter. A general introduction to passenger fares and a description of the CAB's role in coordinating and authorizing the certificated carriers' fare levels and structure are presented in chapter 4. The detailed comparison of the general passenger fares of the certificated and California intrastate carriers is given in chapters 5 through 7. Chapter 5 contains an explicit estimate of the impact of CAB regulation on increasing fares in major U.S. markets. Chapter 6 examines fares in minor markets; chapter 7 compares the increases in airline prices with increases in consumer price indices over the period studied. Promotional fares and price discrimination are covered in chapter 8. The effects of price and service quality differences on market shares are examined in chapter 9. Chapters 10 and 11 examine carrier survival, profits, economies of scale, and relative utilization of resources. In essence, these two chapters indicate the extent and sources of the certificated and California intrastate carriers' cost differences. Finally, chapter 12 summarizes the findings of this study, outlines the market structures existing within California during the period studied, indicates the effects of CAB regulation on social costs, and lists some of those who, in addition to the certificated carriers, benefit from such regulation.[20] The overall findings are that the economic effects of the CAB's regulation of the certificated carriers have been to limit entry and control exit, to reduce the number of firms in existence, to promote service quality, to raise price levels and encourage price discrimination (yielding a complicated fare structure), to decrease the intensity of resource utilization (thereby increasing average costs), and to benefit aircraft manufacturers and other suppliers of resources as well as the regulated airlines themselves. All of these results are consistent with the implications of cartel theory, where the cartel is not perfectly organized. Without regulation, the U.S. airline industry would have, it appears, an oligopolistic market structure with a significant degree of price rivalry, limited price discrimination, and relatively large numbers of specialized airlines providing services whose average quality would be lower than that existing under regulation. In total, the social costs of air transportation seem to have been significantly increased by the CAB's regulatory activities.

[20] Two short studies have been made of certain aspects of the California intrastate carriers' operations. See CAB, *Traffic, Fares, and Competition, Los Angeles-San Francisco Air Travel Corridor*, Staff Research Report No. 4 (Washington, D.C., August 1965); and M. E. Levine, "Is Regulation Necessary? California Air Transportation and National Regulatory Policy," *Yale Law Journal* 74, no. 8 (July 1965), pp. 1416-47.

Entry and Exit

2

Introduction

There is no question that the CAB controls airline entry and exit. No airline may provide scheduled, interstate air transportation with aircraft having a maximum gross take-off weight over 12,500 pounds (about one-half that of a DC-3) unless the CAB specifically authorizes such service. Also, no such airline may terminate service without the Board's permission.[1] Given this, the relevant questions become: Has CAB regulation served to prevent or significantly delay potential producers from actually entering the industry? Has it influenced the manner in which exit occurs? Have the CAB's actions reduced the number of airlines in the industry at any given time?

During 1965, 40 airlines possessed authorizations from the CAB to operate large, fixed-wing aircraft in domestic air transportation. These airlines were classified into four groups: 11 trunk, 13 local service, 3 all-cargo, and 13 supplemental carriers.[2] Of these domestic carriers, in 1965 the trunk and local service carriers accounted for about 96 percent of total domestic transport revenues[3] and 98.6 percent of total scheduled and nonscheduled revenue passenger-

[1] See Table 1-1. CAB policy regarding carriers providing service with aircraft weighing 12,500 pounds or less (air taxi operators) is summarized in 14 CFR 298. Also, see CAB, *Handbook of Airline Statistics*, p. 467.

[2] CAB, *Air Carrier Analytical Charts and Summaries* VII–4 (December 31, 1965), pp. 19, 31, and 32.

[3] Calculated from data presented in CAB, *Handbook of Airline Statistics*, p. 94. The supplemental carriers' total transport revenues were allocated between domestic and international on the basis of overall revenue ton-mile data given on p. 36 of this handbook.

14

miles.[4] Since such a large part of the regulated airlines' domestic revenues was earned by the trunk and local service carriers in 1965 and in previous years, excluding the all-cargo and supplemental carriers from this study does not unduly reduce its coverage of the domestic regulated airlines. Also, since almost all of the California intrastate carriers' traffic came from passenger operations (they were not allowed to carry mail, and little air freight moved over their systems), the exclusion of the all-cargo and supplemental carriers eliminates those domestic airlines that are most unlike the California carriers. Taken together, the trunk, local service, and California intrastate carriers transported virtually all of the passengers legally carried in scheduled operations performed with large aircraft within the 48 contiguous states between 1946 and 1965;[5] and passenger traffic comprised the major source of revenues for each group of carriers. Overall, limiting this study to these three carrier classes results in the inclusion of the great majority of domestic airline operations and a substantial increase in the homogeneity of the carriers studied. The latter is particularly important since it means that differences between otherwise similar regulated and nonregulated airlines can be more properly attributed to differences in regulation.

Certificated Carrier Entry and Exit

A total of 16 certificated trunk carriers operated during all or part of the period from 1946 through 1965. During this period, five of the carriers were acquired by or merged with another trunk carrier, so that by June 1, 1961, only 11 trunk carriers remained in operation. All of the 16 trunk carriers received their certificates of public convenience and necessity from the CAB in 1939, with a retroactive effective date of August 22, 1938.[6] No other airline has

[4] CAB, *Air Carrier Analytical Charts and Summaries* VII-4 (December 31, 1965), pp. 33 and 34.

[5] Southeast Airlines operated scheduled service with large, two-engine aircraft within Tennessee during 1959 and part of 1960; Lone Star Airlines operated such service within Texas during most of 1960. *Official Airline Guide*, North American Edition, 15, no. 4 (January 1959), p. C 387; 16, no. 5 (February 1960), p. C 408; 16, no. 11 (August 1960), p. C 427; and 17, no. 1 (October 1960), p. C 442.

[6] CAB, *Handbook of Airline Statistics*, pp. 1, 2, 33, 462, and 506. The five exiting carriers were Inland Air Lines (merged with Western on April 10, 1952), Mid-Continent Airlines (merged with Braniff on August 16, 1952), Chicago and Southern Air Lines (merged with Delta on May 1, 1953), Colonial Airlines (acquired by Eastern on June 1, 1956), and Capital Airlines (merged with United on June 1, 1961).

since received such a certificate authorizing it to provide comparable trunk-type service. Apparently the necessary and sufficient condition for an airline to have obtained a certificate for the performance of interstate trunk carrier operations was for it to have been in operation between May 14 and August 22, 1938—the "grandfather" period specified in the 1938 Act.[7]

In contrast to the trunk carriers, the local service carriers were initially certificated by the CAB without benefit of a "grandfather" clause. Beginning with Pioneer Air Lines (then named Essair, Inc.) on November 5, 1943, and ending with Ozark Air Lines on September 26, 1950, the CAB authorized 21 carriers to provide subsidized, experimental, "local feeder" service connecting smaller communities with larger cities, which, in turn, were generally connected by the trunk carriers.[8] Except for a few isolated instances, the local service carriers were not permitted to provide nonstop, terminal-to-terminal service or to operate in direct competition with the trunk carriers during the period covered by this study.[9]

Of the 21 local service carriers receiving certificates from the Board, 13 were still in existence at the end of 1965. Of the 8 that ceased operations, 4 terminated service when the CAB canceled their certificates or denied their requests to extend or renew temporary certificates, and 4 merged with another certificated carrier.[10] These terminations and mergers all occurred before the enactment of Public Law 38 on May 19, 1955, which required the CAB to issue perma-

[7] Section 401(e)(1), 52 Stat. 988. Also, see *ibid.*, p. 462.

[8] Following Pioneer's certification in 1943, nine local service carriers were certificated in 1946, two in 1947, six in 1948, two in 1949, and one (Ozark) in 1950. CAB, *Handbook of Airline Statistics*, pp. 1, 2, and 506–8. Also, CAB, *Annual Report* (1946 ed.; Washington, D.C.), pp. 3–4 & Appendix B; (1947 ed.), pp. 3–5 & Appendix B; (1948 ed.), p. 4 & Appendix B; (1949 ed.), pp. 11–13 & Appendix B; (1950 ed.), pp. 7–9 & Appendix B; (1951 ed.), p. 31; (1952 ed.), pp. 3–6 & Appendix III; (1953 ed.), pp. 6–8; (1955 ed.), p. 5.

[9] This policy was modified in early 1968 when the CAB adopted Subpart M of its Procedural Regulations Part 302, which established an expedited procedure for modifying or removing certain limitations on nonstop operations contained in local service carriers' certificates. CAB Regulation No. PR-104 (effective January 19, 1968).

[10] CAB, *Handbook of Airline Statistics*, pp. 506–7. The four carriers that lost their temporary certificates were Florida Airways (March 29, 1949), Parks Air Lines (July 28, 1950), Mid-West Airlines (May 16, 1952), and Wiggins Airways (August 1, 1953). The four carriers that ceased operations through merger were Arizona Airways and Challenger Airlines (merged with Monarch Air Lines to form Frontier Airlines on June 1, 1950), Empire Air Lines (merged with West Coast on August 4, 1952), and Pioneer Air Lines (merged with Continental, a trunk carrier, on April 1, 1955).

nent certificates to the surviving local service carriers.[11] There was no further exit from the ranks of the local service carriers throughout the remainder of the period covered by this study. During 1967 and 1968, however, the CAB authorized three more mergers among these carriers, so that by mid-1968 only 9 local service carriers remained in operation.[12]

Overall, it is clear that entry into the ranks of the certificated carriers has been limited to a single time period for each class of carriers, and so long as a departing carrier possessed a CAB operating certificate, exit has been via merger with or acquisition by some other certificated carrier. However, entry during a single period and exit through merger or acquisition may not be unique to regulated airlines; they may also be characteristics of nonregulated airlines. Therefore, before it is possible to say that this experience provides evidence that regulation has helped the certificated carriers limit the number of airlines entering interstate air transport markets and explicitly reallocate or transfer market shares of departing carriers through mergers or acquisitions, it is necessary to examine the patterns of entry and exit experienced by the relatively nonregulated California intrastate carriers during these same years to determine whether they differed appreciably from those of the certificated carriers.

Intrastate Carrier Entry and Exit

Between 1946 and 1965, a total of 16 California intrastate carriers provided scheduled, common-carrier service with DC-3's or larger aircraft. Appendix 1 lists these carriers and gives their dates of entry and exit and the dates that they served various cities on their routes. Two important facts emerge from comparing the intrastate carriers with the certificated carriers. First, even though the California intrastate market was much smaller than the national market available to the certificated carriers, the number of intrastate carriers equals the number of trunk carriers in existence during these years and is not much smaller than the number of local service carriers certificated by the CAB. Second, rather than entering during a single

---

[11] CAB, *Annual Report* (1955 ed.), p. 18.

[12] On September 1, 1967, the CAB authorized the merger of Central Airlines into Frontier (CAB Order No. E-25626); on February 23, 1968, it authorized Bonanza and West Coast to merge with Pacific to form Air West (CAB Orders Nos. E-26625 and E-26626, approved by the President on April 4, 1968); and on June 24, 1968, it approved the merger of Lake Central into Allegheny (CAB Order No. E-26967).

period, the intrastate carriers entered at various times from 1946 through 1964, with most entry occurring during 1949 and early 1950, and between May 1962 and September 1964.

The first intrastate carrier to enter the California market was Pacific Air Lines, which began DC-3 service between Burbank and Sacramento on March 6, 1946, extended service to San Francisco on June 1 of that year, and then on October 22, 1946, inaugurated service to Fresno, Modesto, and Stockton.[13] Little information is available regarding Pacific's operations. It scheduled two to four round trips daily over its system and, unlike the later intrastate carriers, charged the same fares the certificated trunk carriers charged for their first-class service (coach service was not provided by the trunk carriers at that time).[14] Pacific remained in service until June 3, 1947, and its termination of service was followed by involuntary bankruptcy.

The calm that descended over the California intrastate market following the demise of Pacific Air Lines lasted for a year and a half. It was rippled on December 1, 1948, when California Central Airlines (CCA) filed a tariff with the PUC for low-fare, coach-type service.[15] Then, between January 2, 1949, when CCA inaugurated the first coach service within California, and January 21, 1950, a total of eight intrastate airlines inaugurated service. Six of those eight operated for less than ten months (four operated less than six months), but the two survivors of that period—California Central Airlines and Pacific Southwest Airlines—played decisive roles in the development of California intrastate air service. A large part of this study concerns the operations of those two carriers.

The six intrastate carriers that operated for less than ten months terminated service for a variety of reasons and did so in several different ways. Western Air Lines of California (WALC) operated

---

[13] See Appendix 1 of this book. Unless specified to the contrary, all data presented in this section are from this appendix. Pacific Air Lines, the California intrastate carrier, should not be confused with the CAB-certificated, local service carrier that changed its name from Southwest Airways to Pacific Air Lines in 1958. CAB, *Handbook of Airlines Statistics*, p. 508.

[14] *American Aviation Air Traffic Guide* 2, nos. 9–12, and 3, nos. 1–9 (June 1946 to June 1947), pp. 90, 169, 177, 183, 185, 177, 177, 177, 167, 167, 168, 170, and 190, respectively. Also, see Pacific Air Lines tariffs, C.R.C. No. 1 (April 14, 1946), and C.R.C. No. 2 (June 17, 1946).

[15] California Central Airlines tariff, Cal. P.U.C. No. 1 (issued December 1, 1948, effective January 1, 1949). Even though the PUC did not regulate airline fares during the years prior to 1949, it did require all airlines operating within the state to file tariffs showing existing rules, fares, and charges.

from August 19, 1949, through May 31, 1950. It terminated service when Western Air Lines (the certificated trunk carrier) canceled the lease agreement under which it had provided all of WALC's equipment, facilities, and personnel. On the following day, Western began operating a coach service identical to the one it had performed for WALC.[16] A study of the inception and operation of WALC shows that it was essentially an arm of Western that came into existence because during 1949 the CAB refused to allow Western to match the low coach fares of the California intrastate carriers. As soon as a change in CAB policy permitted Western (and United Air Lines) to equal the fares of the intrastate carriers, WALC went out of existence (see chapter 5).

Three of the six short-lived carriers were closely associated with large irregular (nonscheduled) interstate airlines. California Skycoach had the same management as Trans American Airways; Robin Airways was associated with Robin Airlines; and California Arrow was a part of Arrow Airways. California Skycoach operated within California for about one month in early 1949; Robin Airways lasted from March 16 to September 12, 1949; California Arrow's service extended from May 23, 1949, to December 7, 1949, when one of its DC-3's crashed with the loss of nine lives. All three large irregular carriers continued interstate operations after their intrastate associates withdrew from the California markets. Apparently they found it advantageous to transfer their equipment from scheduled service within California back to nonscheduled interstate operations.[17]

The last two of the six short-lived carriers were Channel Airways and California Pacific Airlines. Channel Airways operated between Long Beach and San Francisco from May to August 1949. It terminated service simply because it failed to generate adequate traffic to support even its small rate of operations.[18] California Pacific oper-

---

[16] So far as passengers were concerned, the only difference between Western's and WALC's coach services was the name on the ticket issued to them. Fares, aircraft, personnel, reservations procedures, etc., were identical.

[17] Robin Airlines continued nonscheduled interstate service until April 18, 1952, when the Civil Aeronautics Administration suspended its commercial operator certificate after one of its aircraft crashed with the loss of 29 lives (*The Los Angeles Times* [November 5, 1952], part II, p. 2). The CAB revoked the letter of registration of Arrow Airways effective February 15, 1951 (12 CAB 405, 414 [1951]). In the case of Arrow Airways, California Arrow's crash was probably the precipitating factor in its decision to terminate intrastate service and concentrate on nonscheduled interstate operations.

[18] Channel carried about 1,200 passengers during its 12 weeks of operation—only about 100 one-way passengers per week, or 10 passengers per flight. California Public Utilities Commission, *Intrastate Scheduled "Coach Class" Air*

ated between Burbank and Oakland for about a month in early 1950. It withdrew from this market when its management learned that United Air Lines and Western Air Lines planned to introduce coach service at fares equaling those then charged by the intrastate carriers.[19]

Of the two carriers that survived the initial period of major entry, Pacific Southwest Airlines (PSA) continued to operate and grow throughout the years covered by this study. The other carrier, California Central Airlines (CCA), went bankrupt and terminated service on February 14, 1955, after over six years of large-scale operations. During those six years, it was the largest of the intrastate carriers. CCA will be studied at length in the following chapters. The important consideration at this point is that when it did terminate service it did so through bankruptcy proceedings, and its aircraft were bought by two local service carriers (Allegheny and Pacific).[20] There was no offer from another carrier to merge with CCA or to buy it and maintain service over its routes.

The next airline to enter the California market was the second of the two whose entry did not coincide with the two major periods of entry. Actually, this carrier, California *Coastal* Airlines, was the direct successor of the bankrupt California Central Airlines. It was organized by Colonel and Mrs. C. C. Sherman, the owners of California Central, just before California Central was adjudicated bankrupt. It purchased the right to use the name "California Central Airlines" together with the defunct company's station, office, and ground equipment, telephone numbers, etc. (but not its aircraft).[21] On or about March 15, 1955, California Coastal, doing business as California Central Airlines, inaugurated DC-3 service over the original California Central routes. This service was maintained until August 9, 1957.

Both California Central and California Coastal were closely associated with the large irregular (supplemental) carrier, Airline Transport Carriers (ATC). All three airlines were owned by the Shermans

---

Carriers, by C. J. Astrue, Exhibit No. 1-C, Cal. PUC Case No. 4994, *et al.* (San Francisco: PUC, 1949, mimeographed), pp. 34 and 41.

[19] Telephone conversation with Mr. D. W. Mercer, former manager of California Pacific Airlines, October 13, 1965.

[20] U.S. District Court, Southern District of California, files of the Court Clerk, Bankruptcies Nos. 59560-PH and 59561-PH, Order Confirming Sale of Assets (dated February 14, 1955). Note that Pacific was named Southwest Airways at that time.

[21] Memorandum of Airline Transport Carriers, Inc., *in re* Motion to Consolidate (filed May 28, 1955), *ibid.*

and there was a full exchange of aircraft between California Central/ Coastal and ATC. After California Coastal terminated service, ATC continued to operate for several years with particular emphasis on charters for the U.S. Military Air Transport Service. Thus, California Coastal's termination was probably another case of management's finding more lucrative markets outside of California and simply transferring operations to those markets. California Coastal's increasingly erratic schedule performance and its 1956–57 record of delays in refunding unused tickets indicate that its California operations had become unprofitable.[22]

The second major period of airline entry was initiated by Paradise Airlines on May 14, 1962, when it began service between Oakland, San Jose, and Lake Tahoe. Futura Airlines followed on June 15, 1962, with service between Los Angeles and Lake Tahoe via Bakersfield, Fresno, Sacramento, and Oakland; and on August 15, 1962, Trans California Airlines (TCA) began flying between Burbank and Oakland. Futura operated two Constellation L-049's for about three months before going bankrupt (its leased aircraft were repossessed by their owner and later leased to Paradise).[23] Paradise operated first DC-3's and then the two Constellation L-049's until it was forced to discontinue operations when the Federal Aviation Agency (FAA) suspended its commercial operator certificate following the crash of one of the L-049's near Lake Tahoe on March 1, 1964, with the loss of 85 lives. The efforts of Paradise's owner to have the FAA's suspension lifted indicate either that the company was currently profitable or expected significant future profits.[24] Its departure from the California scene at that time may therefore be attributed to administrative action rather than economic forces.

The specific factor causing Trans California to terminate service on October 7, 1964, was an FAA decision not to renew its commercial operator certificate. Beginning in 1964, the FAA required air-

---

[22] Federal Aviation Agency, Western Region, records concerning Airline Transport Carriers, Inc. Also, see 55 Cal. PUC 602 (1957).

[23] U.S. District Court, Southern District of California, files of the Court Clerk, Bankruptcy No. 147405-WB, Futura Airlines Company Records. Also, U.S. District Court, Northern District of California, files of the Court Clerk, Case No. 43394, *Peerless Insurance Co.* v. *Paradise Airlines*, Paradise Airlines Company Records. The two L-049's were owned by Nevada Airmotive, Las Vegas, Nevada.

[24] See the transcript of the hearings before CAB Hearing Examiner S. Thomas Simon in: *N. E. Halaby, Administrator, Federal Aviation Agency, Complainant* v. *Paradise Airlines, Inc., Respondent*, Docket No. SE-462, March 20–April 7, 1964 (Washington, D.C.: CAB).

lines to meet certain minimum financial standards as a condition for obtaining the required annual renewal of their commercial operator certificates.[25] The inability of TCA to meet these requirements caused its existing owner to transfer his stock to TCA's major creditor, resign as president, and leave the company. With this, the FAA canceled TCA's temporary certificate extension and insisted upon a complete re-evaluation of the carrier before issuing a certificate to the new owners.[26] This procedure put TCA out of business. Thus, the specific reason for TCA's exit from the California market was the FAA's administrative action. Whether economic factors would have eventually caused TCA's demise is, of course, unknown.

The next intrastate entrant was Blatz Airlines, which began serving Truckee and the North Shore of Lake Tahoe from Burbank on July 5, 1963. Before finally terminating intrastate service on or about December 26, 1963, it also provided service to Lake Tahoe on the south shore of the lake. Blatz was a large irregular/supplemental carrier from May 14, 1947, until October 23, 1962, when the CAB canceled its supplemental certificate.[27] Thus, it did not enter the California market until after the CAB excluded it from supplemental interstate operations. As of the end of 1965, Blatz was still operating out of Burbank as a private carrier, implying that it found uses for its aircraft that were more profitable than scheduled intrastate operations.[28]

Mercer Enterprises and California Time Airlines were the last two carriers to inaugurate intrastate service with large aircraft prior to September 17, 1965. Mercer Enterprises began scheduled weekend

[25] The applicable Federal Aviation Regulation reads as follows: "(b) The Administrator may deny an application for a certificate under this subpart if he finds . . . (3) in the case of an applicant for a commercial operator certificate, that for financial reasons the applicant is not able to conduct a safe operation" (14 CFR 121.51 [1965]). In addition, at about this same time the FAA began to refuse commercial operator certificates to intrastate carriers whose operations were questioned by the CAB as possibly being interstate. Therefore, since 1964 the FAA's operating/safety regulation has come to support CAB economic regulatory policies, thereby taking on some of the characteristics of direct economic regulation. Overall, this late development had little impact on this study.

[26] FAA, Western Region, telegram to Trans California Airlines, October 8, 1964. Also, conversation with Mr. L. A. Mudgett, former President of TCA, May 24, 1965.

[27] FAA, Western Region, Status Reports for Blatz Airlines (September 1962 and January 1963).

[28] FAA, Western Region, Air Carrier and Commercial Operator Reports for Blatz Airlines (June and December 1963). Also, telephone conversation with Mr. F. A. Blatz, President of Blatz Airlines, October 28, 1965.

service between Burbank and Brown Field (located just south of San Diego) on April 18, 1964. It is still providing this limited scheduled service in conjunction with various charter operations, thereby demonstrating that it is possible for a very small airline to be commercially successful.

California Time initiated service between San Jose, Burbank, and Palm Springs on September 19, 1964, and began serving Oakland the following November. FAA records indicate that California Time's maximum schedule frequency was no more than 15 flights per month with a Martin 202.[29] Apparently little traffic was attracted, and this service was discontinued in January 1965, during the peak of the Palm Springs tourist season. This appears to be an example of departure from the market for economic reasons.

It is clear that the California intrastate carriers differed significantly from the certificated carriers in terms of entry and exit. Whereas the entry of both the regulated trunk and local service carriers was limited to a single time period for each class, the intrastate carriers entered throughout the 1946–65 period, although there were two major periods of activity separated by about a dozen years. Note that both of the major periods occurred when there were large stocks of obsolescent transport aircraft available at low prices, which lowered the economic barriers to entry.

Among the 14 California intrastate carriers that terminated service through 1965, there is not a single case of one being merged with or acquired by another airline, in sharp contrast to the fact that *all* of the trunk carriers terminating service did so through merger or acquisition. Similarly, except when exit resulted from the CAB's canceling or refusing to renew a temporary certificate, all local service carriers terminating service also did so through merger with another certificated carrier. So long as a regulated airline has held a certificate of public convenience and necessity, its means of exit has been through merger or acquisition. Without such a certificate from the government, the California experience shows that airline exit occurs by means of bankruptcy, transference of operations to other geographic areas (physically, a simple matter for airlines), or the sale of assets to firms which may or may not operate as air carriers.[30] It

[29] FAA, Western Region, Monthly Air Carrier Aircraft and Engine Utilization Reports for California Time Airlines (September 1964 through February 1965).

[30] It is necessary to differentiate between the means of exit and the cause of exit. This latter factor includes the termination of commercial operator certificates by the FAA (something that has never happened to a CAB-certificated carrier), the incurring of losses, or the expectations of greater profits (or smaller losses) elsewhere.

seems that the asset of an airline that is of unique value to other airlines is its CAB certificate of public convenience and necessity, not its aircraft, facilities, or good will, etc.[31]

This clear contrast between the experiences of the certificated carriers and of the California intrastate carriers shows that the CAB did have a significant impact on interstate airline entry and exit. It did limit the number of airlines authorized to offer interstate air service and the periods during which such carriers were allowed to enter. In addition, CAB regulation controlled exit from the industry with each departing carrier's market share (routes) being transferred to a remaining certificated carrier through merger or acquisition.

Number of Airlines in Existence

The evidence pertaining to entry and exit cannot be applied to the question of whether regulation limited the total number of airlines operating at any given time. Although the entry of certificated carriers was limited by the CAB, the number terminating service also appears to have been reduced by regulation. In contrast, a relatively large number of intrastate carriers entering the California market was accompanied by an almost equal number of service terminations. Also, the fact is that there have certainly been many more trunk and local service carriers in operation at any one time than California intrastate carriers. Thus, the question remains: would there have been even more interstate airlines in existence at any given time had it not been for CAB regulation?

Evidence Derived from System Sizes. If regulation does limit the number of airlines, one would expect to find each of a fewer number of regulated airlines serving more cities and covering broader geographic areas than each of a larger number of nonregulated airlines. It is impossible to make direct comparisons between the certificated and the California intrastate carriers in this matter because the intrastate carriers are restricted by the borders of California, which effectively limit the sizes of their route structures. Also, of course, the California traffic potential is much smaller than that of the national

---

[31] As this book goes to press, the first proposed merger of two California intrastate carriers is under consideration, with Air California to be merged into PSA. Both of these carriers hold permanent certificates of public convenience and necessity issued by the PUC in accordance with the provisions of Assembly Bill No. 413. See N. S. Himmel, "Merger Could Reshape California Market," *Aviation Week & Space Technology* 92, no. 2 (January 12, 1970), pp. 42 and 47.

airline market. Overall, California comprises only 5.3 percent of the total land area of the 48 contiguous states; its 1950 population was 7.0 percent of the total for these states, whereas its 1960 population was 8.8 percent of the total.[32] Given this, it is necessary to rely upon indirect comparisons to obtain evidence about the effects of CAB regulation on the number of carriers.

Table 2-1 gives for each of the three carrier classes the number of carriers that provided service during any portion of a year, the sum of the average number of airports served annually by each carrier, and the sum of the average number of route miles operated by each carrier during a year.[33] This table shows that, from 1946 through 1965, a decreasing number of trunk carriers provided a more dispersed coverage of the 48 contiguous states (more route miles operated) and, from 1959 through 1964, a less intense coverage (fewer airports served). The geographic coverage of a similarly decreasing number of local service carriers also became more dispersed, but their intensity of coverage increased over the entire period. Beginning in 1962, however, the increase in the average number of airports served by the local service carriers was not enough to offset the decrease in the number served by the trunk carriers, so that the overall coverage of all certificated carriers began to decrease in that year. In contrast, starting in 1949 the average coverage of one to seven California intrastate carriers fluctuated between 452 and 1,343 route miles operated, and from 3.4 to 12.0 airports served, with no apparent trend in either of those measures or in the number of carriers operating.

The data presented in Table 2-1 provide the basis for making two very rough quantitative estimates of the effects of CAB regulation in limiting the number of interstate airlines. This can be done by comparing the actual number of certificated carriers operating between 1949 and 1965 with estimates of the potential number of interstate airlines that could have existed without CAB regulation. The first estimate of the potential number of airlines is made by dividing the average number of airports served by each California intrastate carrier (about four airports per carrier) into the sum of the

---

[32] Calculated from data presented in *Cosmopolitan World Atlas* (Chicago: Rand McNally & Company, 1962), pp. 189 and 198.

[33] The airport and route-mile averages in Table 2-1 should not be compared directly to the number of carriers in any year that entry or exit occurred. This limitation is required because the airport and route-mile data were weighted by the number of days in a year that service was actually provided by each carrier. In contrast, a carrier was fully counted in each year it provided service even if it operated for only one day.

Table 2-1

Overall System Sizes for Each Class of Carriers
Trunk, Local Service, and California Intrastate
1946-1965

| Year | No. of Carriers[a] | | | Sum of Each Carrier's Weighted Average No. of | | | | | |
| | | | | Airports Served[b] | | | Route Miles Operated[c] | | |
	Trunk	Local	Intra.	Trunk	Local	Intra.	Trunk	Local	Intra.
1946	16	5	1	454.1	11.9	2.7	48,168	950	326
1947	16	8	1	514.9	91.7	1.8	51,066	5,127	181
1948	16	12	–	567.8	165.8	–	54,622	9,602	–
1949	16	19	7	589.1	222.8	9.6	55,643	13,482	1,343
1950	16	19	4	603.5	336.7	8.5	56,072	18,744	1,068
1951	16	17	2	603.8	372.1	9.8	55,867	20,763	1,009
1952	16	17	2	605.1	361.2	10.0	55,583	21,227	1,030
1953	14	15	2	592.2	374.9	9.8	54,525	22,205	986
1954	13	14	2	587.6	380.8	8.7	54,354	22,682	918
1955	13	14	3[d]	587.7	371.7	6.6	54,922	22,276	856
1956	13	13	2	602.6	384.8	7.8	58,438	23,660	897
1957	12	13	2	611.3	404.7	4.4	60,693	25,563	651
1958	12	13	1	612.3	417.5	3.4	61,341	26,953	452
1959	12	13	1	601.4	462.0	4.0	63,396	30,409	454
1960	12	13	1	589.7	499.1	4.2	63,265	33,433	457
1961	12	13	1	563.7	548.2	4.3	65,190	35,794	457
1962	11	13	4	542.3	552.9	7.2	67,033	36,582	787
1963	11	13	4	527.1	554.5	12.0	66,948	37,049	1,251
1964	11	13	5	500.4	561.2	10.5	66,228	37,818	1,022
1965	11	13	3	n.a.	n.a.	8.3	66,190	37,670	641

n.a.—not available.

[a]Any airline that operated during any portion of a year is counted for that year.
[b]The sum of the number of days each airport was served by each carrier during the year, divided by 365 or 366 days. One airport served throughout the year by three carriers is counted three times, once by each carrier.
[c]The sum for all carriers of the shortest distance connecting all of the points served by each carrier on all of its routes. These data are weighted for the time element involved in route changes during each year.
[d]The combined operations of two of these three carriers (California Central and California Coastal Airlines) resulted in almost continuous service by the equivalent of one carrier during 1955.

Sources: CAB, *Handbook of Airline Statistics* (June 1960 ed.), pp. 2 and 21; (1965 ed.), p. 404; and (1967 ed.), pp. 33, 394, 506, and 507. (Note: Information given on pp. 506-7 of the 1967 edition was used to correct an apparent error on p. 33 regarding the number of local service carriers operating during 1952.) CAB, Bureau of Accounts and Statistics, Research and Statistics Division, *Route Miles—Trunks*, and *Route Miles—Local Service* (unpublished worksheets). CAB, Bureau of Accounts and Statistics, Research and Statistics Division, *Record of Computation of Route Miles Operated* (unpublished worksheets). Calculated from information presented in Appendices 1 and 13 of this book.

average number of airports served each year by all of the certificated carriers. The second estimate is made by dividing the average number of route miles served by representative intrastate carriers (about 450 miles per carrier) into the sum of the average number of route miles served by all of the certificated carriers. The assumption underlying these calculations is that the traffic generated at four airports or over route systems averaging 450 miles in length should be adequate to support an interstate airline if the traffic proved adequate to support airlines operating within California. The first method yields estimates ranging from 203 to 278 potential nonregulated interstate airlines, while the second yields estimates of from 154 to 231 such carriers. The overall range is 154 to 278 potential airlines. Since the actual number of certificated carriers ranged from 35 in 1949–50 down to 24 in 1961–65, the estimates of potential carriers imply that between 4 and 12 times the actual number of certificated carriers could have existed had there been no regulation.

These estimates of the number of potential interstate airlines are surprisingly large, and few would accept them without question. But, then, their purpose is not to provide accurate estimates of the number of airlines that could have existed in the U.S. without regulation; rather, it is to provide evidence of whether CAB regulation served to limit the number of interstate airlines. This they do.

Still another way to gain insight into this matter is to see how large a California intrastate carrier would have to be to approximate the size of the average certificated carrier on the basis of airports served. Calculations using data in Table 2-1 show that the average certificated carrier served between 23 and 45 airports from 1949 through 1964 (37 to 51 for the average trunk carrier, and 12 to 43 for the average local service carrier). No California intrastate carrier came anywhere near serving such a large number of airports. In fact, there were generally fewer than 40 airline airports in all of California during those years.[34] Therefore, in order to equal the coverage of an average regulated airline, an intrastate carrier would have had to serve almost every airline airport in the state. Of course, no intrastate carrier even began to approach that degree of coverage.

It can be argued that one reason the intrastate carriers served such a small number of airports was that the certificated carriers were already established at the majority of California airline airports prior to the entry of the early intrastate carriers. Since the CAB subsidized much of the certificated carrier service at the many small airports served by only one carrier, it really was not feasible for the

---

[34] Airline route maps contained in CAB, *Annual Report*, various years.

intrastate carriers to attempt to enter those monopoly markets. Had it not been for this coverage by the certificated carriers, perhaps each successful California intrastate carrier would have served a greater number of airports with larger route miles than they actually did serve. This, in turn, would lower the above estimates of the number of potential interstate airlines that would have existed without CAB regulation. It is difficult, however, to believe that excluding certificated carriers from the California intrastate markets would have resulted in only one or two California carriers serving all of the airline airports in the state, especially since some intrastate carriers were able to survive while limiting their service to three or four airports. Thus, it seems reasonable to conclude that the existence of the certificated carriers within California did not affect the sizes of the individual California carriers enough to change substantially the estimates of the number of potential interstate airlines.

Another argument could be that the small size of the California intrastate carriers might be attributed to their service being limited to only the largest California markets, including three of the largest in the United States. Appendix 1, however, shows that the intrastate carriers served a number of small markets within California as well as the large ones. In fact, they provided the first common-carrier airline service (regulated or nonregulated) at Inyokern and Edwards AFB (California Central beginning in 1951), Lake Tahoe (Paradise and Futura beginning in 1962), Truckee-Tahoe North Shore (Blatz in 1963), and Brown Field near San Diego (Mercer beginning in 1964). In contrast, Pacific Air Lines (the local service carrier) did not inaugurate service at Inyokern until 1953, and at Lake Tahoe until October 1963.[35] The other three small airports listed above were never served by a certificated carrier.

Overall, the above analyses do provide evidence that CAB regulation resulted in the existence of fewer airlines than would have existed without such regulation. Also, it appears that the individual certificated carriers generally provided scheduled service to more airports over larger route structures than individual nonregulated airlines would have provided had they been able to operate throughout the United States.

Evidence Derived from Airline Traffic and Production. There are two measures of passenger traffic commonly used by the airlines: revenue passenger originations (the number of passengers boarding

[35] CAB Orders Nos. E-14593 (adopted October 29, 1959) and E-19963 (adopted August 29, 1963). TWA operated between San Francisco and Lake

aircraft at the points of initial enplanement on each carrier's system, with the return portion of a round trip counted as another origination) and revenue passenger-miles (the number of passengers flying on each aircraft multiplied by the airport-to-airport distances traveled). Available seat-miles (ASM) provide the standard measure of airline production for passenger operations. This measure is calculated by multiplying the number of seats available in each aircraft by the airport-to-airport distances for all segments flown.[36] These three measures provide information that may be used to derive some further indication of whether the CAB's entry and exit control has served to limit the total number of airlines providing interstate air transportation.

Table 2-2 presents the overall increases in these three measures from 1949 through 1965 for each carrier class. Clearly, all three groups of carriers experienced substantial growth during this period, with the local service carriers' growth rate being by far the largest, followed by that of the California intrastate carriers.

Table 2-2

Growth in Total Passenger Originations, RPM, and ASM from 1949 to 1965
Trunk, Local Service, and California Intrastate Carriers
Scheduled Domestic Service

Carrier Class	Growth from 1949 to 1965					
	Passenger Originations		Revenue Passenger-Miles		Available Seat-Miles	
	Number (millions)	Percent	Number (billions)	Percent	Number (billions)	Percent
Trunk	55.9	398%	42.42	646%	77.61	698%
Local Service	11.6	1,717	2.49	1,845	5.08	1,062
Calif. Intrastate	1.7	903	.53	868	.85	923

Sources: Calculated from data presented in CAB, *Handbook of Airline Statistics*, pp. 46, 47, and 78; and in Appendices 2, 3, and 4 of this book.

Tahoe during 1961, but it only provided contract service for Harrah's Club. See CAB Order No. E-16205 (adopted December 30, 1960).

[36] The use of available seat-miles as a measure of airline production has some theoretical shortcomings. In the case of a good that perishes as soon as it is produced, is it possible to measure production independently of consumption? Rottenberg discusses this problem in his article "The Baseball Players' Labor Market," *Journal of Political Economy* 64 (June 1956), p. 255, where he argues that the professional baseball product is the game played weighted by the number of customers who attend the game. This implies that if no one attends, there

Despite their larger growth rates, the local service carriers and the California intrastate carriers did not gain appreciably in terms of relative market shares. The trunk carriers were so much larger than the other two carrier groups in 1949 that their more modest percentage increases served to maintain their dominant position in the total airline industry. This is shown in Table 2-3, which gives the percentage share of total industry traffic and production accounted for by each class of carrier during various years. Even though the trunk carriers did lose 3.2 percentage points in their share of total RPM and 1.9 percentage points in their share of total ASM from 1949 to 1965, they still accounted for well over 93 percent of total domestic scheduled RPM and ASM during 1965. Obviously, the domestic carriers initially certificated by the CAB back in 1938 are still the dominant suppliers of air transportation service to domestic travelers. This, of course, is consistent with the implications of the cartel hypothesis. One would expect that the original cartel members would be protected from undue incursion by new members of the cartel (the local service carriers in this case) and that firms outside the cartel would be contained (here done by confining the intrastate carriers to operating within the borders of California).

Table 2-3 also shows that the trunk carriers experienced a much greater decrease in their share of total revenue passenger originations than in their share of RPM from 1949 to 1965—that is, 11.0 vs. 3.2 percentage points. By far the largest portion of the trunk carriers' overall decrease in market share occurred after 1958. In that year the trunk carriers as a group began to reduce the number of domestic points that they served. In 1957, a high of about 373 points received service from one or more trunk carriers; by 1964 only about 242 points had trunk service.[37] It seems truly remarkable that a 35 per-

---

is no production even though 18 individuals decide to play nine innings of baseball. The same reasoning may be applied to theatrical productions, university lectures, medical services, and transportation. Aside from the nebulous value of having space available should it be demanded, is the transporting of empty seats from point A to point B productive? If not, then revenue passenger-miles measure production as well as consumption. Given this idea of their theoretical limitations, however, it is believed that ASM do provide an indication of airline production that will be useful for the purpose of this study.

[37] CAB, Office of the Secretary, Schedules and Records Unit, *Suspensions and Points Authorized (Exclusive and Combination)*, unpublished worksheets. This measure was calculated by taking the simple average of the number of authorized points actually served by trunk and local service carriers as of February 15, May 16, August 15, and November 15 of each year. Any point served through two or more airports (New York, Chicago, Los Angeles, etc.) was still considered to be only one point. A summary of the average number of points

Table 2-3

Percentage Distribution of Total Passenger Originations, RPM, and ASM
Trunk, Local Service, and California Intrastate Carriers
Scheduled Domestic Service, Selected Years 1949-1965

| | Percent of Total Domestic | | | | | | | | |
| Year | Passenger Originations | | | RPM | | | ASM | | |
	Trunk	Local	Intra.	Trunk	Local	Intra.	Trunk	Local	Intra.
1949	94.1%	4.6%	1.3%	97.1%	2.0%	0.9%	95.1%	4.1%	0.8%
1952	91.9	7.0	1.1	96.6	2.7	0.7	94.6	4.8	0.6
1955	91.7	7.8	0.5	97.0	2.7	0.3	95.9	3.8	0.3
1958	89.6	9.7	0.7	96.4	3.2	0.4	95.5	4.2	0.3
1961	86.1	12.5	1.4	94.9	4.3	0.8	93.6	5.8	0.6
1964	83.4	14.4	2.2	93.7	5.1	1.2	93.1	6.0	0.9
1965	83.1	14.7	2.2	93.9	5.0	1.1	93.2	5.8	1.0

Sources: Calculated from data presented in CAB, *Handbook of Airline Statistics*, pp. 46, 47, and 78; and in Appendices 2, 3, and 4 of this book.

cent decrease in the number of points served should have been accompanied by a reduction of less than three percentage points in share of total domestic RPM. This implies that the trunk carriers terminated service at the low-traffic generating points where unit costs are high.[38] In addition, the greater reduction in the passenger origination share than in the RPM share means a relative increase occurred in the average passenger trip length.[39] Overall, it appears that the trunk carriers mainly "lost" short-haul passengers generated at small, high-cost stations. It seems likely that their reductions in market shares have resulted in increased profits (or decreased losses) over what they would have attained had this traffic not been "lost."

These market-share data provide another means of making a simplistic estimate of the number of potential interstate airlines that could have existed had there been no CAB regulation. If one percent or less of total domestic RPM has been adequate to support one or two California intrastate carriers producing even smaller percentages of total ASM without direct subsidy (compare Tables 2-1 and 2-3), it would seem reasonable to expect that the other 99 percent of total

served by certificated carriers from 1949 through 1964 is given in Jordan, *Economic Effects of Airline Regulation*, pp. 512-17.

[38] A number of these small points were transferred from the trunk carriers to the subsidized local service carriers. The local service carriers' average number of points served increased from 388 in 1957 to 464 in 1964. Jordan, *Economic Effects of Airline Regulation*, pp. 512-17.

[39] CAB, *Handbook of Airline Statistics*, p. 84.

domestic RPM could support between 100 and 200 carriers, instead of the 24 to 35 that actually existed from 1949 to 1965. As in the case of the estimates based on airports served and route-miles operated, the accuracy of this estimate can be questioned, but the consistency among the results derived from using the three different estimating methods is noteworthy. In addition, the results are all consistent with what one would expect if CAB regulation did serve to limit the number of interstate airlines in existence at any given time.

Conclusion

The evidence regarding the effects of the CAB's regulation of entry is unambiguous. Clearly, the CAB has allowed fewer airlines to provide interstate passenger service than would have tried to do so had the CAB not existed. If 16 airlines tried to enter the geographically restricted California market between 1946 and 1965, one can well conclude that a great many more would have tried to enter the much larger interstate market. Yet, only 37 airlines were allowed to operate as trunk or local service carriers during this period. Also, in the case of each of the two classes of certificated carriers, entry was restricted to a single, discreet time period, in contrast to the entry of intrastate carriers at various times from 1946 through 1964.

The difference between the certificated carriers and the California intrastate carriers in terms of the means by which exit occurred also provides convincing evidence that CAB regulation did affect exit. If only one California intrastate carrier had terminated service via merger or acquisition, or if only one certificated carrier had left the industry through some means other than these, one could question the impact of regulation in this area. But the contrast is not complicated by exceptions. In the case of the regulated airlines, each departing carrier was consistently merged with or acquired by a remaining certificated carrier; in the case of relatively nonregulated airlines, exit always occurred through bankruptcy, sale of assets, or the transferal of operations to other areas.

The evidence is not as clear whether the number of certificated carriers in existence at any one time was limited by CAB regulation. There is no question, however, that some intrastate carriers have been able to survive for appreciable time periods even when serving a much smaller number of airports, connected by many fewer route miles than that of the smallest of the certificated carriers. Also, intrastate carriers survived even though the average traffic carried by them was much less than that of the smallest trunk carrier and even smaller than that of most subsidized local service carriers. These findings imply that the existing certificated carriers, especially the trunk carriers, are much larger than required for economic survival and that without CAB regulation the number of interstate airlines would have substantially exceeded the number that actually existed.

Additional insight can be obtained by contrasting the CAB's regulatory actions to those that might be expected if the consumer-protection hypothesis was predictive of the effects of CAB regulation. This hypothesis implies that if airlines could be located that offered reliable service at fares lower than those of existing regulated airlines the CAB would allow the new carriers to expand their operations into regulated markets in order to benefit a larger number of travelers. Later chapters will show that several of the intrastate carriers did offer reliable service at fares lower than those of the certificated carriers. The CAB, however, never allowed a California intrastate carrier to expand its service beyond the state borders. Quite the contrary, it refused to allow California Central to extend its existing route from San Diego to Tijuana, Mexico (about 20 miles);[40] it filed a cease and desist order against PSA to prevent its carrying connecting interstate passengers on its intrastate flights;[41] and it directly or indirectly (through FAA actions) prevented two or three intrastate carriers from operating to Lake Tahoe (on the California side of the California–Nevada border) on the grounds that their passengers might actually be destined for Nevada and, thus, would be interstate passengers.[42]

The CAB's effective control of entry and exit provides ample evidence that the no-effect hypothesis does not describe the effects of CAB regulation. Thus, of the three hypotheses proposed in chapter 1, the evidence presented in this chapter is most consistent with the implications of the cartel hypothesis. Overall, it is clear that regulation does prevent potential airlines from entering markets, compels interstate airlines to join a specific group of carriers, prevents carriers from leaving the regulated industry if they intend to continue interstate service, and provides for the transferal of the routes and markets of departing carriers to remaining regulated carriers. In addition, it appears to limit the number of airlines in existence at any one time. Thus, CAB regulation has solved some very important problems for the certificated carriers, problems that cartels must solve in order to be effective.

[40] CAB Order No. E-8782 (adopted November 24, 1954).

[41] CAB Order No. E-19655 (adopted June 10, 1963).

[42] CAB Order No. E-22387 (adopted June 30, 1965). Also, telephone conversation with employee of Holiday Airlines, July 20, 1967.

Rivalry through Service Quality

3

Introduction

The Civil Aeronautics Board's direct power over service has always been limited. This regulatory shortcoming would probably not be significant if the CAB permitted the certificated carriers to pool their output and explicitly allocate industry profits on the basis of some predetermined formula. In such a situation, the carriers would simply endeavor to provide levels of service that maximized industry profits under the prices authorized by the CAB—that is, they would seek to maintain levels of service at which the industry's marginal revenues from improved service equaled the marginal costs of the improvements. The CAB, however, has allowed little output pooling and even less allocation of industry profits.[1] Therefore, if two or more certificated carriers serve the same markets without market shares being specified, it is reasonable to expect rivalry among them for larger traffic shares and profits.[2] Given the Board's limited control

---

[1] The main examples of output pooling and profit allocation among the certificated carriers are to be found in the few equipment interchange agreements authorized by the CAB and in the Mutual Aid Strike Pact. See Caves, *Air Transport and Its Regulators*, pp. 185, 196, 203-4, and 243; and CAB, *Handbook of Airline Statistics*, pp. 470 and 500. For information on the more extensive airline pooling in Europe, see S. Wheatcroft, *The Economics of European Air Transport* (Cambridge, Mass.: Harvard University Press, 1956), pp. 249-68; and S. Wheatcroft, *Air Transport Policy* (London: Michael Joseph, 1964), pp. 102-3.

[2] The CAB can and has limited the ability of carriers to obtain traffic in various multi-carrier markets by imposing operating restrictions on their authorizations. For example, it may prohibit one carrier from operating nonstop service between a city pair, or it may forbid turnaround service while allowing other

over service, in contrast to its full control of prices, it is in the area of service that one should look for certificated carrier rivalry to be expressed, resulting in high levels of service quality.

The CAB can influence a carrier's output and profit through its regulation of entry. The more markets the Board allows a carrier to serve, other things held constant, the greater the carrier's share of total industry traffic. If every market (pair of cities) were awarded to just one carrier, an explicit allocation of industry output and profits (or losses) would result, and there would be little incentive for carrier rivalry. This is essentially what the CAB did with the local service carriers throughout the period studied. Because these carriers were granted monopoly rights in most of their markets (mainly short-haul, low-density markets), their traffic potential was well defined and there was little carrier rivalry for traffic. A much different situation existed in the major interstate markets. The CAB generally reserved these markets for the trunk carriers, but since World War II, the number of such markets served by only one trunk carrier has steadily decreased. Indeed, an increasing number of the major markets (and some of the smaller ones) have been served by three, four, or more trunk carriers.[3] Since the CAB has not explicitly allocated traffic shares to the trunk carriers serving each market, it is not surprising to find substantial rivalry among these carriers to attract passengers. Furthermore, given the CAB's control of prices, it is not surprising to find this carrier rivalry concentrated on improving service quality rather than on reducing prices. The California intrastate carriers also experienced great carrier rivalry in their major markets, both with certificated carriers and among themselves. But, since the California Public Utilities Commission did not restrict price decreases, this rivalry could be expressed through lower fares as well as through service improvements.

The above differences in carrier rivalry and in the degree and type of regulation provide the basis for predicting that the trunk carriers' service was superior to that of both the local service carriers and the California intrastate carriers during the period studied, while the California airlines' prices were lower than those of the certifi-

---

carriers to provide unrestricted service. See Richmond, *Regulation and Competition in Air Transportation*, pp. 82–85 and 272.

[3] Richmond in *ibid.*, provides a thorough study of the 514 city pairs in which the CAB authorized new or improved multiple-carrier service in fourteen decisions made between September 1, 1955, and December 31, 1956. (See chapter VII of that book.) As a result of these decisions, the number of trunk carriers authorized to serve the New York–Washington market increased from four to nine (*ibid.*, pp. 36, 174, and 282).

cated carriers. This chapter will describe the differences in service quality among the three carrier groups; the following chapters will describe the differences in price levels and structures.

Airline Innovation

The airlines have adopted innumerable innovations of varying importance affecting the quality of their service. Such a volume and diversity of innovation makes it impossible to calculate one inclusive measure of service quality. In this section, therefore, the trunk, local service, and California intrastate carriers will be compared in terms of their adoption of four major innovations that appear to have greatly influenced service quality since 1945. Then, in the following section, the California intrastate carriers' safety record will be compared with that of the certificated carriers.

Three factors are relevant in comparing the adoption of innovations by airlines. These factors are the date the innovation was initially adopted, the rate at which it was adopted, and the extent to which it was adopted. Clearly, a late and token adoption of some innovation has less impact on service quality than an early, rapid, and extensive adoption. With regard to safety, a relatively low passenger fatality rate yields a superior quality of service. Comparing the three carrier groups in terms of their adoption of selected innovations and their relative safety records provides a basis for ranking them in terms of their quality of service from 1946 through 1965.

Table 3-1 lists the four major innovations selected for comparison and gives the date that each was initially adopted by the three carrier groups. The pressurized aircraft innovation was selected for comparison because by eliminating many of the effects of altitude on passenger comfort it greatly increased the appeal of air travel. In addition, by insulating passengers from altitude effects, it substantially increased the flexibility and efficiency of airline operations. Except for the Martin 202, all large transport aircraft types produced after World War II were pressurized.

The adoption of turbine-powered aircraft (especially large turbojet/fan aircraft) resulted in greatly increased speeds, reduced cabin noise and vibration, and lower seat-mile operating costs. The truly major dimensions of this innovation will become clear later in this section.

The inauguration of single-class coach service, when only first-class service had been provided previously, resulted in a *lower* quality of service. However, because this inferior service was offered at lower fares, passengers who valued travel comfort relatively less than other

Table 3-1

Adoption Dates of Four Major Airline Innovations
by the Trunk, Local Service, and California Intrastate Carriers

Innovation	Trunk	Date of Adoption Local Service	Calif. Intrastate
Technological			
Pressurized aircraft	Feb. 15, 1946[a]	July 1, 1955	Nov. 20, 1959[b]
Turbine-powered aircraft			
Turboprop	July 26, 1955	Sept. 28, 1958	Nov. 20, 1959
Turbojet/fan	Dec. 10, 1958	July 15, 1965	Apr. 9, 1965
Class of Service			
Single-class coach	Nov. 4, 1948	April 1952	Jan. 2, 1949
Mixed-class	Aug. 18, 1955	_[c]	_[c]

[a]Excludes five pressurized Boeing B-307's operated briefly by TWA beginning July 8, 1940, and then reintroduced without pressurization on April 1, 1945, following wartime service.
[b]Excludes one Lockheed L-049 operated jointly by Airline Transport Carriers and California Central Airlines from July 17, 1952 through July 3, 1953. CCA accounted for only about four percent of this aircraft's total revenue mileage during those 12 months, i.e., about 20 round trips between Burbank and San Francisco.
[c]These carriers did not adopt mixed-class service during the period studied.

Sources: CAB, *Handbook of Airline Statistics* (June 1960 ed.), p. 94; (1967 ed.), pp. 440, 444–45, and 490–91. Mohawk Airlines, *The Air Chief* 13, no. 6 (November–December 1965), p. 3. *Pedigree of Champions, Boeing Since 1916*, D6-8988 (Seattle: The Boeing Company, November 1963), pp. 46–47. U.S. District Court, Southern District of California, files of the Court Clerk, Bankruptcies Nos. 59560-PH and 59561-PH, California Central Airlines and Airline Transport Carriers Combined Aircraft Utilization, 1952 and 1953, unpublished report (n.d.).

goods were provided a price/product combination that differed significantly from that previously available. Since much of the certificated carriers' early single-class coach service was offered in older aircraft and was operated at generally less convenient hours of the day (often at night), it was possible for these carriers to differentiate their product into two fairly distinct types. The coach type attracted one segment of the overall market without unduly "diverting" from the other, which was comprised of individuals willing to pay higher fares for first-class service.

The major contribution of mixed-class (or combination) service was to break down the product differentiation that the trunk carriers had been able to establish with single-class service. The offering of both first-class and coach service in the same aircraft meant that schedule convenience was the same for both types of service, while differences in passenger comfort were reduced. This, combined with the lower coach fares, resulted in the rapid growth of the trunk carriers' coach traffic at the expense of first-class, until coach service came to dominate total operations.

Pressurized Aircraft. Table 3-1 shows that the trunk carriers adopted pressurization over nine years before the local service carriers and almost fourteen years before the California intrastate carriers. Table 3-2 indicates that the trunk carriers' adoption of this innovation was rapid and extensive. By 1949, the third full year in which pressurized aircraft were operated, 53.5 percent of the trunk carriers' total ASM were produced in such aircraft (mainly four-engine aircraft). From a total of 3.8 billion ASM, produced entirely with nonpressurized aircraft in 1945,[4] the trunk carriers' total output increased by 7.3 billion ASM (193 percent) in four years. Of this increase, 6.0 billion ASM were accounted for by new pressurized aircraft. Similarly, the 18.9 billion (170 percent) increase in total ASM over the six years from 1949 to 1955 was all accounted for by pressurized aircraft (again, largely by four-engine aircraft). During 1955, 88.8 percent of the trunk carriers' output was in pressurized aircraft. Thus, by the ninth full year after its introduction, this significant improvement in service quality had been almost completely adopted by the trunk carriers.

In addition to being nine years behind the trunk carriers in adopting pressurized aircraft, the local service carriers adopted this innovation at a much slower rate. It took them six (rather than three) years to produce half of their total ASM in pressurized aircraft; during the ninth full year after initial adoption, they produced 76.3 percent in such aircraft, compared with the 88.8 percent that the trunk carriers produced in a similar period. Without doubt, throughout the years covered by this study, the local service carriers' service was markedly inferior to that of the trunk carriers with respect to pressurization.

The California intrastate carriers adopted pressurization even later than the local service carriers. If one ignores the insignificant amount of service temporarily produced by California Central in an L-049 during 1952-53, it can be said that the California airlines did not adopt pressurized aircraft until November 20, 1959. Once intro-

[4] CAB, *Handbook of Airline Statistics*, p. 46.

Table 3-2

Percent of Total Available Seat-Miles Produced with Pressurized Aircraft Trunk, Local Service, and California Intrastate Carriers Scheduled Domestic Service, Selected Years 1947–1965

Carrier Class and Aircraft Type	1947	1949	1952	1955	1958	1961	1964	1965
					Year			
A. Total Available Seat-Miles (billions)								
Trunk	9.15	11.12	18.07	29.98	40.70	52.53	75.24	88.73
Local Service	0.16	0.48	0.91	1.18	1.79	3.23	4.84	5.55
California Intrastate	n.a.	0.09*	0.13*	0.09*	0.14	0.32	0.71*	0.94*
B. Percent of Total ASM Produced with Pressurized Aircraft								
Trunk								
Piston								
2-Engine	13.4%	9.4%	14.3%	20.1%	14.1%	5.4%	1.9%	1.5%
4-Engine	—	44.1	57.4	68.6	78.0	30.3	12.9	8.4
Turbine								
Propeller	—	—	—	0.1	5.1	13.9	11.0	9.5
Jet/fan	—	—	—	—	0.02	50.1	74.2	80.6
Total	13.4	53.5	71.7	88.8	97.22	99.7	100.0[a]	100.0[a]
Local Service								
Piston								
2-Engine	—	0.0	0.0	1.6	6.4	30.3	56.3	55.1
Turbine								
Propeller	—	—	—	0.0	0.9	20.7	20.0	25.8
Jet/fan	—	—	—	—	0.0	0.0	0.0	1.4
Total	—	0.0	0.0	1.6	7.3	51.0	76.3	82.3
California Intrastate								
Piston								
4-Engine	0.0	0.0	0.5*	0.0	0.0	4.2*	8.5*	0.0
Turbine								
Propeller	—	—	—	0.0	0.0	95.8*	91.3*	66.6*
Jet/fan	—	—	—	—	0.0	0.0	0.0	33.2*
Total	0.0	0.0	0.5*	0.0	0.0	100.0	99.8*	99.8*

n.a.—not available.
*Partially estimated.
[a] Approximately 0.05% of total trunk ASM were produced in nonpressurized DC-3's in 1964 and 1965.

Sources: Air Transport Association of America (ATA), *Comparative Statement of Flight and Traffic Statistics* (12 Months Ending December 31, 1947, 1949, 1952, and 1955). ATA, *Quarterly Comparative Statement of Air Carriers' Aircraft Operating Statistics* (12 Months Ending December 31, 1958, 1961, 1964, and 1965). CAB, *Handbook of Airline Statistics*, p. 46. Appendices 4 and 5 of this book.

duced, however, the rate and extent of adoption was impressive. Pacific Southwest Airlines (PSA) was the only intrastate carrier operating at that time, and it completely replaced its fleet of non-pressurized DC-4's with pressurized Electras within about two months. During 1960, over 98 percent of PSA's total ASM were produced with Electras.[5] Some of the intrastate carriers that entered in 1962–64 operated nonpressurized aircraft, but at no time after 1960 did such aircraft account for more than one percent of total ASM produced by all California airlines. Thus, prior to 1960, these carriers' service quality with respect to pressurization was inferior to that of the trunk carriers; from 1955 to 1959, it was also inferior to that of the local service carriers. From 1960 to 1965, however, the California intrastate carriers' service quality in this regard was fully comparable to that of the trunk carriers and was far superior to that of the local service carriers.

Turbine-Powered Aircraft. Since all turbine-powered aircraft were pressurized, the percentages for these aircraft in Table 3–2 can be used to summarize the rate and extent to which the turbine-engine innovation was adopted by the three carrier groups. Capital Airlines' introduction of the English-built Vickers Viscount on July 26, 1955, began the trunk carriers' initially slow adoption of turbine-powered aircraft. By 1958, only about five percent of total trunk ASM were produced with this turboprop aircraft. The introduction of turbojet aircraft by National Airlines on December 10, 1958, brought about a complete change in the adoption rate of turbine-powered aircraft. During 1962 (the fourth full year of turbojet/fan operations), the trunk carriers produced as many ASM (38.6 billion) with these aircraft as they produced with all piston-powered aircraft during 1958—the peak year of piston-powered output.[6] By 1965, the trunk carriers produced more than twice as many ASM as in 1958, and turbojet/fan aircraft accounted for 80.6 percent of the total, with turboprop aircraft producing an additional 9.5 percent. This left piston-powered aircraft with less than ten percent of the total. Changes of this magnitude and rapidity might better be characterized as "revolution" rather than "innovation."

Returning briefly to the development of turboprop operations, the introduction of the American-built Lockheed Electra (on Decem-

[5] Pacific Southwest Airlines, Company Records.

[6] Air Transport Association of America (ATA), *Quarterly Comparative Statement of Air Carriers' Aircraft Operating Statistics* (12 Months Ending December 31, 1958, and 1962).

ber 30, 1958) resulted in a quadrupling of turboprop output between 1958 and 1960, but from 1960 through 1965 turboprop output remained essentially constant at around eight billion ASM.[7] Obviously, the growth of turbine-powered aircraft output since 1960 has been due to the expansion of turbojet/fan service. By the end of 1965 some of the trunk carriers had already decided to phase their turboprop aircraft out of service.[8]

The local service carriers introduced turbine-powered aircraft on September 27, 1958, when West Coast Airlines began using the turboprop Fairchild F-27. This was just over three years after the first turboprop aircraft had been introduced by Capital Airlines, but it was about three months *before* the trunk carriers inaugurated service with American-built turbojet and turboprop aircraft. Thus, in terms of American-built aircraft, the local service carriers adopted the turbine-powered aircraft innovation at about the same time as the trunk carriers. Unlike the trunk carriers during these years, however, the local service carriers' rate and extent of adoption of these new aircraft were quite low. Between 1958 and 1961, there was a net addition of 19.8 percentage points to the local service carriers' turboprop aircraft share of total ASM, compared to a 58.9 percentage point increase in the trunk carriers' turbine-powered aircraft share. Between 1961 and 1964, the local service carriers replaced large numbers of their obsolete DC-3's with pressurized Convair and Martin piston-powered aircraft (purchased secondhand from the trunk carriers) but added only a few turboprop aircraft to their fleets. As a result, the turboprop percentage of their total ASM actually declined in 1962 and 1963 before recovering to 25.8 percent of the total in 1965.[9]

One reason for the low rate and extent of adoption of turbine-powered aircraft by the local service carriers is that no more than six out of the thirteen carriers flew such aircraft at any one time through 1964.[10] During 1965, however, three more local service carriers added turboprop aircraft to their fleets, and on July 15, 1965, Mohawk Airlines introduced the turbofan BAC-111 to local service

[7] *Ibid.* (12 Months Ending December 31, 1958, through 1965).

[8] For example, in late 1965, Continental Air Lines arranged to sell its 11 Viscount 812 aircraft to Channel Airways Ltd., a British airline. CAB Order No. E-23147 (adopted January 21, 1966).

[9] In 1962 and 1963, turboprop aircraft accounted for 21.3 and 19.4 percent, respectively, of total local service carrier scheduled ASM. ATA, *Quarterly Comparative Statement of Air Carriers' Aircraft Operating Statistics* (12 Months Ending December 31, 1962, and 1963).

[10] *Ibid.* (12 Months Ending December 31, 1959, through 1964).

operations (6½ years after the trunk carriers began flying turbojet aircraft).[11] By January 1966, all local service carriers had placed orders for a total of 152 turboprop and turbofan aircraft to be delivered in that and the following two years.[12] Therefore, whereas all of the trunk carriers were operating turbine-powered aircraft by 1959,[13] it took all of the local service carriers about eight additional years to adopt this innovation.

Clearly, as in the case of pressurization, the slowness of the local service carriers to adopt turbine-powered aircraft resulted in their service quality being significantly inferior to that of the trunk carriers in this respect. Furthermore, if the service superiority of turbojet/fan aircraft over turboprop aircraft is also taken into consideration, the differences in service quality between these two carrier groups become even greater than indicated by the comparison of all turbine-powered aircraft.

As already mentioned, the California intrastate carriers' adoption of turbine-powered aircraft and pressurized aircraft took place simultaneously when PSA replaced its DC-4's with Electras beginning on November 20, 1959. This was about a year after American-built turbine-powered aircraft were introduced by the trunk and local service carriers and coincided with the adoption of such aircraft by the last of the trunk carriers. Since PSA retired all of its DC-4's by February 1960, and was the only intrastate carrier operating at that time, the rate and extent of adoption of the turbine-powered aircraft innovation by this class of carriers could hardly have been greater. None of the intrastate carriers inaugurating service in 1962–64 operated turbine-powered aircraft, but PSA was so much larger than these carriers that the overall extent of adoption of the turbine-engine innovation by the intrastate carriers as a group substantially exceeded that of the trunk and local service carriers from 1960 through 1965. Table 3–2 shows that by 1965, 99.8 percent of total intrastate carrier ASM were produced in turbine-powered aircraft,

[11] *Ibid.* (12 Months Ending December 31, 1965). Also, see Mohawk Airlines, *The Air Chief* 13, no. 6 (November–December 1965), p. 3.
[12] *Aviation Week and Space Technology* (October 25, 1965), pp. 146–49; (November 8, 1965), pp. 40 and 57; (January 24, 1966), p. 37; and (February 7, 1966), p. 35. Table 1 of CAB Press Release No. 68-69 (June 18, 1968) shows that by December 31, 1967, all local service carriers operated turbine-powered aircraft (with Southern Airways' three turbofan aircraft comprising the smallest turbine-powered fleet), and that 253 out of a total of 414 aircraft were turbine-powered.
[13] ATA, *Quarterly Comparative Statement of Air Carriers' Aircraft Operating Statistics* (12 Months Ending December 31, 1959).

compared to 90.1 percent for the trunk carriers and only 27.2 percent for the local service carriers.

PSA's adoption of turbine-powered aircraft differed from that of the trunk carriers in one important respect. Whereas the trunk carriers emphasized turbojet/fan rather than turboprop aircraft, PSA expanded its turboprop fleet from three to six Electras by buying an additional aircraft in 1961, 1962, and 1963, even though new turbojet/fan aircraft were available during those years. It did not take delivery of its first pure jet aircraft, a Boeing 727-100, until April 6, 1965 (inaugurating service three days later); however, it received four more B-727-100's in the next four months and a sixth on March 7, 1966.[14] Obviously, once started, PSA also adopted turbofan aircraft at an extremely rapid rate, but the fact remains that it postponed adopting such aircraft for several years.

There seem to be at least two reasons for PSA's delay in adopting turbojet/fan aircraft. The first is that its Electra schedule time between Los Angeles and San Francisco was within two to five minutes of the schedule times advertised by United and Western for their turbofan service,[15] while, until September 27, 1964, the trunk carriers' jet-coach service in this, the largest California, market cost up to $11 more than PSA's Electra service.[16] Apparently this fare differential was sufficient to outweigh the service quality differences in the opinion of many travelers. The second reason is that the three-engine Boeing 727 was the first American turbojet/fan aircraft designed for "medium-range" rather than nonstop coast-to-coast flights. As a result, it has a smaller fuel capacity and lighter structure than four-engine turbojet/fan aircraft. With an operating weight

[14] PSA, Company Records.

[15] PSA's schedule time for Electras was 60 minutes. United's B-727 schedule time was 55 minutes, and Western's B-720B time was 58 minutes. See *Official Airline Guide*, North American Edition, 22, no. 7 (April 1966), various pages for these carriers. There is some question about the comparability of PSA's schedule times with those of United and Western. The trunk carriers have agreed (through the Air Transport Association) to quote schedule times on a block-to-block basis. PSA's times, on the other hand, are measured from block-to-touchdown—that is, they exclude the time required to taxi to the terminal after landing. Another factor favoring PSA is that in the great majority of times their Electras were operated under the FAA's visual flight rules (VFR) while the certificated carriers (again by industry agreement) flew under the more time-consuming instrument flight rules (IFR). It is thought that these two factors reduced PSA's advertized schedule times by about 10 minutes. Perhaps half of this saving is illusory (due to differences in definitions), while the other five minutes are real (resulting from different operating procedures).

[16] See chapter 5, and Appendices 6(B), 6(C), and 7 of this book.

empty of about 86,500 pounds, a Boeing 727-100 can hold up to 122 seats (passengers), yielding an average of 709 pounds per seat. In comparison, the operating weight empty per seat of a Boeing 720B (neither the largest nor the longest-range four-engine turbofan aircraft) is about 798 pounds (116,500 pounds divided by a maximum capacity of 146 seats).[17] It seems reasonable to expect that, other things being equal, this 13 percent difference in operating weight empty per seat would be reflected in higher direct operating costs. This should be particularly important to a carrier, such as PSA, that always provided service at relatively low fares.

In conclusion, the California intrastate airlines (in the form of PSA) adopted the turbine-powered aircraft innovation at about the same time the trunk and local service carriers adopted American-built turbine-powered aircraft, and their rate and extent of adoption in the early 1960's was much greater than that of the CAB-regulated airlines. PSA's early reliance on turboprop rather than turbojet/fan aircraft makes it difficult, however, to specify whether the trunk or the California intrastate carriers offered a higher average level of service quality with respect to the overall turbine-powered aircraft innovation. The trunk carriers operated a much larger proportion of the superior turbojet/fan aircraft, but because they retained a number of piston-powered aircraft their total turbine-powered aircraft percentages were appreciably lower than those of the California intrastate carriers as a group. This difficulty in objectively specifying relative superiority leads to the conclusion that the average service quality of these two carrier groups, with respect to turbine-powered aircraft, was roughly the same from 1960 through 1965. There is no such difficulty in ranking the local service and California intrastate carriers. Obviously, beginning in 1960 the intrastate carriers were much superior to the local service carriers in terms of turbine-powered aircraft.

Class of Service. The CAB classifies passenger service into two general categories: first-class and coach plus economy. First-class service is defined as "transport service established for the carriage of passengers at standard fares, premium fares, or at reduced fares such as family-plan and first-class excursion for whom standard or premium quality services are provided."[18] In every postwar aircraft

---

[17] Boeing Company specifications for the B-727-100 and the B-720B. A 98-seat Electra has an operating weight empty of about 61,000 pounds, or only about 622 pounds per seat (Lockheed Aircraft Corporation specifications). These specifications were located in Western Air Lines Company Records.

[18] CAB, *Handbook of Airline Statistics*, p. 536.

operated by the trunk carriers, first-class service has been characterized by four-abreast seating with a seat pitch of 36 to 40 inches.
Coach plus economy service is defined as passenger service at fares
and quality of service below first-class service.[19] This combines the
conventional coach service having five- and six-abreast seating with
off-peak, reduced-fare services performed in first-class configured aircraft and with such services as standard-class, business-class, air bus,
Air Shuttle, commuter, and Thriftair. Thus, the development of
coach plus economy service reflects the growth of a group of services
much more heterogeneous than those included under the first-class
service classification. In this study, this more heterogeneous group of
services will be referred to simply as coach service.

Table 3-1 shows that the trunk carriers were the first of the
three carrier groups to provide scheduled, high-density coach service.
Capital Airlines introduced this service on November 4, 1948, and
was followed by nine more trunk carriers during 1949.[20] The rate
and extent of adoption of single-class coach service, and of coach
service offered in mixed-class aircraft, are shown in Table 3-3. It
took 13 years (until 1961) for coach to account for more than half
of the total ASM, and it required both the single-class coach and the
mixed-class service innovations to achieve this degree of penetration.
Between 1949 and 1952, and again between 1952 and 1955, the
single-class coach share of total ASM increased by about 15 percentage points. From 1955 to 1958, however, it increased by only
2.5 percentage points, indicating an important reduction in the rate
at which this innovation was adopted.

The introduction of mixed-class service (offered in aircraft configured to provide both first-class and coach service as joint products) destroyed the possibility of maintaining first-class as the dominant type of service offered by the trunk carriers. It also served to
reduce greatly the importance of single-class coach service in trunk
carrier operations. Mixed-class coach service was introduced by Eastern Air Lines on August 18, 1955, and accounted for only 4.6
percent of total trunk ASM by 1958.[21] However, its share of total
output exploded to 36.1 percent in 1961, while single-class coach
service declined from 35.4 percent of total ASM in 1958 to only
17.9 percent in 1961. This change in the relative importance of
single-class and mixed-class aircraft in producing coach service was

[19] *Ibid.*

[20] For a description of the early development of coach service by the trunk
carriers, see Cherington, *Airline Price Policy*, pp. 186–289.

[21] CAB, *Handbook of Airline Statistics* (June 1960 ed.), p. 94.

Table 3-3

Percent of Total Available Seat-Miles Produced in Coach Service
Trunk, Local Service, and California Intrastate Carriers
Scheduled Domestic Service, Selected Years 1949–1965

	Percent of Total ASM Produced in Coach Service				
Year	Trunk			Local Service	Calif. Intrastate
	Single-Class Aircraft	Mixed-Class Aircraft	Total	Single-Class Aircraft[a]	Single-Class Aircraft[a]
1949	3.2%	—	3.2%	0.0%	100.0%
1952	17.3	—	17.3	0.1	100.0
1955	32.9	0.2%	33.1	0.0	100.0
1958	35.4	4.6	40.0	3.1	100.0
1961	17.9	36.1	54.0	1.7	100.0
1964	20.1	48.8	68.9	0.6	100.0
1965	13.2	58.1	71.3	0.02	100.0

[a]These carriers did not operate mixed-class configured aircraft during this period.

Sources: ATA, *Comparative Statement of Flight and Traffic Statistics* (12 Months Ending December 31, 1947, 1949, 1952, and 1955). ATA, *Quarterly Comparative Statement of Air Carriers' Aircraft Operating Statistics* (12 Months Ending December 31, 1958, 1964, and 1965). Appendix 4 of this book.

largely due to the almost universal introduction of turbojet/fan aircraft in mixed-class rather than single-class configuration.[22] Thus, as turbojet/fan aircraft replaced four-engine, piston-powered aircraft, both coach and first-class service were offered where only first-class service had been previously available. Not only that, but turbojet/fan service was so far superior to piston service that many passengers were "diverted" from the remaining first-class, piston-powered flights to coach service in turbojet/fan aircraft. This trend continued throughout the early 1960's, so that by 1965, 71.3 percent of the total ASM were produced in coach service, 58.1 percent of which were accounted for by mixed-class aircraft and only 13.2 percent by single-class aircraft.

Taken together, the two class-of-service innovations resulted in an increase in the coach share of total output of around five percentage points per year from 1949 to 1964 (except for a lower rate between 1955 and 1958). This was a much lower rate than those at which the trunk carriers adopted the two technological innovations

[22] CAB, *Handbook of Airline Statistics*, p. 445.

(see Table 3-2), but it was quite consistent with the trunk carriers' emphasis on high service quality. Clearly, to the extent the trunk carriers delayed replacing first-class with coach service, their overall quality of service was enhanced. Similarly, their rapid adoption of the most modern pressurized and turbine-powered aircraft also served to improve their service quality.

Table 3-3 shows that the local service carriers provided little coach service through 1965. Except for a very small amount produced by Bonanza Air Lines from April 1952 to April 1953, this carrier group delayed introducing single-class coach service until July 1956, almost eight years after the first trunk carrier inaugurated such service.[23] In addition, since these carriers did not adopt the mixed-class service innovation during these years, they did not experience the great expansion in coach service that the trunk carriers experienced with that innovation. Between July 1956 and the end of 1965, only four local service carriers offered any coach service, and one, Pacific Air Lines, accounted for the majority of the coach ASM produced.[24] In 1962 and 1963, coach ASM reached a peak of about 3.5 percent of total local service output.[25] The coach share then fell to less than one percent of the total in 1964 and to almost nothing in 1965. Overall, the local service carriers' adoption of the single-class coach innovation was late and their rate and extent of adoption very limited.

One problem faced by the local service carriers in providing coach service during this period was the inflexible seating capacity of their two-engine, propeller aircraft. Unlike the trunk carriers with their four-engine aircraft, the local service carriers could not add an extra one or two seats per row when providing coach rather than first-class service. Thus, the profit potential of their coach service was relatively restricted. Perhaps an even more important factor influencing the local service carriers' limited adoption of coach service was the lack of airline rivalry over their routes. The large irregular

[23] *Ibid.*, pp. 442 and 444.

[24] These four carriers were Pacific Air Lines (July 1956 to April 1964), Trans-Texas Airways (June 1962 to October 1963), Central Airlines (July to December 1964), and Ozark Air Lines (March to May 1965). *Ibid.*, pp. 444 and 482. CAB, *Air Carrier Traffic Statistics* XI-2 (February 1965), p. 49; and XI-6 (June 1965), pp. 20 and 48. It is significant that because Pacific's routes are located largely within California it was subject to the rivalry associated with the extensive and early development of coach service by the California intrastate carriers (see below, p. 49).

[25] Calculated from data presented in CAB, *Handbook of Airline Statistics*, p. 135.

airlines never operated over these low-density routes, and with just a few exceptions, through 1965 the CAB did not allow direct rivalry between two or more carriers in markets assigned to a local service carrier. Because of this lack of rivalry, it was relatively easy for the local service carriers to limit the variety and range of their services and fares.

Evidence consistent with the lack-of-rivalry hypothesis can be found in the differing policies adopted by the first trunk carrier and the first local service carrier to introduce two-engine turbofan aircraft. In 1965, for the first time in history, a trunk carrier (Braniff) and a local service carrier (Mohawk) introduced a new aircraft (the BAC-111) at essentially the same time. Braniff operated its BAC-111's in a mixed-class configuration having 24 four-abreast, first-class seats in the front of the cabin, and 39 five-abreast coach seats in the rear, for a total of 63 seats.[26] In contrast, Mohawk inaugurated BAC-111 service with first-class seating only. Its first-class configuration, however, consisted of alternating rows of four-abreast and five-abreast seats throughout the cabin, and a total of 69 such seats were installed.[27] Thus, Mohawk utilized the cabin of its BAC-111's more intensively than did Braniff, but did so without providing its passengers the advantage of coach service at fares lower than first-class fares. Obviously, Mohawk's decision not to provide coach service in its BAC-111's was not due to the physical limitations of its aircraft.

In summary, it can be seen that the local service carriers were able to maintain a higher service quality than the trunk carriers with respect to class of service by offering mainly first-class service. Their slowness in adopting pressurized and turbine-powered aircraft, however, served to make their service quality markedly inferior to that of the trunk carriers with respect to those innovations.

Back in 1946 and 1947, the service of the first California intrastate carrier (the original Pacific Air Lines) was comparable to the first-class service of the certificated carriers. Pacific adopted the same first-class fares as the trunk carriers, and at that time, its DC-3's were fairly modern aircraft for short-haul operations. In contrast, the ser-

[26] Letter from Mr. Cecil C. Carter, Administrative Assistant, Economic Planning, Braniff Airways (dated November 24, 1965). The 39 coach seats were arranged in seven rows each having five seats, plus one row with four seats. Braniff inaugurated BAC-111 service on April 25, 1965. *Ibid.*, p. 493.

[27] Letter from Mr. William H. Lohden, Director of Information, Mohawk Airlines (dated November 24, 1965). The 69 seats were arranged in seven rows each having five seats, eight rows with four seats, and one row with two seats. Mohawk inaugurated BAC-111 service on July 15, 1965 (see Table 3-1).

vices of the subsequent 15 intrastate carriers clearly conformed to the CAB's definition of coach service since they were all provided at fares lower than the certificated carriers' standard or premium fares.[28] Thus, California Central Airlines' inauguration of operations on January 2, 1949, introduced scheduled single-class coach service to California just two months following its introduction by Capital over the Chicago–Pittsburgh–New York route (see Table 3–1).

Table 3–3 shows that while the trunk and California intrastate carriers adopted coach service at the same time, they differed greatly in the rate and extent of their adoption of this innovation. That of the trunk carriers was controlled, took placed over a number of years, and required the mixed-class service innovation to make coach the major type of service. In contrast, when the California airlines adopted coach service, they did so completely and permanently and never operated mixed-class configured aircraft. Thus, with regard to class of service, the California intrastate carriers consistently provided service inferior to that of the certificated carriers to the extent these latter carriers provided first-class service. There was no such consistency associated with the two technological innovations. In terms of both the pressurized aircraft and the turbine-powered aircraft innovations, the intrastate carriers' service was much inferior to that of the trunk carriers through 1959, although comparable or only slightly inferior to that of the local service carriers. From 1960 through 1965, however, the service quality of the California intrastate carriers as a group became roughly equal to the trunk carriers in terms of these two technological innovations and greatly exceeded that of the local service carriers.

Safety

A widely used measure of airline safety is the rate of passenger fatalities per 100 million passenger-miles flown. Passenger fatality rates for the trunk, local service, and California intrastate carriers are

---

[28] A full description of relative fares in the California markets is given in chapters 5 and 6 of this book. The crucial importance of fares in determining the type of service provided by the certificated carriers can be seen most clearly with respect to the local service carriers. From 1956 through 1965, these carriers' aircraft were operated with identical four-abreast seating for both first-class and coach service. Whether the service was classified as first-class or coach depended on whether the fare charged was equal to or less than the established first-class fare. The same was true for the trunk carriers' night-coach service. Here aircraft that provided first-class service in the daytime were often used to provide coach service at lower than first-class fares during the night.

presented in Table 3–4. This table shows that for the period from
1949 through 1965 the intrastate carriers' rate of 2.67 passenger
fatalities per 100 million RPM was much higher than the 0.45 rate of
the trunk carriers and the 0.92 rate of the local service carriers. It
seems, therefore, that the intrastate carriers have had a much poorer
safety record (and thus lower service quality) than the regulated
airlines.

Table 3–4

Passenger Fatalities and Fatality Rates
Trunk, Local Service, and California Intrastate Carriers
Scheduled Domestic Service, 1949–1965

Carrier Group	Number of Passenger Fatalities[a]	Total Revenue[b] Passenger-Miles (000)	Passenger Fatality Rate per 100 Million RPM
Trunk	1,809[c]	402,736,593	0.45
Local Service	151	16,392,377	0.92
California Intrastate			
All Carriers	87	3,254,630[d]	2.67
Excluding Paradise	6	3,240,710[d]	0.19

[a]Includes both revenue and nonrevenue passengers.
[b]Nonrevenue passenger-miles are not available for the California intrastate
carriers.
[c]108 passenger deaths occurring in dynamite/sabotage accidents are excluded.
[d]Partially estimated.

Sources: CAB, *A Statistical Review and Briefs of U. S. Air Carrier Accidents,
Calendar Year 1965* (Washington, D.C., March 1966), Section I, pp. 7
and 8 (and predecessor publications with similar titles for calendar
years 1949–1964). CAB, *Aircraft Accident Report*, SA-378, File No.
1-002 (adopted July 12, 1965, released July 15, 1965), pp. 1 and 2.
CAB, *Handbook of Airline Statistics*, p. 47. CAB, *Resume of U. S.
Carrier Accidents (Calendar Year 1950)* (Washington, D.C., August
1951), p. 23. Appendix 3 of this book.

Before accepting this conclusion, however, it is desirable to
realize that throughout this period there were only two fatal accidents among all of the California intrastate carriers. The first occurred on December 7, 1949, when a California Arrow DC-3 crashed
near Vallejo, California, killing six passengers (including the wife and

son of the airline's owner) and three crew members.[29] The second took place more than 14 years later, on March 1, 1964, when a Constellation L-049 of Paradise Airlines crashed near Lake Tahoe with the loss of 85 lives (81 passengers and four crew members).[30] As mentioned in chapter 2, both airlines ceased operations almost immediately following their crashes. Paradise accounted for less than one-half of one percent of all RPM carried by the California intrastate carriers during these years but provided 93 percent of the total passenger fatalities. Should its record be excluded, Table 3-4 shows that the fatality rate of the remaining intrastate carriers was 0.19 per 100 million RPM, or less than half that of the trunk carriers' rate. In contrast, the overall fatality rates of the trunk and local service carriers would not be reduced to a level of 0.19 per 100 million RPM by merely excluding the one carrier in each group having the highest passenger fatality rate.

Between 1949 and 1965, the certificated and the California intrastate carriers operated under essentially identical direct safety regulations exercised by the Civil Aeronautics Administration (until 1958) and the Federal Aviation Agency. Thus, to the extent overall government regulation had an impact on relative safety, this impact must have been due mainly to economic regulation rather than to direct safety regulation. It is not clear, however, that economic regulation by the CAB served to motivate increased airline safety, even though it may have increased the resources available for this purpose. On the one hand, carrier rivalry expressed through higher service quality should result in an emphasis on improving safety. On the other hand, since no certificated carrier has ever been forced to terminate service following a fatal accident (due either to decreased passenger traffic or to the suspension of its commercial operator certificate by the CAA/FAA), it seems reasonable to assume that managers of certificated carriers (unlike those of the California airlines) had little reason to expect their companies would be put out of business following one or even several accidents. Furthermore, the CAB's economic regulation may even have prevented the full application of sanctions otherwise applicable under federal safety regulations or available to consumers. With respect to service termination, if a carrier possesses a CAB certificate of public convenience and necessity, does the FAA really have the power to suspend its operations following one or

[29] CAB, *Resume of U.S. Carrier Accidents (Calendar Year 1950)* (August 1951), p. 23. Also, *The Los Angeles Times* (December 9, 1949), part 1, p. 1.

[30] CAB, *Aircraft Accident Report*, SA-378, File No. 1-002 (adopted July 12, 1965, released July 15, 1965; mimeographed), pp. 1 and 2.

more fatal accidents (as in the case of Paradise), or are the FAA's corrective powers effectively limited to fines, increased surveillance of operations, etc.? In terms of consumer choice, since carriers with low passenger fatality rates are prohibited by the CAB from quickly extending operations over the routes of a carrier having a relatively high fatality rate, do air travelers have as many opportunities under CAB regulation to express their concern over one carrier's poor safety record by using other carriers having superior records?

It may be that economic regulation has no impact on safety per se but does have an effect on who bears the onus of incurring a relatively greater number of accidents. For example, by requiring the local service carriers to specialize in providing service in short-haul markets (with many more take-offs and landings per 100 million RPM) and at small airports having fewer air traffic aids, the CAB may be requiring this group of carriers to incur greater risks than the trunk carriers, regardless of the overall level of airline safety.

It seems inappropriate to draw definite conclusions regarding relative safety (and service quality) from the above data and reasoning. Clearly, the intrastate carriers had a higher passenger fatality rate than the certificated carriers following the 1964 crash, but their record for the 1950–63 period was superior to that of the certificated carriers, and, again, they experienced no fatal accidents from 1965 through 1969 (as this is being written).[31] Actually, the small volume of traffic for the California intrastate carriers relative to that of the certificated carriers may well make it improper to compare their passenger fatality rates. With a relatively small RPM base, one accident (such as Paradise's) has a large impact on the overall rate, whereas small volumes of operation also provide opportunities for the achievement of perfect safety records, even though performance may not be perfectly safe. At the same time, the complete absence of

---

[31] Extending the period covered in Table 3-4 by only three years, through 1968, results in the following passenger fatality rates per 100 million RPM: trunk carriers = 0.33, local service carriers = 1.28, California intrastate carriers = 1.29 (0.09 if Paradise is excluded). However, the California intrastate carriers operated under the increased regulatory powers of the PUC during these last three years, so the 1949–68 data for these carriers cover two dissimilar periods with respect to economic regulation. (The passenger fatality and RPM data for 1966–68 were obtained or calculated from: CAB, *Air Carrier Traffic Statistics* [December 1967 and 1968]; PSA, *Annual Report* [1966–68]; Air California, *Annual Report* [1967–68]; PUC, *Intrastate Passengers of Scheduled Air Carriers*, Report No. 1511 [Quarters Ended December 31, 1966, and 1967]; National Transportation Safety Board, *Annual Review of U.S. Air Carrier Accidents* [Calendar Years 1966 and 1967]; and NTSB, *A Preliminary Analysis of Aircraft Accident Data, U.S. Civil Aviation, 1968*.)

fatal accidents by PSA during 16 years of unregulated operations, and by California Central/Coastal during their 8½ years of existence, does indicate that economic regulation is not a necessary condition for airline safety, while the varying experiences of individual certificated carriers show that such regulation is not a sufficient condition for superior safety performance.

Conclusion

It is easy to rank the service quality of the three carrier groups in terms of the two technological innovations. The trunk carriers were consistently the first to introduce each innovation. In fact, they introduced all but two of the over 40 aircraft types operated by all three carrier groups between 1946 and 1965.[32] In addition, they adopted these innovations rapidly and extensively. The local service carriers, on the other hand, were slow to introduce the two innovations and their rates of adoption were low. By 1965, they had not yet completely adopted pressurized aircraft, and their turbine-powered aircraft service was still limited, even though they first operated turboprop aircraft seven years earlier. The California intrastate carriers fluctuated between the two certificated carrier groups in their adoption of the technological innovations. Prior to 1960, they were like the local service carriers in operating nonpressurized, piston-powered aircraft. From 1960 through 1965, however, they were comparable to the trunk carriers, so that, considering the entire period, they ranked second after the trunk carriers but ahead of the local service carriers with respect to service quality based on technological innovations.

The service quality rankings based on the class-of-service innovations differ appreciably from the above rankings. Here the local service carriers were superior to the other two carrier groups, since they offered little if any coach service. Starting with their adoption of coach service in late 1948, the trunk carriers consistently ranked below the local service carriers, whereas the California

[32] W. A. Jordan, "Competition—A Two-Edged Sword in Improving Air Transportation Performance?" in J. de S. Coutinho (Chm.), *Transportation: A Service* (New York: New York Academy of Sciences, 1967), pp. 167–68. The two aircraft not introduced by the trunk carriers during this period were the turboprop Fairchild F-27 and Nord 262 which were first operated by the local service carriers. In addition, the local service carriers introduced modified Convair 240, 340, and 440 aircraft equipped with turboprop rather than their original piston-powered engines. The turboprop versions have been designated Convair 540, 580, 600, and 640, depending upon the type of turboprop engine installed.

intrastate carriers' complete adoption of coach service in 1949 put them well down in third place in terms of service quality based on class of service.

The evidence is contradictory with regard to relative safety. The California intrastate carriers as a group had the highest passenger fatality rate because of one accident in 1964. Individually, however, most intrastate carriers had enviable safety records compared with the certificated carriers. Overall, it seems fair to say that passengers could expect high levels of safety regardless of which type of carrier they flew and that such expectations were generally fulfilled.

Since the two technological innovations represent a multitude of other postwar innovations, it seems reasonable to give them more weight than the class-of-service innovations in obtaining overall rankings. Therefore, it is concluded that the trunk carriers consistently offered the highest quality of service, followed by the California intrastate carriers (especially beginning in 1960), and then by the local service carriers.

The above rankings are consistent with the implications of the cartel hypothesis of regulation. The local service carriers operated under prices controlled by the CAB, entry was restricted, and traffic potential was determined by the CAB's awarding monopoly rights in most markets. Thus, there was little carrier rivalry and no reason to emphasize service quality in order to obtain larger market shares and higher profits at the expense of other carriers. The predictable result was relatively low levels of service quality. In contrast, the large portion of the cartel composed of the trunk carriers was imperfectly organized since two or more carriers were authorized to serve most major markets without traffic shares and industry profits being explicitly allocated. The relative lack of service-quality regulation allowed individual trunk carriers to attempt to obtain greater profits by offering superior service under the prices controlled by the CAB. The introduction of coach service was an example of pricing rivalry associated with a reduction in service quality. This gave a second level of service which, once established, improved essentially in parallel with first-class service as various innovations were adopted. The eventual dominance of coach service through the widespread adoption of mixed-class service on turbojet/fan aircraft indicates that the majority of passengers preferred to forego some service quality in exchange for lower fares.

The California intrastate carriers, like the trunk carriers, also experienced great intercarrier rivalry in their major markets. Since, however, the PUC did not regulate price reductions or service quality, carrier rivalry could be expressed interchangeably through lower prices and improved service. Also, since entry was not controlled, any intrastate carrier believing it had a more preferred price/service combination could test its belief by inaugurating service within California. The complete adoption of coach service by the 15 intrastate carriers operating between 1949 and 1965, and their delays in adopting pressurized and turbojet/fan aircraft, indicates that their managers thought low prices were more effective than high-quality service in attracting passengers.

The California intrastate carriers' service quality actually appears to have been affected less by carrier rivalry than by the desire or need of these carriers to achieve low operating costs. The intrastate carriers contented themselves with obsolescent DC-3's and DC-4's, or the nonpressurized Martin 202, until the prices of used, pressurized piston-powered aircraft fell drastically in the early 1960's. In contrast, the turboprop Electra was adopted by PSA soon after it became available, but this was a case in which low operating costs per seat-mile offset a high purchase price.[33] On the other hand, turbojet/fan aircraft were not adopted until a medium-range turbofan aircraft was developed that had relatively low operating costs for short stage lengths. This delay resulted in the sacrifice of some service quality to lower operating costs, just as occurred during the piston aircraft era.

After allowing for the different distances involved, the development of the California intrastate carriers' fleets provides an indication of the types of aircraft the interstate carriers would have operated had there been no CAB regulation. It seems reasonable to conclude that without regulation the nonpressurized DC-3's and DC-4's would have had longer lives, especially in short-haul markets. Pressurized, piston-powered aircraft would have been adopted, particularly for medium- and long-range operations, but the final series of these aircraft (the DC-7's, later model L-1049's, and the L-1649's—those aircraft powered with turbo-compound piston engines) would not have been adopted because their small improve-

---

[33] FAA, *Direct Operating Costs and Other Performance Characteristics of Transport Aircraft in Airline Service, Calendar Year 1964* (Washington, D.C.: September 1965), pp. 18 and 19. The findings of this publication are based on averages of accounting data submitted by the certificated carriers. Since differences in operating procedures, average stage lengths, aircraft utilization and seating configurations, accounting policies, etc., all have some impact on the data, the cost levels reported in this study may not be fully accurate. While one may question the degree, however, these data do show that turbine-powered aircraft have significantly lower seat-mile costs (excluding depreciation) than piston-powered aircraft.

ments in speed over the DC-6's, DC-6B's, L-749's, etc., were obtained through very much higher operating costs. Turbine-powered aircraft, however, would have been adopted in much the same manner that actually occurred since this innovation offered both superior service quality and lower seat-mile costs—a potent combination.

CAB Fare Authorizations

4

Introduction

The Civil Aeronautics Board may exercise direct control over airline pricing in two ways. First, it can simply respond to carrier initiatives by approving or suspending (and investigating) fares filed by individual carriers. Second, it can set exact fares or maximum and/or minimum fares following the completion of a formal hearing.[1] In both cases, the Board provides a forum in which the airlines can openly discuss and evaluate fare proposals prior to the Board's decision. The first procedure, used more frequently than the second in changing fares, is facilitated by the requirement that a minimum of 30 days elapse between the public filing of fare changes with the Board and the effective date of such proposals. During the first 12 days of this period, any carrier or other interested party may file statements supporting or opposing the new fare proposal.[2] In the case of complicated alternative fare filings by several carriers, the Board may even permit or sponsor a meeting with the certificated carriers' presidents or other officers to discuss the effects of alternative fare changes.[3] By approving a proposed tariff change or by

---

[1] Section 1002(g) and Section 1002(d), 72 Stat. 788.

[2] 14 CFR 221.160 and 302.505.

[3] An example of a CAB meeting with airline presidents to discuss fare changes occurred on January 13 and 16, 1969. The result of this two-day meeting was the across-the-board fare increase that became effective on February 20, 1969. See CAB Press Release No. 69-3 (January 16, 1969), and CAB, *Report on Meetings Between the Civil Aeronautics Board and the Domestic Trunkline Carriers on Domestic Passenger Fares* (Washington, D.C.: n.d., mimeographed). In addition, Cherington, *Airline Price Policy*, pp. 84–110, reviews how the carriers and the CAB used fare filings and meetings to determine fare changes between 1947 and 1954.

announcing the decision reached at a fare meeting, the Board publicizes its acceptance of new fares which may then be adopted by the certificated carriers. In this situation, the individual carriers have only to decide whether their profits will be enhanced if they and the other carriers accept the new fares, or whether the retention of the existing fares will be more beneficial.

With respect to the economic effects of CAB regulation, the relevant questions do not concern *how* the certificated carriers and the CAB manage to establish airline fares, but whether regulated fares are higher than, the same as, or lower than nonregulated fares, and whether CAB *authorized* (as distinct from CAB *ordered*) fare changes have indeed been adopted by all or most of the certificated carriers. This chapter will describe the major CAB fare decisions and indicate the extent to which they have been adopted by individual carriers. The matter of comparative fare levels will be examined in the following three chapters.

Types of Passenger Fares

Passenger fares can be classified into two major types or groups. The first of these includes those fares available to all travelers with little or no restriction—that is, first-class and coach fares (on propeller or turbojet/fan aircraft) and the more recent coach-fare variations such as commuter, Thriftair, air bus, and economy. In this study, fares of this type will be called *general* fares.

The second type of fares is comprised of the so-called *promotional* fares. They have one common characteristic. Unlike the general fares, they are not available to all travelers but are restricted to persons having some identifiable characteristic and/or conforming to some specified travel pattern. Examples of persons having an identifiable characteristic are: members of the military traveling in uniform, ministers, a family traveling together, and persons under or over some specified age. Examples of specified travel patterns include: travel limited to between Monday noon and Friday noon, the well-known round-trip requirement, and the limitation that a return journey cannot begin sooner than the calendar week following the date of departure. Promotional fares are usually derived by applying some percentage discount to one of the general fares.

The division between general and promotional fares is not always clear-cut. For example, night-coach fares usually have been restricted to flights departing between the hours of 10:00 P.M. and 4:00 A.M. These late departure times tend to limit the use of such fares to individuals preferring money (representing other goods) relatively more than travel convenience. Should night-coach fares be classified as general or promotional? A similar question may be asked about those excursion fares which merely limit travel to round trips that must be taken on certain days of the week, with added restrictions concerning the elapsed time allowed for return travel.

Even though restrictions on night-coach fares and excursion fares may be a matter of degree, there does seem to be an operational basis for classifying a fare as a general fare or a promotional fare. Night-coach fares are for a corresponding class of service, are available to all who wish to use that service, and may be combined with fares for other types of services that may be utilized with night-coach service in the course of a given trip. In contrast, there is no excursion type of service corresponding to an excursion fare, and this fare often cannot be combined with other fares. Passengers qualifying for excursion fares utilize some general type of service (first-class, coach, etc.), but pay fares that are lower than those paid by other passengers sitting in adjacent seats, making the identical trip on the same flight. Obviously, promotional fares conform to the traditional economic requirements for discriminatory pricing.[4]

The differences between general and promotional fares bring up another important aspect of airline pricing. This is the concept of fare *level* as opposed to fare *structure*. Generally speaking, the fare level pertains to the average fare or revenue earned by an airline for all of its services. One measure of it can be calculated by dividing total passenger revenues by total revenue passenger-miles for some period. The result of such a calculation is called the average yield per mile. In contrast, fare structure pertains to the many different fares available within the group of general fares (first-class, coach, economy, etc.), plus the various promotional fares that are available. Thus, the fare structure reflects the range and variation of fares actually available. Obviously, a change in the fare level may occur through an overall increase or decrease in all fares (a direct change in the level), through additions to or deletions from the various types of

---

[4] The necessary conditions for price discrimination may be summarized as follows: (1) the ability to keep identifiable groups of buyers separate (at relatively low cost) to prevent a buyer in one group from reselling to a buyer in another group at a price under the higher discriminatory price charged the second group; (2) differing price elasticities of demand for the various groups; (3) a monopoly, or at least some agreement among rival suppliers not to lower the price available to the group(s) being discriminated against. See J. Robinson, *The Economics of Imperfect Competition* (London: Macmillan and Co., 1933), pp. 179–81; and A. C. Pigou, *Economics of Welfare* (4th ed.; London: Macmillan and Co., 1932), p. 279.

fares comprising the fare structure, or through changes in the relative amounts of service offered under individual fares.

General Fares

Prior to late 1948, the certificated carriers offered only first-class service. During those years, there were a few examples of different first-class fares in individual markets when older aircraft were operated in competition with newer aircraft (for example, when the Boeing 247 was competing with the Douglas DC-3 in 1940).[5] Also, the introduction of the Constellation and DC-6 pressurized aircraft was accompanied by a 10 percent service charge.[6] In general, however, the early fare structure of the certificated carriers was uncluttered by different kinds of general fares.

This situation came to an end in November 1948 when scheduled coach service was introduced by Capital Airlines, which was followed by the other trunk carriers. This resulted in the replacement of the simple first-class fare structure by a structure featuring first-class, night-coach, and day-coach fares. From 1948 through 1965, at least 15 different fare types were added to the original first-class fares. These fares and their dates of introduction are summarized in Table 4-1. Notice that most of them were introduced after mid-1959. A number of these fares, such as the no-meal, Thriftair, and business fares, have been offered by only one or a few airlines over a limited number of routes, for relatively short time periods. Others, such as the day-coach fares, have been offered by all trunk carriers over all or many of their routes for a number of years. Throughout this period, however, the first-class fare for service in propeller aircraft was the one fundamental type of general fare filed between all points on each carrier's system; most of the other fare types were related to it in some direct or indirect manner.

Even without considering the surcharges and the many promotional fares that have been introduced since the end of World War II, it is clear that the fare structure has become much more complicated since 1948; therefore, it has become increasingly difficult to trace the overall change in airline fares. The common practice is to calculate the average yield, either for all services combined or for first-class and coach service separately, and compare the changes in yield over time. The drawback to this approach is that it fails to measure the full impact of lower-fare service on prices actually available to

[5] CAB, *Handbook of Airline Statistics*, p. 477.
[6] Cherington, *Airline Price Policy*, pp. 88–91 and 360–68.

Table 4-1

Types of General Passenger Fares Introduced by
the Domestic Certificated Carriers from 1948 to 1965

General Passenger Fare	Date of Introduction
Night (Off-peak)-Coach	November 4, 1948
No-Meal First-Class	February 1, 1949
Day-Coach	December 27, 1949
Local Commuter	October 4, 1959
Jet Coach	October 1-7, 1960
Air Bus	October 12, 1960
Air-Shuttle	April 30, 1961
Thriftair	June 1, 1962
Business	August 24, 1962
Economy	August 24, 1962
One-Class	March 10, 1963
Club Coach	January 27, 1964
Standard	August 9, 1964
Jet Commuter	September 27, 1964
Executive Shuttle	October 1, 1964

Sources: CAB, *Handbook of Airline Statistics*, pp. 478-85. Cherington, *Airline Price Policy*, pp. 94, 274, and 275. Western Air Lines tariff, Cal. P.U.C. No. 2, sixth revised p. 19, effective Feb. 1, 1949; and Cal. P.U.C. No. 26, originally effective June 1, 1962. Eastern Air Lines, *Local "Executive Shuttle" Tariff*, C.A.B. No. 160, originally effective October 1, 1964.

the traveling public. For example, consider a city pair originally having only first-class service at, say, 8 cents per passenger-mile. Should this market be favored with new coach service at 6 cents per passenger-mile, which is then utilized by half of the passengers in the market, the average yield would be reduced by 12.5 percent to 7 cents per mile. The reduction in the lowest widely-available fare, however, would actually be 25 percent—that is, from 8 to 6 cents per passenger-mile. From the point of view of the demand for airline services, the 25 percent decrease in the lowest widely-available fare would be the relevant change, not the 12.5 percent reduction in average yield. Continuing with this same market, suppose that in a later period coach service is expanded until 75 percent of all travel is via such service. This would further reduce the average yield from 7 to 6.5 cents per passenger-mile, although the lowest widely-available fare would not be decreased at all. Compound this situation with many fare types (including promotional fares and surcharges) and with thousands of city pairs—each with its own pattern of service—

and the limitations inherent in using average yield to study fare changes become obvious.

In this study, the comparison of fare levels and fare structure over time will be done on an individual city-pair basis using actual fares rather than average yields. Although this method will severely limit the number of markets studied, the limitation will be more than offset by the increased accuracy and applicability of the data being used.

Adoption of CAB-Authorized Across-the-Board Fare Changes

It was not until February 27, 1943, that the CAB took its first major action in passenger fares by issuing an order to 11 of the 16 certificated carriers then operating to show cause why passenger fares should not be reduced.[7] As a result of this order, five trunk carriers lowered their passenger fares between 6 and 7.6 percent on July 15, 1943; most of the other carriers followed suit by the end of that year. A second CAB show-cause order (issued January 2, 1945) resulted in the larger trunk carriers lowering their fares in the spring of 1945, this time by 6.5 to 17 percent, and restoring the 5 percent, round-trip discount that had been canceled shortly after the outbreak of war. As before, these fare decreases were adopted by the other carriers operating between city pairs served by the larger carriers. The final World War II fare reduction became effective on August 20, 1945. It resulted in system-wide reductions of about 7 percent, the effects of which were partially offset by the elimination of the 5 percent, round-trip discount.[8]

One important by-product of these early Board actions, particularly the first, was the certificated carriers' adoption of a uniform, airport-to-airport mileage rate for constructing fares between all city pairs on their systems.[9] Since, however, through fares were obtained by totaling the local fares for *all* intermediate segments on the route, *nonstop* rates per mile still differed, with adjacent city pairs having lower nonstop rates than long-haul city pairs that were joined by a zigzag route connecting several intervening points. Further differences in nonstop rates resulted from the fact that the fare for a city pair served by two or more carriers was usually set by the all-stop mileage of the carrier having the most direct route.

[7] CAB Order No. 2164 (adopted February 26, 1943).

[8] CAB, *Handbook of Airline Statistics*, pp. 477–78.

[9] *Ibid.*, p. 477. Also, see Cherington, *Airline Price Policy*, pp. 82–84.

Even with the simple fare structure existing in 1946, there is some question about the actual airport-to-airport mileage rate in effect at that time. The CAB's *Handbook of Airline Statistics* states that the average fare level was about 4.35 cents per mile after the August 20, 1945, fare reduction.[10] Cherington, on the other hand, claims that fares were based on a 4.58 cents-per-mile rate.[11] The fare data presented in this study yield rates per mile during 1946 of from 4.51 to 4.68 cents, with a median value of 4.61 cents.[12] Thus, they support Cherington's estimate.

This review of the Board's early passenger fare activities provides the basis for studying the across-the-board fare changes that were authorized by the CAB between 1946 and 1965. A summary of these fare changes is presented in Table 4-2. Eight of the 19 fare changes authorized during this period were applicable to all domestic markets, while the applicability of the remaining eleven depended upon the type of service offered (first-class vs. coach), the aircraft type utilized (propeller vs. jet), the distance between city pairs, and the specific airline providing service. Clearly, the eight fully applicable fare changes differed in degree from the eleven limited changes, and it is these eight that will be studied in the following analysis to indicate the extent to which CAB-authorized, across-the-board fare changes were actually adopted by the certificated carriers.[13]

Tariff experts and those familiar with airline pricing generally assert that the eight fare changes (all increases) were adopted by all the certificated carriers in virtually every applicable market.[14] This writer's own experiences and research support this assertion. It is beyond the resources of this study to examine thoroughly even one percent of all the fares filed between the thousands of domestic city pairs by all certificated carriers since 1946 to verify that the eight fare increases were widely adopted. Indeed, a substantial effort was

---

[10] CAB, *Handbook of Airline Statistics*, p. 478.

[11] Cherington, *Airline Price Policy*, p. 84. Also, pp. 143 and 146.

[12] Calculated from data presented in Appendices 6(A), 8(A), 11, and 13 of this book. Also, see United Air Lines, "Chronology of United's First-Class Fare Level, 1938 to Date," Exhibit No. U-11, in Cal. PUC Application No. 39775 (submitted March 12, 1958). This exhibit specified a rate of 4.64¢ per mile effective August 20, 1945, which also supports Cherington's estimate.

[13] Of the eight fare changes applicable to all markets, seven pertained to general fares and one concerned promotional fares. This change in promotional fares was effective October 20, 1958. It reduced the round-trip and family plan discounts.

[14] For example, see Cherington, *Airline Price Policy*, pp. 380–416. Also, see Caves, *Air Transport and Its Regulators*, pp. 144–52.

Table 4-2

Summary of the Across-the-Board Passenger Fare Changes
Authorized by the Civil Aeronautics Board
for Domestic Services, 1946-1965

Effective Date	Domestic Passenger Fare Changes Authorized
1947	
Apr. 1	Increase of approximately 10 percent.
Dec. 12	Increase of approximately 10 percent.
1948	
Sept. 1– Oct. 15	Increase of from 2 to 11.5 percent, for an average increase in general fares of approximately 10 percent. Five percent, round-trip discount re-established. Ten percent DC-6 and Constellation surcharges canceled by some carriers.
Nov. 4	Night-coach fares introduced at a level of approximately 4 cents per passenger mile, compared to the first-class average fare level of about 6 cents per passenger-mile.
1949	
Dec. 27	Day-coach fares introduced at a level of approximately 4.5 cents per passenger-mile.
1950	
Nov. 15	Increase in minimum night-coach fare level to 4.5 cents per passenger-mile.
1952	
Apr. 1	Decrease in night-coach fare level to 4 cents per passenger-mile.
Apr. 16–27	Increase of $1.00 per one-way ticket.
1953	
Oct. 5	Air-coach fare policy revised from the specified cents-per-mile levels to the standard that new coach fares should not exceed 75 percent of the corresponding first-class fare.
1958	
Feb. 10	Increase of 4 percent plus $1.00 per one-way ticket.
Oct. 20	Elimination of discounts on first-class fares for round trips, circle trips, and open-jaw trips. (These discounts had never been applicable to coach fares.) Also, the discount for family-plan travel was reduced from 50 to 33 1/3 percent. It was estimated that the overall result of these actions was to increase the fare level by about 3.5 percent.
Dec. 10	Introduction of surcharges for travel on jet aircraft ranging from $1.00 to $10.00 per ticket.

Table 4-2 (continued)

Effective Date	Domestic Passenger Fare Changes Authorized
1959 May 15– Nov. 29	Eight trunk carriers increased all day-coach fares by 25¢ to $2.50, depending upon distance ($1.00 was the usual increase), and began serving "complimentary" meals to coach passengers. The other trunk carriers (Continental, Trans World, United, and Western) initially limited these new coach-meal fares to their premium coach services, but between late 1960 and 1964, they also adopted them completely.
1960 July 1	Increase of 2.5 percent plus $1.00 per one-way ticket.
Oct. 1–7	Increase in long-haul jet coach fares to 75 percent of first-class fares *before* the adjustments for the three $1.00-per-ticket increases, the coach-meal increase, and the jet surcharge.
1961 Aug.–Oct.	Gradual extension to short-haul markets of the increase in jet coach fares to 75 percent of first-class fares before adjustments.
1962 Feb. 1	Increase of 3 percent.
1964 Jan. 15 and Aug. 1, 1965	Decrease of from 4.5 to 14 percent in first-class fares on flights over 700 miles in length. American introduced this decrease system-wide on this date. United made a similar reduction on August 1, 1965. In both cases, other carriers made similar reductions in the affected markets.
1965 Jan. 15	Increase and decrease of fares in the eastern part of the nation when Eastern was authorized to decrease all fares by 5 percent and then add $2.50 per ticket. Carriers serving the same markets Eastern served adopted the resulting reductions in fares that had been more than $50, but not the increases in fares that had been less than $50.

Sources: CAB, *Analysis of Domestic Fare Structure and Historical Fare Data* (Washington, D.C.: April 21, 1966, mimeographed), p. 1. CAB, *Handbook of Airline Statistics*, pp. 468, 478, and 485. CAB, Press Release No. 51-10 (February 5, 1951). Cherington, *Airline Price Policy*, pp. 85-97 and 360-68. *Official Airline Guide*, North American Edition, 15-21 (various dates from 1959 through 1964). J. B. Walker, Agent, Air Traffic Conference of America, *Local and Joint Passenger Fares Tariff*, No. PF-5, C.A.B. No. 44, originally effective April 28, 1957, various pages effective during 1959 and 1960.

required to obtain complete fare information for just the 17 markets studied in this book (see Appendices 6 to 12). Of these 17 markets, only nine were served continuously by certificated carriers between 1947 and 1962 when the eight fare increases occurred. The fare histories of these nine markets do, however, provide some evidence to test the assertion about the widespread adoption of the CAB's across-the-board fare increases.

Three of the nine city pairs are major interstate markets located on the East Coast, while six are located within California. In Table 4-3, the dates that the CAB authorized the eight major across-the-board fare increases to become effective are compared with the dates that various carriers actually increased their fares in these nine markets. With one minor and brief exception (see note d in Table 4-3), the two trunk carriers (American and Eastern) carrying the majority of the traffic in the three East Coast markets consistently adopted the Board's authorized fare increases in those markets as early as possible. This was true for both first-class and coach service (after coach service was inaugurated in late 1953).

In contrast, several of the effective dates for the fares of the certificated carriers operating in the six California intrastate markets differed from those authorized by the CAB. Looking initially at the first-class fares, it can be seen that the three earliest across-the-board fare increases were implemented by United and Western on the effective dates authorized by the CAB. Starting April 1952, however, these trunk carriers began to delay implementing the authorized fare increases. The first delay was only about two weeks long, but the implementation of the following four fare increases were delayed from 47 to 192 days. It was no coincidence that the 1952 fare increase was the first one authorized by the CAB following the PUC's assertion of jurisdiction over the intrastate fares of the certificated carriers.[15] Without doubt these delays were due to the trunk carriers having to obtain the PUC's permission before increasing their fares within California. This is shown in Table 4-4, which compares the dates on which the CAB announced its authorization of the last four major fare increases with the dates that United, Western, and Pacific filed applications with the PUC requesting permission to adopt these increases. Clearly, the trunk carriers generally filed their PUC applications shortly after the CAB's announcement regarding each fare increase. Furthermore, comparing the PUC's decision dates with the

---

[15] 50 Cal. PUC 563 (1951). Also, see chapter 5 of this book for a detailed description of the PUC's actions to extend its jurisdiction over the California fares of the certificated carriers.

Table 4-3

Dates the CAB Across-the-Board Fare Increases Were Authorized To Become Effective Compared with the Dates Fares Were Actually Increased in Markets Selected for Analysis in This Study

CAB Authorized Effective Date of Increase	Actual Effective Date for				No. of Days between Actual and Authorized Dates			
	3 Interstate City Pairs[a]		6 California City Pairs[b]		3 Interstate City Pairs[a]		6 California City Pairs[b]	
	First Class	Coach	First Class	Coach	First Class	Coach	First Class	Coach
4/ 1/47	Same[c]	n.a.	Same[c]	n.a.	0	–	0	–
12/12/47	Same[c]	n.a.	Same[c]	n.a.	0	–	0	–
9/ 1/48[d]	Same[d]	n.a.	Same[e] 3/11/51[f]	n.a. n.a.	0[d]	–	0[e] 920[f]	–
4/16-27/52	Same[c]	n.a.	4/30/52[g] 5/ 5/52[h] 9/ 6/54[f]	Ignored[g] Ignored[h] n.a.	0	–	14[g] 17[h] 876[f]	– – –
2/10/58	Same[c]	Same[c]	7/ 7/58	7/ 7/58	0	0	147	147
10/20/58	Same[c]	n.a.	3/ 1/59[e] 5/ 8/60[f]	n.a. n.a.	0	–	132[e] 567[f]	– –
7/ 1/60	Same[c]	Same[c]	1/ 9/61	1/ 9/61	0	0	192	192
2/ 1/62	Same[c]	Same[c]	3/20/62[e] 7/14/63[i]	3/20/62[e] 7/14/63[i]	0	0	47[e] 528[i]	47[e] 528[i]

n.a.—not applicable.

[a] Boston–New York/Newark, Boston–Washington, D.C., and New York/Newark–Washington, D.C. Dates are for the fares of American and Eastern airlines.

[b] Long Beach–San Diego, Long Beach–San Francisco/Oakland, Los Angeles/Burbank–San Francisco/Oakland, Los Angeles/Burbank–San Diego, Los Angeles/Burbank–San Jose, and San Diego–San Francisco/Oakland. Dates are for the fares of United, Western, and Pacific airlines.

[c] Effective the same date as that authorized by the CAB.

[d] The CAB did not decide on a precise policy nor a definite effective date for this increase. Rather, it indicated its preference for a 10 percent increase and invited all carriers to file proposals for its consideration. American, Inland, Trans World, United, and Western immediately filed for a 10 percent increase effective September 1, 1948. The last carrier to file, Eastern, did so on October 8, with an effective date of October 15, 1948.

[e] United Air Lines and Western Air Lines.

[f] Pacific Air Lines.

[g] Western Air Lines.

[h] United Air Lines.

[i] Pacific intentionally omitted Los Angeles/Burbank–San Jose (and two other city pairs) when adopting this fare increase. It stated that this was done pending the completion of an economic study of these markets; however, it had yet to implement this fare increase in these city pairs by the end of 1965.

Sources: Appendices 6, 8, 9, and 11 of this book.

Table 4-4

Dates That Across-the-Board Fare Increases Were Announced by the CAB
Compared with the Dates that United, Western, and Pacific Filed
Applications with the PUC for These Increases, and the Dates
of the PUC's Decisions Authorizing These Increases, 1958-1963

Major Fare Increase	Date of CAB Announcement	Car-rier	Public Utilities Commission			
			Application		Decision	
			Number	Date[a]	Number	Date
4 percent plus $1.00	1/24/58	UAL	39775	2/ 3/58	56849	6/17/58
		WAL	39776	2/ 3/58	56849	6/17/58
		PAC	39807	2/11/58	56849	6/17/58
Discounts reduced	10/14/58[b]	UAL	40490	10/ 6/58[b]	57990	2/ 9/59
		WAL	40536	10/23/58	57990	2/ 9/59
		PAC	41983	2/25/60	59929	4/12/60
2.5 percent plus $1.00	6/17/60	UAL	42461	7/14/60	61224	12/20/60
		WAL	42417	6/29/60	61224	12/20/60
		PAC	42750	10/13/60	61225	12/20/60
3 percent	12/28/61	UAL	44104	1/15/62	63315	2/23/62
		WAL	44118	1/19/62	63315	2/23/62
		PAC	45071	12/28/62	65589	6/18/63

[a]Date application was received by the PUC. The application was usually
mailed by the carrier two or more days prior to this date.
[b]This announcement was in response to fares filed by several carriers beginning on September 12, 1958. Apparently UAL also filed for this increase with
the PUC prior to the CAB's announcement.

Sources: CAB Press Releases Nos. 58-5 (January 24, 1958) and 60-13 (June 17,
1960). CAB Order No. E-17885 (adopted December 28, 1961), p. 4.
56 Cal. PUC 779, 780 (1959). Cal. PUC, records for the specified
applications.

dates the trunk carriers' fare increases actually became effective within California (see Table 4-3) shows that the trunk carriers generally
implemented the fare increases immediately after the minimum publication period required by the PUC.

Table 4-3 shows that Pacific Air Lines also increased its first-
class fares at the same time the trunk carriers did in four out of the
eight fare authorizations. It delayed adopting the other four
increases, however, for periods exceeding those of the trunk carriers
by 435 to 920 days. Obviously these longer delays were due to
factors other than having to obtain the PUC's approval of the increases. They indicate that one or more local service carriers were not

as prompt as the trunk carriers in adopting several of the across-the-board fare increases. This conclusion is supported by the minority statement in *Local-Service Carrier Fare Increases—Statement Issued February 7, 1962*, which mentioned that of all the local service carriers, Bonanza, Ozark, and Pacific did not file the 3 percent, across-the-board fare increase in accordance with the CAB announcement of December 28, 1961.[16] However, these three carriers did eventually adopt the increase.[17] Pacific's Vice President–Traffic stated during an interview that their delay in adopting the authorized fare increases was the result of certain policies of that firm and that, to his knowledge, the other local service carriers did not have similar policies.[18] Despite the fact that a few local service carriers did delay adopting some of the CAB-approved fare increases, no evidence was found during this study of any of the local service carriers failing to adopt such a fare increase eventually.

Table 4–3 also shows that the certificated carriers' California coach fares were increased at the same time as their first-class fares in 1958, 1960, and 1962.[19] The April 1952 fare increase, however, was completely "ignored" by the certificated carriers for their coach service within California. The reasons for this exception will be described at length in the next chapter. Suffice it to say here that from 1950 through 1957 the trunk carriers both *decreased* and *increased* their coach fares within California, and in no instance was a change caused by a CAB-authorized, across-the-board fare change. Also, the California coach fare changes during those years were not duplicated in any interstate market in which the CAB had exclusive jurisdiction over fares.

Overall, the fare histories of the nine city pairs support the assertion that the CAB-authorized, across-the-board fare increases were adopted by all certificated carriers. In the case of the trunk carriers' interstate fares, this occurred on the effective date specified by the Board, whereas their California intrastate fares were increased as soon as possible after the PUC approved each across-the-board increase. In the case of the local service carriers, there were several

---

[16] 35 CAB 877, 1n (1962).

[17] Pacific adopted this fare increase for its interstate markets on February 1, 1963 (Cal. PUC Decision No. 65589 [dated June 18, 1963], p. 5 [mimeographed]). Ozark implemented it in mid-1963 (*Official Airline Guide*, North American Edition, 19, no. 9 [June 1963], p. C 268). Bonanza finally adopted it in June 1965 (*Air Travel* 21, no. 10 [July 1965], p. 70).

[18] Mr. R. E. Costello, Vice President–Traffic, Pacific Air Lines, September 13, 1966.

[19] The October 20, 1958, fare increase did not apply to coach fares.

other delays indicating occasional reluctance on the part of some of these carriers to raise fares in their short-haul markets. Every one of the CAB fare increases, however, appears to have been adopted eventually by all of the local service carriers.

Enforcement of Fare Agreements

Given the widespread adoption of across-the-board fare changes authorized by the CAB, and through this the ability of the certificated carriers to solve the problem of how to obtain agreement on fares, the possibility still exists that a carrier may officially adopt the CAB-approved fares, file tariffs accordingly, but then proceed to charge favored customers fares lower than those in its tariffs—that is, carriers can "cheat" on their agreements. Of course, a problem that must be solved by a cartel is how to detect, punish, and prevent violations in its agreements. Moreover, this function of a viable cartel must be carried out at relatively low cost to the industry for it to be worthwhile.

This study will not examine the methods whereby price agreements are enforced by the CAB and the certificated carriers. Given that tariff violations are misdemeanors (criminal offenses),[20] and that the CAB's auditing and investigating staffs have the right of access to almost all records of the certificated carriers,[21] it is not surprising to find few examples of illegal price cutting among these carriers. Also, the Air Traffic Conference (ATC) of the Air Transport Association of America carries out additional enforcement of airline agreements. In her review of the enforcement activities of the CAB and the ATC, Kleiger found that most of these activities since 1938 concerned violations of agreements involving service, advertising matters, and travel agents rather than price agreements.[22] Of course, this does not mean that there have been no rebates or other tariff violations. Rather, it means that direct price violations have been limited and that other areas of rivalry bulk larger in the CAB's and the ATC's enforcement activities.

Conclusion

The major conclusion of this chapter is that CAB-authorized, across-the-board fare changes were adopted essentially system-wide by all or most certificated carriers immediately after these changes

---

[20] Section 902(d), 72 Stat. 784.

[21] Section 407(e), 72 Stat. 766.

[22] Kleiger, *Maximization of Industry Profits*, pp. 115–38, esp. 130–33.

were authorized. Indeed, it seems clear that the general fares of these carriers through 1965 were the direct result of the CAB's fare decisions during World War II (which set a common mileage base for first-class fares), the Board's postwar across-the-board fare increases, and its policies regarding coach fares and other general fares. A few local service carriers did delay adopting one or more of these fare increases, and beginning in 1952, the certificated carriers experienced delays in obtaining the additional permission required from the PUC to increase fares within California. These exceptions, however, largely serve to emphasize the general applicability of the CAB's fare actions. The further unique exception of coach fares in the major California markets will be treated at length in the next chapter.

It would not be correct to imply that the CAB alone determined the fares of the certificated carriers during the period covered by this study. The carriers also played a major role in establishing fares through the submission of tariff changes, through formal and informal discussions with the Board and its staff, through discussions with each other as authorized by the CAB, and through various public announcements, etc. Actually, the majority of the postwar across-the-board fare increases were precipitated by the actions of various carriers. In addition, state and local government agencies, chambers of commerce, congressional representatives, etc., have influenced the Board's decisions.[23]

It would also be incorrect to imply that all fare changes during these years were the result of across-the-board fare authorizations. There have been examples of unilateral fares filed by individual certificated carriers which have been approved by the CAB and implemented without an overall fare change. The economy and business fares introduced in 1962–63 by Continental Air Lines over the Los Angeles–Chicago and Los Angeles–Houston routes are prime examples of unilateral fare filings.[24] Eastern Air Lines' Air-Shuttle fares between Boston, New York, and Washington comprise another example (see chapter 5); however, these unilateral fare actions have had two common characteristics. First, they generally involved the introduction of a new type of general fare (associated with an allegedly different class of service) rather than a change in an existing general fare. This is clearly reflected in Table 4–2.[25] Second, they

---

[23] An indication of the impact of a Congressional investigation on the CAB is given in Caves, *Air Transport and Its Regulators*, pp. 149–50.

[24] CAB Orders Nos. E-18706 (adopted August 15, 1962), E-19313 (adopted February 21, 1963), and E-20821 (adopted May 8, 1964).

[25] Also, see Caves, *Air Transport and Its Regulators*, p. 372.

were widely recognized and discussed within the industry as fare innovations—that is, they were exceptions to the general rule and thus stood out from the majority of fares in effect at the time they were introduced. The majority of fares were, of course, those that resulted from the across-the-board fare increases and coach policies of the CAB during the postwar years.

The CAB's across-the-board fare authorizations do provide a mechanism through which one of the major problems of a cartel may be solved: how to obtain agreement on the prices to be charged by all cartel members. The CAB provides a forum where fare proposals may be discussed and evaluated by the certificated carriers and other interested parties. Following this discussion and evaluation, the Board's decision is binding on all carriers. If any certificated carrier wishes to increase his fares he must adopt the CAB's authorized fare increase; therefore, once the Board has issued its decision, no carrier is required to evaluate an authorized fare change on the basis of whether it serves to maximize its profits. The evaluation is limited to estimating which of two alternative sets of fares will yield greater profits (or smaller losses). The almost universal adoption of the CAB's across-the-board fare authorizations demonstrates that the regulated carriers generally considered the newly authorized fares to be more profitable to them than the previously existing fares.

Fares in Major Markets

5

Introduction

Even though the Civil Aeronautics Board facilitated the establishment and enforcement of fare agreements, it does not necessarily follow that the resulting fares of the certificated carriers were higher than they would have been without the Board's regulation. Indeed, effective regulation could well have resulted in lower fares. Since the Public Utilities Commission did not control fare decreases, while CAB authorization was required for any change in interstate fares (whether an increase or a decrease), price regulation within California was much more limited than it was in interstate markets. A comparison of the California intrastate carriers' fares with those of the certificated carriers, therefore, provides a method for estimating the effects of CAB regulation on prices. This comparison will be undertaken in this and in the next three chapters.

Overall, three major and about 40 minor city pairs within California received service from one or more of the intrastate carriers between 1946 and 1965.[1] This chapter presents the fare histories for the three major markets: Los Angeles/Burbank–San Francisco/Oak-

[1] In this count of city pairs, Los Angeles and Burbank are considered to be only one city, as are San Francisco and Oakland. This combining of two adjacent cities was done for two reasons. First, the fares available at the two cities were usually identical. Second, in the CAB's origin and destination traffic statistics, Burbank's traffic has been combined with that of Los Angeles, while Oakland's O & D passenger data have been combined with those of San Francisco. Thus, individual traffic data are not available for these adjacent cities. If these two combinations of cities should be disregarded, it could be said that service was provided in about 58 rather than 43 California city pairs. (See Appendix 1 of this book.)

land, Los Angeles/Burbank–San Diego, and San Diego–San Francisco/Oakland (henceforth to be referred to simply as Los Angeles–San Francisco, Los Angeles–San Diego, and San Diego–San Francisco);[2] chapter 6 analyzes the fares for eight of the minor markets. The three major markets are by far the largest in California (measured by the annual number of passengers flying between them), and Los Angeles–San Francisco was the largest single market in the entire United States for the latter part of the period studied.[3] They are also the only markets that have had continuous service from intrastate carriers since 1949.

The first three sections of this chapter contain detailed descriptions of the fare histories of the three major markets and indicate the roles individual carriers, the CAB, and the PUC played in establishing or influencing fares. Then, based on the CAB across-the-board fare authorizations described in chapter 4, hypothetical coach fares are calculated to show what the coach fares in these markets would have been had the California intrastate carriers not existed—that is, if the only air service available within California from 1946 through 1965 had been provided by the regulated interstate airlines. Finally, a quantitative estimate of the CAB's impact on general fare levels is obtained by comparing the hypothetical coach fares with the coach fares that actually existed without CAB regulation.

Los Angeles–San Francisco Fare History

Figure 5–1 depicts the one-way passenger fares in effect between Los Angeles and San Francisco from 1946 through 1965. Some very minor or temporary fares not drawn in this figure may be found in the detailed fare summaries given in Appendices 6(A), 6(B), 6(C), and 7. Actually, the fares contained in the appendices are converted to fares *per mile* in Figure 5–1. Since fares increase with distance, the

---

[2] The letter codes for these markets are LAX/BUR–SFO/OAK, LAX/BUR–SAN, and SAN–SFO/OAK, respectively.

[3] In 1965, a total of 3,023,000 on-line O & D passengers flew between Los Angeles and San Francisco, compared with 1,986,000 such passengers flying between Boston and New York/Newark, the nation's second largest airline market at that time. Boston–New York/Newark was the largest market in the 1940's and early 1950's, but it was replaced by Los Angeles–San Francisco sometime prior to 1959 (generally comparable data are not available for both markets from 1949 through 1958). See Appendices 14(A), 14(B), and 14(C) of this book; CAB, *Competition Among Domestic Air Carriers* (1959–65) (Washington, D.C.: Air Transport Association of America, 1960-66); and CAB, *Domestic Origin-Destination Survey of Airline Passenger Traffic* (1946-58) (Washington, D.C.: ATA, 1947-59).

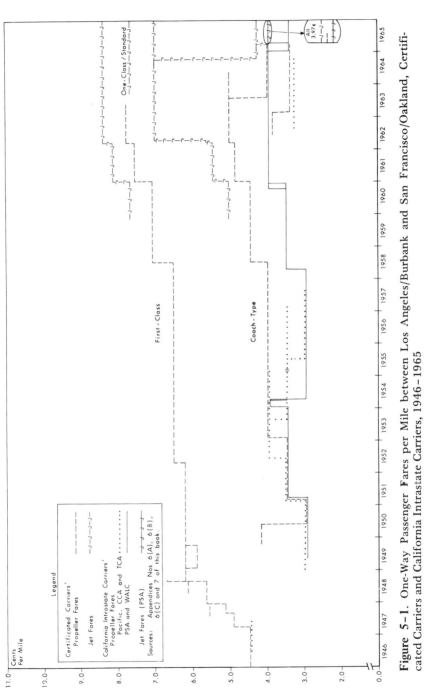

Figure 5–1. One-Way Passenger Fares per Mile between Los Angeles/Burbank and San Francisco/Oakland, Certificated Carriers and California Intrastate Carriers, 1946–1965

calculation of fares per mile serves to remove the effect of the distance variable and permits direct comparisons of fare levels among
different markets.[4]

First-Class Fares. The first-class fares per mile are depicted by the
top line in Figure 5-1. With the exception of Pacific Air Lines (the
intrastate carrier) in 1946-47, only the certificated carriers offered
such fares in this market. It is easy to follow the changes in the
propeller first-class fares of United and Western from 1947 through
1962.[5] There were four increases in 1947 and 1948. These consisted
of the three 10 percent, across-the-board fare increases authorized by
the CAB, plus an increase in mid-1947 that resulted when these two
carriers transferred their major operations from the Lockheed Air
Terminal at Burbank to the Los Angeles International Airport.[6]
During the next ten years, only the $1.00 per ticket, across-the-board
fare increase of 1952 marred the stability of first-class fares.[7] Then,
in mid-1958, early 1961, and early 1962, the last three CAB-
authorized, across-the-board fare increases (for the period studied)
were implemented, following the delays required to obtain the PUC's

[4] Nonstop airport-to-airport distances are given in Appendix 13 of this
book. The mileages used for the three major California markets are those based
on the Los Angeles, San Diego, and San Francisco airports. This introduces
minor inaccuracies for the Burbank and Oakland fares per mile. From 1946
through 1965, however, an increasing majority of passengers utilized the Los
Angeles and San Francisco airports, so that fares per mile based on these larger
airports are the most representative for the three major markets.

[5] Trans World Airlines was also authorized to operate between Los Angeles
and San Francisco throughout this period. Until it received turnaround authority in the *Pacific-Southwest Local-Service Case*, 35 CAB 50 (1962), however,
TWA had a long-haul restriction that required it to originate or terminate all Los
Angeles–San Francisco flights at, or east of, Albuquerque. Despite its change in
operating rights, TWA continued to limit its service in this market to flights
operated as part of its transcontinental schedules. In the Los Angeles–San Diego
market, American, Delta, and National airlines have also been authorized to
provide service—American throughout the postwar period, and Delta and
National since 1961 (see the *Southern Transcontinental Service Case*, 33 CAB
701 [1961]). The authorizations of all three of these carriers, however, contained long-haul restrictions.

[6] As explained in chapter 4, at this time the fares of the certificated carriers
were set by multiplying a given mileage rate by the all-stop route mileage
between city pairs. The Los Angeles International Airport is 13 miles farther
from San Francisco than is the Lockheed Air Terminal in Burbank.

[7] The dip in the first-class fare during 1949 depicts Western's no-meal fare
of that period. As shown, United retained the previously established first-class
fare with meal service.

approval of these increases.[8] Propeller first-class service was terminated in this market on May 31, 1963, thereby ending the effectiveness of this type of fare. Over the 17-year period from 1946 through 1962, the one-way, propeller first-class fare increased 73.9 percent from 4.46 to 7.75 cents per mile ($15.15 to $26.35).

The turbojet/fan (hereafter called "jet") first-class fares are drawn immediately above the propeller first-class fares from October 31, 1959, through 1965.[9] These jet fares (which include the jet surcharges) were also increased in 1961 and 1962 in response to the CAB's across-the-board fare authorizations. As a result, the jet first-class fare per mile increased from 7.63 cents in 1959 to 8.37 cents by early 1962 ($25.95 to $28.45). Comparing the 8.37-cent rate of 1962 with the 4.46-cent per mile fare for the best-available (DC-4) service back in 1946, it can be seen that the fares for the best-available first-class service increased by 87.8 percent between those years.[10] Clearly, the history of first-class fares in this market has been one of substantial increases in accordance with the across-the-board fare authorizations of the CAB.

Coach Fares. The certificated carriers' coach fares and the California intrastate carriers' fares for this market are also drawn in Figure 5–1. A comparison of the changes in the certificated carriers' coach and first-class fares shows that important differences occurred in the development of these two types of general fares. Still other important differences can be seen between the changes in the California intrastate carriers' fares and the changes in the coach fares of the certificated carriers. The following description of these differences shows the impact the California intrastate carriers had on the coach fares adopted by the certificated carriers in this market between 1949

---

[8] Since only one-way fares are drawn on the figures in this chapter, the adoption of the 5 percent, round-trip discount on September 1, 1948, is not shown, nor is its elimination on March 1, 1959.

[9] Trans World Airlines was actually the first carrier to operate jet aircraft in this market. It inaugurated Boeing 707 service between Los Angeles and San Francisco on or about June 1, 1959, at the same fare subsequently adopted by United on October 31, 1959. See *Official Airline Guide*, North American Edition, 15, no. 9 (June 1959), pp. C 325–38.

[10] On August 1, 1947 (after the first 10 percent across-the-board fare increase had been adopted), United introduced DC-6 service in this market with a $1.50 service charge added to its first-class fare (see Appendix 6[C]). If the resulting 5.35-cent per mile fare for that service is compared with the 8.37-cent per mile fare for jet service in 1962, one obtains a 56.4 percent increase in fares from DC-6 to DC-8 service.

and 1965, and indicates how these fares diverged from fares established through the CAB.

On January 2, 1949, California Central Airlines (CCA) inaugurated day-coach service between Burbank and San Francisco at a fare of 2.94 cents per mile ($9.99). This fare was less than half of the 6.19-cent per mile ($21.05) fare then charged by the certificated carriers for their first-class service in this market. Ten and one-half months later, on October 16, 1949, Western inaugurated the first coach service operated by a certificated carrier within California. This service was limited to a single round-trip night flight between Los Angeles, Burbank, San Francisco, Oakland, Portland, and Seattle. Western charged $14.10 between Los Angeles and San Francisco/Oakland. Based on the 340 miles between Los Angeles and San Francisco, this works out to 4.15 cents per mile, but adding the 12 miles between the San Francisco and Oakland airports reduces the fare per mile to 4.01 cents—the level then required by the CAB for new night-coach services.[11] Seven months later, on May 14, 1950, United introduced day-coach service at a one-way fare of $9.95, thereby equaling the lowest coach fare the intrastate carriers had adopted in 1949. This fare averaged 2.93 cents per mile—well under the CAB's prescribed 4-cent per mile minimum. Western also adopted this $9.95 fare on June 1, 1950, the day after it terminated the various services it had been operating for Western Air Lines of California.[12]

Without question, the certificated carriers' inauguration of coach service was in response to the services and fares introduced by the California intrastate carriers in 1949. The following quotation from a memorandum submitted to the CAB by Western in March 1950 testifies to this fact:

> Experience has demonstrated that, if such service ($9.95 air coach service performed with high-density aircraft) is not offered by Western—the oldest air carrier in the nation—under its certificate of public convenience and necessity authorizing it to provide transportation between the metropolitan areas in question, an abundance of such service will continue to be offered

[11] See chapter 4, Table 4–2.

[12] Western's $9.95 fare was initially filed to be applicable to intrastate passengers only, thereby retaining the $14.10 night-coach fare for interstate passengers traveling in this market. Before the $9.95 fare became effective, however, Western canceled this provision and made the low fare available to interstate as well as intrastate passengers. See Western Air Lines tariffs: Cal. P.U.C. No. 4, originally effective June 1, 1950, canceled by Supplement No. 1, effective May 17, 1950; and Cal. P.U.C. No. 3, originally effective October 15, 1949, 3d revised p. 7.

by unregulated intrastate air carriers apparently not subject to the economic jurisdiction of the Civil Aeronautics Board. In this connection, it is important to recognize that the reported gain of air travel over surface transportation on this segment during 1949 was principally the result of the availability of $9.95 air coach service. The market for such an operation, on a profitable basis, exists. The question to be answered is whether the public interest requires that such service be provided by a certificated carrier operating under a tariff filed with and approved by the Civil Aeronautics Board, or should the unregulated intrastate operators be permitted to enjoy "exclusive rights" to said traffic.[13]

During September 1950, the CAB decided to require that minimum coach fares be based on a 4.5-cent per mile rate rather than the 4-cent rate that had been in effect since November 1948. In the press release announcing this decision the Board stated:

> The conclusion that the fares for coach service should be increased in certain instances was reached after a thorough study of the results of coach operations to date and their impact on the financial results of the air carriers. . . . Except where special conditions or circumstances may necessitate exceptions, the Board believes that the 4.5 cent minimum fare level should prevail.[14]

Special circumstances obviously existed in California, since United and Western did not respond to this authorized increase in coach fares until, four months later, the CAB specifically urged them (as well as California Central and Pacific Southwest Airlines) to do so.

> The Civil Aeronautics Board announced today that it has urged all the airlines offering coach service between San Francisco and Los Angeles to increase their fare by one-half cent per mile, which would raise it from the present $9.95 to $11.70.
> The Board urged the increase in recognition of mounting costs of operations and for the purpose of bringing the fare more nearly into line with air coach fares elsewhere in the United States, which were raised a half cent, from 4 to 4.5 cents per mile, as of November 15, 1950.
> The Board acknowledged the special nature of operations between those points and noted that the present extremely low fare, approximately 3 cents per mile, which has prevailed for some time, reflects these special circumstances and is by far the lowest in the country. However, during the past year and the early part of this year, costs have risen to the point where, in the opinion of the Board, the proposed increase would be required if these operations are to continue on an economically sound basis.

[13] Western Air Lines, "Memorandum on Behalf of Western Air Lines, Inc., to Accompany Special Intrastate Air Coach Tariff for Service between Los Angeles and San Francisco–Oakland Filed with the Civil Aeronautics Board on March 27, 1950," p. 11.

[14] CAB Press Release No. 50-56 (September 27, 1950). Also, see chapter 4, Table 4-2.

The request was made to both the interstate air carriers, United Air Lines and Western Air Lines, and to both the intrastate airlines, California Central Air Lines and Pacific Southwest Air Lines, offering this service. The Board urged prompt action and suggested that the new rate should be established to be effective March 1, 1951.[15]

In response to this action by the CAB, United, Western, California Central, and Pacific Southwest (PSA) all filed applications with the PUC for permission to implement the suggested fare increase.[16] In addition, United and Western filed tariff revisions with the CAB containing the new fare. The CAB, of course, approved the increase, effective March 1, 1951. The PUC did not act by that date, however, and for the first time, United and Western found themselves with a discrepancy between a fare filed in their CAB tariffs and an intrastate fare authorized by the PUC. Their response to this dilemma was to follow their CAB tariffs, apparently believing that in the case of such conflict the CAB had primary jurisdiction. In addition, despite the fact that the PUC had not yet approved this fare increase, and even though it had no CAB tariff, California Central also increased its fare as of March 1, 1951. Only PSA retained the $9.95 fare, until the PUC authorized it to adopt the $11.70 (3.44 cents per mile) fare effective March 28, 1951.[17]

On March 6, 1951, the PUC reacted to this challenge to its authority by instituting the landmark Case No. 5271, in which it investigated the actions of California Central, United, and Western. As a result of its decision,[18] which was upheld by the California Supreme Court,[19] and which the U.S. Supreme Court decided not to review "for want of a substantial federal question,"[20] the PUC clearly extended its jurisdiction over all fares filed for service entirely within California by certificated as well as by intrastate carriers.

The question arises why California Central (unlike PSA) followed the wishes of the CAB rather than waiting for the PUC to act. The answer probably lies in the fact that at that time CCA had pending before the CAB an application for a certificate of public convenience

---

[15] CAB Press Release No. 51-10 (February 5, 1951).

[16] United filed with the PUC for this fare increase on February 9, 1951; Western filed on February 7, 1951; and California Central filed on February 20, 1951. See Exhibits Nos. 12, 13, and 14, submitted in Cal. PUC Case No. 5271.

[17] Cal. PUC Fare Authorization No. 20-12-121 (March 20, 1951). See 50 Cal. PUC 565 2n (1951).

[18] 50 Cal. PUC 565 (1951).

[19] 42 Cal. 2d 621 (1954).

[20] 342 U.S. 908 (1952).

and necessity to provide scheduled air transportation of persons, property, and express between San Diego, Los Angeles, Oakland, and San Francisco.[21] In addition, on November 22, 1949, the Board had instituted an investigation to determine whether the owners of California Central, Mr. and Mrs. C. C. Sherman, also controlled Airline Transport Carriers (which, as a large irregular carrier providing interstate service, was subject to the CAB's jurisdiction), and to determine whether a cease and desist order should be issued with respect to any violations that may have occurred through joint ownership. This case was in progress during 1951.[22] Overall, it seems evident that at this time the CAB was in a position to influence the decisions of California Central's management.

The second increase in the coach fare between Los Angeles and San Francisco occurred a little over a year later. There is no indication that it was introduced because of CAB pressure; however, it may have been related to the $1.00 per one-way ticket, across-the-board fare increase of April 16–27, 1952, which was approved by the Board in response to a number of tariff filings made during the previous month.[23] The certificated carriers applied this interstate fare increase to all of their first-class fares within California but not to their coach fares in the three major California markets.

California Central was the initiator of the second coach fare increase in this market. It had replaced its DC-3's with Martin 202 aircraft on August 31, 1951, and had enjoyed a 43 percent increase in traffic with those postwar (but nonpressurized) aircraft during the seven months from September 1951 through March 1952, compared with the same period a year earlier (even though its $9.99 fare had been in effect during most of the earlier period and the $11.70 fare was effective throughout the second period).[24] Whether because of

[21] California Central Airlines, "Application for Certificate of Public Convenience and Necessity," CAB Docket No. 4482 (filed May 19, 1950).

[22] A decision favorable to the Shermans was handed down on June 6, 1952. See *Charles C. Sherman and Edna K. Sherman—Interlocking Relationship and Stock Ownership in Airline Transport Carriers, Inc., and California Central Airlines*, 15 CAB 876 (1952).

[23] The March 1952 filings of the certificated carriers were for a $1.00 per one-way ticket fare increase plus the deletion of the 5 percent, round-trip discount. By a three-to-two vote, the Board approved the $1.00 per ticket increase but rejected the termination of the round-trip discount. Cherington, *Airline Price Policy*, pp. 99–102.

[24] U.S. District Court, Southern District of California, files of the Court Clerk, Bankruptcies Nos. 59560-PH and 59561-PH (filed January 27, 1954), California Central Airlines, *History, Development and Analysis of California Central Airlines* (n.d.), Appendices A-II and A-III.

this traffic growth, because of increasing costs during these Korean War years, because of a belief that the increased first-class fares of the certificated carriers would permit a higher coach fare, or because of other reasons, California Central decided to increase its Los Angeles–San Francisco fare from 3.44 to 3.97 cents per mile ($11.70 to $13.50). On April 29, 1952, the PUC approved California Central's application for this increase, which was implemented on June 15, 1952.[25]

The former general sales manager of California Central has asserted that the certificated carriers advised CCA of their intention to adopt this fare increase at about the same time,[26] and the following quotation from a CCA memorandum does imply that this may have been the belief of its management:

> It is not *officially* known at this time whether the other airlines that have been operating at a comparable fare between the above mentioned points (Los Angeles/Burbank and San Francisco/Oakland) are going to increase their fares in proportion. However, it is *intimated* that they will at an early date, as their costs have increased considerably.[27] (Italics added.)

United and Western did not, however, adopt the $13.50 fare until February 1, 1953, 7½ months after California Central.[28]

The period from mid-1952 to 1956 saw several changes in coach fares in this market that were independent of any CAB across-the-board fare authorization and were usually introduced by a single carrier. On August 25, 1953, California Central reintroduced DC-3, "tourist-class" service between Burbank and San Francisco/Oakland at the 3.44-cent per mile ($11.70) fare still offered by PSA for its DC-3 service. On January 15, 1954, PSA finally adopted the $13.50

[25] Cal. PUC Fare Authorization No. 20-12-146 (April 29, 1952).

[26] Conversation with Mr. Robert P. Hubley, October 14, 1965.

[27] U.S. District Court, Southern District of California, files of the Court Clerk, Bankruptcies Nos. 59560-PH and 59561-PH (filed January 27, 1954), California Central Airlines, "Memorandum To: All Travel Agents, All Sales Representatives, All Employees; From: General Sales Manager; Subject: Increase in Fare" (dated June 14, 1952). On July 22, 1952, California Central filed a complaint with the PUC regarding the retention of the $11.70 fare by United and Western. The complaint was withdrawn on March 30, 1953. 52 Cal. PUC 455 (1953). A similar complaint regarding PSA's retention of the $11.70 fare was rejected by the PUC on May 5, 1953. 52 Cal. PUC 509 (1953).

[28] Caves states (without specifying a source) that "under pressure from the Board, Western and then United and TWA followed California Central's increase." Caves, *Air Transport and Its Regulators*, p. 371. This writer has been unable to locate any source to confirm that the CAB did pressure Western, United, and TWA to adopt CCA's fare increase.

fare but shortly thereafter, on March 24, 1954, partially abandoned this higher level and reduced its fare to $11.70 for service on Monday through Thursday. Then, two weeks later, on April 8, 1954, both the $13.50 weekend and the $11.70 midweek fares were reduced by PSA to $9.99—the 2.94-cent per mile fare that had been introduced in January 1949 and discarded in March 1951. PSA retained the $9.99 fare with no changes for the following four years.

California Central maintained the dual fare structure of $13.50 for Martin 202 service and $11.70 for DC-3 service until February 14, 1955, when its operating assets were sold in bankruptcy. California Central's successor, California Coastal Airlines, inaugurated service with DC-3's around March 15, 1955, charging the $11.70 fare. On July 6, 1955, however, it lowered its Burbank–San Francisco fare to $9.99 (thereby meeting PSA's fare and service at Burbank) and then, on January 4, 1956, extended this lowest fare to service between Burbank and Oakland. The $11.70 fare was applicable between Los Angeles and San Francisco/Oakland (where PSA did not yet operate) until service was terminated at Los Angeles on February 3, 1957. Finally, after terminating service at San Francisco on February 17, 1957, California Coastal maintained the $9.99 Burbank–Oakland fare for six more months until it ceased all intrastate operations around August 9, 1957.

The certificated carriers' coach fare increase to $13.50 in February 1953, was the last time until mid-1962 that these carriers changed their coach fares without a CAB across-the-board fare authorization. The increase to 4.43 cents per mile ($15.05) on July 7, 1958, resulted from the 4 percent plus $1.00 across-the-board authorization; the 2.5 percent plus $1.00 increase raised the fare to 4.84 cents per mile ($16.45) on January 9, 1961; and, finally, effective March 20, 1962, the 3 percent across-the-board authorization carried this fare up to 4.99 cents per mile ($16.95). Thus, all of the major across-the-board fare increases of this period were adopted by United and Western in this market. Neither carrier, however, adopted the coach-meal fare increase (of $1.00 in this case) for their intrastate propeller coach service, even though they eventually did so in their interstate markets (see chapter 4, Table 4-2).

In 1959 the certificated carriers added a $2.00 per ticket surcharge for the new jet coach service, just as they did for jet first-class service. The resulting jet coach fares increased with other fares in response to the CAB's across-the-board fare authorizations, including the authorization which allowed jet coach fares in short-haul markets to be increased to 75 percent of corresponding first-class fares, before adjustments for the three $1.00 per ticket fare increases, the jet surcharge, and the coach-meal charge. This last increase was approved by the PUC to become effective on April 7, 1962, just 18 days after fares were increased by the 3 percent fare authorization. It appears to be an innocuous adjustment, but it raised jet coach fares in the Los Angeles–San Francisco market by almost 25 percent— from 5.60 to 6.97 cents per mile ($19.05 to $23.70). As a result, by April 7, 1962, the jet *coach* fare almost equaled the propeller *first-class* fare ($23.95) that had been in effect from mid-1958 through 1960.

Overall, between mid-1950 and mid-1962, the propeller coach fare charged by United and Western in this market increased by 70.3 percent. During the same period, the increase in the fare for the *best-available* coach service (provided with DC-4's in 1950 and with jet aircraft in 1962) was 137.9 percent. The first of these percentages is almost equal to the 73.9 percent increase in propeller first-class fares from 1946 to 1962, whereas the second is in a class by itself.

Returning to the California intrastate carriers, Figure 5–1 and Appendix 7 show that, effective April 14, 1958, the PUC authorized PSA (the only intrastate carrier then operating) to increase its fare from 2.94 to 3.47 cents per mile ($9.99 to $11.81), followed on December 12, 1960, by a second increase to 3.97 cents per mile ($13.50). In each of these two cases, PSA's fare increase became effective shortly before the certificated carriers implemented an across-the-board fare increase within California (on July 7, 1958, and January 9, 1961). This indicates that PSA led the certificated carriers in the fare increases for 1958 and 1960–61; however, closer study shows that this was not the case. During March 1957, seven certificated carriers asked the CAB to authorize a flat 6 percent fare increase; Capital and Eastern also requested an additional $1.00 per ticket increase. The CAB suspended these fare applications and, following an investigation, denied them on September 25, 1957.[29] On June 22, 1957, about three months after the certificated carriers' March filings, PSA applied for PUC permission to increase its fare to 3.47 cents per mile ($11.81), and nine months later, on March 25, 1958, the PUC approved its application.[30] In the meantime, on January 24, 1958, the CAB announced that it would authorize the "temporary" 4 percent plus $1.00 increase (to $15.05 in this mar-

[29] *Suspended Passenger Fare Increase Case*, 25 CAB 511 (1957). The seven carriers were Braniff, Capital, Delta, Eastern, Northwest, Trans World, and United.

[30] Pacific Southwest Airlines, Application No. 39172 (filed June 22, 1957). 56 Cal. PUC 214 (1958).

ket), and the certificated carriers quickly filed for this increase with both the CAB and the PUC.[31] The new fares became effective in interstate markets on February 10, 1958, but the PUC delayed their effective date within California to July 7, 1958.[32] Thus, PSA "led" the certificated carriers in adopting a fare increase within California simply because the CAB denied the certificated carriers' initial request for an increase, while the PUC granted PSA's somewhat later application.

The 1960 fare application also demonstrates that PSA was not a leader in increasing fares. PSA's filing with the PUC on May 17, 1960, occurred at about the same time the certificated carriers filed with the CAB for fare increases in response to the CAB's tentative decision on April 29, 1960, in the *General Passenger Fare Investigation*.[33] The Board's resulting 2.5 percent plus $1.00 across-the-board fare increase was effective in interstate markets on July 1, 1960, and Western and United filed for this increase with the PUC on June 29 and July 14, 1960, respectively.[34] Thus, because of the PUC's relative slowness in processing applications, PSA's fare increase *followed* the CAB-approved increase in interstate markets by more than five months, but because United and Western delayed their PUC filings for 1½ and two months, PSA led these carriers by a month within California.

PSA did not increase its fare in 1962 when the certificated carriers adopted the 3 percent across-the-board increase, and $13.50 was the highest fare charged by an intrastate carrier in this market through 1965. Therefore, over the period from 1950 through 1962,

---

[31] CAB Press Release No. 58-5 (January 24, 1958). The certificated carriers applied for this increase with the PUC on February 3 and 11, 1958 (see chapter 4, Table 4-4).

[32] See chapter 4, Table 4-3.

[33] Pacific Southwest Airlines, Application No. 42253 (filed May 17, 1960, amended August 8, 1960), 58 Cal. PUC 248 (1960); and CAB Press Release No. 60-10 (April 29, 1960). Caves states that PSA's application for the 1960 fare increase was filed *before* the Board's decision in the *General Passenger Fare Investigation*. (Caves, *Air Transport and Its Regulators*, p. 372.) He is correct in terms of the Board's final decision, which was issued on November 25, 1960. However, the dates of the CAB's tentative decision in this case and the subsequent across-the-board fare authorization (CAB Press Release No. 60-13 [June 17, 1960]) are more relevant than the date of the final decision. On the other hand, Caves is quite right in pointing out that PSA amended its original application (thereby raising the requested Los Angeles–San Francisco increase from 90 cents to $1.69) following the Board's across-the-board authorization on June 17, 1960.

[34] See chapter 4, Tables 4-2 and 4-4.

while United and Western increased their propeller coach fares by 70.3 percent, the Los Angeles–San Francisco fares of the intrastate carriers increased only 35.7 percent (calculated from the same base fare of $9.95). After the 3 percent fare increase became effective on March 20, 1962, the propeller coach fare of the certificated carriers was 25.6 percent higher than the comparable PSA fare ($16.95 vs. $13.50), while after April 7, 1962, their jet coach fare was 75.6 percent higher than PSA's fare for service on its turboprop Electras ($23.70 vs. $13.50).

Throughout the period from mid-1954 to 1962, the differences in fares charged by the certificated carriers and by PSA were striking, and the inauguration of Electra service by PSA in late 1959 substantially reduced the differences in service quality. More and more travelers turned to PSA until, in 1961, 32 percent of all passengers flying between Los Angeles and San Francisco utilized this intrastate carrier.[35] The first response of the certificated carriers to PSA's growing incursions was Western's introduction of Thriftair service on June 1, 1962. This service, conducted with DC-6B aircraft, was initially differentiated from Western's regular DC-6B coach service by somewhat different reservation and ticketing procedures, but even those differences were soon eliminated. As shown in Figure 5–1, Western's initial Thriftair fare of 3.81 cents per mile ($12.95) was slightly under PSA's 3.97-cent per mile ($13.50) fare. Since this difference proved to be insufficient to counteract the greater speed and comfort of PSA's Electras, on February 25, 1963, Western decreased its Thriftair fare to 3.36 cents per mile ($11.43), which was 15.3 percent lower than PSA's fare and 32.6 percent under the certificated carriers' regular propeller coach fare. Then, on August 1, 1963, Western reduced its propeller (Electra) coach fare to $13.50 to equal PSA's Electra fare.[36]

Given the substantial decreases in Western's fares, one would predict that its market share would increase at the expense of all the other carriers in the market. It happened, however, that while Western's market share did increase from 14.7 percent in 1961 to 30.8 percent in 1964, PSA's market share also increased, rising from 32 percent in 1961 to 43 percent in 1962–63, and 41.5 percent in

[35] Calculated from data presented in Appendix 14(A) of this book.

[36] The certificated carriers' propeller coach fares were relatively unimportant by this time. United was operating only jet aircraft in this market so that the only propeller day-coach service was Western's three daily round trips with Electras. *Official Airline Guide*, North American Edition, 19, no. 12 (September 1963), p. C 401. Western retained the $16.95 fare for Los Angeles–Oakland propeller coach service.

1964. Only United suffered a reduction in relative traffic over the entire period, with its market share falling from 44.4 percent in 1961 to 18 percent in 1963 and 15.6 percent in 1964. Therefore, it is understandable why, on September 27, 1964, United introduced Jet Commuter service with Boeing 727-100 aircraft at a fare of 4.26 cents per mile ($14.50). Also, on October 10, 1964, it lowered its jet coach fare on dual-configured aircraft to $14.50.

The last important coach fare adjustments during the period studied occurred in early 1965. On January 5, 1965, PSA reinaugurated service to Oakland with Electra aircraft, using the 3.36-cent per mile ($11.43) fare that Western introduced with its Thriftair service. On April 9, 1965, the first of PSA's Boeing 727-100's was placed in service at the 3.97-cent per mile ($13.50) fare. Then, on April 20, PSA carried out its earlier announced plan to lower the Los Angeles/Burbank–San Francisco Electra fare to $11.43, while retaining the $13.50 fare for jet service.[37] Meanwhile, United lowered its Jet Commuter fare to $13.50 on April 1, 1965, and on the same day, Western introduced its new Boeing 720B commuter service at the $13.50 fare (which it had filed on March 26, 1965) and terminated all Thriftair service.

After this relative storm of new fares and services, the remainder of 1965 was calm, with jet commuter service being offered by all carriers at the $13.50 fare, and with PSA operating Electra service at the $11.43 fare.[38] The only other development for that year occurred on December 7, when Western filed a propeller commuter fare of $11.43 between Los Angeles and Oakland, to be effective on January 6, 1966. On that latter date, Western terminated its Fanjet Commuter service to Oakland and inaugurated propeller commuter service with Electras.[39]

Before ending this description of the fare changes in the Los Angeles–San Francisco market, mention should be made of Trans

---

[37] On December 28, 1964, PSA filed a revision to its PUC tariff lowering its Electra fare to $11.43, effective May 17, 1965. This date was later advanced to April 20, 1965. PSA tariff, C.P.U.C. No. 1, 20th revised p. 13 (issued December 28, 1965).

[38] Western retained a single round-trip Electra coach flight between Los Angeles and San Francisco until June 30, 1965. The intrastate fare for this flight was $13.50. It is relevant to note that any passenger whose journey originated or terminated outside of California still had to pay the CAB-authorized fare of $16.95 to use this service.

[39] *Official Airline Guide*, North American Edition, 22, no. 5 (February 1966), p. C 500. Western Air Lines tariff, Cal. P.U.C. No. 25, 2d revised p. 2-B (issued December 7, 1965).

California Airlines' fare. TCA inaugurated service between Los Angeles/Burbank and Oakland on August 15, 1962, charging a one-way fare of 3.23 cents per mile ($10.99) for propeller coach service on Lockheed L-749 Constellations (see Figure 5-1 and Appendix 7). This was the lowest fare available at that time, and, initially, TCA's service was fairly successful. When, however, Western inaugurated Thriftair service between Los Angeles and Oakland on June 10, 1964,[40] TCA's traffic began to decrease, and this indirectly resulted in its service termination on October 7, 1964 (see chapter 2).

In summary, the net result of 17 years of coach fare increases and decreases (from 1949 to the last three quarters of 1965) was an increase of just 14.9 percent in fares for propeller service (from $9.95 to $11.43), while the increase in fares for the best-available coach service (provided with DC-4's in 1950 and jets in 1965) was 35.7 percent (from $9.95 to $13.50). The changes in fares for first-class service for another 17-year period (from 1946 to the last three quarters of 1962, but extending on to 1963–65) were 73.9 percent for propeller service and 87.8 percent for best-available service (from $15.15 to $26.35 and $28.45). The repeated first-class fare increases were clearly the direct result of the CAB's across-the-board fare increases. In contrast, the coach fare changes in this market (including all of the fare decreases) were often the result of independent actions by individual certificated and intrastate carriers, undertaken without the guiding influence of CAB fare authorizations.

Los Angeles–San Diego and San Diego–San Francisco Fare Histories

The average fares per mile for the Los Angeles–San Diego and San Diego–San Francisco markets are drawn in Figures 5-2 and 5-3 (pp. 90–91). Looking initially at the lines representing the certificated carriers' first-class fares, it is obvious that the changes in these fares were the same as those for the Los Angeles–San Francisco first-class fares (see Figure 5-1). Each of the CAB-authorized, across-the-board fare increases is in evidence, together with Western's no-meal fares in 1949, and United's DC-6 service charge in 1948 (for the Los Angeles–San Diego market). In fact, between mid-1947 (when fares were adjusted to reflect the greater use of the Los Angeles International Airport over the Lockheed Air Terminal in Burbank) and April 1952, the first-class fares per mile for all three of these city pairs were identical (ranging from 5.12 cents per mile in mid-1947 to 6.19 cents per mile from 1949 to early 1952).

[40] *Official Airline Guide*, North American Edition, 20, no. 9 (June 1964), p. C 415.

The $1.00 per one-way ticket increases, comprising the 1952 and, in part, the mid-1958 and early 1961 across-the-board fare increases, introduced a "taper" to the certificated carriers' fare structure by increasing the fares per mile for short-haul markets more than those for long-haul markets. As a result, after the across-the-board fare increase of March 1962, the 109-mile Los Angeles–San Diego market had a propeller first-class fare of 9.82 cents per mile, compared with 7.75 cents per mile for the 340-mile Los Angeles–San Francisco market, and 7.53 cents per mile for the 449-mile San Diego–San Francisco market—an overall difference of 30 percent from the lowest to the highest fare, where ten years before the fares per mile had been the same.

Propeller first-class service was terminated between May 31, 1963, and April 25, 1964, in all three of these major markets. Thus, while propeller first-class fares were retained in the certificated carriers' tariffs for fare construction purposes, they became irrelevant to this study as of early 1964.

Jet first-class service was inaugurated at San Diego on September 13, 1960 (see note n of Appendix 6[A]), and single-plane, jet first-class service was operated between Los Angeles and San Diego throughout the remainder of the period studied. Such service, however, was terminated between San Diego and San Francisco on April 27, 1963. In both markets, the jet surcharge was adopted together with the across-the-board fare increases of 1961–62. Between 1960 and early 1962, the first-class jet fares increased from 9.27 to 10.78 cents per mile ($10.10 to $11.75) in the San Diego–Los Angeles market, and from 7.35 to 8.00 cents per mile ($33.00 to $35.90) in the San Diego–San Francisco market.

Table 5–1

Percentage Increases in the Certificated Carriers' First-Class Fares
in the Three Major California Markets
from 1946 to 1962[a]

Market	Percentage Increase, 1946–1962[a]	
	Propeller	Best-Available[b]
LAX/BUR–SFO/OAK	73.9%	87.8%
LAX/BUR–SAN	92.8	111.7
SAN–SFO/OAK	63.3	73.4

[a]April-December, 1962.
[b]DC-4 propeller aircraft in 1946 and jet aircraft in 1962.

Source: Calculated from data presented in Appendix 6(A) of this book.

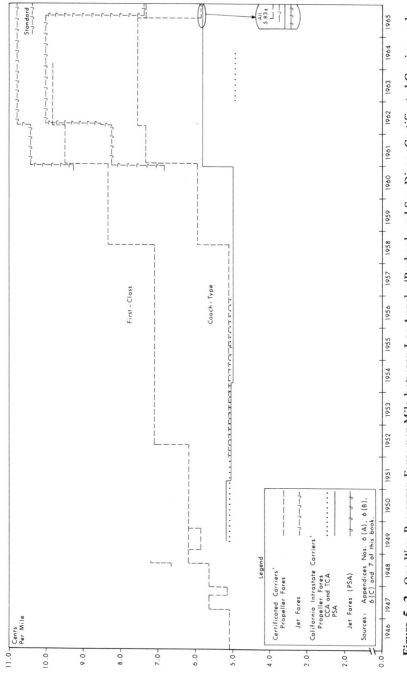

Figure 5–2. One-Way Passenger Fares per Mile between Los Angeles/Burbank and San Diego, Certificated Carriers and California Intrastate Carriers, 1946–1965

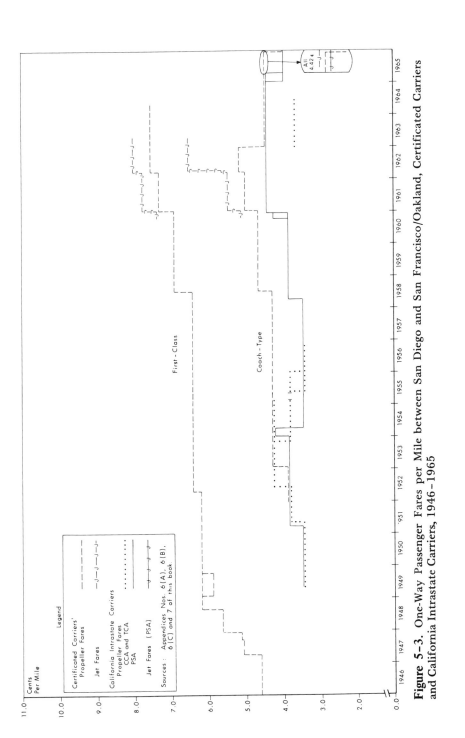

Figure 5–3. One-Way Passenger Fares per Mile between San Diego and San Francisco/Oakland, Certificated Carriers and California Intrastate Carriers, 1946–1965

Overall, between 1946 and April 1962, the first-class fares of the certificated carriers increased substantially in all three major California markets, the greatest percentage increases occurring in the short-haul Los Angeles–San Diego market. These increases are summarized in Table 5-1. Because there were no changes in first-class fares in any of these markets between April 1962 and 1965, the above increases would also have applied through 1965 had it not been for service terminations. As it was, only the 87.8 and 111.7 percent increases for best-available service between Los Angeles–San Francisco and Los Angeles–San Diego were still applicable by 1965.

Coach Fares of Intrastate Carriers. The California intrastate carriers introduced coach service to the two San Diego markets in May 1949, 2½ years before the first certificated carrier (Western) did so. The history of the intrastate carriers' fares in the Los Angeles–San Diego market is easily summarized. California Central and California Coastal charged only one fare in this market throughout their periods of operation between May 1949 and November 1956. This fare was 5.09 cents per mile ($5.55). PSA did change its fare twice during those early years, but its changes were both merely 10-cent *decreases*, which dropped its fare per mile from 5.18 to 5.09 to 5 cents ($5.65 to $5.55 to $5.45). The 5-cent per mile fare was adopted by PSA on April 8, 1954, when it slashed its Los Angeles–San Francisco fare to 2.94 cents per mile ($9.99). Only one fare increase was implemented in this market by a California airline through 1965. That occurred on December 12, 1960, when PSA increased its fare from 5 to 5.83 cents per mile ($5.45 to $6.35). This increase coincided with the increase from 3.47 to 3.97 cents per mile ($11.81 to $13.50) in the Los Angeles–San Francisco fare.

The introduction of service by Trans California on January 4, 1963, resulted in a decrease in the lowest fare available between San Diego and Los Angeles. TCA's fare of 4.95 cents per mile ($5.40) was just under the fare that had been in effect throughout the 1950's. TCA's limited amount of service,[41] however, made its fare relatively unimportant; the fare was canceled on June 14, 1964, when TCA stopped serving San Diego. The California airlines adopted no other fare change between Los Angeles and San Diego during the period studied. In fact, when PSA introduced jet service in April 1965, it retained the 5.83-cent per mile ($6.35) fare for *both* propeller and jet service.

---

[41] See the DC-6, L-749 intrastate coach schedule data for August 1, 1963, given in Appendix 15(B) of this book.

While the intrastate carriers' fares in this short-haul market have been very stable, they have also yielded the highest fares per mile charged by these carriers in the three major California markets. The initial 5.09-cent per mile fare was well above the early 2.93-cent per mile ($9.95) fare between Los Angeles and San Francisco, while the 5.83-cent per mile fare in effect after December 12, 1960, was still much higher than the 3.97-cent per mile ($13.50) fare, which was the highest intrastate carrier fare between Los Angeles and San Francisco. The 5.09-cent per mile fare was even higher than the 4.0 and 4.5-cent per mile minimum coach fares authorized by the CAB until October 1953. By December 1960, however, the CAB minimum propeller coach fare for a 109-mile intrastate market would have been about 8.39 cents per mile ($9.15—see Table 5-7 below), far surpassing the 5.83-cent per mile fare then in effect between Los Angeles and San Diego.

The California intrastate carriers' fare changes in the long-haul San Diego–San Francisco market differed significantly from the Los Angeles–San Diego fares. Their fares in this long-haul market have always been obtained by simply combining the local fares in the two intermediate markets. Thus, as can be seen by comparing Figure 5-3 to Figures 5-1 and 5-2, the stability of the Los Angeles–San Diego fares meant that changes in the San Diego–San Francisco fares resulted mainly from the changes in the Los Angeles–San Francisco fares.

The intrastate carriers' fares between San Diego and San Francisco increased from the 3.46-cent per mile ($15.54) fare introduced by CCA on May 5, 1949 (PSA's initial fare was $15.64), to 3.84 cents per mile ($17.25) in early 1951 (resulting from the $1.71 Los Angeles–San Francisco fare increase). CCA further increased its fare to 4.24 cents per mile ($19.05) on June 15, 1952 (when adopting its $13.50 Los Angeles–San Francisco fare), followed by PSA on January 15, 1954. In late 1953, CCA returned to the 3.84-cent per mile ($17.25) fare for its DC-3 service, and in its major retrenchment on April 8, 1954, PSA reduced its fare to 3.44 cents per mile ($15.44). On June 2, 1955, California Coastal adopted a 3.43-cent per mile ($15.39) fare between San Diego and San Francisco, while retaining the 3.84-cent per mile fare from San Diego to Oakland (which was no longer served by PSA). The 3.43-cent per mile fare was extended to Oakland on January 4, 1956, and was retained in both markets until California Coastal suspended service at San Diego on November 1, 1956. PSA's increases to 3.84 cents per mile ($17.26) on April 14, 1958, and to 4.42 cents per mile ($19.85) on December 12, 1960, corresponded to its Los Angeles–San Francisco fare increases (to

$11.81 and $13.50) on those dates. Finally, in early 1965, PSA decreased its fare for Electra service to 3.96 cents per mile ($17.78) between San Diego and Oakland (on January 5) and San Francisco (on April 20), while retaining the 4.42-cent per mile ($19.85) fare for jet service. To complete the record of the intrastate carriers' fares it is again necessary to mention Trans California's fare of 3.65 cents per mile ($16.39) during 1963 and early 1964. Again, however, TCA's limited service makes its fare for this market unimportant to this study.[42]

Table 5-2 summarizes the percentage changes in the intrastate carriers' fares from 1949 to the end of 1965 for all three major California markets. Comparing these percentages with those presented in Table 5-1, shows that the intrastate carriers' percentage fare increases for this 17-year period were only a fraction of the increases in the certificated carriers' first-class fares for the earlier 17-year period ending in 1962.

Table 5-2

Percentage Increases in the California Intrastate Carriers' Fares
in the Three Major California Markets
from 1949 to the End of 1965

Market	Percentage Increase, 1949-1965	
	Propeller	Best-Available[a]
LAX/BUR–SFO/OAK	14.9%	35.7%
LAX/BUR–SAN	14.4	14.4
SAN–SFO/OAK	14.4	27.7

[a]DC-3 propeller aircraft in 1949 and B-727-100 jet aircraft in 1965.

Source: Calculated from data presented in Appendix 7 of this book.

Coach Fares of Certificated Carriers. Western Air Lines began operating propeller coach service at San Diego on December 10, 1951 (see Appendix 6[B]), 1½ years after the certificated carriers matched the intrastate carriers' low fares between Los Angeles and San Francisco. Given this timing, it is not surprising to find that Western established coach fares in the Los Angeles–San Diego and San Diego–San Francisco markets equal to the fares already adopted

_____

[42] See the L-749 intrastate coach schedule data for August 1, 1963, given in Appendix 15(C) of this book.

by CCA and PSA—that is, 5.09 and 3.84 cents per mile ($5.55 and $17.25) respectively. When United inaugurated propeller coach service in these markets (briefly in 1952 and then permanently on April 25, 1954), it too adopted the prevailing fares of the intrastate carriers.

Turning first to the certificated carriers' Los Angeles–San Diego propeller coach fares (as drawn in Figure 5-2), we can see that their fares essentially equaled those of CCA and PSA until mid-1958. Thus, they did not adopt the 1952 across-the-board fare increase, and the increase to $13.50 in the Los Angeles–San Francisco fare was not reflected in a comparable increase in this short-haul market (with its already relatively high fare per mile).[43] Starting in 1958, however, the certificated carriers began to adopt the familiar pattern of CAB-authorized, across-the-board increases for their coach fares in this market, as well as in their other California markets. Each of the three 1958–62 fare increases is clearly depicted in Figure 5-2.[44] As was the case for the other major California markets, however, the coach-meal fare increase (of 75 cents for this market) was not adopted by United and Western. This figure also shows the large increase in the jet coach fare that occurred on April 7, 1962 (as a result of the jet coach fare being increased to 75 percent of the first-class fare, before adjustments). As of April 1962, the certificated carriers' propeller coach fare between Los Angeles and San Diego had risen to 7.57 cents per mile ($8.25), while the jet coach fare was 10 cents per mile ($10.90).

Looking now at the San Diego–San Francisco market (Figure 5-3), it appears that the pattern of certificated carriers' coach fare increases in this market was almost identical to that just described for Los Angeles–San Diego through 1962. The only difference was the increase on February 1, 1953, which raised the San Diego–San Francisco fare from 3.84 to 4.24 cents per mile ($17.25 to $19.05),

---

[43] Note that this long-lived coach fare was equal to the $5.55 first-class fare in effect in this market prior to the first postwar across-the-board fare increase in early 1947.

[44] Actually, there was one minor discrepancy between the CAB's across-the-board fare increases and the increases adopted in this market. The 1958 4 percent plus $1.00 fare increase should have yielded a fare of $6.80 rather than the $6.50 fare that was adopted. The reason for this was that the PUC held United's fare increase to a maximum of 17 percent to conform to the limit that United imposed upon itself in its then pending application for a permanent fare increase (the 4 percent plus $1.00 supposedly being only an interim increase). For short-haul markets, such as Los Angeles–San Diego, the 17 percent limit proved to be more restrictive than the 4 percent plus $1.00 request—that is, $5.55 x 1.17 = $6.50, as opposed to $6.80. See Cal. PUC 374, 379 (1958).

while the Los Angeles–San Diego fare was unchanged. This single difference occurred because at this time the certificated carriers' San Diego–San Francisco coach fares were also obtained simply by combining the fares for the two intermediate markets. Therefore, the $1.80 increase in the Los Angeles–San Francisco fare on this date caused an equal increase in the San Diego–San Francisco fare but had no effect on the Los Angeles–San Diego fare. Overall, the certificated carriers' propeller coach fares increased from 3.84 cents per mile ($17.25) in 1952 to 5.14 cents per mile ($23.10) by March 20, 1962, while the jet coach fare was 6.51 cents per mile ($29.25) as of April 7, 1962, following its increase to 75 percent of the first-class fare (before adjustments).

Table 5–3 summarizes the percentage increases in the certificated carriers' coach fares for all three major California markets from 1952 to the last nine months of 1962. It is obvious that the certificated carriers' coach fares increased much more in this 11-year period than the intrastate carriers' fares increased in a 17-year period (see Table 5–2). This, of course, can also be seen in Figures 5–1, 5–2, and 5–3. The much higher fares of the certificated carriers, together with the substantial improvement of PSA's service with its adoption of Electras, allowed PSA to capture an increasing portion of the total traffic in these markets. By 1962, PSA carried 37.5 percent of the Los Angeles–San Diego passengers and 79.3 percent of the long-haul San Diego–San Francisco passengers.[45]

The decisions of United and Western to respond to PSA's rivalry by lowering their coach fares and instituting new coach-type services has already been described for the Los Angeles–San Francisco market. As can be seen in Figures 5–2 and 5–3, they carried out similar reductions in fares for the two San Diego markets. On January 1, 1963, Western lowered its 5.14-cent per mile ($23.10) propeller (Electra) coach fare between San Diego and San Francisco to equal PSA's 4.42-cent per mile ($19.85) fare. This fare equality was maintained until early 1965, when PSA reduced its propeller fare to 3.96 cents per mile ($17.78), while Western delayed meeting this reduction until December 12, 1965. United literally withdrew from the San Diego–San Francisco market when it canceled its last single-plane schedule on April 27, 1963. This withdrawal lasted until June 4, 1965, when United introduced Jet Commuter service at the same fare that PSA charged for its then new jet service, namely, the 4.42-cent per mile ($19.85) fare (see Appendix 6[C]). Thus, by the

---

[45] Calculated from data presented in Appendices 14(B) and 14(C) of this book.

Table 5-3

Percentage Increases in the Certificated Carriers' Day-Coach Fares
in the Three Major California Markets
from 1952 to 1962[a]

| Market | Percentage Increase, 1952–1962[a] | |
	Propeller	Best-Available[b]
LAX/BUR–SFO/OAK[c]	44.9%	102.6%
LAX/BUR–SAN	48.6	96.4
SAN–SFO/OAK	33.9	69.6

[a]April-December 1962.
[b]DC-4 propeller aircraft in 1952 and jet aircraft in 1962.
[c]The percentage increases given for this market are based on the $11.70 fare
in effect during 1952. Should the $9.95 fare of May 1950-February 1951 be
used as the base figure, the percentage increases would be 70.4% and 138.2% for
propeller and best-available fares, respectively.

Source: Calculated from data presented in Appendix 6(B) of this book.

end of 1965, United was providing jet service in this market at a fare
equal to PSA's jet fare, while Western was matching PSA's Electra
fare on its Electra coach service.

The certificated carriers chose to delay meeting PSA's fares in the
short-haul Los Angeles–San Diego market until mid-1965. On June
4, 1965, United introduced Jet Commuter service with a 5.83-cent
per mile ($6.35) fare, which was equal to PSA's fare in this market,
and a month and a half later, on July 21, it also lowered its propeller
coach fare to 5.83 cents per mile and decreased its regular jet coach
fare from 10 to 7.25 cents per mile ($10.90 to $8.00). Western
contented itself with meeting United's 7.25-cent per mile fare on
both its propeller coach and jet coach services, effective August 1,
1965. Both United and Western retained their jet first-class fares at
the previous 10.78-cent per mile ($11.75) level. The percentage *de-
creases* in the certificated carriers' coach fares from 1962 to 1965 are
summarized in Table 5-4. These decreases range from 20.4 to 43
percent of the 1962 peak fares. Obviously, changes of such magnitude served to reduce greatly the overall fare increases of the certificated carriers from 1950/52 to 1965, compared with the percentage
increases given in Table 5-3 for the shorter 1952–62 period which
ended at the peak of the CAB-authorized fares. The extent of these
differences in increases is shown in Table 5-5. Reductions in overall
fare increases of from 30.8 to 102.5 percentage points for the period

Table 5-4

Percentage Decreases in the Certificated Carriers' Coach Fares
in the Three Major California Markets
from 1962 to 1965[a]

Market	Percentage Decrease, 1962-1965[a]	
	Propeller	Jet
LAX/BUR–SFO/OAK	20.4%[b]	38.8%[d]
	32.6[c]	43.0[e]
LAX/BUR–SAN	23.0[f]	26.6[g]
	–	41.7[h]
SAN–SFO/OAK	23.0[i]	32.1[h]

[a]From April-December 1962 to the specified periods in 1965.
[b]January 1-June 30, 1965 (Western propeller coach).
[c]January 1-March 31, 1965 (Western Thriftair).
[d]January 1-December 31, 1965 (United jet coach).
[e]April 1-December 31, 1965 (United and Western jet commuter).
[f]July 21-December 31, 1965 (United propeller coach).
[g]July 21 and August 1-December 31, 1965 (United and Western jet coach).
[h]June 4-December 31, 1965 (United Jet Commuter).
[i]December 12-31, 1965 (Western propeller coach).

Sources: Calculated from data presented in Appendices 6(B) and 6(C) of this book.

ending in 1965, compared with that ending in 1962, are substantial, and they provide important evidence regarding the impact of the California intrastate carriers on the long-term growth of the certificated carriers' fares in these markets. If PSA (or some other intrastate carrier) had not developed into such an important rival in the early 1960's, it is clear that the CAB-authorized across-the-board fare increases of 1958, 1960, and 1962 would have been retained in the three major California markets, yielding much higher coach fares without any appreciable difference in the quality of available coach service.

Relative Roles in Determining Fares

The fare histories for the three major California markets show that first-class fares were set by the CAB through its across-the-board

Table 5-5

Percentage Increases in the Certificated Carriers' Coach Fares
in the Three Major California Markets
for the Period Ending in 1962[a] Compared with That Ending in 1965[b]

Market and Time Period	Fare per Mile			Percentage Increase	
	Base Year	Final Year			
		Propeller	Jet	Propeller	Best-Available[c]
LAX/BUR–SFO/OAK					
1950–1962[a]	2.93¢	4.99¢	6.97¢	70.4%	138.2%
1950–1965[b]	2.93	3.36	3.97	14.9	35.7
Reduction		1.63	3.00	55.5	102.5
LAX/BUR–SAN					
1952–1962[a]	5.09	7.57	10.00	48.6	96.4
1952–1965[b]	5.09	5.83	5.83	14.4	14.4
Reduction		1.74	4.17	34.2	82.0
SAN–SFO/OAK					
1952–1962[a]	3.84	5.14	6.51	33.9	69.6
1952–1965[b]	3.84	3.96	4.42	3.1	15.1
Reduction		1.18	2.09	30.8	54.5

[a]April-December 1962.
[b]Various time periods in 1965. See notes c, f, and i (for propeller fares), and e and h (for jet fares) in Table 5-4.
[c]DC-4 propeller aircraft in 1950/52, and jet aircraft in 1962/65.

Source: Calculated from data presented in Appendices 6(B), 6(C), and 13 of this book.

fare authorizations. With the exception of Western's no-meal fare in 1949, there were no deviations from these industry-wide fares by individual certificated carriers serving California, and the only impact the PUC had on changes in authorized first-class fares was to delay their implementation within California.

In contrast, starting with the intrastate carriers' coach fares in 1949, the levels of coach fares in these markets differed from those set elsewhere by the CAB. The California airlines' initial Los Angeles–San Francisco coach fare per mile of 2.94 cents was 26.5 percent lower than the CAB's original 4-cent per mile minimum, and the certificated carriers found it necessary to adopt this lower fare in order to operate effectively in this market. The CAB did request and coordinate the March 1951 fare increase, the adoption of which the PUC attempted to delay, but every fare change in these markets from then until 1958 was determined by individual carriers with little regard to CAB actions and without restraint by the PUC. CAB fare actions regained relevancy from 1958 to early 1962, when the certificated carriers adopted the CAB-authorized, across-the-board fare increases of that period (except for the coach-meal increase), again after PUC-imposed delays. PSA adopted somewhat different fare increases in actions that were closely related to the CAB's first two authorizations of that period, but it ignored the third authorization and did not adopt jet surcharges when introducing jet service in 1965. Starting in mid-1962 and continuing through 1965, the certificated carriers once again responded to the intrastate carriers' pricing practices by independently implementing a series of fare decreases (unmatched elsewhere in the U.S.) that lowered their coach-type fares down to or below those of the intrastate carriers. Finally, Trans California introduced its own low fares in the three markets in 1962–63, and in early 1965 PSA responded to the fare and service rivalry of the certificated carriers by lowering its Electra fares to equal Western's Thriftair fare.

Overall, the fare histories show that regulation did not play a role in reducing coach fares. The CAB repeatedly authorized coach fare increases, and the main result of the PUC's regulation was merely to delay the implementation of carrier requests for increases, since it did eventually approve every such request. Rather, the main role was played by the individual carriers, who were able to play this role because the CAB did not have jurisdiction over intrastate operations and because the PUC did not control airline entry and fare reductions. The unrestricted entry of intrastate carriers in 1949 brought about the initial low coach fares eventually matched by the certificated carriers in 1950. Then, the several independent (and unregulated) reductions from 1953 through 1957 provided the low base from which PSA's increases of 1958 and 1960 merely served to return its fares to the level existing in 1952–54—a level that the certificated carriers eventually felt compelled to adopt.

Fares within California
Had There Been No Intrastate Carriers

Had it not been for the low fares charged by the intrastate carriers, the coach fares of United and Western would have been much higher at the end of 1965 than they actually were. The question arises, how much higher? One answer could be derived simply by extending the peak 1962 fares of these carriers on into 1965—that is, by eliminating the fare reductions that occurred between mid-1962 and 1965. There is, however, another, more accurate answer that will be described and tested in this section.

It has been shown that the intrastate carriers had no impact on the first-class fares adopted by United and Western in the three major California markets. In addition, since the April 7, 1962, jet coach fare authorization increased such fares to 75 percent of jet *first-class* fares (before the three $1.00 per ticket, jet surcharge, and coach-meal charge adjustments), it follows that the jet coach fares also were not influenced by the intrastate carriers' fares from that date until October 10, 1964, when United began to lower its jet coach fares. One can conclude, therefore, that the California intrastate carriers' influence was limited to the following fares of the certificated carriers: propeller coach fares, other coach-type fares, and jet coach fares in effect prior to April 7, 1962, and after October 10, 1964.

The CAB's first policy regarding coach fares became effective on November 4, 1948. As stated in chapter 4, Table 4-2, it held that such fares should not be lower than 4 cents per mile and that they should be limited to night-coach flights. This policy was adopted by Western when it became the first certificated carrier to offer coach service within California. Western's original coach fares for the three major California markets were filed on September 1, 1949, but were revised on October 1, before the initial effective date of October 15, 1949. Both of these filings are summarized in Table 5-6. Each of these fares can be derived by multiplying the appropriate airport-to-airport mileage by 4 cents per mile. The main difference between the September 1 and October 1 fares is an extra 50 cents that was added to the two city pairs that include San Francisco/Oakland. Appar-

Table 5-6

Western Air Lines' Original Coach Fare Filings
for the Three Major California Markets
Issued September 1, and Revised October 1, 1949

Market	Coach Fare Filed on	
	September 1, 1949	October 1, 1949
LAX/BUR–SFO/OAK	$13.60	$14.10
LAX/BUR–SAN	4.35	4.40
SAN–SFO/OAK	17.95	18.50

Source: Western Air Lines, Inc., *Local Air Coach Passenger Tariff No. 1*, C.A.B. No. 5, Cal. P.U.C. No. 3, originally effective October 15, 1949, original p. 7 and 1st revised p. 7.

ently the initial filing was based on mileages to the San Francisco airport, while the second contained an extra 50 cents to cover the 12 additional miles to Oakland. Also, fares in the first filing were rounded down to the nearest 5 cents, while those in the second were rounded up, as was customary. The CAB suspended all of Western's fares involving San Diego but authorized the Los Angeles–San Francisco fare to go into effect.[46]

This adoption of the CAB's original coach fare policy by Western provides base fares for these markets to which all subsequent CAB across-the-board fare authorizations may be applied serially to compute the hypothetical coach fares that would have been adopted by the certificated carriers had the California intrastate carriers not existed. These hypothethical fares are given in Table 5–7.

The hypothetical fares calculated for February 1, 1962, are all higher than the propeller coach fares in existence after March 20, 1962 (the effective date authorized by the PUC for the 3 percent, across-the-board fare increase). Appendix 6(B) shows that the actual propeller coach fares for these three major markets at that time were $16.95, $8.25, and $23.10, respectively—that is, $4.75, $1.20, and $4.05 lower than the hypothetical fares. The following are the reasons for these differences—and thus the reasons the actual 1962 fares do not provide an accurate estimate of the 1965 fares the certificated carriers would have charged had it not been for the California intrastate carriers' low fares in these markets. (1) The CAB across-the-board fare increases of 1958–62 were applied to base fares that had been established in response to the California intrastate carriers' fares rather than to the CAB's early coach fare policies; (2) the 1952 $1.00 per ticket across-the-board fare increase was not adopted for coach fares (but the independent $1.80 increase of February 1, 1953, in the Los Angeles–San Francisco and San Diego–San Francisco markets may have been associated with that increase); (3) the coach-meal fare increase in 1959 was also not adopted.

Test of the Hypothetical Fares. The obvious way to test the hypothetical fares calculated in Table 5–7 is to compare them with CAB-authorized fares actually in existence between interstate city pairs having characteristics similar to those of the California markets. Two of the most important characteristics would seem to be airport-

---

[46] Western's tariff also included night-coach fares for Long Beach, Portland, and Seattle. The Long Beach fares were also suspended, but the Portland and Seattle fares were approved. CAB Order No. E-3419 (adopted October 12, 1949).

Table 5-7

Hypothetical Propeller Coach Fares of the Certificated Carriers
for the Three Major California Markets
Assuming the California Intrastate Carriers Had Not Existed

CAB Effective Date[a]	Authorized Increase	One-Way Propeller Coach Fare[b]		
		LAX/BUR–SFO/OAK	LAX/BUR–SAN	SAN–SFO/OAK
10/15/49	Original (4¢/mile)	$14.10	$4.40[c]	$18.50[c]
11/15/50	0.5¢ per mile	15.85	4.95	20.80
4/ 1/52	Day-Coach[d]	15.85	4.95	20.80
4/16/52	$1.00 per ticket	16.85	5.95	21.80
10/ 5/53	New coach fares not to be above 75% of first-class fare[e]	(16.80)	(6.10)	(21.85)
2/10/58	4% plus $1.00	18.55	7.20	23.70
July '59[f]	Coach-Meal	19.55	7.95	24.70
7/ 1/60	2.5% plus $1.00	21.05	9.15	26.35
2/ 1/62	3%	21.70	9.45	27.15

[a]Had the California intrastate carriers not existed, it seems reasonable to assume that the CAB would have retained primary jurisdiction over the certificated carriers' fares within California and would have determined the effective dates of those fares.

[b]All fares that do not calculate out to an exact multiple of five cents are rounded up to the next higher multiple of five cents.

[c]The $4.40 and $18.50 fares are shown as the original fares for these two San Diego markets notwithstanding their suspension in 1949, since the CAB policy between 11/4/48 and 11/15/50 specified a minimum rate of four cents per mile which yields the above fares.

[d]On this date, the night-coach fare per mile was reduced to four cents leaving the day-coach fare at 4.5 cents per mile. These and all subsequent fares are for day-coach service.

[e]Derived by subtracting the $1.00 per ticket fare increase of 1952 from the applicable first-class fare *before* taking 75% of the remaining number, and then adding back the $1.00 per ticket increase to obtain the corresponding coach fare. The hypothetical fares after this date are based on the 4/16/52 fares (and the earlier policies) since it is believed that coach service would have been inaugurated in these markets before the end of 1953. In any case, by 2/1/62 the greatest difference between fares based on the alternative policies would have been only 20 cents (for LAX/BUR–SAN).

[f]American increased its Los Angeles–San Diego fare for interstate passengers on July 24, 1959, while United adopted the coach-meal increase for its premium interstate custom coach service on July 31, 1959. Western delayed adopting this increase in all its propeller coach services until 1964.

Sources: Calculated from data presented in Tables 4–2 and 5–6, and in Appendix 6(A) of this book.

to-airport distances and annual passenger traffic. Because of the very large sizes of the three major California markets' passenger traffic, only the top 20 or so interstate city pairs are comparable in this respect. Three of these markets have been selected as being similar enough to the California markets to provide a useful comparison of fares. The chosen city pairs are those comprising the major East Coast markets—Boston–New York/Newark, Boston–Washington, and New York/Newark–Washington. The 1965 on-line O & D passenger traffic and airport-to-airport mileages for these city pairs are compared in Table 5–8.

The three California markets have a greater range of airport mileages and passenger traffic than the major East Coast markets. The differences in range of passenger traffic during the overall period studied, however, were smaller than indicated by the 1965 data, since in the early years the Boston–New York traffic exceeded that for Los Angeles–San Francisco. In each case the population of the intermediate city is much larger than the other two, and the long-haul market has the smallest passenger traffic. Also relevant is the fact that each group has had a large number of turnaround, commuter-type flights scheduled for individual markets, has had flights serving all three city pairs as a unit, and has also been served by a number of long-haul flights connecting these cities with other cities located beyond the immediate geographic area.

American Airlines and Eastern Air Lines have been the certificated carriers accounting for the majority of traffic in the three major East Coast markets. Cherington describes in some detail their reluctance to comply with the CAB's coach fare policy when they introduced coach service in these markets.[47] Initially, in the spring of 1953, both carriers sought to charge first-class fares for coach service between Boston, New York/Newark, and Washington provided on extensions of long-haul flights that also served these cities. The CAB decided that two different fares for the same class of service on the same flight was unduly discriminatory, so it suspended the fares and instituted the *Short-Haul Coach Fare Case*.[48] American then submitted coach fares for these markets ranging from 5.15 to 6.05 cents per nonstop mile (vs. 6.40 to 6.70 cents per mile for first-class service). These fares were well above the CAB's existing policy which set coach fares at approximately 4.5 cents per mile,[49]

[47] Cherington, *Airline Price Policy*, pp. 432–35.
[48] CAB Order No. E-7333 (adopted April 24, 1953) for Eastern; and CAB Order No. E-7377 (adopted May 14, 1953) for American.
[49] See chapter 4, Table 4-2.

Table 5-8

1965 On-Line Origin and Destination Passenger Traffic[a]
and Nonstop Airport-to-Airport Mileages
for the Major California and East Coast Markets

Three Major California Markets

Market	Airport Mileage	On-Line O & D Pax.[b]
LAX/BUR–SFO/OAK[c]	340	3,023,341
LAX/BUR–SAN[c]	109	637,447
SAN–SFO/OAK	449	359,025

Three Major East Coast Markets

Market	Airport Mileage	On-Line O & D Pax.
BOS–NYC/EWR	184	1,985,680
NYC/EWR–DCA	215	1,663,850
BOS–DCA	399	435,920

[a]On-line O & D passenger data show where passengers originate and terminate their journeys on *individual carriers*. Passengers using two or more carriers for their trips are counted as on-line O & D passengers in two or more city pairs—one for each carrier. See note a of Appendix 14(A).

[b]The sum of the on-line O & D passengers carried by the certificated carriers and the California intrastate carriers.

[c]Includes a small amount of traffic originating and terminating at Long Beach.

Sources: Appendices 13, 14(A), 14(B), and 14(C). CAB, *Competition Among Domestic Air Carriers* (1965).

and they were also suspended by the Board. On October 5, 1953, before this case went to hearing, the CAB announced its revised coach fare policy which established the standard that new coach fares should not exceed 75 percent of first-class fares in the same market. American and Eastern accepted this policy but gave it an interesting interpretation. Instead of basing the 75 percent on the published first-class fare, they first subtracted the $1.00 per ticket across-the-board fare increase that had been authorized in 1952, took 75 percent of the remainder, and then added back in the $1.00 per ticket increase to obtain the coach fare, thereby gaining 25 cents on each fare. The result of this was coach fares in these three markets ranging from 4.89 to 5.16 cents per mile—76.3 to 77.4 percent of the published first-class fares. Since the Board allowed these fares to go into effect in early December 1953, it can only be assumed that this approach was acceptable to it.[50]

As shown in chapter 4, Table 4-3, American and Eastern applied the three major across-the-board fare increases of 1958, 1960, and 1962 to their initial coach fares in these markets. In addition, they also adopted the coach-meal fare increase on June 1 (Eastern) and July 24 (American), 1959, which added $1.00 to each fare.[51] The resulting fares that were effective as of February 1, 1962, provide the basis for testing the hypothetical propeller coach fares in the three major California markets following the adoption of the 3 percent, across-the-board fare increase.

It is incorrect to make comparisons between the certificated carriers' propeller coach fares for the major California and East Coast markets until appropriate adjustments are made to remove the fare taper (resulting from the various $1.00 per ticket increases) and to eliminate the effects of the differing airport-to-airport mileages by converting the adjusted fares to fares per mile. These adjustments are made in Table 5-9 for the actual and hypothetical 1962 fares of the major California markets and for the actual 1962 fares of the East Coast markets.

Comparing the adjusted hypothetical California fares per mile given in Table 5-9 with the adjusted actual East Coast fares per mile shows that they are very similar. In fact, they are almost identical. All

[50] The first-class and coach fares for these three East Coast markets are presented in Appendices 8(A) and 8(B) of this book.

[51] The only deviation from the across-the-board fare increases occurred on August 20, 1961, when Eastern lowered its Boston–Washington propeller coach fare by 5 cents, from $23.90 to $23.85. It retained this small differential compared with American even after the 3 percent fare increase of February 1, 1962. (See Appendix 8[B] of this book.)

six of these adjusted fares per mile fall within an interval of only 0.16 cents and deviate by no more than 1.8 percent from their simple average of 5.08 cents. In contrast, the adjusted actual Califor-

Table 5-9

Adjusted Actual and Hypothetical Propeller Coach Fares per Mile
for the Major California and East Coast Markets
Effective February 1[a] and March 20[b], 1962

Market	Unadjusted 1962 Fare	$1.00 Taper Adjustments[c]	Adjusted 1962 Fares One-Way	Per Mile
	A. Actual California Fares			
LAX/BUR–SFO/OAK	$16.95	$2.10	$14.85	4.37¢
LAX/BUR–SAN	8.25	2.10	6.15	5.64
SAN–SFO/OAK	23.10	2.10	21.00	4.68
	B. Hypothetical California Fares			
LAX/BUR–SFO/OAK	$21.70	$4.28	$17.42	5.12¢
LAX/BUR–SAN	9.45	4.01	5.44	4.99
SAN–SFO/OAK	27.15	4.28	22.87	5.09
	C. Actual East Coast Fares			
BOS–NYC/EWR	$13.50	$4.28	$ 9.22	5.01¢
NYC/EWR–DCA	15.35	4.28	11.07	5.15
BOS–DCA	24.65	4.28	20.37	5.11

[a]Hypothetical California and actual East Coast fares.
[b]Actual California fares.
[c]These adjustments are calculated by taking each $1.00 per ticket fare increase and tracing it through all subsequent percentage fare increases while rounding fractions to the next highest penny, i.e.:

Fare Increase of					Adjustments		
					California		E. Coast
4/16/52	2/10/58	July '59	7/1/60	2/1/62	Actual	Hypoth.	Actual
$1.00	$1.04	n.a.	$1.07	$1.11	n.a.	$1.11	$1.11
	1.00	n.a.	1.03	1.07	$1.07	1.07	1.07
		$1.00*	1.03	1.07	n.a.	1.07	1.07
			1.00	1.03	1.03	1.03	1.03
			Total Adjustment		$2.10	$4.28*	$4.28

n.a.—not applicable.
*75¢ for LAX/BUR–SAN yielding a total adjustment of $4.01
($1.11 + 1.07 + .80 + 1.03) for this market.

Sources: Tables 4-2 and 5-7; and Appendices 6(B) and 8(B) of this book.

nia fares per mile all fall well outside the range of the adjusted actual East Coast fares per mile, with deviations of from minus 14 to plus 11 percent from the simple average of the East Coast fares per mile (5.09 cents).[52] Thus, the results of this test are consistent with the hypothesis that the hypothetical fares derived in Table 5-7 represent the propeller coach fares that would have existed in the three major California markets in 1962 had the CAB's coach fare policies and across-the-board fare increases been applicable to these markets.

Since there were no general across-the-board fare changes between mid-1962 and 1965, it follows that, given the sole right to provide scheduled air transportation within California, the certificated carriers would have maintained their hypothetical 1962 fares on into 1965. American's unchanging fares for the East Coast markets from early 1962 through 1965 support this conclusion.[53] The findings of Table 5-7, therefore, can be extended on to 1965 to determine how much higher the California fares per mile would have been at that time had it not been for the intrastate carriers' rivalry. This will be done in the following section.

Those familiar with the three East Coast markets may properly point out that in 1965 the relevant fares in the Boston–New York/Newark and the New York/Newark–Washington markets were those for Eastern's dominant Air-Shuttle service, rather than for propeller coach service. Therefore, it could be argued that the Air-Shuttle fares should be used to test the accuracy of the hypothetical California fares. This argument warrants consideration and, for that reason, Appendix 8(C) presents Eastern's Air-Shuttle passenger fares between Boston, New York/Newark, and Washington from the date of the inauguration of this type service, on April 30, 1961, through

[52] The differences in the adjusted actual California fares per mile reflect the different mileage rates in the early fares for these markets. Recall that the certificated carriers' original Los Angeles–San Diego coach fare of 5.09 cents per mile matched that of the California airlines at a time when the Los Angeles–San Francisco rate was 3.44 cents per mile. The CAB's approval of both these rates when its coach fare policy specified a rate of 4.5 cents shows that within California it accepted violations of its policy on the high as well as the low side. Increasing the Los Angeles–San Francisco and San Diego–San Francisco fares by $1.75 in 1951 and $1.80 in 1953 reduced the original fare taper in these markets and brought their fares per mile closer to that for Los Angeles–San Diego, but they did not eliminate the differences in rates.

[53] On January 15, 1965, Eastern increased its first-class and coach fares in these markets to conform to its "minus 5 percent, plus $2.50" across-the-board fare adjustment (see chapter 4, Table 4-2). American did not adopt these changes, and on June 5, 1965, Eastern rescinded its Boston–Washington increase but retained the increases in the two short-haul markets.

1965. Comparing the regular, or "on-peak," Air-Shuttle fares with the corresponding propeller coach fares in these markets (Appendix 8[B]) shows that the Air-Shuttle fares were not affected by the across-the-board fare increase of February 1, 1962, and that the Boston–New York/Newark and the New York/Newark–Washington Air-Shuttle fares were indeed $0.77 to $2.19 lower than propeller coach fares from April 1961 through 1963.[54] Effective January 8, 1964, however, Eastern increased the regular Air-Shuttle fares so that they were only 9 to 17 cents under the propeller coach fares, and on January 15, 1965, it increased them to about $1.75 *above* American's propeller coach fares and almost equal to Eastern's new propeller coach fares in these two markets. Thus, while it is certainly possible that some type of special shuttle service might have been instituted in the major California markets had there been no intrastate carriers, and that the fares for such service might have been changed independently of CAB across-the-board authorizations, there is nothing in the East Coast Air-Shuttle record to indicate that fares for such a service would have been significantly under those charged for regular propeller coach service during 1965. Thus, the hypothetical propeller coach fares calculated in Table 5–7 still seem to be a reasonable estimate of the fares that would have existed in the three major California markets had the California intrastate carriers not existed.

Quantitative Estimates of Fare Reductions

The fare histories for 1949 through 1965 and the testing of the hypothetical coach fares provide persuasive evidence that one result of the California intrastate carriers' operations was lower coach fares in the three major California markets. Quantitative estimates of the extent to which the lowest widely-available fares were reduced in 1949 and during the early 1950's may be obtained by comparing the fares of the California intrastate carriers with the certificated carriers' first-class fares. Then, starting sometime in the 1950's, the comparison with the intrastate carriers' fares should be transferred from the certificated carriers' first-class fares to their hypothetical coach fares given in Table 5–7. Of course, no one knows when the certificated carriers would have introduced coach service in these markets had the intrastate carriers not existed; however, if the major

[54] This was not the case for the Boston–Washington regular Air-Shuttle and Executive Shuttle fares. From the beginning of single-plane shuttle service in this market on February 1, 1962, until its termination on April 25, 1965, the applicable shuttle fares were approximately equal to the propeller coach fares.

East Coast markets are any indication, it would not have occurred much before the end of 1953. Regardless of when coach service might have been introduced had these markets been served only by certificated carriers, there certainly would have been extensive coach service by 1965. A comparison of differences in actual and hypothetical coach fares for the last eight months of that year, therefore, provides a measure of the cumulative effects of CAB price regulation relative to the cumulative effects of nonregulated price rivalry within California.

Table 5-10 summarizes the hypothetical and actual first-class and coach fares for the period from April 20 to December 31, 1965—the period that includes the operation of jet coach service at the lowest fares in all three major markets, together with the operation of Electra coach service at fares that were generally below those for jet service. Since the first-class fares were determined by CAB across-the-board fare authorizations and were not influenced by price rivalry within California, the actual and hypothetical first-class fares in Table 5-10 are the same. In contrast, there are large differences between the actual coach/commuter fares of PSA, United, and Western and the calculated hypothetical coach fares of the certificated carriers. For example, instead of paying a hypothetical fare of about $21.70 (plus tax) to fly on a propeller coach flight between Los Angeles and San Francisco during this period, an air traveler was actually able to make such a trip for only $11.43 (plus tax), 47 percent lower than the hypothetical fare. Similarly, the actual jet coach fare at this time of $13.50 was 43 percent lower than the hypothetical (and, for Western, actual) jet coach fare of $23.70. Table 5-11 presents the differences between the hypothetical coach fares and the lowest actual coach fares in effect in the three major California markets during most of 1965.

The findings of the previous sections and Tables 5-10 and 5-11 are thought-provoking. Given the general applicability of the CAB's coach fare policies and across-the-board fare authorizations, it follows that the great majority of interstate propeller coach fares were comparable to the hypothetical fares calculated for the three major California markets (after allowing for fare taper and adjusting for mileage differences). Therefore, if the actual California fares were the result of limited regulation, it can be concluded that had this degree of regulation existed throughout the country from 1946 to 1965, one would find coach fares for comparable interstate markets roughly equaling the actual rather than the hypothetical coach fares for the three major California markets. In other words, under California-type regulation these interstate coach fares during the last

Table 5-10

Hypothetical and Actual One-Way Passenger Fares
of United, Western, and Pacific Southwest Airlines
for the Three Major California Markets
from April 20 to December 31, 1965

| Market | Service | One-Way Passenger Fares | | PSA |
| | | United and Western | | Actual |
		Hypothetical	Actual	
LAX/BUR–SFO/OAK	First Class–Jet	$28.45	$28.45	none
	Prop.	26.35	26.35[a]	none
	Coach–Jet	23.70	14.50 & 23.70	$13.50[c]
	Prop.	21.70	13.50[b]	11.43
	Commuter–Jet	n.a.	13.50	13.50[c]
LAX/BUR–SAN	First Class– Jet	11.75	11.75	none
	Prop.	10.70	10.70[a]	none
	Coach–Jet	10.90	8.00	6.35[c]
	Prop.	9.45	6.35 & 8.00	6.35
	Commuter–Jet	n.a.	6.35	6.35[c]
SAN–SFO/OAK	First Class– Jet	35.90	35.90[a]	none
	Prop.	33.80	33.80[a]	none
	Coach–Jet	29.25	29.25[a]	19.85[c]
	Prop.	27.15	19.85 & 17.78[d]	17.78
	Commuter–Jet	n.a.	19.85	19.85[c]

n.a.—not applicable.

[a]This class of service was not operated in this market during this period. Therefore, this fare was not actually available.

[b]This class of service was terminated effective July 1, 1965. Therefore, this fare was not actually available for this service as of that date.

[c]PSA's service in its Boeing 727-100 aircraft (with 122 seats) is considered to be comparable to both the certificated carriers' jet coach and their jet commuter services.

[d]Western's $17.78 fare became effective on December 12, 1965. The $19.85 fare was in effect prior to that date.

Sources: Table 5-7 and page 101 above. Appendices 6(A), 6(B), 6(C), and 7 of this book.

eight months of 1965 would have been between 32 and 47 percent lower than what they actually were.

There is danger in extrapolating from a small and perhaps unusual sample. It is difficult to believe, however, that differences of 32 to 47 percent can be entirely accounted for by nonregulatory differences between the major California markets and all the other domestic markets. This is especially true given the common

Table 5-11

Differences between Hypothetical Coach Fares and
the Lowest Actual Coach Fares for the Three Major California Markets
from April 20 to December 31, 1965

Market	Coach Service	One-Way Coach Fare Hypothetical	Actual	Difference Amount	Percentage[a]
LAX/BUR–SFO/OAK	Jet	$23.70	$13.50	$10.20	−43.0%
	Prop.	21.70	11.43	10.27	−47.3
LAX/BUR–SAN	Jet	10.90	6.35	4.55	−41.7
	Prop.	9.45	6.35	3.10	−32.8
SAN–SFO/OAK	Jet	29.25	19.85	9.40	−32.1
	Prop.	27.15	17.78	9.37	−34.5

[a]Based on the hypothetical fare. This gives the percentage reduction of the actual fare from the hypothetical fare.

Source: Table 5-10.

development of the certificated carriers' coach fares, which served to establish a consistent fare base for the application of the percentage fare differences.

The implications of these findings can be carried one step further. If such differences existed between the actual and hypothetical coach fares for travel in the relatively short-haul California markets, how much lower might interstate fares have been had California-type regulation existed in long-haul, high-density markets? The operating costs of large- and medium-sized jet aircraft are significantly lower for 1,500- to 2,500-mile flights than for flights of under 450 miles. Would such lower costs be reflected in even lower fares for long-haul markets under conditions of limited regulation? One example will suffice to indicate what this would mean. The February 1, 1962, across-the-board fare increase yielded a one-way jet coach fare of $145.10 between New York and the major California cities, and this fare was still in effect on December 31, 1965.[55] A 43 percent reduction in this fare (based on the Los Angeles–San Francisco jet coach fare difference) would yield a fare of only $82.70—3.31 cents per mile for a 2,500-mile market compared to 3.97 cents per mile for the 340-mile California market.[56]

[55] *Official Airline Guide*, North American Edition, 22, no. 3 (December 1965), p. C 569.

[56] New York is 2,446 miles from Los Angeles and 2,566 miles from San Francisco. This yields a simple average of 2,506 miles. CAB, *Handbook of Airlines Statistics*, p. 399.

This may appear to be unrealistically low; however, in April 1967, World Airways (a supplemental airline) applied to the CAB for authority to operate scheduled nonstop service between California and the East Coast with Boeing 707 aircraft at a "thrift service" fare of $79.50 (about 3.2 cents per mile), which would have been 45.6 percent under the existing $145.10 fare.[57] This is consistent with the above analysis and does indicate that through 1965 one major effect of CAB regulation was to preclude reductions in long-haul coach fares that would have been at least as great as the percentages indicated by the California experience.

Conclusion

Widely available coach fares were obviously lower in the three major California markets under the PUC's limited regulatory power than they would have been had the CAB exercised control over air transportation in these markets. This conclusion is supported by the adherence of the certificated carriers' first-class and (in 1962–64) jet coach fares to the CAB's fare policies and across-the-board authorizations, by the reduction of the certificated carriers' coach fares in response to the price rivalry within California, and by the comparison of the adjusted hypothetical California fares per mile with the adjusted fares per mile actually adopted in the three major East Coast markets. During the last eight months of 1965, the coach fares in the major California markets were 32 to 47 percent lower than what they would have been had the CAB's fare policies and across-the-board authorizations been adopted over the years. Extrapolations of these calculations, supported by the 1967 fare proposal of World Airways, suggest that even greater differences would have existed in the high-density, long-haul transcontinental markets had California-type regulation been in effect there. Thus, it seems clear that CAB regulation has resulted in higher prices for many of the certificated carriers' interstate services. This, of course, is consistent with the implications of the cartel hypothesis, thereby providing additional evidence that CAB regulation has helped the certificated carriers act as a cartel.

Although one important result of the CAB's extensive regulation has been higher fares in many interstate markets, it does not follow that the CAB has failed to hold fares down below what they would have been given its other direct and indirect regulatory powers over entry and service, and given its administrative procedures. The World War II fare reductions and the occasions during the postwar period

---

[57] *Aviation Week and Space Technology* 86, no. 18 (May 1, 1967), p. 27.

when the CAB suspended or refused carrier requests for fare increases both indicate that the Board did hold down prices within the market structure that its regulatory powers did so much to create. However, when CAB-authorized fares are compared with fares for similar services provided in a different market structure, it becomes evident that, overall, the Board was relatively ineffective in achieving low fares.

It can be argued that the lower general coach fares within California were due more to effective regulation by the PUC than to the relative lack of regulation. There is little evidence, however, to support this position and much to oppose it. First, the fare histories indicate that the PUC eventually approved every fare increase requested by either the certificated or the intrastate carriers. As shown in chapter 4, Table 4-3, its only measurable impact on applications for fare increases was to delay the implementation of some of the across-the-board authorizations of the CAB. Second, the fare histories show that the low fares within California stemmed largely from the original fares introduced by those intrastate carriers inaugurating service in 1949. The PUC had no control over their entry and, moreover, had to accept their initial fares (providing their tariffs were technically correct). This shows that open entry was an important determinant of fare levels during this period.[58] Finally, the PUC's lack of control over fare decreases facilitated the fare reductions of California Central in 1953, of PSA in 1954, California Coastal in 1955-57, Western in 1962-63, United in 1964, and of all existing carriers in 1965. This is not a record of active fare regulation. Quite the contrary, it is a record of essentially passive response to carrier or CAB decisions. Clearly, it was the independent fare policies and actions of the intrastate carriers and, eventually, the certificated carriers—working in an environment of limited regulation—that determined the low coach fares in the major California markets.

---

[58] The PUC could investigate initial fare filings and, if they were found to be unreasonable, could cancel them even though they had been in effect throughout the investigation. Only one example of such an investigation was discovered, and that concerned the 1949 filings. The PUC's decision that the $9.95/9.99 fares were reasonable certainly aided the development of low-fare air transportation within California, but this should not obscure the fact that it was the intrastate carriers who introduced those fares and provided the evidence that permitted the PUC to arrive at its decision. See Cal. PUC Case No. 4994 et al.; 49 Cal. PUC 494 (1950).

Fares in Minor Markets

6

Introduction

An examination of passenger fares in minor California markets provides evidence pertaining to both pricing and entry aspects of airline regulation. With regard to price, comparing the passenger fares of the certificated carriers with those of the California intrastate carriers in minor markets yields additional information about relative fare levels (thereby extending the analysis of chapter 5). Also, comparing the intrastate carriers' fares in minor markets with their fares in major markets adds further insights into the pricing performance of airlines operating under little or no effective regulation. With regard to entry, studying intrastate carriers' fares in minor markets generates evidence about the assertion that nonregulated airlines merely "skim the cream" by serving only the largest and most profitable markets. This assertion underlies the internal subsidy argument which reasons that the Civil Aeronautics Board must control entry and allow the certificated carriers to make large profits in major markets in order to cover losses incurred in serving low-density markets, and that without this effect of regulation small markets would not be served. This rationale for regulation is challenged to the extent the relatively nonregulated intrastate carriers served minor as well as major markets within California.

The California intrastate carriers served a total of about 40 minor city-pair markets at various times from 1946 through 1965.[1] Fare histories are presented for only eight of these markets. The other 32

[1] This number is calculated by combining Burbank with Los Angeles and Oakland with San Francisco to make one city each, despite the fact that service was provided through two airports. (See footnote 1 of chapter 5.)

are excluded either because they were served for less than seven months (usually by a minor carrier), or because the two cities were located within 30 miles of each other, such as Burbank-Long Beach and Oakland-San Jose, thereby resulting in negligible local traffic. In addition, the 1946-47 fares of Pacific Air Lines (the intrastate carrier) are excluded since the important fares for this study are those that existed between 1949 and 1965.

The eight markets to be studied are divided into two groups. The first group is composed of three markets in which no alternative airline service was available at adjacent cities. In other words, if someone wished to fly between the cities comprising each market, he could not use substitute service provided by the same or another airline at a nearby city. In contrast, for each of the five markets in the second group, a variety of substitute airline services were available to potential passengers through adjacent cities.

Table 6-1 summarizes the fares per mile of the certificated and the California intrastate carriers in these eight minor markets. The time periods covered generally encompass the dates that the intrastate carriers served these markets. It can be seen from this table that the intrastate carriers' fares per mile for the first group of markets (those without alternative airline service) were much higher than their fares per mile for the second group. In fact, the fares per mile for the second group of markets (those with good alternative airline service) were roughly equal to the low fares per mile then available in the alternative major California markets. This difference in fares, associated with the availability or lack of availability of substitute service, provides a basis for analyzing the fares existing in the minor markets.

Markets without Alternative
Airline Service at Adjacent Cities

Burbank/Los Angeles-Inyokern. Part A of Table 6-1 shows that California Central's fares between Burbank and Inyokern were 6.67 or 7.62 cents per mile ($7.00 or $8.00) during the 2½ years it served this market (from February 1951 through July 1953). This was substantially higher than the 4.76-cent per mile ($5.00) fare that Pacific Air Lines (the local service carrier, then named Southwest Airways) charged when it replaced California Central in this market on August 3, 1953. The traffic moving over this route was comprised mainly of government-employed or contract personnel traveling to or from the Naval Ordnance Test Station at Inyokern. In fact, the CAB did not even allow Pacific to provide common carriage service for nongovern-

Table 6-1

Fares per Mile of the Certificated and California Intrastate Carriers
in Eight Minor California Markets
Various Time Periods, 1951-1965

City Pair[a]	Carrier[b]	Time Period	Mileage	Fare per Mile Intrastate	Fare per Mile Certificated
		A. Markets without Alternative Airline Service at Adjacent Cities			
BUR/LAX-IYK	CCA	2/25/51- 7/ 9/52	105[c]	6.67¢	—
	CCA	7/10/52- 7/30/53	105[c]	7.62	—
	PAC	8/ 3/53- 7/ 7/54	105[c]	—	4.76¢
	PAC	7/ 8/54- 9/30/56	105[c]	—	5.48
	PAC	10/ 1/56-11/30/60	122[d]	—	5.53
	PAC	4/24/62- 7/16/63	122[d]	—	8.52
	PAC	7/17/63-12/31/65	122[d]	—	8.81
TVL-SFO/OAK	PAR	5/14/62- 3/ 3/64	145[e]	7.21	—
	PAC	10/27/63-12/31/65	164[f]	—	10.06[f]
TVL-SJC	PAR	11/ 1/62- 3/ 3/64	149	7.01	—
	PAC	10/27/63-12/31/65	196[g]	—	9.44[g]
		B. Markets with Good Alternative Airline Service at Adjacent Cities			
BUR/LAX-BRF	Mercer	4/14/62-12/31/65	139	5.14¢	—
LGB-SFO/OAK	WAL	2/ 1/53- 7/ 6/58	355	—	4.01¢[h]
	PSA	10/ 1/53- 1/14/54	355	3.93	—
	PSA	1/15/54- 4/ 7/54	355	4.01	—
	PSA	4/ 8/54- 6/16/54	355	3.58	—
LGB-SAN	WAL	2/ 1/53- 7/ 6/58	94	—	5.11[h]
	PSA	10/ 1/53- 4/ 7/54	94	5.11	—
	PSA	4/ 8/54- 6/16/54	94	4.83	—
LAX/BUR-SJC	PAC	1/ 9/61- 4/25/64	309	—	5.11
	PAC	4/26/64-10/30/65	309	—	7.57[i]
	PAC	10/31/65-12/31/65	309	—	5.02
	PSA	10/ 8/65-10/11/65	309	3.70	—
SAN-SJC	PAC	9/ 1/62- 1/17/63	418[j]	—	5.36
	PAC	1/19/63- 7/13/63	418[j]	—	7.24[i]
	PAC	7/14/63-12/31/65	418[j]	—	7.46[i]
	PSA	10/ 8/65-10/11/65	418[j]	4.25	—

[a]See note b, Appendix 1, for an explanation of the city codes used in this table.

[b]California Central Airlines (CCA), Mercer Enterprises (Mercer), Pacific Air Lines (PAC), Pacific Southwest Airlines (PSA), Paradise Airlines (PAR), and Western Air Lines (WAL).

[c]Burbank-Inyokern.

[d]Los Angeles-Inyokern.

[e]Lake Tahoe-Oakland. Paradise did not serve San Francisco.

[f]Lake Tahoe-San Francisco. The CAB exemption that authorized Pacific to provide this service required an intermediate stop at Sacramento (CAB Order No. E-19963, adopted August 29, 1963). The given mileage reflects this route requirement. The fare for the 157-mile nonstop routing would be 10.51 cents per mile.

[g]The limited service provided by Pacific between Lake Tahoe and San Jose was operated via Sacramento and San Francisco. The given mileage is for this routing. The fare for the 149-mile nonstop routing would be 12.42 cents per mile.

[h]Propeller coach fare. United also operated in this market during this period. However, it provided only first-class service at a higher fare.

[i]Propeller first-class fare. Pacific did not operate coach service in this market during this period.

[j]Via the Los Angeles International Airport.

Sources: Calculated from data presented in Appendices 9(A), 9(B), 10, 11, 12, and 13 of this book.

118   AIRLINE REGULATION IN AMERICA

ment traffic until October 1959.[2] The large fare difference and the
"co-ordination" of service termination by CCA and inauguration by
Pacific (rather than a period of rivalry) indicates that the navy found
a lower priced supplier and transferred its contract accordingly.
Eleven months after inaugurating service, Pacific increased its fare
per mile to 5.48 cents ($5.75), followed by a minor increase to 5.53
cents ($6.75) when the southern terminal of the route was moved
from Burbank to the Los Angeles International Airport. Both of
these fares were much lower than CCA's last fare, and the 5.53-cent
rate was retained until Avalon Air Transport took over the operation
on December 1, 1960.

When Pacific reinstituted service to Inyokern on April 24,
1962, it did so on a regular common carrier basis without the benefit
of the navy's minimum-passenger guarantee (but with its traffic). The
one-way fare adopted by Pacific at that time was 8.52 cents per mile
($10.40), 54 percent higher than its fare in 1960, and 12 percent
higher than California Central's 1953 fare per mile. Then, on July 17,
1963, Pacific raised this fare to 8.81 cents per mile ($10.75) in
response to the 3 percent, across-the-board fare increase. When one
considers that Pacific's operations were heavily subsidized by the
CAB,[3] the 7.62-cent per mile fare charged by California Central back
in 1953 does not seem to be unduly high. The fact remains, however,
that it was much higher than the fares per mile existing in the major
California markets at that time, and this warrants investigation.

It happens that there were several similarities between California
Central's Burbank–Inyokern operation and its operation over the
major Burbank–San Diego route. First, CCA operated the same aircraft types in both markets. Second, the nonstop distance between
Burbank and Inyokern is not much different than that between Burbank and San Diego (105 vs. 123 miles), and because of airway
routes and air traffic control requirements, the difference in actual
miles flown by CCA may have been even less than that indicated by
the nonstop mileages. This, plus the fact that CCA specified identical
schedule times for nonstop flights between the two city pairs (50

---

[2] CAB Order No. E-14593 (adopted October 29, 1959). Pacific's intrastate
tariff filing for this service became effective on May 8, 1960 (see note c, Appendix 9[A] of this book). Until that date, therefore, Pacific's traffic potential
was more limited than that of California Central.

[3] From 1954 through 1965, 30.6 percent of Pacific's overall operating revenues were comprised of direct subsidy (as adjusted) paid to it by the CAB.
CAB, *Handbook of Airline Statistics* (1963 ed.), p. 265, and (1967 ed.), p. 254.

minutes for DC-3's and 40 minutes for Martin 202's),[4] makes it seem likely that aircraft flight costs were very similar. Third, the two routes shared a common airport (at Burbank), so that they had the same operating costs at one terminal. The only other possible cost differences were those resulting from differences in landing fees and ground handling costs at Inyokern and San Diego,[5] the extra costs that CCA incurred in operating some Burbank–San Diego flights via the Los Angeles International Airport, and any travel agent commissions paid for Burbank–San Diego passengers. Overall, the similarities seem to be more important than the possible differences, so that a basis exists for evaluating CCA's pricing practices during the early 1950's by comparing its Burbank–Inyokern fares with its fares for Burbank–San Diego.

Despite these similarities, the Burbank–Inyokern fares per mile (6.67 and 7.62 cents) were 48 and 69 percent higher than the 4.51-cent per mile fare in effect between Burbank and San Diego during the same period.[6] It could be that these much higher fares per mile resulted from CCA's attempting to obtain economic profits by setting fares well above average costs in a market where it provided monopoly service. It appears, however, that this was not the case. Rather, it seems that these higher fares per mile were required to cover the higher costs per *passenger-mile* (as opposed to seat- or aircraft-mile costs) resulting from the very much lower volume of traffic flying on CCA to Inyokern than to San Diego. These large differences in traffic volumes are shown in Table 6–2. While only about 1,000 passengers per month flew between Burbank and Inyokern during each time period, CCA carried an average of from 2,600 to 3,400 monthly passengers to and from San Diego (55 percent of which were long-haul, San Diego–San Francisco passengers). Clearly, there were fewer passengers to share the fixed costs of

---

[4] *California Central Airline Guide*, supplement effective September 3, 1952; and the *Official Airline Guide*, North American Edition, 11, no. 2 (November 1954), p. 491.

[5] Data were not available to determine landing fees at Inyokern relative to San Diego in the early 1950's; however, during that period, landing fees at California airports were generally quite low.

[6] The 4.51-cent per mile fare is obtained by dividing the Burbank–San Diego fare of $5.55 by the 123 nonstop miles separating the Burbank and San Diego airports. The Burbank–San Diego mileage is used in place of the 109 miles between the Los Angeles International Airport and San Diego because of Burbank's role as the common terminal of both routes.

Table 6-2

Comparison of Passenger Volumes over the Burbank-Inyokern
and Burbank-Los Angeles-San Diego Routes
California Central Airlines, March 1951 to July 1953

Time Period	BUR-IYK Route	Number of One-Way Passengers			
		BUR-LAX-SAN Route			
		BUR-SAN	LAX-SAN	SAN-SFO/OAK	Total
Mar.-Dec. 1951	9,900*	7,277	2,483	16,040	25,800
Calendar 1952	11,400*	15,018	4,362	21,414	40,794
Jan.-July 1953	6,900*	6,834	2,272	9,554	18,660

*Partially estimated.

Sources: U.S. District Court, Southern District of California, files of the Court Clerk, Bankruptcy No. 59561-PH (filed January 27, 1954); CCA, *History, Development and Analysis of California Central Airlines* (n.d.), Appendices A-II, A-III, and A-IV. CCA, unpublished exhibits, worksheets and station reports, including Exhibit B of an unknown document pertaining to Burbank-Inyokern service.

operating the Burbank-Inyokern route than there were for the Burbank-San Diego route.

A similar situation existed with regard to variable costs, such as direct aircraft operating costs. The following quotation from an article written in mid-1952 provides an indication of California Central's segment load factors at that time:[7]

> For the first six months of 1952, CCA carried a total of 93,864 passengers as against 61,283 passengers in the first six months of 1951, a gain of 32,581 passengers.
>
> Current load factors on CCA's three segments as compared to a year ago are as follows:

	1951 (28-pass. DC-3's)	1952 (44-pass. 2-0-2's)
Los Angeles-San Francisco	74.6%	82.7%
San Diego-Burbank	40.6%	51.9%
Burbank-Inyokern	30.9%	31.2%

Although it is not clear from the article whether the segment load factors were for the first six months of 1951 and 1952, or for some shorter period, there is no question that the Burbank-Inyokern load factors were consistently much lower than those for CCA's other two

[7]*American Aviation* 16, no. 5 (August 4, 1952), p. 24.

routes. Thus, even if variable costs per *aircraft* mile were equal, variable costs per *passenger*-mile for service between Burbank and Inyokern were much higher than between Burbank and San Diego. Therefore, a higher fare per passenger-mile was required to cover the variable costs for the Burbank–Inyokern service.

The above fares per mile and load factors are used in Table 6-3 to estimate and compare California Central's revenues per aircraft mile for these two routes. In 1951, the higher fare per mile between Burbank and Inyokern served to more than offset the lower load factor experienced over that segment. This was especially true since the navy's ten-passenger guarantee for each flight resulted in a minimum revenue per aircraft mile of 66.7 cents. By 1952, however, with Martin 202 service, the Burbank–San Diego route's increased average load factor resulted in higher revenues per aircraft mile than the Burbank–Inyokern route. This may be why, effective July 10, 1952, CCA increased its fare in the Burbank–Inyokern market to 7.62 cents per mile. Assuming a completely inelastic short-run demand in this essentially government-travel market, this fare increase would

Table 6-3

Estimated Revenues per Aircraft Mile for California Central Airlines'
Burbank–Inyokern and Burbank–San Diego Routes
Early 1951 and 1952

Year	Route	Load Factor	Seats per Aircraft	Avg. Number of Passengers per Flight	Fare per Mile	Est. Revenue per Aircraft Mile
1951	BUR–IYK	30.9%	28[a]	8.7[b]	6.67¢	58.0¢[b]
	BUR–SAN	40.6	28[a]	11.4	4.51[c]	51.4
1952	BUR–IYK	31.2	44[d]	13.7	6.67	91.4
	BUR–SAN	51.9	44[d]	22.8	4.51[c]	102.8

[a]DC-3.
[b]The Department of the Navy guaranteed payment to CCA for ten passengers per one-way flight over this route. This served to increase CCA's *minimum* revenues to 66.7 cents per aircraft mile in 1951. Due to traffic fluctuations, CCA's average revenues were probably somewhat higher than this minimum.
[c]Since the SAN–SFO/OAK fare was derived by combining the two local intermediate fares, it is assumed that the BUR–SAN fare per mile also applied to the through passengers flying over that segment. Note that the BUR–SAN fare was not changed on June 15, 1952.
[d]Martin 202.

Sources: Table 6-1, footnote 7 (above), and Appendices 7 and 13 of this book.

have raised CCA's revenue per aircraft mile to about 104.4 cents, just a little above that for its Burbank-San Diego route.

Obviously, the above figures are only rough approximations, but they do show that the higher fares per mile in the low-density Burbank-Inyokern market gave CCA revenues per aircraft mile about equal to those achieved in the major Burbank-San Diego market with a much lower fare per mile. If the Burbank-Inyokern market had higher fixed costs per passenger than the Burbank-San Diego market, and roughly equal costs and revenues per aircraft mile, it follows that even with the higher fares per mile, Burbank-Inyokern service was less profitable to CCA than Burbank-San Diego service.

The fact that the average fare per mile for the even denser Los Angeles/Burbank-San Francisco market was lower than the Burbank-San Diego fare per mile (see chapter 5) provides further evidence that CCA was fully aware of the importance of traffic density in the profitable operation of low-fare air service. Where traffic density was high, CCA's fares were relatively low, and, as shown by Burbank-Inyokern, low traffic density was associated with much higher fares.

Lake Tahoe-San Francisco/Oakland and San Jose. Turning now to the other two city pairs in this first group of minor markets, it appears that in some respects the Lake Tahoe-San Francisco/Oakland and the Lake Tahoe-San Jose markets were similar to the Burbank-Inyokern market. The nonstop distances were relatively short (just under 150 miles for the Lake Tahoe markets vs. 105 miles for Burbank-Inyokern), and both services connected a major population center with a lightly populated area having a special reason for supporting air service. (The Naval Ordnance Test Station provided the basis for service to Inyokern, while the gambling casinos located in Nevada did so for Lake Tahoe.) There was a significant difference, however, in traffic densities. Paradise Airlines carried just under 12,000 passengers into and out of Lake Tahoe in October 1963 (its peak month), with 8,000 passengers a month being the average for the period from August 1963 through February 1964.[8] This compares with CCA's average of about 1,000 passengers per month between Burbank and Inyokern. In addition, an important difference eventually developed in the equipment operated by the two carriers. Both began operations with DC-3's having 28 (CCA) or 30 (Paradise)

_____

[8] U.S. District Court, Northern District of California, files of the Court Clerk, Case No. 43394, *Peerless Insurance Co.* v. *Paradise Airlines:* Paradise Airlines Company Records, including station reports.

seats. But, while California Central temporarily replaced its DC-3's with 44-seat Martin 202's for about 11 months, Paradise expanded into 81-seat, L-049 Constellations beginning April 6, 1963. From that date until its service was terminated on March 4, 1964, Paradise operated both DC-3's and L-049's to Lake Tahoe, the Constellations gradually becoming the aircraft used for the majority of flights.[9]

Table 6-1 shows that CCA's Burbank–Inyokern 6.67- and 7.62-cent per mile fares were similar to Paradise's one-way fares of 7.21 cents per mile between Lake Tahoe and Oakland, and 7.01 cents per mile for Lake Tahoe–San Jose.[10] The one-way fares, however, may not provide a complete basis for comparison because, unlike most other California intrastate carriers, Paradise adopted important promotional (discriminatory) fares. Instead of charging $20.90, or twice the one-way fare for round trips (the usual practice), Paradise's round-trip fare was $19.00, or 6.55 and 6.38 cents per mile, for the two city pairs—that is, about the same as the earliest Burbank–Inyokern fare per mile. Also, effective September 13, 1963, Paradise offered an even lower round-trip excursion fare. If a passenger agreed to complete his round trip within 24 hours after initial departure, and if he carried no luggage, he could fly from Oakland or San Jose to Lake Tahoe and return for only $15.00 (5.17 and 5.03 cents per mile, respectively).[11] The attractiveness of this excursion fare was greatly enhanced by the offer of Harrah's Club to give a $10 cash "bonus," free limousine service to and from the airport, and two free cocktails to any person utilizing the excursion fare on any day but Saturday and possessing a return reservation on a flight leaving Lake Tahoe within 12 hours after arrival.[12] This excursion fare in particu-

[9] *Ibid.* Also, U.S. Federal Aviation Agency, Western Region, Systemsworthiness Inspection Report, Paradise Airlines (dated June 17, 1963), pp. 27–28.

[10] Since the published fares for these two Lake Tahoe markets were identical ($10.45), the difference in the fares per mile was due entirely to the four mile greater distance from Lake Tahoe to San Jose compared to Oakland (see Appendices 10 and 13 of this book).

[11] This is a 28.2 percent discount from the one-way fare. See chapter 8, Table 8-2 of this book.

[12] Paradise Airlines, counter schedule (n.d.). Also, Paradise Airlines, "Motion for Disclaiming Jurisdiction," to be consolidated with CAB Docket No. 147066 (dated October 26, 1963), p. 5. The limousine service provided by Harrah's Club (which is located on the boundary between California and Nevada) arrived and departed at the Club's California entrance. This was not the first time Harrah's Club promoted air service to Lake Tahoe. CAB Order No. E-16205 (adopted December 30, 1960) gave TWA an exemption to provide *contract* service for the club for a period of one year. It is believed that a large number of passengers flying on Paradise after September 13, 1963, did use the excursion fare. Of the

lar raises the problem of fare level vs. fare structure mentioned in chapter 4, and since it was clearly a promotional fare, its consideration will be postponed until chapter 8, where such fares are studied at some length.

Paradise's one-way and round-trip fares provide another example of an intrastate carrier operating over a relatively low-density route at average fares per mile that were higher than those charged at the same time for service over routes having much greater traffic densities. For example, PSA's traffic volume to and from San Diego in 1963 was about six times larger than Paradise's traffic at Lake Tahoe (362,000 vs. 63,000).[13] With this greater density it is not surprising to find that PSA's Los Angeles–San Diego fare per mile was lower than Paradise's fares per mile in the Lake Tahoe markets. Perhaps the surprising thing is the small differences in fares per mile relative to the large differences in traffic densities. Paradise's fares were 7.21 and 7.01 cents per mile (for one-way fares), and 6.55 and 6.38 cents per mile (for round-trip fares), compared with PSA's Los Angeles–San Diego fare of 5.83 cents per mile. But, of course, the Los Angeles–San Diego market always had the highest fares per mile of the three major California markets.

The fares filed by Pacific Air Lines in these two markets provide another way to evaluate the relative level of Paradise's fare.[14] Pacific's fares of $16.50 (Lake Tahoe–San Francisco) and $18.50 (Lake Tahoe–San Jose) were 58 and 77 percent higher than Paradise's $10.45 fare for both markets, and Pacific did not offer a round-trip discount, so the differences for round-trip passengers were even greater.[15] Pacific's fares per mile in the two Lake Tahoe markets (10.06 and 9.44 cents per mile based on actual flight mileages, or 12.42 and 10.51 cents per mile based on nonstop mileages) were even higher than its concurrent fare of 8.81 cents per mile between Burbank and Inyokern. One possible reason for this is that Pacific's

---

81 passengers on board the Constellation that crashed on March 1, 1964, all but one is said to have been flying on an excursion ticket (telephone conversation with Mr. Degarde of Nichols, Williams, Morgan and Degarde; attorneys for Peerless Insurance Company, February 7, 1966). Paradise's Income Journal for 1964 shows average revenues per ticket of $8.38 in January and $9.65 for February. This implies a particularly heavy use of the excursion fare in January, with less use in February.

[13] See Appendices 2, 11(D), and 14(C) of this book.

[14] Pacific inaugurated service at Lake Tahoe on October 27, 1963, in accordance with an exemption issued in CAB Order No. E-19963 (adopted August 29, 1963).

[15] See Appendices 9(A) and 10 of this book.

Burbank-Inyokern service qualified for subsidy payments from the CAB, whereas its service to Lake Tahoe was specifically excluded from all subsidy computations and payments.[16] Regardless of the reason(s), this does provide another case of a certificated carrier's fares being substantially higher than the fares of a California intrastate carrier. Unfortunately, the abrupt termination of Paradise's service four months after Pacific began operating at Lake Tahoe makes it impossible to determine whether carrier rivalry would have eventually resulted in a narrowing of the fare differences in these markets, just as such rivalry narrowed the fare differences in the major California markets.

Markets with Good Alternative Airline Service at Adjacent Cities

Burbank/Los Angeles-Brown Field. The minor markets having good alternative airline service at adjacent cities are listed in Part B of Table 6-1. The alternative to Mercer Enterprises' weekend service between Burbank/Los Angeles and Brown Field was the multiple daily flights operated between Lindbergh Field in San Diego and Los Angeles/Burbank. Given the much greater flight frequency at San Diego, the superiority of Electra and jet aircraft over Mercer's DC-3's, and the fact that Brown Field is located only about 20 miles by road southeast of Lindbergh Field, it seems reasonable to find Mercer's one-way Burbank/Los Angeles-Brown Field fare of $7.14 to be quite close to PSA's fare of $6.35 between San Diego and Los Angeles/Burbank (based on Burbank-Brown Field and Burbank-San Diego mileages, these work out to 5.14 and 5.16 cents per mile, respectively).[17]

As of mid-1969, Mercer had been able to sustain its service to Brown Field for over five years. This indicates that, despite the very low traffic density (around 8,000 passengers for all of 1965) and the very limited schedule frequency of about three round trips each weekend, the fare has been high enough to cover the operating costs

---

[16] CAB Order No. E-19963 (adopted August 29, 1963), p. 3. Also, CAB Order No. E-23819 (adopted June 15, 1966), p. 4 of the attached certificate of public convenience and necessity for local service.

[17] See Appendices 7, 12, and 13 of this book, and Table 6-1, above. The Burbank-Brown Field and Burbank-San Diego mileages are used because most of Mercer's passengers originated at Burbank. Brown Field is located about four miles from the border crossing to Tijuana, Mexico, while Lindbergh Field is approximately 18 miles from the crossing. *Map of San Diego and Vicinity* (1964 ed.; San Jose, Calif.: H. M. Gousha Co.).

of this service.[18] In addition to this weekend scheduled service, however, Mercer performs substantial (for its size) contract charter operations. For example, during the last quarter of 1965 and during 1966, Mercer had contracts with the Military Air Transport Service to perform weekday service between Point Mugu and San Nicolas Island or Vandenberg AFB, and between Long Beach and San Clemente Island.[19] Thus, while Mercer's scheduled service probably could not be maintained as a completely independent operation, it was viable when operated in conjunction with contract services.

Long Beach–San Francisco/Oakland and San Diego. The alternative airline service for the Long Beach–San Francisco/Oakland and Long Beach–San Diego markets was the high frequency, high quality, and low fare service operated to San Francisco/Oakland and San Diego through the Los Angeles International Airport, which is located about 22 road miles northwest of the Long Beach Municipal Airport.[20] Associated with this geographic proximity was the certificated carriers' practice during the early 1950's of providing coach service to Long Beach on flights that operated between San Diego and Oakland via Long Beach, Los Angeles, Burbank, and San Francisco.[21] Thus, to avoid charges of undue discrimination, the Long Beach–San Francisco/Oakland fares had to fall somewhere between the San Diego–San Francisco/Oakland and Los Angeles–San Francisco/Oakland fares, while the Long Beach–San Diego fare could be no more than the Los Angeles–San Diego fare.[22] Also, it was the

[18] See Appendices 14(B) and 16(E) of this book. Also, Mercer Enterprises, Application No. 48157 (filed December 28, 1965), p. 2. (Cal. PUC Decision No. 71490 [dated November 1, 1966].)

[19] U.S. Department of the Air Force, Headquarters, Military Air Transport Service, Negotiated Contracts Nos. 11(626)-733 (effective 5 October 1965) and 11(626)-735 (effective 4 January 1966).

[20] *Map of Los Angeles and Vicinity* (1965 ed.; San Jose, Calif.: H. M. Gousha Co.).

[21] See the schedules for United and Western published in the *Official Airline Guide* for these years.

[22] The reality of this constraint was demonstrated in the early 1960's when Western failed to provide coach service between Long Beach and San Francisco at fares comparable to the fares existing between Los Angeles and San Francisco for its Thriftair and propeller coach services. Long Beach and Oakland filed complaints with the PUC alleging the low Los Angeles–San Francisco fares discriminated against them. In Decision No. 67077, 62 Cal. PUC 553 (1964), the PUC ordered Western to terminate this discrimination. Western did so by extending Thriftair service to Oakland, and by reducing its Long Beach–San Francisco propeller coach fare from $17.80 to $14.10 (compared with $13.50 for Los Angeles–San Francisco). See Appendices 6(B), 6(C), and 11 of this book.

established custom of that period to base fares on airport-to-airport distances (see chapter 4). Therefore, when Western Air Lines inaugurated coach service at Long Beach on December 10, 1951, it was natural for it to adopt propeller coach fares that were similar to those available at Los Angeles. Since, as shown in chapter 5, the low coach fares then available at Los Angeles were the direct result of the California intrastate carriers' pricing practices, there seems to be little doubt that the low coach fares introduced by Western at Long Beach were the result of the intrastate carriers' activities at Los Angeles and Burbank, rather than an example of aggressive pricing on the part of a certificated carrier.[23]

When Pacific Southwest Airlines inaugurated the first intrastate carrier service at Long Beach on October 1, 1953, its Burbank–San Francisco/Oakland fare for DC-3 service was only $11.70, compared with the certificated carriers' and California Central's fare of $13.50 for DC-4 and Martin 202 service. As shown in Table 6-1, PSA's initial Long Beach–San Francisco/Oakland fare of $13.95 (3.93 cents per mile) was slightly under Western's then current fare of $14.25 (4.01 cents per mile), but it was above what would be expected, given its $11.70 Burbank fare. This discrepancy was eliminated on January 15, 1954, when PSA increased its San Francisco/Oakland fares to equal those of the certificated carriers and CCA. As described in chapter 5, this equality of fares lasted less than three months. In its major fare retrenchment on April 8, 1954, PSA lowered all of its fares to levels below those in effect prior to January 15, 1954. Although it slashed its Burbank–San Francisco/Oakland fare by $3.51, to $9.99 (3.06 cents per mile based on Burbank), the decrease in its Long Beach–San Francisco/Oakland fare was only $1.53, to $12.72 (3.58 cents per mile).[24] Two months later it terminated all service to Long Beach after having operated there for 8½ months. No intrastate carrier provided service to Long Beach from that time through 1965.

[23] Western's coach fares in these markets as of December 10, 1951, were: LGB–SFO/OAK–$12.45 (3.51 cents per mile); LAX/BUR–SFO/OAK–$11.70 (3.44 cents per mile); LGB–SAN–$4.80 (5.11 cents per mile); LAX/BUR–SAN–$5.55 (5.09 cents per mile). The through San Diego–San Francisco/Oakland fare was $17.25, regardless of whether it was obtained by combining the intermediate fares via Long Beach or Los Angeles. See Appendices 6(B) and 11 of this book.

[24] PSA's reductions in its Burbank–San Diego and Long Beach–San Diego fares were quite small. The Burbank–San Diego fare was reduced from $5.55 to $5.45, while the Long Beach–San Diego fare went from $4.80 to $4.54. See Appendices 7 and 12 of this book.

Relative traffic volumes again suggest why PSA maintained some-what higher fares per mile at Long Beach than at Burbank, and why, despite these higher fares, it terminated service after less than nine months of operation. Table 6–4 gives the average number of passengers that PSA originated and terminated daily at Burbank and at Long Beach during this general time period. With PSA's average daily traffic volumes at Long Beach ranging from only 25 to 35 percent of the volumes at Burbank, the somewhat higher fares per mile at Long Beach would seem to be inadequate to cover what were doubtless very much higher average costs at Long Beach. Since substantially higher fares were precluded by Long Beach's proximity to the Los Angeles International Airport, PSA's low and directionally unbalanced traffic volumes at Long Beach made the termination of its service understandable.

Table 6-4

Average Daily Number of Passengers Originating and Terminating
on Pacific Southwest Airlines at Burbank and Long Beach
1953 and 1954

Year	Number of Days of Service	Base City	Avg. Daily Number of Passengers Flying between Base City and	
			San Francisco/Oakland	San Diego
1953	365	Burbank	115.9	64.7
	92	Long Beach	39.0	7.3
1954	365	Burbank	104.6	40.3
	167	Long Beach	41.8	7.9

Sources: Appendices 1, 14(A), and 14(B) of this book.

San Jose-Los Angeles/Burbank and San Diego. Los Angeles/Bur-bank–San Jose and San Diego–San Jose are the last two markets listed in Table 6-1. In total, PSA served these two markets for just four days during 1965, October 8-11. This is such a brief period of time that one could argue for the exclusion of these two city pairs from this study. The following factors, however, make the introduction of intrastate carrier service at San Jose relevant to this analysis. First, PSA suspended service involuntarily because the PUC ordered it to do so, not because the service appeared to be unprofitable. [25]

[25] Cal. PUC Decision No. 69764 (dated October 7, 1965).

Second, after the PUC finally authorized service to be reinstituted effective May 18, 1966, PSA's weekly schedule frequency was increased from the originally proposed 60 one-way Electra flights to 106 one-way Electra flights as of June 20, 1966.[26] Obviously, without the intervention of the PUC, acting under its newly acquired power to control entry, the October 8, 1965, inauguration would have been the beginning of an extended period of operation by PSA at San Jose. Thus, this attempt to inaugurate service can be considered the last example of entry that would have occurred in California under open entry conditions, while the October 11, 1965, termination is the first example of the effective control of entry by the PUC.

The alternative to air service at San Jose is that available at San Francisco and Oakland. The San Francisco International Airport is located about 35 freeway miles northwest of San Jose Municipal Airport, whereas the Metropolitan Oakland International Airport is about 33 miles distant.[27] As shown in Appendices 9(A) and 9(B), Pacific Air Lines has provided service at San Jose since March 1947, with coach service being available between July 20, 1956, and April 25, 1964, followed by the introduction of Commutair service on October 31, 1965. Most of Pacific's Los Angeles/Burbank–San Jose flights made one or more intermediate stops between these two cities, but beginning on March 1, 1958, Pacific did schedule a limited number of nonstop flights in this market.[28]

During the years it operated coach service between Los Angeles/ Burbank and San Jose, Pacific's coach fares generally ranged from $2.30 to $3.51 higher than PSA's fares for nonstop Los Angeles/ Burbank–San Francisco service. First-class fares, of course, gave even greater differentials, ranging from $6 to $10 higher than the intrastate carriers' fares at San Francisco from 1949 through 1965.[29]

While it had a monopoly at San Jose, Pacific's peak traffic year was 1962, when it carried about 73,000 on-line origin and destination passengers between Los Angeles/Burbank and San Jose. In 1963 (the year Western introduced its $11.43 Thriftair fare), Pacific's

[26] Cal. PUC, "Proposed Report" by Examiner Richard D. Gravelle, Application No. 47843, *et al.* (dated February 28, 1966), p. 27 (mimeographed). (Cal. PUC Decision No. 70657 [dated May 3, 1966].) Also, PSA, Flight Schedule (June 20, 1966).

[27] *Map of San Francisco and Vicinity* (1965 ed.; San Jose, Calif.: H. M. Gousha Co.).

[28] *Official Airline Guide*, North American Edition, 14, no. 6 (March 1958), pp. 572–73.

[29] Compare the fares presented in Appendices 7, 9(A) and 9(B) of this book.

traffic in this market decreased to 65,000 O & D passengers; in 1964 (the year Pacific suspended coach service), its O & D passenger volume fell to 61,000; and in 1965 (the year low-fare jet service became widely available at San Francisco), it declined to 59,000 passengers.[30] These are large volumes of traffic compared with some of the minor markets studied in this chapter. By themselves they hardly indicate substantial underdevelopment of the market. Between May 18, 1966 (when PSA was allowed to reinstitute service at San Jose), and December 31, 1966, however, PSA carried 258,454 passengers between San Jose, on the one hand, and Los Angeles and San Diego on the other![31] In addition, Pacific carried approximately 72,000 passengers in these markets during the year (thereby approaching its 1962 high).[32] This makes a total of over 330,000 passengers for 1966—5½ times that flying in 1965—despite PSA's service being limited to the last 7½ months of the year. Clearly, the traffic potential of the San Jose Airport area was not developed while Pacific had a monopoly at that airport.[33]

It is obvious that San Jose generates sufficient traffic to support profitable low-fare service to Los Angeles/Burbank and to San Diego. PSA's $11.43 Electra and $13.50 Boeing 727-100 fares between Los Angeles and San Jose were identical to its fares for comparable service between Los Angeles/Burbank and San Francisco/Oakland during 1966. Since it is only 309 miles from Los Angeles to San Jose

---

[30] See Appendix 14(A) of this book. While it cannot be shown that the decreases in passenger volume in 1963, 1964, and 1965 were largely due to Western's Thriftair service, the cancellation of Pacific's coach fares, and the widespread operation of low-fare jet service at San Francisco, the evidence is at least consistent with these hypotheses.

[31] PSA, Exhibit No. 9, submitted in Application No. 49001. (Cal. PUC Decision No. 73487 [dated December 19, 1967].)

[32] Cal. PUC, Transportation Division, *Intrastate Passengers of Scheduled Air Carriers*, Report No. 1511 (Quarter and Twelve Months Ended December 31, 1966). As shown in Appendix 14(C), Pacific consistently carried fewer than 500 passengers annually between San Diego and San Jose.

[33] It is not possible to determine from available information the extent to which the passengers utilizing the San Jose Airport in 1966 were diverted from the San Francisco and Oakland airports or were generated by the improved service and lower fares provided by PSA and Pacific at San Jose. The immediate response to PSA's service, however, (together with this writer's personal experience) indicates that many of the passengers were existing air travelers who had formerly used the other airports. The City of San Jose forecast that 450,234 passengers would fly between San Jose and Los Angeles/Burbank during 1966, assuming full service throughout the year. The actual performance during the last 7½ months of that year indicates that this "optimistic" forecast was remarkably accurate. See City of San Jose, Exhibit No. 1-12, submitted in Application No. 47843, *et al.* (Cal. PUC Decision No. 70657 [dated May 3, 1966].)

(compared with 340 miles between Los Angeles and San Francisco), these fares yield somewhat higher fares per mile than the San Francisco/Oakland fares. But at 3.70 and 4.37 cents per mile, they were still only about half as high as Pacific's first-class fares in this market, and a similar relationship held for the fares between San Diego and San Jose. Of course, the "$64,000" question is, and will remain: how many undiscovered "San Joses" are there within California and within the remainder of the United States?[34]

Conclusion

In one sense the intrastate carriers did "skim the cream" in the major California markets. They did so by diverting substantial traffic from the certificated carriers[35] and by motivating them to provide extensive coach service at much lower fares than would have existed had the CAB's fare policies and across-the-board authorizations been applied in these markets (this latter effect left much of the "cream" with the consumer). It seems likely that the certificated carriers' average revenues were reduced more than their average costs in these markets, so that they had smaller profits available for subsidizing service in minor, loss-producing markets, if, indeed, this was where some of the greater profits would have been applied.

On the other hand, the data presented in this chapter show that, contrary to the "skim-the-cream" argument, the relatively nonregulated intrastate carriers did not limit their service to the major markets. Rather, they provided extended service to eight minor California markets and operated briefly in 32 other minor markets where, apparently, their services quickly proved to be economically unviable. Not only that, the intrastate carriers were the first to provide scheduled service at Inyokern and Lake Tahoe, and they were the only carrier group to do so at Brown Field.[36] This shows that CAB-

[34] One such market within California appears to have been discovered following the period covered by this study. In September 1966, the PUC authorized Air California to provide service between Santa Ana (located in the southern portion of the Los Angeles Metropolitan Area) and San Francisco (Cal. PUC Decision No. 71310 [dated September 20, 1966]). Air California inaugurated scheduled service in this market with two Electras on January 16, 1967 (*The Wall Street Journal*, Pacific Coast Edition, 76, no. 10 [January 16, 1967] p. 7). During 1967, Air California carried 293,604 passengers in this market (Air California, *Annual Report*, 1967–68, pp. 5 and 6).

[35] See Appendix 14 of this book for relative traffic volumes in the major California markets.

[36] California intrastate carriers were also the only airlines to provide scheduled served at Edwards AFB (California Central 8/1/51–1/14/52), Truckee/

type regulation is not a necessary condition for airline service to be provided in low-density markets, and it challenges the internal subsidy argument that the CAB needs to protect the trunk carriers from competition in profitable, high-density markets so that service will be provided in low-density markets. The intrastate carriers were not protected in major markets, yet they provided service in minor markets.

Of course, while the intrastate carriers did operate in various minor markets, their voluntary termination of service at Inyokern and Long Beach indicates that they did not intentionally subsidize service in such markets. The fragmentary evidence available (see Table 6-3) implies that high fares were adopted in the minor markets in order to generate revenues per aircraft mile about equal to those in much larger markets. It appears that so long as comparable aircraft-mile revenues were attained, the intrastate carriers were willing to provide service in low-density markets at high fares as well as in high-density markets at low fares.

It is certainly true that the certificated carriers have served many more minor markets within California than have the intrastate carriers. It is not clear, however, whether this greater coverage was due to internal subsidy (made possible by CAB regulation) or to the Board's explicit payment for such service through direct subsidy. In any case, the data in Table 2-1 of chapter 2 show that between 1958 and 1964 the largely unsubsidized trunk carriers transferred service to subsidized local service carriers at a large number of airports.[37] Therefore, whatever internal subsidy may have existed in the 1950's, certainly much less existed by the mid-1960's. To the extent that the more extensive coverage of small markets has been the result of direct subsidy rather than internal subsidy, the regulation of price, service, and entry and exit by the CAB has been unnecessary to achieve this objective. Indeed, the evidence of this chapter suggests that without CAB-type regulation, but with direct subsidies, service would be provided in the existing subsidized airline markets at fares lower than those now prevailing.

Tahoe (Blatz 7/5/63-9/25/63), and Van Nuys (Futura 8/31/62-9/19/62). See Appendix 1 of this book.

[37] The average number of domestic points (as distinct from airports) served by the trunk carriers decreased from a high of 373 in 1957 to 242 in 1964, while the local service carriers' points increased from 388 to 464 in the same period. CAB, Office of the Secretary, Schedules and Records Unit, *Suspensions and Points Authorized (Exclusive and Combination)* (unpublished worksheets). This information is summarized in Jordan, *Economic Effects of Airline Regulation,* pp. 512-17.

The other major finding of this chapter concerns absolute and relative price levels. Obviously, it is not correct to say that the California intrastate carriers were invariably the champions of low fares in an absolute sense. In three of the eight minor California markets, their one-way fares ranged from 6.67 to 7.62 cents per mile, compared with fares of from 3.58 to 5.14 cents per mile in the other five minor markets, and compared with their low fares of 2.93 to 3.97 cents per mile for the high-density Los Angeles/Burbank–San Francisco/Oakland market. The characteristic distinguishing the minor markets with high absolute fares from those with lower fares appears to have been the lack of alternative airline service at adjacent cities. Where substitute airline service was available, an effective limit existed on how high fares could be raised, and service that could not be provided within this limit was terminated.

The intrastate carriers' performance was much more impressive in terms of relative fares. Generally speaking, their fares in the minor markets were significantly lower than the fares of the certificated carriers, regardless of whether substitute service was available at adjacent cities.[38] Here, again, the limited regulation of the PUC was associated with fares that were low relative to the fares of the CAB-regulated airlines. This is consistent with the findings of chapter 5 regarding relative fares in the major California markets. Overall, it seems proper to conclude that CAB regulation has been associated with relatively high fares, in minor markets as well as in major markets.

[38] There are three possible exceptions to this statement among the markets studied in this chapter. However, in the case of two of these (Long Beach–San Francisco/Oakland and Long Beach–San Diego), Western's low fares prior to PSA's entry were the result of the intrastate carriers' low fares at Los Angeles/Burbank rather than an example of price leadership by a certificated carrier. Therefore, these two markets should probably not be considered exceptions. Pacific's early fares between Burbank and Inyokern seem to be the single real exception to the conclusion that the intrastate carriers' fares were generally lower than those of the certificated carriers. But even this exception is not clear-cut, since the role of the Department of the Navy in influencing fares is unknown.

Overall Price Changes

7

Introduction

To this point, the study of airline pricing has been limited to determining the effects of regulation on airline fares. By themselves, however, current dollar fares do not accurately measure the prices paid by passengers over time. First, since October 10, 1941, a federal transportation tax has been assessed on airline fares,[1] and the resulting 5, 10, or 15 percent tax rate must be applied to fares to yield the prices actually paid by passengers at any given time. Second, it is necessary to adjust current dollar prices to delete the effects of inflation in order to measure the extent to which airline prices have changed in real terms over the period studied. The effects of these two factors on airline prices will be examined in this chapter.

Effects of the Federal Transportation Tax

The federal transportation tax rates for the years 1941 through 1965 are listed in Table 7-1. Applying these tax rates to the various fares for the major California and East Coast markets yields the prices actually paid in current dollars.[2] Dividing these prices by the appropriate airport-to-airport mileages then yields prices per mile for

---

[1] CAB, *Handbook of Airline Statistics*, p. 477.

[2] The prices in the eight minor California markets will not be covered in this chapter since most of them did not have continuous airline service throughout the period studied. All tax and price index adjustments made to the fares and prices of the major markets, however, are equally applicable to those of the minor markets.

Table 7-1

U.S. Federal Transportation Tax Rates
1941-1965

Effective Date	Tax Rate
October 10, 1941	5%
November 1, 1942	10
April 1, 1944	15
April 1, 1954	10
November 16, 1962	5

Source: CAB, *Handbook of Airline Statistics*, pp. 477, 479, and 483.

such services. Table 7-2 contains the prices per mile for first-class and coach services in these six major markets for the years 1946 (first-class only), 1950, early 1954 (coach only), and 1965. While the transportation tax served to make prices 5, 10, or 15 percent higher than fares, the reduction in tax rates on April 1, 1954, and November 16, 1962, resulted in smaller increases in prices than in fares for any period encompassing one or both of these tax reductions. Overall, between 1946 and 1965, the increases in first-class prices per mile were 14.1 to 26.0 percentage points lower than the increases in comparable fares per mile. Similarly, the increases in coach prices per mile were 9.8 to 14.6 percentage points less than the increases in fares per mile from 1950 (California markets) and early 1954 (East Coast markets) to 1965.[3]

Airline Price Changes Relative to General Price Changes

Various consumer price indices provide some basis for evaluating the changes in airline prices in relation to price changes in the overall economy. Table 7-3 gives the Consumer Price Index for all items, private transportation, and public transportation for 1946, 1950, 1954, and 1965, together with the percentage increases in these indices for the resulting time periods ending in 1965.

This table shows that through 1965 the percentage increases in the price index for public transportation were more than twice the increases for the all-items and private-transportation indices. If the price increases for public transportation in general are representative

---

[3] Calculated from data presented in Table 7-2, and in Appendices 6(A), 6(B), 6(C), 7, 8(A), 8(B), 8(C), and 13 of this book.

Table 7-2

One-Way Passenger Prices per Mile
in the Major California and East Coast Markets
First-Class and Coach Service, 1946, 1950, Early 1954, and 1965

| | | One-Way Passenger Prices per Mile | | | | | |
| | | California Markets | | | East Coast Markets | | |
Year	Aircraft	LAX-SFO	LAX-SAN	SAN-SFO	BOS-NYC	NYC-DCA	BOS-DCA
		A. First-Class Service					
1946	Propeller	5.12¢	5.85¢	5.30¢	5.22¢	5.38¢	5.30¢
1950	Propeller	7.12	7.12	7.12	6.97	7.18	7.08
1965	Propeller	8.14[a]	10.31[a]	7.90[a]	8.82	8.77	7.95
	Jet	8.79	11.32	8.40[a]	10.02	9.79	8.50
		B. Coach or Coach-Type Service					
1950	Propeller	3.37	5.85	3.98	—	—	—
1954[b]	Propeller	4.57	5.85	4.88	5.88	5.94	5.62
1965[c]	Propeller	3.53	6.12	4.16	7.71	7.50	6.49
	Shuttle[d]	—	—	—	8.70	8.37	—
	Jet	4.17	6.12	4.64	8.90	8.01	7.00

[a]This service was terminated in this market during 1963 or 1964; therefore, this price per mile was not available in 1965, even though the underlying fare remained in the carriers' tariffs.

[b]January-March 1954. The reduction in the federal transportation tax from 15 to 10 percent was effective April 1, 1954. Also, PSA's major fare reductions took place on April 8, 1954.

[c]April 20-December 31, 1965, for the California markets; entire year for the East Coast markets. Due largely to Eastern's fare change of January 15, 1965, several of American's fares in the East Coast markets differed from those of Eastern. Since American's fares were based on the across-the-board increases adopted nation-wide by the certificated carriers, they have been used wherever available. American's jet fares became effective with service inaugurations in middle and late 1965, but they had been filed in its tariff since 1962.

[d]Eastern's propeller Air-Shuttle fares effective January 15, 1965.

Sources: Calculated from data presented in Table 7-1, and in Appendices 6(A), 6(B), 6(C), 7, 8(A), 8(B), 8(C), and 13 of this book.

Table 7–3

Consumer Price Indices for
All Items, Private Transportation, and Public Transportation
1946, 1950, 1954, and 1965

Commodity Group	Consumer Price Index (1957–59 = 100)				Percent Increase		
	1946	1950	1954	1965	1946– 1965	1950– 1965	1954– 1965
All Items	68.0	83.8	93.6	109.9	61.6%	31.1%	17.4%
Private Transportation	61.8	82.6	91.5	109.7	77.5	32.8	19.9
Public Transportation	45.5	64.6	86.5	121.4	166.8	87.9	40.3

Source: U.S. Department of Commerce, Office of Business Economics, *Business Statistics* (Washington, D.C., 1967), pp. 38 and 40.

of the increases for the intercity component of this index,[4] it provides a partial explanation why intercity private transportation has grown so much more rapidly than intercity public transportation. In 1946, private autos accounted for 71.1 percent of total intercity passenger traffic. By 1955 this had increased to 88.5 percent, and in 1965 it was 89.9 percent of a total traffic volume that was 2.7 times larger than in 1946. (Calculated from data in Table 7–4.) The great improvement in highways during this period would also serve to promote private auto transportation.

The Bureau of Labor Statistics does not publish an airline price index that would allow direct comparisons to be made between it and consumer price indices. It is possible, however, to obtain an idea of the extent of airline price changes relative to changes in the prices of all items, public transportation, and private transportation from 1946 to 1965 by comparing the percentage increases in prices for the major California and East Coast markets (given in Table 7–5) with the percentage increases in the three price indices (see Table 7–3).

---

[4] The price index for public transportation currently includes city bus, streetcar, and subway fares, taxicab fares, railroad coach fares, intercity bus fares, and airplane fares. Federal, state, and city taxes are added wherever they are imposed. Airplane and intercity bus fares, the most recent additions to the index, were added in January 1964, when the number of goods and services included in the all-items index was increased from 325 to 400; therefore, the changes in airline prices are not part of the index prior to this date. The private-transportation index measures price changes for items used to provide private automobile transportation. See U.S. Department of Commerce, Office of Business Economics, *Business Statistics* (Washington, D.C., 1967), explanatory notes for p. 38.

Table 7–4

Domestic Intercity Passenger-Miles (in Millions)
Travelled in Public and Private Transportation, 1946, 1955, and 1965

Years	Public					Private Auto	Grand Total
	Intercity Bus	Railroad	Water Carrier	Airline	Total		
1946	25,576	66,262	2,327	5,910	100,075	253,570	353,645
1955	25,519	28,695	1,738	19,804	75,756	585,817	661,573
1965	23,775	17,557	3,101	52,204	96,637	858,641	955,278

Sources: U.S. Interstate Commerce Commission, *Annual Report*, 1948, p. 15; 1957, p. 11; 1967, p. 55. CAB, *Handbook of Airline Statistics*, p. 47. Appendix 3 of this book.

For passengers utilizing first-class service in 1965 (either voluntarily or because they flew between smaller cities where only first-class service was available), the percentage increases in first-class prices are the relevant ones to be compared with the Consumer Price Indices. In Table 7–5, percentage increases in airline prices are listed in order of airport-to-airport mileages, and it can be seen that an inverse relationship exists between distance and increases in first-class prices. This, of course, resulted from the fare taper introduced by the CAB's three $1.00 per ticket, across-the-board fare increases. Even for the 109-mile Los Angeles/Burbank–San Diego market, the 76.2 and 93.5 percent price increases for propeller service and best-available (propeller in 1946 and jet in 1965) service were well below the 166.8 percent increase in the comparable public-transportation price index. The 77.5 percent increase in the private-transportation price index was also greater than the increase in propeller first-class prices for all six markets and was greater than the price increases for best-available service for distances over about 300 miles (where jet service was pre-eminent). The 61.6 percent increase in the all-items price index was also higher than the increases in first-class service in markets over 300 miles (propeller service) or 400 miles (best-available service). Clearly, by 1965 first-class air travel was much less costly relative to public transportation in general than it was in 1946. In addition, since in 1964, 52.6 percent of all first-class passengers flew 300 miles or more,[5] it appears that about half of those utilizing first-class service paid comparatively less for their air travel in 1965 than in 1946, relative to the prices for private transportation and for all items in the Consumer Price Index.

[5] Based on data for true origin and destination passengers. CAB, *Handbook of Airline Statistics*, p. 406.

Table 7-5

Percentage Increases in Prices per Mile
for the Major California and East Coast Markets
between 1946 and 1965

| Market | Mileage | Percent Increase in Prices per Mile, 1946-1965 | | | |
| | | First-Class in 1965 | | Coach in 1965[a] | |
		Propeller	Best-Available[b]	Propeller	Best-Available[c]
LAX/BUR-SAN	109	76.2%[d]	93.5 %	4.6 %	4.6 %
BOS-NYC/EWR	184	69.0	92.0	47.7[e]	70.5
NYC/EWR-DCA	215	63.0	82.0	39.4[f]	48.9
LAX/BUR-SFO/OAK	340	59.0[d]	71.7	-31.1	-18.6
BOS-DCA	399	50.0	60.4	22.5	32.1
SAN-SFO/OAK	449	49.1[d]	58.5[d]	-21.5	-12.5

[a]April 20-December 31, 1965, for the California markets; entire year for the East Coast markets. (See note c of Table 7-2.)
[b]Service provided with propeller aircraft in 1946 and jet aircraft in 1965, both operated in first-class configurations.
[c]Service provided with first-class configured propeller aircraft in 1946, and with coach configured jet aircraft in 1965.
[d]Because this service was terminated in this market during 1963 or 1964, this percentage increase actually applies to a somewhat shorter period than that indicated.
[e]66.7% using Eastern's Air-Shuttle price per mile in 1965. During 1965, Eastern carried 76.9% of total true O & D coach passengers flying in this market.
[f]55.6% using Eastern's Air-Shuttle price per mile in 1965. During 1965, Eastern carried 87.2% of total true O & D coach passengers flying in this market.

Sources: Calculated from data presented in Table 7-2; and in CAB, *Domestic Origin-Destination Survey of Air Passenger Traffic* (1965).

In 1964, 59 percent of all true origin and destination passengers flying on trunk and local service carriers utilized coach service for all or part of their journeys,[6] and, of course, all passengers flying on the California intrastate carriers also flew coach. Therefore, the percentage increases in prices calculated using first-class prices in 1946 and coach prices in 1965 represent the price changes for the majority of all passengers. Two important facts are brought out by the percentage changes in propeller prices given in the next-to-last column in Table 7-5. First, every change in propeller prices was smaller than the increase in any of the three general price indices—even the in-

[6]*Ibid.*

crease in the all-items index.[7] Second, and of great significance to
this study, two out of the three major California markets actually
experienced decreases of 21.5 and 31.1 percent in their lowest,
widely-available prices over this period. These were impressively dif
ferent from the 22.5 to 47.7 percent increases in the propeller prices
of the three major East Coast markets. Even the 4.6 percent increase
in the short-haul Los Angeles/Burbank–San Diego market was negligible compared with the increases in the East Coast markets. This, of
course, reflects the impact of the airline price rivalry within California during most of this period.

Turning now to the changes in prices for best-available service, it
is possible to obtain an idea of relative price increases for those
airline markets where coach service was provided mainly (or entirely)
by jet aircraft in 1965. Again, whereas the major California markets
enjoyed price decreases or only a small increase, the East Coast markets had rather large price increases. Even so, the 1946–65 price
increases for the East Coast markets were either roughly equal to or
less than the increases for the all-items and private-transportation
indices, while being much smaller than the large increase in the
public-transportation price index.

Other time periods would provide percentage price changes that
differ from those given in Table 7–5. Data for such other time
periods, however, would not change the conclusion that, overall, the
percentage price increases of the certificated carriers compared favor-
ably with the increases in the all-items and private-transportation
indices and were very much lower than the large increase in the
public-transportation price index.[8] On the other hand, the fact remains that the achievement of the certificated carriers in holding
down increases in their interstate prices (with the help of a 10 percentage point tax reduction) falls far short of the outstanding record
of price decreases and small increases experienced in the three major
California markets, where price rivalry existed under the limited regulation of the PUC.

[7] Any exceptions to this finding would be limited to very short-haul markets
and to special situations. Two such special situations are the increases derived by
using Eastern's Air-Shuttle prices for 1965 (see notes e and f of Table 7–5). If
these prices are adopted for 1965, the percentage price increases in the BOS–
NYC/EWR and NYC/EWR–DCA markets for 1946–65 (66.7 and 55.6 percent,
respectively) are just about equal to the increase in the all-items index for that
period.

[8] It would be interesting to investigate the extent to which the prices
comprising the public-transportation index are regulated by some government
commission compared with the extent to which prices for goods included in the
private-transportation and all-items indices are so regulated.

Changes in Constant Dollar Prices

As a final means of evaluating the changes in airline prices over the period covered by this study, the lowest, widely-available, current dollar prices for the major California and East Coast markets will be deflated by the all-items Consumer Price Index to obtain an estimate of changes in *constant* dollar prices. Since the lowest current dollar fares available in the California markets were those introduced by the intrastate carriers in 1949 and adopted by the certificated carriers in 1950, it seems appropriate to express all prices in terms of constant 1950 dollars to yield a direct comparison with the prices available "in the good old days" when coach service was first available on all carriers in the California markets. This is done in Table 7-6.

One surprising fact shown by these data is that the low coach prices introduced in the major California markets in 1949 and 1950 were actually *higher* than the constant-dollar, propeller and jet coach prices in 1965. In other words, the effects of the transportation tax decreases and inflation resulted in a coach passenger having to forego fewer other consumer goods (on average) to fly a jet aircraft in these markets in 1965 than to fly a DC-3 or DC-4 back in 1949-50. A review of all the constant dollar prices presented in Table 7-6 shows

Table 7-6

Estimated Lowest, Widely-Available, Constant Dollar Prices per Mile[a]
in the Major California and East Coast Markets
1946, 1950, Early 1954, and 1965

Market	Mileage	Prices per Mile Measured in 1950 Dollars[a]					
		1946 First-Class	1950 Coach	Early 1954[b] Coach	1965[c] Prop. Coach	Air-Shuttle	Jet Coach
LAX/BUR–SAN	109	7.21¢	5.85¢	5.24¢	4.67¢	–	4.67¢
BOS–NYC/EWR	184	6.44	–	5.26	5.88	6.64¢	6.79
NYC/EWR–DCA	215	6.63	–	5.32	5.72	6.38	6.11
LAX/BUR–SFO/OAK	340	6.31	3.37	4.09	2.69	–	3.18
BOS–DCA	399	6.54	–	5.03	4.95	–	5.34
SAN–SFO/OAK	449	6.54	3.98	4.37	3.17	–	3.54

[a]Current dollar prices per mile divided by the following Consumer Price Indices for all items (1950 = 100): 1946 = 81.1, 1950 = 100.0, 1954 = 111.7, and 1965 = 131.1.
[b]January-March 1954. (See note b of Table 7-2.)
[c]April 20-December 31, 1965, for the California markets; entire year for the East Coast markets. (See note c of Table 7-2.)

Sources: Calculated from data presented in Tables 7-2 and 7-3.

that they generally decreased or registered only small increases for the various time periods. The extent of these changes is summarized in Table 7-7.

While it is true that three-quarters of the lowest, widely-available, constant dollar prices actually decreased during the three time periods, summarizing the price changes by market groups shows that by far the largest decreases occurred in the major California markets, whereas all of the increases were in the major East Coast markets. The price changes for the three California markets ranged from minus 57.4 to minus 5.6 percent, with a median value of about minus 21 percent. In contrast, the price changes for the East Coast markets ranged from minus 24.3 to plus 29.1 percent, with a median value of about plus 2 percent (plus 4 percent if Eastern's Air-Shuttle prices are included).

There is no need to dwell upon the comparisons of price changes for the two market groups. It is obvious that the combination of the inauguration of coach service, decreases in federal transportation taxes, and inflation (as measured by the all-items price index) re-

Table 7-7

Percentage Changes in the Lowest, Widely-Available, Constant Dollar Prices per Mile
in the Major California and East Coast Markets
between 1946, 1950 or Early 1954, and 1965

Market	Mileage	Percent Change in Lowest, Widely-Available Constant Dollar Prices Per Mile					
		1946 to 1965[a]		1950 to 1965[a]		1954[b] to 1965[a]	
		Propeller	Best-Avail.[c]	Propeller	Best-Avail.[c]	Propeller	Best-Avail.[c]
A. Major California Markets							
LAX/BUR–SAN	109	−35.2%	−35.2%	−20.2%	−20.2%	−10.9%	−10.9%
LAX/BUR–SFO/OAK	340	−57.4	−49.6	−20.2	− 5.6	−34.2	−22.2
SAN–SFO/OAK	449	−50.9	−45.9	−20.4	−11.1	−27.5	−19.0
B. Major East Coast Markets							
BOS–NYC/EWR	184	− 8.7[d]	5.4	−	−	11.8[f]	29.1
NYC/EWR–DCA	215	−13.7[e]	− 7.8	−	−	7.5[g]	14.8
BOS–DCA	399	−24.3	−18.3	−	−	− 1.6	7.9

[a]April 20-December 31, 1965, for the California markets. Entire year for the East Coast markets. (See note c of Table 7-2.)

[b]January-March 1954. (See note b of Table 7-2.)

[c]Propeller aircraft in the base year, and jet aircraft in 1965.

[d]3.1% using Eastern's Air-Shuttle price per mile in 1965.

[e]−3.8% using Eastern's Air-Shuttle price per mile in 1965.

[f]26.2% using Eastern's Air-Shuttle price per mile in 1965.

[g]19.9% using Eastern's Air-Shuttle price per mile in 1965.

Source: Calculated from data presented in Table 7-6.

sulted in reductions in widely-available, constant dollar prices in all markets from 1946 to 1965. However, when the effect of the coach service innovation is eliminated by comparing changes in coach prices from 1954 to 1965, the major California markets still show large decreases in constant dollar prices, while the major East Coast markets are mainly characterized by price increases. Again, consistent with the findings of chapter 5, the extensive regulation of the CAB was associated with relatively small decreases and some increases in constant dollar prices for the various time periods, while the much more limited regulation of the PUC was associated with significantly greater price decreases and not a single increase.

Conclusion

The federal transportation tax served to make actual prices paid by passengers 5, 10, or 15 percent higher than airline fares during the period studied, but the 10 percentage point reduction in tax rate (from 15 percent prior to April 1954 to 5 percent after mid-November 1962) caused significant reductions in overall price increases. With the assistance of the two tax rate reductions and the coach service innovation, both the certificated and the California intrastate carriers were generally able to keep their increases in lowest, widely-available prices well under the increases in the all-items, private-transportation and, especially, the public-transportation price indices (which also reflect tax changes). In 1965, passengers enjoyed higher quality service at constant dollar prices that were usually lower than those in effect in 1946.

There were, however, significant differences within this overall creditable performance. In the three major East Coast markets (representing interstate markets), the certificated carriers' constant dollar prices for jet coach service in 1965 ranged from minus 18.3 to plus 5.4 percent of 1946 propeller first-class prices. Taken alone, this might well be considered an outstanding performance, one that the CAB could point to with pride as a laudable result of its regulatory activities. But, this record pales when compared with the minus 49.6 to minus 35.2 percent decreases in constant dollar prices for the same period and services in the three major California markets where the PUC's limited regulation allowed active price rivalry. Thus, while the airline industry in general has earned kudos for holding down or reducing constant dollar prices (with the aid of decreased tax rates), this achievement should not be attributed to government regulation.

Promotional Fares

8

Introduction

Promotional fares, unlike general fares, are not available to all persons. Only air travelers having some specified personal characteristic, conforming to a restrictive travel pattern, utilizing standby (no-reservation) service,[1] or having a combination of these distinguishing criteria, may qualify for these lower discriminatory fares. The purpose of promotional fares is to increase profits (or decrease losses) by lowering prices to groups of persons whose price elasticities of demand are relatively high, while requiring those with more inelastic demand to pay higher general fares. In all cases, the ideal is to set prices so as to increase total revenues until marginal revenues for the various groups are equal and are also equal to marginal cost.

Two conditions pertaining to demand characteristics are necessary for effective price discrimination in the sale of some good (or service). First, groups of customers with differing price elasticities of demand must be identified and an appropriate structure of discriminatory prices established for these buyers. Second, it must be possi-

---

[1] Standby fares are classified as promotional fares under the definition adopted in this study. It may be argued that standby service is available to all who wish to use it and that it differs from reserved-space service provided under general fares so that the differences in prices are proportional to differences in marginal costs, thereby eliminating any discrimination. (Stigler defines price discrimination as "the sale of two or more similar goods at prices which are in different ratios to marginal cost." *The Theory of Price* [3d ed.], p. 209.) As shown in Table 8-1, certain standby fares have ranged from 7 to 38 percent under general fares for otherwise identical reserved-space service. It is hard to believe that differences in marginal costs may actually be as great as 38 percent, but it is impossible to determine this from available data.

ble to prevent (at low cost) those buyers enjoying low prices from undercutting the original suppliers by reselling to other buyers who are charged the higher, discriminatory prices. There is a third necessary condition for effective price discrimination, but it pertains to an aspect of supply rather than to demand. That is, there must be sufficient monopoly power in the industry to prevent some existing or new firm from offering lower prices to the buyers being discriminated against.[2] This may not be a major problem for monopolists, but it is an important problem when several suppliers exist or when entry is easy. These latter situations need enforceable agreements among the suppliers (a cartel) to obtain the necessary power to prevent price cutting by rival suppliers.

In this chapter the extent to which promotional (discriminatory) fares were adopted by the certificated carriers in interstate markets will be compared with the extent to which they were offered by the California intrastate carriers and by the certificated carriers within California. There seems to be no reason to believe that California residents utilizing air service within the state should have significantly different demand characteristics than California and other U.S. residents flying between states. If, therefore, the certificated carriers were able to utilize more promotional fares in interstate markets than they and the intrastate carriers provided in California markets, this will provide evidence that differences existed in these markets in the supply condition necessary for price discrimination—that is, it will indicate that the airlines operating under Civil Aeronautics Board regulation had more monopoly power than the carriers operating in the relatively unregulated environment existing within California prior to September 1965.

Certificated Carriers' Interstate Promotional Fares

A large number of promotional fares have been authorized by the CAB since World War II.[3] Unfortunately, a thorough study of this

---

[2] See p. 59, n. 4. An independent supplier in an industry faces a much more elastic demand curve (and marginal revenue curve) than the remaining suppliers who act together. So long as any discriminatory price set by the industry is somewhat higher than an existing firm's marginal costs, or exceeds a new firm's average costs, a situation exists in which any one firm may increase profits by offering a lower price to those being discriminated against. Effective price discrimination, therefore, provides incentives for price rivalry among suppliers.

[3] On July 1, 1942, the certificated carriers canceled all promotional fares and discounts for the duration of World War II. A few promotional fares were briefly reinstated in 1945, but the widespread adoption of such fares did not begin until 1948. CAB, *Handbook of Airline Statistics*, pp. 477-78.

subject has yet to be published. Enough information is available, however, to permit the listing in Table 8-1 of some of the promotional fares (including several of the major ones) offered by the certificated carriers.

This list is far from exhaustive. Many other promotional fares could have been included, such as the West Coast common fares; triangle fares for travel between the East and West Coasts via Miami, Atlanta, or other Southeastern cities; excursion fares between Las Vegas and Los Angeles, and between Las Vegas and the Southeast; other local service carrier excursion fares; various group fares; 50 percent discount fares to clergymen travelling without reservations; discounts for airline employees, etc. Promotional fares for adult travelers have been in effect continuously since September 1948. Clearly, price discrimination is possible in the airline industry. Not only is it possible, but it has been widely practiced by the certificated carriers in their interstate markets.[4]

California Intrastate Carriers' Promotional Fares

The feasibility of price discrimination in the airline industry is also demonstrated by the history of the promotional fares adopted by the eight major intrastate carriers (those operating nine months or more) since World War II. The extent and variety of price discrimination practiced by these intrastate carriers has, however, been much more limited than that practiced by the certificated carriers. Table 8-2 summarizes *all* of the promotional fares offered by the eight major intrastate carriers between 1946 and 1965 and, for one fare, in 1966.

Two things are apparent from a review of Table 8-2. First, the only promotional fare that was widely adopted by the intrastate carriers was the 50 percent discount for children eleven years of age or younger. Seven out of the eight major carriers did eventually adopt this discriminatory fare, and five of them offered it throughout their entire existence.[5] Most of the other promotional fares were

---

[4] In the first half of 1966, 22.8 percent of all passengers carried by eight trunk carriers utilized promotional fares, while 32.3 percent did so during the same period in 1967. See ATA, *Major U.S. Airlines, 1967-1971 Financial Projections and Requirements*, presentation to the CAB, November 28, 1967, Slide 9.

[5] Five of the major intrastate carriers also adopted the related 100 percent discount for infants under two years of age, provided a seat was not reserved for them. The prevalence of a discount for children in most common carrier modes (as well as in many other personal service industries) suggests that this discrim-

Table 8-1

Promotional Fares Offered by the Certificated Carriers
1946-1965

Promotional Fare	Percent Discount	Date Effective	Date Canceled[a]
A. Personal Characteristics			
Children[b/c]	50%	8/20/45	—
Official military travel[b]	10	7/ 1/49	—
Official military travel-groups of 25[c]	20	7/27/62	—
Visit U.S.A.[b/c]	Depends on use	9/ 1/63	—
B. Travel Pattern			
Round-, circle-, open-jaw trips[b]	5	9/ 1/48	10/20/58
Summer excursion[b]	25 or 33.5	5/15/49	11/ 1/49
Summer excursion[b]	25	7/ 5/50	9/ 1/50
Summer excursion[b]	25	6/ 1/-[d]	11/ 1/-[d]
Night-coach excursion	20*	1/13/58	n.a.
Summer coach excursion	20 or 32.5	4/30/62	12/ 8/62
Transcontinental coach excursion	15* to 20*	9/12/55	mid-1961
Transcontinental jet or propeller coach excursion	8* to 33*	8/16/61	12/16/61
Bonanza's resort and commercial excursion[b]	22* to 39*	4/ 1/61	—[e]
C. Standby Service			
Allegheny's local commuter[b]	27* to 36*	10/ 4/59	—
Northeast's standby[b/c]	7* to 38*	Early 1962	—
D. Personal Characteristics and Travel Pattern			
Family plan[f]	25 to 50	9/13/48	—
Allegheny's 10-member group[b]	33.33	3/ 1/61	—
Mohawk's "Golden Age" excursion[b]	33.33	7/10/61	1/ 1/66
25-member affinity group[c/g]	20	7/27/62	—
E. Personal Characteristics and Standby Service			
Youth (3-hour reservation)[b]	50	8/30/61	12/16/61
Military standby[c]	50 .	3/17/63	—

n.a.—not available.

*Approximate.

[a]The first full day on which the fare was no longer available.

[b]First-class service.

[c]Coach service.

[d]This fare was available for the indicated five-month period during each year from 1951 to about 1957.

[e]Bonanza canceled its resort excursion fares effective July 11, 1965, replacing them with commercial excursion fares.

[f]With one or two very minor exceptions, family-plan fares were available only on first-class service until January 15, 1964, when this promotional fare was generally extended to coach service.

[g]The affinity requirements were gradually canceled beginning in mid-1964.

Source: Jordan, *Economic Effects of Airline Regulation*, pp. 606-18.

Table 8-2

Promotional Fares Offered by the Major California Intrastate Carriers
1946–1965

Promotional Fare	Carrier	Percent Discount	Date Effective	Date Canceled[a]
A. Personal Characteristics				
State personnel	Pacific	15 %	4/ 1/47	6/ 4/47
Children	PSA	50	5/ 6/49	–
	WALC	49.7	5/ 8/50	6/ 1/50
	CCA	50	1/18/52[b]	2/15/55
	C. Coastal	50	3/15/55	8/10/57
	Paradise	50	5/14/55	3/ 5/64
	TCA	50	8/15/62	10/ 8/64
	Mercer	50	4/14/64	–
Military personnel	CCA	9.4	3/ 6/53	2/15/55
	PSA	9.4	3/ 5/54	4/ 8/54
Official military travel	PSA	10 to 22	6/24/53	4/ 8/54
	PSA	4.8 or 8.3	4/29/54	11/16/54
	CCA	10	1/ 5/54	2/15/55
	C. Coastal	10	3/15/55	2/ 3/57
Group commutation (10-trip)	CCA	10	11/14/53	2/15/55
	C. Coastal	10	3/15/55	2/ 3/57
Official government travel	CCA	10	3/13/54	2/15/55
	C. Coastal	10	3/15/55	2/ 3/57
Clergy	TCA	5	8/15/62	10/ 8/64
B. Travel Pattern				
Round trip	Pacific	10	4/ 1/47	6/ 4/47
	Paradise	9.1	5/14/62	3/ 5/64
	TCA	2.4 or 4.5	8/15/62	10/ 8/64
Mid-week excursion	CCA	18.4 or 26	10/14/52	2/ 1/53
Individual commutation (10-trip)	CCA	10	11/14/53	2/15/55
	C. Coastal	10	3/15/55	2/ 3/57
24-hour excursion	Paradise	28.2	9/13/63	3/ 5/64
C. Standby Service				
Bud-jet standby	PSA	15.3	5/ 6/66[c]	–

[a]The first full day on which the fare was no longer available.

[b]Available on Tuesday, Wednesday, and Thursday only from this date through January 13, 1953. Extended to all days of the week effective January 14, 1953.

[c]Originally effective following the end of the period under study.

Source: Jordan, *Economic Effects of Airline Regulation*, pp. 619–28.

offered by only one or two carriers (especially if California Coastal is considered to be an extension of California Central). Second, aside from the children's fare and one minor exclusion,[6] the intrastate carriers offered promotional fares during only two discontinuous periods, the 52 months from mid-October 1952 to early February 1957, and the 29 months from mid-May 1962 to mid-October 1964. Overall, the intrastate carriers offered promotional fares for only six and three-quarters of the 17 years between 1949 and 1965.

There was one central relationship between the intrastate carriers' promotional fares and their general fares: no carrier offered a promotional fare when its general one-way fare between Los Angeles and San Francisco was $9.95 or $9.99 (or some correspondingly low fare per mile in any other California market). This relationship will be emphasized in the following description of their promotional fares.

The California intrastate carriers' first promotional fare (other than for children) was introduced by California Central on October 14, 1952, four months after it had raised its general Los Angeles–San Francisco fare to $13.50 and its San Diego–San Francisco fare to $19.05. This first fare was CCA's "Special Mid-Week Round-Trip Adult Excursion Fare," available on Tuesdays, Wednesdays, and Thursdays. It provided fares equal to the round-trip general fares that had been in effect from 1949 to March 1951 (twice the old one-way fares of $9.99 and $15.54 for Los Angeles–San Francisco and San Diego–San Francisco, respectively). Two things should be noted about this fare. First, it was not offered between Los Angeles and San Diego where CCA's unchanged general fare still equaled that of PSA, United, and Western. Second, it was canceled effective February 1, 1953, the day that United and Western adopted the $13.50 fare for their coach service between Los Angeles and San Francisco (and the $19.05 fare between San Diego and San Francisco), thereby leaving only PSA with lower general fares. Clearly, this promotional fare was a device used by CCA to lessen the adverse impact of its independent fare increase until the other large carriers in these markets increased their fares to the same level.

---

inatory fare has become so much a part of the economic customs of the nation that its adoption by carriers is almost habitual. Overall, it does appear that this fare is not a useful criterion by which to distinguish between these two types of carriers.

[6] The minor exclusion consists of Pacific Air Lines' discounts for state employees and for round-trip passengers that applied from April 1 to June 4, 1947. PSA's Bud-jet standby fare is also excluded from this comparison since it was not introduced until after the end of the period covered by this study.

The role of a lower-price competitor in fostering the adoption of promotional fares can also be seen in CCA's promotional fare for military personnel flying between San Diego and San Francisco. PSA consistently carried more passengers than CCA in this market,[7] and following CCA's June 15, 1952, fare increase, PSA's general fare was lower than CCA's $19.05 fare. Effective March 6, 1953, CCA introduced the $17.25 one-way fare (9.4 percent discount) for military personnel, thereby equaling PSA's general fare. Obviously, this promotional fare was adopted to attract a portion of the large volume of military traffic flying PSA at that time.

Starting in November 1953, CCA adopted four other promotional fares (for official military or government travel, and for group or individual commutation) that provided 10 percent discounts on all of its fares for Martin 202 and DC-3 service. With the single exception of the already relatively high (and unchanged) $5.55 fare between Los Angeles and San Diego, all of these discounts provided fares to qualifying passengers that were generally higher (and were never lower) than the low general fares in effect during the 1949 to early 1951 period. These promotional fares remained in effect until CCA went bankrupt in early 1955.

PSA's first promotional fare was the 10 percent discount for official military travel adopted on June 24, 1953. This was over two years after its Burbank–San Francisco general fare had been increased to $11.70, but it was less than four months after CCA filed its military personnel fare in the San Diego–San Francisco market. The importance to PSA of official military traffic was further demonstrated the following January, when it finally adopted the $13.50 Burbank–San Francisco general fare. Instead of maintaining the 10 percent discount and increasing its promotional fares along with its general fares, PSA filed special military travel fares which held the military fares constant, thereby increasing the discount up to as high as 22 percent.

One result of PSA's January 1954 general fare increase was to make CCA's $17.25 military personnel promotional fare and its DC-3 general fare the lowest fare between San Diego and San Francisco for other than official military travel. Within seven weeks, PSA filed a $17.25 fare (9.4 percent discount) for all military personnel (whether or not on official business) to match CCA's fare in this market.

When PSA slashed its general fares to the $9.99 level on April 8, 1954, it canceled all of its promotional fares, including the official military travel fares. This latter fare was reintroduced three weeks

[7] See Appendix 14(C) of this book.

later in the relatively high fare-per-mile Burbank–San Diego and
Long Beach–San Diego markets. By mid-June 1954, however, all
service to Long Beach had been terminated, and by the middle of the
following November, the official military travel fare between Burbank and San Diego was canceled. PSA did not offer any promotional fares (other than children's fares) during the remainder of the
period covered by this study.

California Coastal's emergence from the ashes of California Central included the adoption of all of CCA's applicable promotional
fares, except for the $17.25 military personnel fare between San
Diego and San Francisco, which became superfluous with the termination of Martin 202 service. California Coastal appears to have
found it difficult to compete with PSA while operating the same
type aircraft (DC-3's) at higher fares ($11.70 vs. $9.99 between
Burbank and San Francisco).[8] Beginning on June 2, 1955, it gradually matched PSA's lower general fares and, as it did so, terminated
its promotional fares in the various markets.

Only three different promotional fares were actually offered
during the second period that such fares existed (from mid-May 1962
to mid-October 1964), and all of them were introduced by two of
the three new major carriers that entered during those years.[9] Both
Paradise and Trans California provided round-trip discounts throughout their existences. These discounts ranged from 2.4 to 9.1 percent
of twice their one-way fares. TCA also offered a 5 percent discount
on one-way fares to members of the clergy. Finally, as mentioned in
chapter 6, Paradise had a 24-hour, round-trip excursion fare that
provided a 28.2 percent discount from twice its one-way fare
($15.00 vs. $20.90). As in the case of most of the earlier promotional fares, these three later fares were all associated with general
fares above the $9.99 (or equivalent) level. Trans California's Los
Angeles–Oakland general one-way fare was $10.99, and Paradise's
fare between Lake Tahoe and Oakland/San Jose was about 7.2 cents
per mile, more than twice the fare per mile derived from the $9.99
Los Angeles–San Francisco fare.

It should be recognized that both TCA and Paradise enjoyed
partial or complete monopolies in their markets. TCA was the only
carrier providing Burbank–Oakland and San Diego–Oakland service

[8] Starting November 10, 1955, and extending over the following three
months, PSA replaced its DC-3's with DC-4's, thereby worsening California
Coastal's competitive position. PSA Company Records. Also, see chapter 3.

[9] The third new carrier, Mercer Enterprises, offered only the children's fare.
There was very little entry of new carriers during the first period of promotional
fares. Only California Coastal might be classified as a new carrier during
1952–57.

at that time, and the certificated carriers operated little coach service between Los Angeles and Oakland until June 1964. Futura offered Paradise a small amount of competition in the summer of 1962, and Pacific (the local service carrier) inaugurated service to Lake Tahoe in October 1963 (at higher general fares), but during the majority of the almost two years that it operated, Paradise was the sole carrier in these markets.

The termination of service by Paradise and TCA brought to an end this second period of promotional fares. During all of 1965 and until PSA introduced the Bud-jet standby fare on May 6, 1966, there were no promotional fares provided by intrastate carriers (other than for children).

To summarize, the offering of promotional fares by the California intrastate carriers has been limited and sporadic and has usually occurred when general fares rose above the minimum levels established in 1949–50. Of the personal characteristic-type fares, four out of six were confined to military or government employees, and only the group commutation fare was available to a broad class of people. Most of the travel pattern-type fares were available for only relatively short time periods, ranging from 3½ to 38 months. Overall, promotional fares of any type were in effect for only 40 percent of the total period from 1949 through 1965.

Certificated Carriers' Promotional Fares within California

A review of the certificated carriers' intrastate tariffs shows that the major promotional fares of the postwar period were offered within California as well as elsewhere in the country.[10] The various promotional fare discounts were, however, with few exceptions, applicable only to those fares which were determined by the across-the-board fare increases authorized by the CAB. Thus, in those markets where no California intrastate carriers operated, and where the regular CAB-authorized fares were charged, the promotional fares of the certificated carriers were also in effect. On the other hand, most of the promotional fare discounts did not apply to the low fares in the major California markets which were adopted by the certificated carriers in response to the price rivalry of the intrastate carriers. Also, in several instances, United Air Lines simply did not make certain discounts applicable to any fare in the major California markets.

---

[10] On January 27, 1966, following the period covered by this study, one major promotional fare (the standby youth fare) was introduced by the certificated carriers in their interstate markets, but was not filed with the PUC for intrastate service wholly within California.

As an example of the certificated carriers' pricing practices in the major California markets, consider the family plan, the military standby, and the group promotional fares offered by United and/or Western in these markets as of December 31, 1965. Table 8-3 compares the lowest fare available under each of these three types of fares with the lowest general fares offered at that time by PSA, United, and Western. This table shows that in the Los Angeles–San

Table 8-3

Comparison of the Certificated Carriers' Promotional Fares
with the Lowest, Widely-Available, General Fares
in the Three Major California Markets
December 31, 1965

| Market | Carrier | Lowest General Fare | Lowest Coach Promotional Fare | | |
			Family Plan[a]	Military Standby	Group[b]
LAX–SFO/OAK	PSA	$11.43[c]	–	–	–
	UAL	13.50[d]	–	$11.85[d]	–
	WAL	13.50[d]	$15.80[d]	11.85[d]	$19.00[d]
LAX–SAN	PSA	6.35[e]	–	–	–
	UAL	6.35[d]	5.80[f]	5.80[f]	8.75[d]
	WAL	8.00[e]	5.80[f]	5.80[f]	6.60[c]
SAN–SFO/OAK	PSA	17.78[c]	–	–	–
	UAL	19.85[d]	–	14.65[d]	–
	WAL	17.78[c]	11.86[c]	14.65[d]	15.90[d]

[a]Fare for the first accompanying member of the family based on the 33-1/3 percent discount available noon Monday through noon Friday. Additional family members 21 years of age or younger traveled at a 66-2/3 percent discount.

[b]The fares shown below are one-half of the required round-trip fares.

[c]Propeller coach service.

[d]Jet coach or commuter service.

[e]Jet and propeller coach service.

[f]Minimum fare allowed irrespective of applicable discount. Same service as shown for general fare.

Sources: Appendices 6(B), 6(C), and 7 of this book. The following tariffs filed with the California PUC: S. J. Rogers, Agent–Cal. P.U.C. No. 1, originally effective July 31, 1959; United Air Lines–Cal. P.U.C. Nos. 22, 25, 29, originally effective Mar. 30, 1963, Nov. 1, 1964, and Apr. 3, 1965, respectively; Western Air Lines–Cal. P.U.C. Nos. 26, 27, 28, originally effective June 1, 1962, Mar. 29, 1963, and June 19, 1963, respectively.

Francisco market a general fare was available that was lower than any of the promotional fares. In the Los Angeles–San Diego market a maximum of 55 cents could be saved by using a promotional fare instead of a widely available general fare. It was only in the San Diego–San Francisco market that promotional fares yielded significant reductions from the general fares.

Apparently, United Air Lines believed that the family plan and the group fares were generally ineffective in these markets, for it offered them only between Los Angeles and San Diego.[11] A similar pattern of application was adopted on March 27, 1966 with the "Discover America" excursion fares. United and Western introduced this 25 percent discount between Los Angeles and San Diego (based on the $8.00 one-way fare) but not in the Los Angeles–San Francisco and San Diego–San Francisco markets.[12]

There are two exceptions to the statement that the certificated carriers did not apply promotional fare discounts to their lowest general fares in the major California markets. One of these exceptions is, of course, the children's fare discounts. The certificated carriers even applied these discounts to their low Thriftair and Jet Commuter fares. The second exception is the 10-trip commuter fare introduced by United on September 27, 1964, when it inaugurated Jet Commuter service between Los Angeles and San Francisco. This fare allowed a frequent traveler to purchase 10 one-way tickets for $137.75, a 5 percent discount from the $145.00 cost of ten Jet Commuter tickets purchased individually. The 10-trip tickets were valid for 90 days after purchase and were nontransferable.[13] They were also valid for travel in the coach section of United's regular jet flights in this market after the one-way fare for that service was reduced from $23.70 to $14.50. When the Jet Commuter fare was decreased to $13.50 on April 1, 1965, it fell below the average charge per trip ($13.78) for the 10-trip commuter fare, and this promotional fare was canceled for Jet Commuter service. It was

[11] United eliminated the Los Angeles–San Diego group fare on March 10, 1966, when it allowed its PUC group fare tariff to expire, thereby deleting this promotional fare in all intrastate California markets. See United Air Lines tariff, Cal. P.U.C. No. 29, originally effective April 3, 1965, original and first revised title page.

[12] United Air Lines tariff, Cal. P.U.C. No. 30, originally effective March 27, 1966. Western Air Lines tariff, Cal. P.U.C. No. 30, originally effective March 27, 1966.

[13] United Air Lines tariff, Cal. P.U.C. No. 23, originally effective September 27, 1964.

retained, however, for regular jet service where the coach fare remained at $14.50.[14]

The pricing practices of the certificated carriers in the major California markets were consistent with those of the intrastate carriers with respect to promotional fares. Low general fares limited the use of promotional fares for both carrier groups. Obviously, as general fares decrease, the possibilities of increasing profits through discriminatory pricing are reduced. The fare rivalry of the intrastate carriers served to reduce the certificated carriers' general fares and, thus, to restrict the use of promotional fares in the major markets. Concurrently, in other markets within California where service was provided solely by certificated carriers, higher general fares were associated with the more extensive use of promotional fares, in the same manner as found in interstate markets.

Conclusion

Clearly, large differences existed between the use of promotional fares in interstate markets and the three major California markets. The certificated carriers have had promotional fares (in addition to those for children) continuously since late 1948, and many of these discriminatory fares were adopted system-wide by all or most of these carriers. In contrast, the intrastate carriers adopted a relatively small number of promotional fares, many of which were offered by only one carrier at any given time, and (again excluding children's fares) such fares were in effect for only 40 percent of the period from 1949 through 1965. Also, the certificated carriers were found to have offered fewer promotional fares in the major California markets than elsewhere; and, with two exceptions, promotional fare discounts did not apply to their special, low general fares adopted as a result of the price rivalry in these markets. Finally, the long lives of some of the certificated carriers' promotional fares in interstate markets indicate that these carriers have been able to reach and enforce effectively agreements with regards to such fares. Thus, since discriminatory pricing requires the existence of monopoly power, it appears that the

[14] United Air Lines tariff, Cal. P.U.C. No. 28, originally effective April 1, 1965. This writer was advised that one reason United did not completely cancel this 10-trip fare when the Jet Commuter fare was reduced to $13.50, was because doing so would have resulted in an official fare increase for regular jet coach service. This would have required a formal hearing before the PUC. It was thought that leaving the fare in effect, but unused, would be less costly than going through the procedure required for its cancellation.

three major California markets were organized in a less monopolistic manner than the markets served only by the CAB-regulated airlines. This, of course, is consistent with the implications of the hypothesis that the CAB has served to facilitate the cartelization of the inter-state airlines.

While the market structure of the major California markets may have been more competitive than that of the markets served only by the certificated carriers, the degree of competition within these major markets seems to have differed over time. During 1949 and 1950, there was a relatively high degree of competition with much entry (and exit), substantial price rivalry yielding low general fares, and no discriminatory pricing. From 1951 to 1957, with only four carriers providing turnaround service in each market, competition was more limited. General fares were increased and promotional fares adopted. In this oligopolistic situation, however, there was sufficient price rivalry to cause general fares to be reduced to historically low levels by PSA and, eventually, by California Coastal, with the concurrent elimination of promotional fares. From 1958 to 1961 the rivalry among PSA, United, and Western was not sufficient to keep the certificated carriers from adopting the three CAB-authorized fare increases of that period, but even following its two fare increases, PSA's general fares were still low enough to discourage it from adopting promotional fares. Finally, the actions of first Western and then United in adopting fares equal to or less than PSA's indicates a renewal of price competition in the major markets during 1962–65.

The entry of Paradise and Trans California in 1962 brought in new promotional fares, contrary to the expectation that additional carriers would increase competition and thereby make discriminatory pricing more difficult. Since, however, these two carriers mainly operated in markets that were not served by other airlines, their entry resulted more in the geographic expansion of monopoly service than in an increase of competition over existing routes. Their promotional fares, therefore, do not provide an exception to the conclusions of this chapter.

Over the long term, the pricing practices of the airlines within California have been consistent with what would be expected in markets where suppliers have little or no monopoly power. The increase in general fares to the $13.50 level back in 1952–53, and the promotional fares of that period, show that the intrastate carriers were just as willing as the certificated carriers to adopt fares that would increase profits. Unlike the experience in the interstate markets, however, such fares were not viable in the major California markets. Given similar demand characteristics, there is no reason why promotional fares should not have survived within California had the necessary supply condition existed. Thus, their disappearance implies that this condition did not exist and that the market structure was not monopolistic.

It is not known whether the low general fares that did exist in the major California markets equaled those that would have developed under a competitive market structure. The information given in this and the previous chapters, however, demonstrates that they were closer to the competitive "ideal" than the fares authorized by the CAB for interstate markets.

Market Shares

9

Introduction

To what extent do differences in price and service quality affect market shares? In contrast to the certificated carriers' almost complete emphasis on improving service quality to obtain larger market shares in interstate markets, the California Public Utilities Commission's policy of not regulating fare decreases permitted carriers to use price rivalry within California in addition to, or as a substitute for, service rivalry to increase their coach market shares. Because of this, the three major California markets provide a rare opportunity to investigate the relative effects of both price and service quality differences in attracting coach passengers, and the findings of one limited study of this matter will be presented in this chapter.

At the outset, it is necessary to warn the reader not to expect conclusive results from this study because there are many unresolved difficulties involved in estimating the relative effects on market shares of price and service quality differences. First, it must be recognized that there are many service quality factors influencing passenger choice. Such factors include flight frequency and the number of available seats, timing of departures and arrivals, aircraft characteristics (speed, pressurization, number of engines, size, age, etc.), locations of ticket offices and terminal facilities, relative convenience of ground services, attractiveness of personnel, food service, aircraft interiors, safety records, and so on. Second, there is the problem of selecting the "proper" measures of price and service quality differences. For example, price differences would seem to be a relatively easy factor to define and measure, but closer examination shows that there are important problems in estimating even this simple variable.

Should price differences be measured on the basis of lowest available prices, or should they be based on an average of prices weighted by the number of seats available under each price? Should the effects of promotional fares somehow be included in average prices? Furthermore, should price differences be expressed in relative (percentage) or absolute (dollar) terms? Measuring service quality differences entails even greater problems than price differences, both because of the larger number of service quality factors and because of difficulties in quantifying these factors. Third, there are factors other than price and service quality which have an impact on consumer choice. The public's general impression of a carrier or a class of carriers, previous travel experiences of passengers and their acquaintances, business and government travel policies, income levels, advertising and promotional activities—all of these factors, and others, influence passengers in selecting a carrier for a particular trip. Finally, it should be recognized that individual factors may have varying effects in different markets.

Obviously, it is impossible to identify and quantify all of the above variables, let alone determine an objective relationship between them and market share. The data presented in this book, however, do provide a few measures of price and service quality differences, and it is desirable at least to investigate whether some consistent relationships can be found between these factors and market share.

The analysis in this chapter will be simplified in two important respects. First, it will be limited to coach market shares in order to eliminate the matter of the rivalry between first-class and coach service. Interclass rivalry occurred *within* carriers (the "diversion" of first-class passengers to coach service) as well as between carriers, and the rapid expansion of coach traffic wherever coach service was widely available indicates that the basic price/product combination of coach service was preferred over that of first-class service by the majority of passengers (see chapter 3). Second, instead of investigating changes in the coach market shares of individual carriers, the carriers will be combined into the customary two groups—the certificated carriers versus the intrastate carriers—and the comparison carried out between these two groups. It is feasible to do this because, even though each carrier sought to increase its market share at the expense of all other carriers, the certificated carriers limited their rivalry with each other to differences in service quality (except from June 1962 through March 1965), whereas their rivalry with the intrastate carriers generally included important differences in both price and service quality. Since the purpose of this chapter is to investigate the relative effects on coach market shares of these two kinds of differences, combining the carriers into two groups facilitates the analysis. In addition, it provides continuity in the intrastate carriers' data that would not be available if only individual carrier data were considered.

Multiple Regression Analyses

Multiple regression analysis provides one method of investigating the simultaneous impact on market share of a number of price and service quality factors. Several such analyses were undertaken while carrying out the research underlying this chapter. The dependent variable (market share) and the four independent variables found to be most useful in these analyses are summarized below. The data for each variable are presented in Tables 9-1 through 9-5.

Y = Market Share—the intrastate carriers' percent of total annual coach passengers in each market (Table 9-1).

X_1 = Price Difference—the dollar difference between the annual weighted average coach prices of the two carrier groups in each market (Table 9-2).

X_2 = Seat Share—the intrastate carriers' percentage of total weekly scheduled coach seats in each market (Table 9-3).

X_3 = Pressurization—the percentage of the certificated carriers' total coach seats in each market provided in aircraft having the same pressurization capability as the intrastate carriers' aircraft (Table 9-4).

X_4 = Seat Speed—the certificated carriers' average coach-seat speed in each market as a percent of the intrastate carriers' average seat speed (Table 9-5).[1]

The overall hypothesis of these regression analyses is that the intrastate carriers' market share has a positive relationship with price difference, seat share, and pressurization, and a negative relationship with seat speed. In other words, the intrastate carriers' market share should increase as the difference between their mean prices and the generally higher mean coach prices of the certificated carriers increases, as their percentage of total weekly coach seats in a market increases, as the certificated carriers operate a greater proportion of

---

[1] Detailed descriptions of these variables (with some minor differences in terminology), indications of their limitations, and reasons for adopting these rather than other measures are given in Jordan, *Economic Effects of Airline Regulation*, pp. 333-62.

Table 9-1

Estimated Number of First-Class and Coach On-Line O & D Passengers Flown by All Carriers in the Three Major California Markets, and the Percent of Total Coach Passengers Flown by California Intrastate Carriers 1949-1965

Year	Estimated Total On-Line O & D Passengers (000)						Intrastate Carriers' Percent of Total Coach Passengers		
	LAX-SFO[a]		LAX-SAN[b]		SAN-SFO[c]		LAX-SFO[a]	LAX-SAN[b]	SAN-SFO[c]
	First-Class	Coach	First-Class	Coach	First-Class	Coach			
1949	291d	170d	78	4	19	10	100.0d%	100.0%	100.0%
1950	192	361	67	14	19	27	39.9e	100.0	100.0
1951	n.a.	n.a.	n.a.	n.a.	n.a.	n.a.	—	—	—
1952	269	464	142	61	24	73	32.8	68.8	76.6
1953	292	398	142	49	28	69	33.0	81.6	89.9
1954	376	476	142	46	31	76	29.8	56.3	84.1
1955	425	554	129	73	37	81	19.0	35.2	70.5
1956	443	579	148	97	35	88	24.5	34.2	78.4
1957	490	666	205	87	41	95	22.8	44.5	82.3
1958	446	725	205	94	43	100	23.1	48.8	83.0
1959	474	855	172	160	40	117	24.0	36.9	77.8
1960	431	1,030	144	219	24	161	39.1	40.1	80.8
1961	312	1,215	71	270	14	176	40.2	34.4	75.0
1962	192	1,514	37	303	6	209	49.1	42.2	81.8
1963	153	2,033	25	389	5	256	50.3	42.2	81.2
1964	138	2,510	25	474	3	295	46.7	43.4	81.3
1965	111	3,063	37	602	2	357	42.2	48.3	78.4

n.a.—not available.

[a] LAX/BUR/LGB/ONT-SFO/OAK/SJC.

[b] LAX/BUR/LGB/ONT-SAN.

[c] SAN-SFO/OAK/SJC.

[d] A small but unknown number of passengers flew on Western's night-coach service between Los Angeles and San Francisco from October 16 through December 31, 1949. These passengers are included in the first-class figure for 1949.

[e] 24.3 percent, excluding Western Air Lines of California.

Sources: Calculated from data presented in Appendices 14(A), 14(B), and 14(C) of this book. Note that the partial and substantial estimates specified in those appendices also apply to these data. The certificated carriers' total on-line O & D passenger data given in these appendices were allocated between first-class and coach on the basis of true O & D data presented in CAB, Domestic Origin-Destination Survey of Air Passenger Traffic (and its predecessor publications), 1949-65. See Jordan, Economic Effects of Airline Regulation, pp. 339-40.

Table 9-2

Annual Weighted Average Coach Prices and Price Differences
for the Certificated and California Intrastate Carriers
in the Three Major California Markets, 1952-1965

Annual Weighted Mean Coach Prices and Price Differences (Dollars)[a]

Year	LAX-SFO Mean Prices			LAX-SAN Mean Prices			SAN-SFO Mean Prices		
	Cert.	Intra.	Diff.	Cert.	Intra.	Diff.	Cert.	Intra.	Diff.
1952	13.46	14.25	-0.79	6.39	6.39	0	19.84	20.44	-0.60
1953	15.36	14.48	0.88	6.39	6.39	0	21.74	20.75	0.99
1954[b]	15.02	13.65	1.37	6.18	6.13	0.05	21.20	19.47	1.73
1955	14.85	11.73	3.12	6.11	6.04	0.07	20.96	17.11	3.85
1956	14.85	11.59	3.26	6.11	6.01	0.10	20.96	16.98	3.98
1957	14.85	10.99	3.86	6.11	6.00	0.11	20.96	16.99	3.97
1958	15.69	12.43	3.26	6.62	6.00	0.62	22.09	18.43	3.66
1959	16.67	13.00	3.67	7.15	6.00	1.15	22.94	18.99	3.95
1960	17.13	13.09	4.04	7.15	6.05	1.10	22.94	19.14	3.80
1961	19.30	14.85	4.45	8.97	6.99	1.98	25.02	21.84	3.18
1962[c]	21.25	14.77	6.48	9.52	6.95	2.57	26.16	21.72	4.44
1963	20.48	13.81	6.67	9.66	6.67	2.99	21.43	20.43	1.00
1964	18.51	13.97	4.54	9.88	6.67	3.21	20.85	20.85	0
1965	15.23	13.10	2.13	8.90	6.67	2.23	20.78	20.11	0.67

[a]Calculated by weighting the various fares plus taxes effective during each year by the proportion of total coach seats operated under each fare by each carrier group. It was assumed that the distribution of seats operated for one period during each year applied throughout that year (see notes a, b, and c of Table 9-3 for exceptions concerning 1964 and 1965).

[b]Transportation tax decreased from 15% to 10% effective April 1, 1954. The average tax for the year was assumed to be 11.25%.

[c]Transportation tax decreased from 10% to 5% effective November 16, 1962. The average tax for the year was assumed to be 9.4%.

Sources: Calculated from data presented in Appendices 6(B), 6(C), 7, 15(A), 15(B), and 15(C) of this book.

Table 9-3

California Intrastate Carriers' Percentage of Total Coach Seats per Week
Scheduled in the Three Major California Markets
Selected Dates 1949-1965

| Date | Intrastate Carriers' Percentage of Total Scheduled Coach Seats per Week | | |
	LAX/BUR/LGB/ONT-SFO/OAK/SJC	SAN	SAN-SFO/OAK/SJC
7/31/49	100.0%	100.0%	100.0%
3/ 1/51	28.9	100.0	100.0
9/ 1/52	38.2	66.4	67.8
9/ 1/53	33.0	83.6	84.2
12/ 1/54	27.2	36.6	56.3
8/ 1/55	18.8	30.1	52.9
8/ 1/56	22.4	26.9	58.8
8/ 1/57	19.5	36.9	81.1
8/ 1/58	16.9	33.2	82.1
8/ 1/59	18.9	25.6	57.7
8/ 1/60	26.1	34.5	69.4
8/ 1/61	28.7	31.1	67.3
8/ 1/62	29.4	35.8	70.6
8/ 1/63	34.2	39.7	89.5
8/ 1/64	37.6	32.8	84.9
10/ 1/64	34.2	33.1	84.9
8/ 1/65	41.5	39.8	71.4
$\overline{X}$ 1964[a]	36.7	32.9	84.9
$\overline{X}$ 1965	40.0[b]	38.5[c]	75.6[c]

[a]Calculated by averaging the data for 8/1/64 (weight = 3/4) and 10/1/64 (weight = 1/4).

[b]Calculated by averaging the data for 10/1/64 (weight = 1/4) and 8/1/65 (weight = 3/4).

[c]Calculated by averaging the data for 10/1/64 (certificated carriers' weight = 5/12, intrastate carriers' weight = 1/3) and 8/1/65 (certificated carriers' weight = 7/12, intrastate carriers' weight = 2/3).

Sources: Calculated from data presented in Appendices 15(A), 15(B), and 15(C) of this book. (Note, the weights used to obtain averages for 1964 and 1965 were based on a review of schedules for those years.)

Table 9-4

Percentage of Certificated Carriers' Total Scheduled Coach Seats
Provided in Aircraft Having the Same Pressurization Capability
as the California Intrastate Carriers' Aircraft
Three Major California Markets, 1952-1965

Year[a]	Percentage of Certificated Carriers' Total Coach Seats Provided in Aircraft Having the Same Pressurization Capability as the Intrastate Carriers' Aircraft		
	LAX/BUR/LGB/ONT– SFO/OAK/SJC	SAN	SAN–SFO/OAK/SJC
1952	100%	100%	100%
1953	100	100	100
1954	77	50	100
1955	79	43	100
1956	73	24	82
1957	28	14	47
1958	4	0	0
1959	2	0	0
1960	100	100	100
1961	100	100	100
1962	100	100	100
1963	100	100	100
1964	100	100	100
1965	100	100	100

[a]Based upon information for the dates specified in Table 9-3.

Sources: Calculated from data presented in Appendices 15(A), 15(B), and 15(C) of this book.

their coach seats in nonpressurized aircraft,[2] and as the certificated carriers' average coach-seat speeds decrease relative to those of the intrastate carriers.

The lack of schedule data for 1950, the nonavailability of the certificated carriers' passenger traffic data for 1951, and the fact that the certificated carriers did not operate coach service at San Diego until late 1951, combine to make 1952 the first year for which data for all variables are available for the three major California markets. Therefore, only the data for the 14 years from 1952 through 1965 were subjected to multiple regression analysis, using the UCLA bio-

[2] This variable is relevant only through 1959, since all carriers operated only pressurized aircraft in these markets beginning in 1960.

Table 9-5

Weighted Average Seat Speeds for the Scheduled Coach Operations
of the Certificated and California Intrastate Carriers
in the Three Major California Markets, 1952–1965

Year[a]	Weighted Mean Coach-Seat Speed (MPH)						Certificated Carriers' Speed Percent of Intrastate Carriers' Speed		
	Nonstop Flights[b]				All Flights[c]				
	LAX/BUR/LGB/ONT– SFO/OAK		SAN		SAN– SFO/OAK		LAX/BUR/LGB/ONT– SFO/OAK	SAN	SAN– SFO/OAK
	Cert.	Intra.	Cert.	Intra.	Cert.	Intra.			
1952	177	175	145	138	116	152	101%	105%	76%
1953	178	168	145	137	113	147	106	106	77
1954	183	168	149	137	114	149	109	109	77
1955	183	153	149	131	117	145	120	114	81
1956	186	168	151	143	124	169	111	106	73
1957	203	174	151	145	128	162	117	104	79
1958	209	177	154	145	155	166	118	106	93
1959	216	177	157	145	154	174	122	108	89
1960	242	296	155	211	151	241	82	73	63
1961	304	296	180	211	176	278	103	85	63
1962	294	296	183	211	225	272	99	87	83
1963	301	283	188	203	254	262	106	93	97
1964d	294	289	201	211	258f	275	102	95	94
1965	336e	321e	206f	213g	250f	291g	105	97	86

[a]Based upon information for the dates specified in Table 9-3.

[b]For each carrier group, calculated by weighting the certificated carriers' scheduled nonstop block-to-block speeds for the various aircraft types operated in these markets, by the number of nonstop coach seats per week scheduled to be provided in each aircraft type.

[c]Calculated by weighting each carrier's scheduled overall block-to-block speeds (including time required for intermediate stops) for the various aircraft types operated in this market, by the number of coach seats per week scheduled to be provided in each aircraft type on flights making three intermediate stops or less.

[d]Calculated by averaging the data for 8/1/64 (weight = 3/4) and 10/1/64 (weight = 1/4).

[e]Calculated by averaging the data for 10/1/64 (weight = 1/4) and 8/1/65 (weight = 3/4).

[f]Calculated by averaging the data for 10/1/64 (weight = 5/12) and 8/1/65 (weight = 7/12).

[g]Calculated by averaging the data for 10/1/64 (weight = 1/3) and 8/1/65 (weight = 2/3).

Sources: Calculated from data presented in Appendices 15(A), 15(B), and 15(C) of this book. Seat speeds obtained from the same sources as specified for these appendices (also, see Jordan, *Economic Effects of Airline Regulation*, pp. 350 and 353).

medical, stepwise regression computer program.[3] Two basic analyses were undertaken. The first assumed a linear relationship among the variables, and the second assumed a nonlinear relationship which was calculated by transforming all variables into their logarithms before carrying out the analysis. The directions of the effects of the four independent variables are hypothesized above, but there seems to be no *a priori* basis for specifying whether the functional relationship should be linear or logarithmic. Actual computations showed that the linear relationship gave results that were equally consistent with the overall hypothesis, while providing higher coefficients of determination (R^2) than the logarithmic relationship. Because of this, only the results of the linear regression analyses are presented and discussed in this chapter.

Table 9-6 summarizes the results of the multiple linear regression analysis for each of the three major California markets when all four independent variables are included. The analysis for the Los Angeles–San Francisco market yields statistically significant coefficients for price difference, seat share, and seat speed, and the signs for these coefficients are consistent with the overall hypothesis. Although the sign of the pressurization coefficient is contrary to that hypothesized, this coefficient is not statistically significant. The regression coefficient and the coefficient of determination (R and R^2) are very high and the standard error of estimate relatively small. Based on this single analysis, one might conclude that, for example, a $1.00 increase in price difference in this market was associated with a 3 percentage point increase in the intrastate carriers' market share—other variables being held constant.[4]

In contrast to the Los Angeles–San Francisco analysis, the results for the other two markets are generally inconsistent with the overall hypothesis. Seat share is the only variable that has a statistically significant coefficient in either market, and in both instances its sign is as predicted. Not only are the coefficients of the other variables not statistically significant, but the signs of the pressurization co-

---

[3] W. J. Dixon (ed.), *BMD Biomedical Computer Programs* (Los Angeles, Calif.: Health Sciences Computing Facility, Dept. of Preventive Medicine and Public Health, School of Medicine, University of California, September 1, 1965), pp. 233ff.

[4] The Los Angeles–San Francisco regression equation also implies that the intrastate carriers would carry 49 percent of the total coach traffic in this market if there was no difference in prices, if they provided 50 percent of the scheduled coach seats, and if the certificated carriers' aircraft had the same pressurization capability (100 percent) and average coach-seat speed (100 percent) as the intrastate carriers' aircraft.

Table 9-6

Multiple Linear Regression Equations for Investigating the Impact of Price and Service Quality Differences on the California Intrastate Carriers' Market Shares Using Four Independent Variables

Market	Regression Equations[a] (and the Standard Errors of the Coefficients)					R	R^2	$\bar{S}_y$
	Constant	Price Diff.	Seat Share	Pressur- ization	Seat Speed			
LAX-SFO	$Y = 25.485$	$+\ 3.049X_1$ (0.338**)	$+\ 1.084X_2$ (0.125**)	$-\ 0.033X_3$ (0.031)	$-\ 0.274X_4$ (0.083**)	.986	.972	2.131
			Durbin-Watson = 1.610					
LAX-SAN	$Y = 4.454$	$+\ 0.347X_1$ (1.866)	$+\ 0.837X_2$ (0.151**)	$-\ 0.031X_3$ (0.070)	$+\ 0.112X_4$ (0.195)	.951	.904	5.102
			Durbin-Watson = 2.591					
SAN-SFO	$Y = 72.059$	$-\ 0.171X_1$ (0.534)	$+\ 0.246X_2$ (0.121″)	$-\ 0.021X_3$ (0.044)	$-\ 0.091X_4$ (0.152)	.600	.359	4.407
			Durbin-Watson = 2.221					

[a] In addition to the specified constant and variable terms, each equation contains a residual term (z) representing the effects of still other variables in causing differences between the observed and calculated market shares. The classical linear model (using least squares estimation procedures) assumes the expected value of z equals zero—that is, it is a random variable. The SAN–SFO regression, however, appears not to conform with this assumption.

″ Significant between 0.10 and 0.05.

** Significant at 0.01 or less.

Sources: Multiple linear regression analyses computed from data for 1952–65 presented in Tables 9–1 through 9–5, using the stepwise regression computer program described in Dixon (ed.), *BMD Biomedical Computer Program*, pp. 233ff. G. W. Snedecor, *Statistical Methods* (5th ed.; Ames, Iowa: The Iowa State University Press, 1956), p. 46. J. Durbin & G. S. Watson, "Testing for Serial Correlation in Least Squares Regression. II," *Biometrica* 38 (1951), pp. 159–77.

efficients are inconsistent with the overall hypothesis, as are the signs for the seat-speed variable for Los Angeles–San Diego and the price-difference variable for San Diego–San Francisco. The Los Angeles–San Diego market has a high R and R^2, but it also has a relatively large standard error of estimate, whereas, unlike the other two markets, the R and R^2 for San Diego–San Francisco are quite small. Given all this, it appears that the three regression analyses do not give consistent results which can be pointed to as strong evidence of the relative impact of price and service quality differences on market shares.

Since the variables used in these regression analyses were obtained from time series, it may be that a statistically significant amount of autocorrelation is present in the data. Should this be the case, there is reason to question the stability of correlation coefficients between series calculated over different time periods and thus the general applicability of the standard errors of these coefficients.[5] The presence of positive autocorrelation was tested by calculating the Durbin–Watson d statistic from the residuals for each regression equation. At the 0.05 level of significance, this test was inconclusive for the Los Angeles–San Francisco market, and indicated no positive autocorrelation for the Los Angeles–San Diego and San Diego–San Francisco markets.[6]

There is some question about using seat share data as an independent variable in the regression analyses. First, the number of scheduled coach seats was used to calculate the weighted average coach-seat prices and coach-seat speeds, and the pressurization variable was based on the percentage of certificated carriers' coach seats that were provided in aircraft having the same pressurization capability as the intrastate carriers' aircraft. Obviously, the number of scheduled coach seats underlies or influences every other independent variable used in the above analyses. Second, it is possible that market share and seat share are little more than two measures of the same thing. Given some quality of service (determined by factors other than the number of seats operated) and some level and structure of prices, if the actual amount demanded in a period is less than expected one would predict a decrease in the quantity of service supplied in following periods until the preferred relationship between amounts supplied and demanded is achieved—that is, until the mar-

[5] M. Ezekiel and K. A. Fox, *Methods of Correlation and Regression Analysis* (New York: John Wiley & Sons, Inc., 1959), p. 327.

[6] J. Durbin and G. S. Watson, "Testing for Serial Correlation in Least Squares Regression. II," *Biometrica* 38 (1951), pp. 161–62, 173.

ginal cost of operating the final unit of seats equals the marginal revenue expected from the sale of some portion of those seats. Thus, a carrier group's seat share may be essentially another measure of its market share, after allowing for some optimal load factor which, in turn, is a function of the level and structure of prices and of service quality. Because of this question about seat share, it seemed appropriate to recalculate the regression analyses excluding seat share as an explicit independent variable. The results of this recalculation are given in Table 9-7.[7]

Comparing the results in Table 9-7 with those in Table 9-6 brings out several important differences. First, the values of R and R^2 for each of the equations with three independent variables are smaller than those for the comparable four-variable equations. In fact, they are so small for the San Diego-San Francisco market that it appears there is little or no relationship between market shares and the three independent variables. Second, the standard errors of estimate are all larger for the more limited analyses than for the analyses based on four independent variables. Third, there are appreciable changes in the signs and statistical significances of the various coefficients. Not only does the pressurization coefficient become statistically significant for the first two markets (especially for the Los Angeles-San Diego market) but its sign in the equations for these markets changes from negative to positive, thereby becoming consistent with the overall hypothesis. On the other hand, the coefficient for the seat-speed variable for Los Angeles-San Francisco changes from being significant at the 0.01 level to just failing to be significant at the 0.10 level. As before, the price-difference coefficient is statistically significant for the Los Angeles-San Francisco market, but it decreases in value from 3.0 to 2.3, indicating a relatively smaller impact of price differences on market share. The most surprising change in the price-difference variable is the negative sign of its co-

---

[7] Even if market share and seat share are completely different variables, there may be reasons to exclude the seat-share variable from the regression analyses. For example, should there be substantial intercorrelation between it and other independent variables, these other variables will pick up most of the significance level attributed to seat share in Table 9-6, thereby retaining the high values of R^2. To the extent this occurs, the multiple regression equations in Table 9-7 should be preferred, statistically speaking, to those in Table 9-6. Or, if, as it happens, the values of R^2 in Table 9-7 are all lower than those of Table 9-6, it still may be desirable at this stage of quantitative research regarding the relative effects of price and service quality, to delete the seat-share variable if by so doing the levels of significance of the "t" statistic of one or more of the other independent variables are increased, thereby indicating an otherwise obscured relationship between them and market share.

Table 9-7

Multiple Linear Regression Equations for Investigating the Impact of
Price and Service Quality Differences on the California Intrastate Carriers' Market Shares
Using Three Independent Variables

Market	Regression Equations[a] (and the Standard Errors of Coefficients)				R	R^2	$\bar{S}_y$
	Constant	Price Diff.	Pressurization	Seat Speed			
LAX-SFO	$Y = 48.780$	$+\ 2.305X_1$ (0.858*)	$+\ 0.138X_3$ (0.068")	$-\ 0.307X_4$ (0.241) Durbin-Watson = 1.060	.860	.739	6.185
LAX-SAN	$Y = -25.021$	$-\ 5.772X_1$ (2.992")	$+\ 0.280X_3$ (0.087**)	$+\ 0.605X_4$ (0.346) Durbin-Watson = 1.432	.760	.577	10.157
SAN-SFO	$Y = 82.949$	$-\ 0.698X_1$ (1.027)	$-\ 0.022X_3$ (0.050)	$+\ 0.008X_4$ (0.165) Durbin-Watson = 2.417	.258	.066	5.046

[a]See note a of Table 9-6.
"Significant between 0.10 and 0.05.
*Significant between 0.05 and 0.01.
**Significant at 0.01 or less.

Sources: Multiple linear regression analyses computed from data for 1952–1965 presented in Tables 9-1, 9-2, 9-4, and 9-5, using the stepwise regression computer program described in Dixon (ed.), *BMD Biomedical Computer Program*, pp. 233ff. Snedecor, *Statistical Methods* (5th ed.), p. 46. Durbin and Watson, "Testing for Serial Correlation in Least Squares Regression. II," *Biometrica* 38 (1951), pp. 159–77.

efficient in the Los Angeles–San Diego equation, even though the coefficient is significant between 0.10 and 0.05. This is inconsistent with the overall hypothesis, since it implies that in this market the intrastate carriers attracted fewer rather than more passengers as the price difference increased—that is, as their fares became lower relative to those of the certificated carriers. Finally, the Durbin–Watson test for positive autocorrelation was inconclusive for both the Los Angeles–San Francisco and the Los Angeles–San Diego markets. Only in the San Diego–San Francisco market did this test indicate no positive autocorrelation at the 0.05 level of significance.

Implications of the Regression Analyses

Obviously, the findings of the regression analyses are inconclusive since they have two important inconsistencies. First, within each set of analyses, the results for the Los Angeles–San Francisco market differ substantially from those for the other two markets. Second, the coefficients between comparable equations in the two sets of analyses experience changes in both signs and statistical significance. These two inconsistencies show that the overall hypothesis excludes important factors which influence market share, and/or that the relationships between the selected variables and market share are not linear (or logarithmic). Even though the findings of the multiple regression analyses are inconclusive, however, an examination of possible reasons for their inconsistencies does shed some light on other factors affecting market shares.

Turning to the short-haul Los Angeles–San Diego market, a logical explanation can be proposed for the inconsistency that was found in the sign of the price difference variable between the two sets of analyses. Table 9–2 shows that this market had the smallest range of price differences among the three major California markets. For the first seven of the 14 years from 1952 through 1965, the average price differences ranged from zero to 65 cents; the next seven years had differences ranging from $1.10 to $3.21, with most of these being less than $2.50. It seems reasonable to believe that these generally small price differences would play a relatively unimportant role in influencing traveler choice in this market. Perhaps there is a "threshold" level of price difference which must be exceeded before this variable has a statistically significant impact on changes in market share. This possibility is supported by the fact that the price difference variable is significant and has the predicted sign in both of the regression equations for Los Angeles–San Francisco where the greatest price differences existed among the three major markets (ranging from minus 79 cents to plus $6.67, with most differences exceeding $3.00).

A similar threshold amount of variation seems to apply to the seat-speed variable in the Los Angeles–San Diego market, which also was not statistically significant in either regression analysis. Calculations based on the data in Table 9–5 show that for all but one year (1960) the average time differences for the nonstop flights operated by the two carrier groups in this market were six minutes or less on flights of 30 to 50 minutes. It seems reasonable to expect that such small absolute differences in elapsed times would have little impact on passenger choice. Both of these examples of threshold amounts of variation call the use of linear regression analysis into question since they imply discontinuous rather than continuous functional relationships.

In contrast to the small differences in prices and seat speeds in this market, there were large differences in pressurization between the two carrier groups. Even over the short distance between Los Angeles and San Diego, aircraft are flown high enough for passengers to experience appreciable changes in atmospheric pressure if their aircraft is not pressurized. One would therefore expect pressurization to influence passenger choice. The statistical significance of the pressurization coefficient in the three-variable regresssion equation for this market is consistent with this reasoning, but the relationship is clouded by the lack of significance when the seat-share variable is included in the four-variable equation. Also, in some ways the usefulness of the pressurization variable in the regression analyses actually suffers from its abrupt fluctuation in value. To the extent that pressurization serves as a proxy for other aircraft characteristics, it is obvious that its great changes in value (from 100 to 0 and back to 100) do not accurately measure the obsolescence of the intrastate carriers' aircraft relative to that of the certificated carriers' aircraft. A smaller fluctuation would have more accurately represented changes in overall aircraft characteristics and would have been better suited for use in computing the regression equations.

A review of the data underlying the regression analyses for the San Diego–San Francisco market indicates that there is even a logical explanation for the inconsistent signs and lack of significant coefficients in the equations for this long-haul market. Table 9–5 shows that the intrastate carriers' (essentially PSA's) policy of usually making only one intermediate stop between San Diego and San Francisco resulted in their offering faster block-to-block speeds than the certificated carriers during each of the years studied, regardless of aircraft operated. Table 9–4 shows that the pressurization capabilities of the certificated carriers' aircraft were comparable to those of the intrastate carriers' aircraft for more years in this market than in the other two markets. During only three years (1957–59) did the certificated carriers enjoy an appreciable advantage in this service quality variable. Table 9–2 shows that the average price differences— while greater than between Los Angeles and San Diego—never exceeded $4.44, compared with the high of $6.67 for Los Angeles–San Francisco. Finally, Table 9–3 shows that the intrastate carriers provided between 52.9 and 89.5 percent of total coach seats scheduled in this market (note that the seat-share coefficient given in Table 9–6 was significant between 0.10 and 0.05). Overall, the intrastate carriers consistently outperformed, outproduced, and underpriced the certificated carriers in this long-haul market. If a traveler wanted to fly between San Diego and San Francisco on coach service, the obvious way to do so was via an intrastate carrier, regardless of any changes that occurred in the intrastate carriers' price and service quality relative to that of the certificated carriers.

The coach market share data given in Table 9–1 clearly illustrate the dominance of the intrastate carriers in this market. From 1952 through 1965, they transported between 70 and 90 percent of all coach passengers, 81 percent being both the median and modal value for these 14 years. Given this situation, it is not surprising that the multiple regression analyses failed to identify any statistically significant variable other than seat share.

Why did the certificated carriers fail to operate more and better coach service in this market and endeavor to carry at least half of the total coach traffic as they did in the other two markets? While San Diego–San Francisco was not as large as the other two major California markets, in 1948 (prior to the massive entry of the intrastate carriers) it was still the eighty-fourth largest market in the United States, and in 1965 it ranked twenty-third in total on-line O & D passenger volume among the nation's markets.[8] Appendix 14(C) of this book shows that the total traffic in this market grew from about 22,000 on-line O & D passengers in 1948 to 359,000 in 1965. Therefore, it would seem large enough to warrant the certificated carriers' best efforts. The answer to the above question primarily involves PSA, since it consistently carried more traffic in this market than any other carrier, and beginning in 1956 it transported more than half of all traffic between San Diego and San Francisco, reaching a high of

[8] CAB, *Airline Traffic Survey* (March and September 1948). San Diego–San Francisco/Oakland ranked eighty-fourth in true O & D passenger volume during both survey periods. Also, CAB, *Competition Among the Domestic Airlines* (1965), and Appendix 14(C) of this book.

79 percent in 1962–64. The key factor appears to lie in the different locations of the operating bases of the carriers serving this market. PSA was (and is) based in San Diego, whereas California Central/ Coastal, Trans California, United, and Western all had their major operating bases at Los Angeles or Burbank.[9] Since base location plays an important role in airline scheduling, it is not surprising to find that until 1960 nearly all of PSA's flights were scheduled to operate between San Diego and San Francisco (via Los Angeles or Burbank), with very few turnaround flights scheduled between Los Angeles/Burbank and San Francisco. Also, PSA was the first carrier to schedule occasional nonstop flights between San Diego and San Francisco (mainly on Friday and Sunday evenings). In contrast, the other carriers scheduled the majority of their California coach service between Los Angeles and San Francisco and generally operated only multistop service between San Diego and San Francisco.[10] Thus, even though PSA was always much smaller than United and Western, and was even smaller than California Central, it appears that its base in San Diego gave it a comparative advantage in serving the San Diego–San Francisco market that the other carriers could not match because of their locations in Los Angeles.

The physical constraints of this book preclude a more thorough study of the relationships between market shares, on the one hand, and price and service quality differences, on the other. They also prevent considering the whole matter of advertising and other demand-increasing marketing efforts, not to mention such factors as service termination by CCA and other intrastate carriers, the public's general opinion of the relative performance of the two carrier groups, changes in business and government travel policies, etc. It isn't even feasible to investigate the evidence provided by the above analyses that individual price and service quality factors may have different effects in different markets.[11] However, by permitting the systematic

[9] United moved its major system maintenance base from Chicago to San Francisco in 1948. This did not, however, result in the replacement of Los Angeles by San Francisco as United's largest operations base in California. Telephone conversation with United Airlines' News Bureau, San Francisco, June 5, 1967.

[10] This schedule information was obtained from the airline schedules listed in the source for Appendix 15 of this book. Also, compare the weekly seat data for PSA with that for the other carriers given in Appendices 15(A), 15(B), and 15(C).

[11] For example, San Diego's relatively large military population may have been attracted by low prices earlier and more rapidly than were the business travelers who probably comprised a larger portion of the traffic generated in Los Angeles or San Francisco. "As of this date we have carried over 63,000 passen-

investigation of the degree to which the factors represented by the four independent variables affect or fail to affect market shares, the multiple regression analyses do provide some basis for indicating where other factors are particularly important; and the above review of what appear to be relevant factors does provide insights into the reasons for the levels and variations of the intrastate carriers' market shares.

Conclusion

It is not easy to understand and predict the actions of individuals, even where such a "simple" matter as choosing between rival carrier groups is concerned. In two of the three major California markets, changes in price differences, as measured here, either had no significant relationship with market shares, or else had a relationship (of limited statistical significance) that was inconsistent with that hypothesized. Only in the Los Angeles–San Francisco market, where the greatest price differences existed, was there an indication that such differences played a significant role in influencing market share in the manner hypothesized. Much the same conclusion applies to service quality factors. Only seat share was statistically significant in every market, but its usefulness as an explanatory variable was reduced by the possibility that it provides little more than just another measure of market share. In the case of the Los Angeles–San Diego market, the inconsistencies in signs and the lack of statistical significance for the price difference and seat speed coefficients can be rationalized by pointing to the small absolute differences existing in these variables in this short-haul market. In the San Diego–San Francisco market, the almost complete lack of association between market share and the independent variables appears to be due to the intrastate carriers' (mainly PSA's) superiority in all aspects of price and service quality. These more detailed studies are helpful in understanding the effectiveness of various means of rivalry in these particular markets, but they are not very useful in predicting the relative importance of price and service quality differences in other markets.

Probably the most important finding of this chapter is that lower prices alone were not enough to allow the intrastate carriers to become ever more effective rivals of the certificated carriers. While

---

gers more than 9,000,000 passenger miles. 65% of these passengers have been enlisted service personnel." Letter to the California PUC from Kenneth G. Friedkin, President of PSA, March 2, 1951. Contained in Exhibit No. 20 (submitted March 27, 1951), Cal. PUC, Case No. 5271. (Decision No. 45624, 50 Cal. PUC 563 [1951].)

price differences (including taxes) in the order of $12.77 ($24.21 vs.
$11.44), such as existed between Los Angeles and San Francisco
during 1949 and early 1950, were sufficient to account for large
diversions of passengers to the intrastate carriers, once the certificated carriers obtained permission from the CAB to operate substantial day-coach service at comparable and then somewhat higher fares,
the rapid growth of the intrastate carriers came to an end (see Table
9–1). It was not until late 1959, when PSA greatly improved the
quality of its service by introducing Electra aircraft, that the intrastate carriers once again began to encroach on the market shares of
the certificated carriers in the Los Angeles–San Francisco and Los
Angeles–San Diego markets. Thus, it appears that in order to become
important participants in a major California market where the certificated carriers operated significant coach service, the intrastate
carriers had to offer *both* significantly lower prices *and* comparable
or superior service quality.

This conclusion can be supported by several specific instances.
For example, Trans California relied on price differences to promote
its service between Los Angeles and Oakland, but lower prices proved
to be insufficient to secure its survival once Western provided substantial Thriftair service in this market. California Central greatly
improved its service quality and market share in late 1951 and early
1952 with the introduction of Martin 202 aircraft. Despite this
superior service, however, CCA's long decline began with its independent fare increase in June 1952, which gave it prices higher than
the coach prices of the certificated carriers and PSA. Finally, PSA
came to dominate the San Diego–San Francisco market by consistently offering lower prices, shorter block-to-block times, and more
coach seats than any other carrier.

A brief review of first-class traffic volumes during these years
adds another perspective to the analysis of coach market shares given
in this chapter. Table 9–1 shows that, despite the rapid expansion of
coach service, first-class traffic continued to increase in absolute
volume in the three major California markets until 1957 or 1958,
whereupon it suffered a rapid decline. Two things happened in the
late 1950's that probably contributed greatly to this sharp decline
during the 1960's. First, the first-class common fares on the West
Coast were terminated in the across-the-board fare increase of
October 1958.[12] This resulted in large increases in the first-class
fares for travel within the California markets for passengers

<hr>

[12] Cherington, *Airline Price Policy*, p. 339. Also, see Table 4–2, chapter 4 of
this book.

originating in the East, thereby increasing the relative appeal of coach service to such passengers. Second, this period saw the great expansion of coach service provided in dual-configured aircraft that coincided with the introduction of jet aircraft in late 1958 and 1959. During the next few years many business firms, governments, etc., adopted policies that required their employees to utilize coach service whenever it was available. Not only did this result in a decrease in first-class traffic—both within California and in interstate markets—but it substantially increased the potential market from which the intrastate carriers could draw traffic. Clearly, PSA's introduction of its high-quality Electra service took place at a time when the demand for its coach service was undergoing a substantial increase—that is, its demand schedule was shifting to the right. It would have been difficult for PSA to have chosen a better time for this move, and its fully comparable, if not superior, coach service quality combined with lower prices proved to be extremely effective in attracting passengers from the certificated carriers.

Survival and Profits

Introduction

Of the sixteen intrastate carriers that operated within California between1946 and 1965, all but two terminated service by the end of 1965. Such a large proportion of failure implies, among other things, that the fares adopted by the intrastate carriers were too low to support profitable operations. However, this high rate of attrition must not be allowed to detract from the fact that two carriers did manage to survive while charging low fares, that some of those who terminated service did so because of noneconomic factors, and that one of the terminating carriers did provide a substantial amount of service for over six years. These examples of economic survival would seem to be more important than the many failures, since the surviving carriers demonstrated that success was possible under the conditions existing within California during this period. It follows that such service could also be successful outside of California under similar circumstances (including the relative lack of regulation).

The first part of this chapter will review the extent to which intrastate carriers survived. Then, the few available financial statements of the major California airlines will be studied to determine the profits (in the accounting sense) made by these carriers. In addition, Pacific Southwest Airlines' (PSA) operating ratios and rates of return on stockholder equity will be compared with those of the certificated carriers to provide a basis for evaluating the performance of the most successful intrastate carrier. Finally, some implications regarding airline economies of scale will be examined. Overall, this chapter investigates the economic viability of low-fare airline service.

The Evidence of Survival

Eight of the 16 carriers that operated large aircraft within California between 1946 and 1965 did so for only one to six months (see Appendix 1 of this book). Their short periods of service would seem to disqualify their being considered viable attempts to become established in the California markets.[1] The remaining eight carriers (the so-called major carriers) survived for nine months or more. One of these, PSA, has managed to survive since May 1949, even though, with the exception of a few years in the early 1960's, it charged the lowest fares per mile available within California. Its performance alone shows that low fares were not a sufficient condition for failure in these markets, a conclusion buttressed by the successful operation of Mercer Enterprises since early 1964.

Of the six major intrastate carriers that terminated service, the information given in chapter 2 shows that at least two of them clearly did so for noneconomic reasons. Paradise Airlines terminated operations because the Federal Aviation Agency suspended its commercial operator certificate following the crash of its Constellation on March 1, 1964. The transcript of the Civil Aeronautics Board hearing in which Paradise unsuccessfully appealed the FAA's action shows that the owner of Paradise was eager to resume operations.[2] He was convinced that Paradise's service under its existing fares was viable and was prepared to test that conviction.

Similarly, there is no question that Western Air Lines of California (WALC) also discontinued service for noneconomic reasons. Its operations were terminated simply because Western Air Lines (the trunk carrier) finally obtained permission from the CAB to introduce day-coach service at fares equal to those offered by WALC and the other intrastate carriers (see chapter 5). Given this permission, Western canceled its extensive leasing arrangements with WALC (thereby causing WALC's demise) and introduced an identical service under its own name. It is hard to believe that Western would have introduced and maintained extensive low-fare coach service in the major California markets had it thought the service provided by WALC (for which it had complete information) was not profitable. The following indicates Western's estimate of the profitableness of its

---

[1] Chapter 2 contains brief summaries of the reasons for the service terminations of these carriers.

[2] Transcript of the hearings before CAB Examiner S. Thomas Simon in: *N. E. Halaby, Administrator, Federal Aviation Agency, Complainant* v. *Paradise Airlines, Inc., Respondent*, Docket No. SE-462, March 20 to April 7, 1964.

proposed service in the Los Angeles/Burbank–San Francisco/Oakland market:

We can, therefore, summarize the estimated results under Methods 2(A) and 2(B) as follows:

	Estimated Profit—Fully Allocated Cost Basis for Year Ended June 30, 1951	
	Method 2(A)	Method 2(B)
Total Revenues	$1,468,406	$1,468,406
Operating Expenses: Direct aircraft operating expense including depreciation	570,628	570,628
Gross profit on direct costs	$ 897,778	$ 897,778
Ground and indirect costs	553,336	573,222
Net profit before taxes	$ 344,442	$ 324,556

We are convinced from our forecast of proposed operation of the special intrastate air coach service between Los Angeles and San Francisco–Oakland *that such operation would prove to be profitable* to Western Air Lines, Inc. We should point out, however, that the forecasted profits do not include any loss to Western as a result of diversion from its first class service. As we have previously stated such diversion would occur in any event. (Italics added.)[3]

It should be noted that while Western believed low-fare service was viable, it did not believe such service maximized the profits available from this market. Clearly, the certificated carriers would have preferred the continuance of the situation existing prior to 1949 when they alone offered service under first-class fares that were more than twice the initial coach fares of the intrastate carriers. Given, however, the introduction of low-fare service by the intrastate carriers and the resulting "diversion" of traffic from first-class to coach service, Western and United chose to match these low fares and service rather than limit themselves to carrying only first-class passengers. They would not have done so had such low-fare service

[3] Western Air Lines, "Memorandum on Behalf of Western Air Lines, Inc., to Accompany Special Intrastate Air Coach Tariff for Service between Los Angeles and San Francisco–Oakland Filed with the Civil Aeronautics Board on March 27, 1950," p. 19. Also, see the quotation associated with footnote 13, page 79, of this book.

been unprofitable, nor would WALC have been sustained by Western had its service incurred significant losses.

Two of the eight major intrastate carriers terminated service through bankruptcy proceedings. Bankruptcy may be a clear indication of uneconomic operations, but it does not tell whether fares were too low or costs too high. Indeed, one of these two carriers, Pacific Air Lines, adopted the certificated carriers' relatively high, first-class fares for its service. For the Burbank–San Francisco market, Pacific's fare in 1946-47 was more than 50 percent higher than the coach fare introduced in 1949 ($15.15 vs. $9.95). Thus, for whatever reasons Pacific went bankrupt, it did not do so because it charged low fares.

California Central Airlines (CCA) was the second of the major carriers to go bankrupt. Of course, it did charge low fares so that they could have been a factor in its service termination. Four factors, however, seem to be relevant in evaluating this possibility. In the first place, during 1952 CCA led the other carriers in *increasing* the Los Angeles/Burbank–San Francisco/Oakland fare from $11.70 to $13.50 (together with the $1.80 increase in the associated San Diego–San Francisco/Oakland fare), and this action was followed by a sharp reduction in its 1953 and 1954 traffic (see Appendix 14 of this book). A former CCA executive asserted that this fare increase played a major role in weakening CCA's financial position.[4] Second, the analysis of CCA's financial statements (see the following section) shows that its costs increased substantially during 1953 even though its traffic volume decreased. Third, the owners of CCA reinstituted service with California Coastal Airlines shortly after CCA's assets had been sold in bankruptcy, and they did so at fares equal to or lower than those in effect prior to the bankruptcy proceeding. This does not indicate that they thought low fares were the crucial factor in CCA's bankruptcy. Finally, it should be remembered that CCA managed to survive for over six years prior to its bankruptcy. Thus, at the very least, its low fares did appear to cover average costs for a significant part of this period.

The evidence from the remaining two major carriers is not as clear. California Coastal Airlines operated for over two years, during which time it lowered rather than increased its fares. Thus, it appears that higher fares were not considered viable by its management. The fact remains, however, that California Coastal did gradually reduce its service and eventually transferred its equipment to the

---

[4] Conversation with Mr. Robert P. Hubley, former General Sales Manager, California Central Airlines, August 19, 1965.

nonscheduled operations of its associated company, Airline Transport Carriers, indicating that more profitable opportunities existed in the services provided by that latter company.

Trans California Airlines (TCA) did not lower its fares during the more than two years it operated from 1962 to 1964. On the other hand, neither did it increase its fares, even though it could easily have done so by merely removing one passenger seat from the cabin of each of its aircraft.[5] The former president of TCA attributed its failure not to its low fares but to the loss of traffic that resulted when Western inaugurated Thriftair service between Los Angeles and Oakland in June 1964.[6]

In summary, two of the eight major intrastate carriers did manage to survive while charging low fares, whereas, of the six carriers that terminated service, two clearly did so because of noneconomic factors. Thus, at most, the attrition due to economic considerations was no more than 50 percent. Of the four carriers whose service terminations appear to have been due to economic factors, one charged high first-class fares, so that low fares cannot be blamed for its failure. The actions of the other three major carriers indicate that at least their managements thought low fares were not the critical factor in their failure to survive. In their cases it appears that either rival service by other carriers prevented their achieving viable levels of output or that their modes of operation were such that average costs exceeded those attainable under alternative operating procedures.

In the evaluation of the viability of economic activities in an open market, it is the fact of survival that is crucially important. Other measures of performance are secondary. This section has shown that some of the intrastate carriers did survive, and this provides hard evidence about the economic viability of low-fare service wherever conditions exist similar to those existing within California during the period studied.

The Evidence from Financial Statements

The earliest available financial information regarding the intrastate carriers is that presented by the PUC's staff in the 1949-50

---

[5] Trans California's PUC-approved tariff provided for a one-way fare of $10.99 between Los Angeles/Burbank–Oakland for piston-powered aircraft having a capacity of 98 or more seats. A fare of $11.49 was specified for a 97-seat piston-powered aircraft. (Trans California Airlines, Inc., tariff, Cal. P.U.C. No. 1, originally effective August 15, 1962, original p. 22.) Throughout its existence, TCA carried 98 seats in its L-749 aircraft.

[6] Conversation with Mr. L. A. Mudgett, May 24, 1965.

investigation of the "reasonableness" of the intrastate carrier's low fares.[7] The conclusion of this study was that the operations of the intrastate carriers as a group during the first ten months of 1949 were profitable, and that CCA and WALC earned rates of return after taxes in excess of 10 percent.[8]

The few individual income statements that could be located for the major intrastate carriers are presented in Appendix 16 of this book. It proved impossible to obtain any financial information for Pacific Air Lines and for California Coastal Airlines, but since Pacific went bankrupt in 1947 and California Coastal gradually terminated its service from 1956 through mid-August 1957, it seems likely that both of their income statements showed losses.

Abbreviated income statements are available for California Central for almost all of its six years of operations (see Appendix 16[A]). Starting with February 1, 1949 (one month after it inaugurated service), and extending through December 31, 1953, CCA's operating revenues totaled $7,172,000, and operating expenses (including depreciation) totaled $7,292,000. This resulted in an overall operating loss of $120,000 and an operating ratio (total operating expenses divided by total operating revenues) of 101.7 percent—hardly an outstanding performance, and one that appears to forecast the approaching bankruptcy of CCA. An inspection of the data for the various time periods, however, shows that CCA had operating profits for the two months ended March 31, 1949, and for the years ended March 31, 1951 and 1952. Indeed, the really major loss (of $126,000) occurred during the nine months ended December 31, 1953, a period in which CCA experienced a 37-day strike of its maintenance employees that curbed operations during July 1953 (a peak traffic month).[9] It should be noted that the fiscal year in which CCA had its greatest profit was that ending on March 31, 1951. This was the last full year of DC-3 operation, and for eleven of the twelve months, the low $9.99 fare was in effect between Los Angeles and San Francisco. CCA's profit performance with the Martin 202 (introduced on August 31, 1951) and with the $11.70 and $13.50 Los Angeles–San Francisco fares was poorer than under its earlier combination of aircraft and fares.

[7] Cal. PUC, *Intrastate Scheduled "Coach Class" Air Carriers*, by C. J. Astrue, Exhibit No. 1-C, pp. 42–60; Exhibit No. 2-C, p. 2; Exhibit No. 5-C, p. 4, Cal. PUC Case No. 4994, *et al.*

[8] 49 Cal. PUC 494, 497 (1950).

[9] U.S. District Court, Southern District of California, Files of the Court Clerk, Bankruptcies Nos. 59560-PH and 59561-PH (filed January 27, 1954), California Central Airlines, *History, Development and Analysis of California Central Airlines* (n.d.), Appendix B, p. 31.

The income statement for the period from January 28 to December 31, 1954, covers the first eleven months that CCA operated under the general direction of the court-appointed bankruptcy referee, although its owners actually controlled operations as debtors in possession.[10] It shows that the large rate of loss experienced during the last nine months of 1953 had been reduced and an operating loss of only $25,000 was incurred during these eleven months. The operating ratio was 101.4 percent, or just under the average for the previous five years. Net nonoperating expenses increased the loss for this period to about $39,000, but noncash depreciation charges of $110,000 resulted in a positive operating cash flow. This indicates that CCA was on the road to regaining a viable operation, but apparently it was too late to overcome the losses of 1953.

It is beyond the scope of this study to delve more deeply into the reasons for CCA's bankruptcy. The effects of the strike were certainly harmful; the one-year lease of an L-049 aircraft from July 1952 through June 1953 (at a fee of $330,000) proved to be extremely detrimental to both Airline Transport Carriers and CCA; the unilateral fare increase of June 15, 1952, resulted in a sharp reduction in traffic, etc. The important point for this study, however, is that through 1952, CCA's operations were marginally profitable under the relatively low fares then in effect.

Western Air Lines of California's income statement for the period from August 19, 1949, through January 31, 1950, shows a loss of $22,800 after taxes on total revenues of $596,500 (see Appendix 16[B]). The monthly breakdown for this 5½-month period shows, however, that most of this loss was incurred in January 1950. Only small losses were experienced in August and November 1949, with profits being earned in the other months. During this period, WALC paid Western Air Lines a total of $556,466 in charter fees. This should be compared with Western's estimate of $570,628 for direct aircraft operating expenses, including depreciation, for a similar, if not identical, schedule pattern covering the *entire year* ending June 30, 1951 (see the above quotation from Western's memorandum to the CAB dated March 27, 1950). This implies that any profits made by WALC's operation were captured by Western through its leasing fees. Of course, this is consistent with the effective control exercised by Western over WALC throughout its lifetime.

The financial information for the major intrastate carriers that operated in the 1960's, Paradise, Trans California, and Mercer Enterprises, are given in Appendices 16(C), 16(D), and 16(E), respectively.

[10] *Ibid.*, "Order of Referee" (filed December 8, 1954).

From April 6 to December 31, 1962, Paradise made a small operating profit, but nonoperating expenses resulted in a loss of $332. The record for all of 1963 indicates operating losses of over $25,000 and total losses of $37,000. But, it is important to note that total revenues in 1963 were $616,000 compared with just over $150,000 for the eight to nine months of service in 1962. This large increase in revenues combined with the extraordinary operating expenses, due to the introduction of L-049 service in April 1963, may have been the reason why the owner of Paradise was so eager to continue service after the fatal accident on March 1, 1964.

The very limited data for Trans California (see Appendix 16[D]), indicate that it enjoyed a net profit before taxes of $22,000 during the eleven months ended March 31, 1964. It happens that this figure may be misleading, since no aircraft leasing charges are shown in this unaudited statement, which was submitted to the FAA in connection with TCA's unsuccessful effort to have its commercial operator certificate renewed. During this eleven-month period, TCA operated 3,120 flight hours with its L-749 aircraft.[11] TCA's leasing agreement with California Airmotive called for a rate of $100 per flight hour to cover aircraft leasing and overhaul charges, plus $50 per hour for maintenance,[12] but only about $65,000 are shown in this income statement for aircraft maintenance (rather than $156,000); and the entire $312,000 leasing/overhaul charge is missing. Since a close relationship existed between TCA and California Airmotive, it is possible that the agreed upon leasing rates were above existing market prices. Regardless of this possibility, it seems clear that the income statement significantly understated TCA's true expenses and that the company did suffer a serious loss during this period. Whether TCA's loss for these eleven months should be attributed to low fares or to other factors cannot be deduced from these data. It is relevant to note, however, that during more than two years of operations, TCA failed to achieve a 50 percent load factor;[13] therefore, it seems proper to conclude that important factors other than low fares contributed to its losses.

Mercer Enterprises was one of the two surviving intrastate carriers as of December 31, 1965. One would expect, therefore, a more favorable income statement for this carrier, and generally speaking,

[11] FAA, Western Region, Monthly Air Carrier Aircraft and Engine Utilization Report, Trans California Airlines (May 1963 to March 1964).

[12] Conversation with Mr. L. A. Mudgett, former President of Trans California Airlines, May 24, 1965.

[13] Calculated from data presented in Appendices 3 and 4 of this book.

that proves to be the case. Mercer's income statements for 1964 and 1965 (see Appendix 16[E]) show total operating revenues of $128,000 and $177,000, respectively, with common carrier revenues being essentially constant at $69,000 and $66,000. An operating profit of almost $41,000 was earned in 1964, with net income before taxes of $38,000. Nineteen sixty-five shows an operating loss of $2,349 with a net income before taxes of just over $12,000, due largely to capital gains. Notice that income taxes are not shown. Since Mercer Enterprises was a sole proprietorship during those years, it is not possible to calculate income taxes without information regarding the owner's personal tax status. Also, note that the expenses for these two years do not include the manager's (owner's) salary.

One reason for the loss shown in 1965 is that during the last quarter of that year Mercer incurred substantial expenses in inaugurating a contract service with the U.S. Military Air Transport Service. Information for the first six months of 1966 shows military contract revenues of $250,000 out of a total of $339,000 and net income before taxes of $62,750.[14] Obviously, Mercer's common-carrier service is only one part of its total operation, but the fact that it has retained this very short-haul, weekend scheduled service implies that it is economically viable, even though offered under low fares.

Table 10-1 summarizes the financial information for PSA that is presented in Appendix 16(F).[15] This table shows that in every year for which information is available PSA made an operating profit and also earned a profit after taxes. True, the profit for 1960 was nearly zero, but this was the first full year of PSA's Electra operations and the year the FAA ordered this aircraft operated at reduced speeds pending the modification of its wing and engine support structure.[16] During this period many passengers shunned the Electra (regardless of the airline operating it). The abnormal situation of that year is emphasized by the large profits PSA earned in the preceding and subsequent years.

The operating ratios given in Table 10-1 appear to have been related to the type of aircraft operated by PSA. Those for both 1950 and 1955 were around 96 percent. During those two years PSA

[14] Cal. PUC, Exhibit No. 5 (submitted August 9, 1966), Application No. 48157. (Decision No. 71490 [dated November 1, 1966].)

[15] Income statements for the years prior to 1957 could not be obtained from PSA, and only limited data for 1950, 1955, and 1956 were available from PUC records.

[16] CAB, *Handbook of Airline Statistics*, p. 491.

Table 10-1

Selected Financial Data, Operating Ratio, and Return on Stockholder Equity
Pacific Southwest Airlines, Various Years 1950-1965

Year	Total Operating Revenues	Total Operating Expenses	Profit after Taxes[a]	Stockholder Equity[b]	Operating Ratio[c]	Return on Stockholder Equity[d]
1950	$ 505,988	$ 489,939	n.a.	n.a.	96.8%	n.a.
1955	1,587,697	1,523,385	$ 243,997[e]	n.a.	95.9	n.a.
1956	2,264,850	2,144,385	58,588	n.a.	94.7	n.a.
1957	3,126,254	2,727,079	196,606	$ 86,550	87.2	227.2%
1958	3,929,921	3,267,309	322,031	n.a.	83.1	n.a.
1959	4,775,993	3,867,215	455,901	1,057,609	81.0	43.1
1960	8,130,483	8,109,688	499	n.a.	99.7	0.0
1961	10,300,293	9,173,116	310,483	n.a.	89.1	n.a.
1962	14,204,915	10,803,179[f]	1,368,770	3,007,734	76.1	45.5
1963	17,852,448	12,900,409[f]	2,251,719	7,429,810	72.3	30.3
1964	20,773,372	14,827,433	2,945,881[g]	10,075,046	71.4	29.2[g]
1965	24,015,261	19,605,184	2,034,932[g]	11,504,770	81.6	17.7[g]

n.a.—not available.

[a]Profit after taxes and special items.
[b]As of December 31, of each year.
[c]Total operating expenses divided by total operating revenues.
[d]Profit after taxes and special items divided by stockholder equity.
[e]Includes gain of $206,150 on sale of DC-3 aircraft. Excluding this gain yields profit after taxes for 1955 of $37,847.
[f]Reported total operating expenses reduced by $100,000 (1962) and $55,000 (1963) by deletion of investment tax credit that was added to provision for obsolescence and depreciation during those years.
[g]Includes provisions for investment tax credit.

Source: Appendix 16(F) of this book.

operated DC-3 aircraft (DC-4's were introduced on November 10, 1955), its fare level was virtually the same (its Burbank–San Francisco/Oakland fare was $9.95 in 1950 and $9.99 in 1955), and it operated over about the same route structure. Thus, it appears that the effects of inflation were balanced by economies resulting from increases in the volume of output and from greater experience in operating DC-3's, and that 96 percent was about as low a ratio as could be attained with DC-3's under such low fares. The operating ratios for DC-4 service started at 94.7 percent in 1956 and fell each year until reaching 81.0 percent in 1959; however, this reduction was helped by the April 14, 1958, fare increase. The introduction of Electras on November 20, 1959, ushered in a new era in PSA's operating ratios. Starting at 99.7 percent in 1960, by 1964, the last full year of all-Electra service, the ratio had declined to 71.4 percent, due in part to the fare increase of December 12, 1960, which raised the Los Angeles–San Francisco fare from $11.81 to $13.50. The mixed operation of Electras and B-727-100's in 1965 raised the operating ratio to 81.6 percent, and its reduction to 76.8 percent in 1966 seemed to maintain the old pattern. The ratio increased, however, to 83.8 and 86.1 percent in 1967 and 1968, when the Electras were retired and PSA's fleet was expanded to include DC-9-30's, B-737-200's, and B-727-200's.[17] Thus, the decreasing trend found with DC-4's and Electras has yet to be established with PSA's all-jet operation.

The very limited information regarding return on stockholder equity suggests an outstanding performance for the years since 1957 (again with the exception of 1960). The 227 percent return of 1957 was due as much to the very low level of stockholder equity for that year (about $87,000) as to the level of profits.[18] But the 43.1 percent return in 1959 was with stockholder equity of over $1 million, and the 45.5 percent return in 1962 was on an equity base of $3 million. These rates of return were too high to sustain, especially in a market with open entry. In fact, these high returns are consistent with the new entry that occurred in 1962 after a seven-year hiatus, and with Western's introduction of Thriftair service in that same year. However, the 30 percent returns of 1963 and 1964, and even the 17.7 percent return of 1965, are still outstanding.

[17] Pacific Southwest Airlines, *Annual Report*, 1966, 1967, and 1968.

[18] The small amount of equity in 1957 indicates that losses may have been incurred by PSA in some of the earlier years for which data are not available. For example, the fluctuations in PSA's fares during 1954 indicate that losses might have been sustained in that year.

PSA Compared with the Certificated Carriers

The certificated trunk and local service carriers' operating ratios and returns on stockholder equity provide yardsticks with which to evaluate PSA's performance. The operating ratios for total trunk and total local service carriers are presented in Table 10-2, together with those for Western Air Lines, Pacific Air Lines (the local service carrier), and PSA. The data for Western and Pacific are presented because they, of all the trunk and local service carriers, had the greatest portions of their operations within California and, so, are more likely than other certificated carriers to be affected by the regional factors (if any) affecting PSA.

A comparison of the median and range for each of these series of operating ratios shows that the trunk carriers generally had lower ratios than did the local service carriers, despite the relatively large direct subsidy payments received by the local service carriers.[19] Within the trunk carrier group, Western usually enjoyed below average (superior) operating ratios (a median value of 88.7 percent for Western vs. 92.0 percent for all trunk carriers). Similarly, during these 17 years, Pacific's median ratio was 95.0 percent, compared with 98.3 percent for all local service carriers. In addition, both Western and Pacific had larger intervals in their ranges of operating ratios than their peers did. This is significant because interval size is mainly determined by the low operating ratio in each series, since high ratios all tend to cluster around 100 percent (airlines having ratios much above 100 percent for significant time periods have difficulty surviving).

It has already been pointed out that PSA's operating ratios appear to have been substantially affected by the type of aircraft it operated. Until late 1955, PSA operated the same type DC-3 aircraft that Pacific and the other local service carriers operated during those same years. Thus, it is not surprising to find that PSA's operating ratios were similar to those of Pacific and of all local service carriers during this period, despite the large subsidies received by the local service carriers. The impact of four-engine aircraft can be seen in PSA's ratios for 1957 (the second full year of its DC-4 service) and

[19] For example, in 1954, the first year in which subsidy payments were segregated from air mail payments, 0.4 percent of the trunk carriers' total operating revenues consisted of subsidy, compared with 43.0 percent for the local service carriers. By 1965, 0.1 percent and 22.7 percent, respectively, of trunk and local service carriers' total operating revenues were derived from subsidy payments. Calculated from data presented in CAB, *Handbook of Airline Statistics* (1961 ed.), pp. IV-4 and IV-7; and (1967 ed.), pp. 222 and 225.

Table 10-2

Operating Ratios for Total Trunk and Local Service Carriers
Western Air Lines, Pacific Air Lines, and Pacific Southwest Airlines
1949–1965

| Year | Operating Ratio[a] | | | | |
| | Trunk Carriers[b] | | Local Service Carriers | | |
	Total	Western	Total	Pacific	PSA
1949	94.6%	92.2%	102.1%	94.4%	n.a.
1950	88.1	88.7	97.8	88.2	96.8%
1951	83.9	83.4	97.9	98.4	n.a.
1952	87.6	83.8	102.6	95.0	n.a.
1953	89.9	88.7	103.1	104.0	n.a.
1954	89.8	92.3	97.1	92.2	n.a.
1955	89.2	85.9	98.8	96.0	95.9
1956	92.0	90.8	100.9	103.1	94.7
1957	97.0	88.1	100.9	100.9	87.2
1958	93.7	95.9	98.3	103.4	83.1
1959	94.1	81.5	99.5	97.5	81.0
1960	98.2	90.9	98.5	102.8	99.7
1961	100.5	97.6	94.7	91.6	89.1
1962	96.7	90.6	93.5	93.8	76.1
1963	94.7	81.5	94.7	95.0	72.3
1964	89.4	78.4	93.3	90.2	71.4
1965	87.2	82.4	91.7	90.0	81.6
Median	92.0	88.7	98.3	95.0	85.2[c]
Range	83.9–100.5	78.4–97.6	91.7–103.1	88.2–104.0	71.4–99.7*

n.a.—not available.
*Estimated.

[a]Total operating expenses divided by total operating revenues.
[b]Domestic operations only.
[c]Based on data for 12 years rather than 17 years.

Sources: Calculated from data presented in Appendix 16(F) of this book; and
in CAB, *Handbook of Airline Statistics* (June 1960 ed.), pp. 111, 116,
and 134; (1961 ed.), pp. IV–26, IV–31, and IV–44; and (1967 ed.),
pp. 93, 95, 245, and 254.

for later years. From 1957 through 1965, PSA's ratios were much
more comparable with those of the trunk carriers than with those of
the local service carriers. In fact, they were even *lower* than the

operating ratios of the trunk carriers and Western, even though PSA's fares per mile were significantly lower than those of these larger carriers, and it did not receive any air mail revenue. Overall, to the extent that operating ratios indicate efficiency, it appears that PSA was generally more efficient than the trunk or the local service carriers. Not only did it have the lowest median operating ratio (85.2 percent) but the interval of its range (28.3 percentage points) exceeded Western's interval (19.2 percentage points) as well as the interval for the total trunk carriers (16.6 percentage points).

The returns on stockholder equity for these same carriers and carrier groups are summarized in Table 10-3. These data show that, at least since 1957, PSA has generally achieved higher rates of return than those of the certificated carriers. Rates above 30 percent appear to have been common for it in contrast to the highs of 21.6 percent for total trunk carriers, 25.5 percent for Western, and in comparison with the 18 percent cost of equity specified by the CAB as being fair and reasonable for the smaller trunk carriers.[20] The negligible return of 1960 was due to the Electra problem and was not repeated in subsequent years; 1965 seems to be the only other year during the period studied when PSA's rate of return was below those of the two total carrier groups and Western. The 1965 results are not surprising, however, considering the greatly increased service and price rivalry given PSA by United and Western (see chapters 5 and 9), and considering the fact that PSA added five B-727-100's to its fleet between April and August 1965, thereby more than doubling its capacity and incurring the costs of introducing a new aircraft type.

Implications Regarding Economies of Scale

The above financial data and the experience of the California intrastate carriers indicate that most economies of scale attainable in airline operations can be achieved by small airlines operating a few aircraft over small (in terms of the number of cities served) route structures. If large operations are required to achieve major economies of scale, then the operating ratios of PSA should have been higher than those of Western (which has always been much bigger than PSA) and even higher than those of Pacific during the 1950's

---

[20] In its 1960 decision in the *General Passenger Fare Investigation,* Docket No. 8008, the CAB found the fair and reasonable cost of equity to be 16 percent for the Big Four trunk carriers and 18 percent for the remaining trunk carriers. Assuming, as did the CAB, that the Big Four accounted for two-thirds of total trunk investment, the weighted average cost of equity for all trunk carriers would be 16.7 percent. 32 CAB 291, 300 (1960).

Table 10-3

Return on Stockholder Equity for Total Trunk and Local Service Carriers
Western Air Lines, Pacific Air Lines, and Pacific Southwest Airlines
1951–1965

| Year | Return on Stockholder Equity[a] | | | | |
| | Trunk Carriers[b] | | Local Service Carriers | | |
	Total	Western	Total	Pacific	PSA
1951	17.9%	17.5%	13.5%	6.6%	n.a.
1952	18.5	15.0	−1.9	10.3	n.a.
1953	14.0	8.3	−6.3	−7.5	n.a.
1954	13.9	14.4	14.2	10.3	n.a.
1955	14.8	17.0	7.5	18.9	n.a.
1956	11.9	22.5	−4.4	−6.6	n.a.
1957	4.8	15.5	−11.4	2.1	227.2%
1958	7.7	9.2	10.7	−7.2	n.a.
1959	9.6	24.8	0.5	23.6	43.1
1960	0.0	8.5	14.8	−10.9	0.0
1961	−5.2	2.2	21.2	15.2	n.a.
1962[c]	1.2	11.7	19.2	6.1	45.5
1963[c]	1.9	21.6	13.0	−0.9	30.3
1964[c]	17.1	25.5	16.3	26.4	29.2
1965[c]	21.6	19.6	19.3	14.2	17.7
Median	11.9	15.5	13.0	6.6	n.a.
Range	(−)5.2–21.6	2.2–25.5	(−)11.4–21.2	(−)10.9–26.4	0.0*–227.2*

n.a.—not available.
*Estimated.
[a]Profit after taxes and special items divided by stockholder equity. The certificated carriers' return is based on the arithmetic mean of stockholder equity at the end of the 12-month period a year ago and at the end of each quarter of the current 12-month period. PSA's return is based on stockholder equity as of December 31, of each year.
[b]Domestic operations only.
[c]Includes provisions for investment tax credit.

Sources: Calculated from data presented in Appendix 16(F) of this book. Also, CAB, *Handbook of Airline Statistics*, (1961 ed.), pp. IV–4, IV–7, IV–26, IV–31, and IV–44; (1967 ed.), p. 385.

(when Pacific was bigger than PSA). This was not the case, however. PSA's operating ratios were generally equal to Pacific's during the years they both operated DC-3's (despite Pacific's larger size, higher fares, and subsidy receipts), and they were consistently lower than Western's once PSA adopted four-engine aircraft.

It might be argued that PSA's lower operating ratios for 1957-59 compared with 1950 and 1955, and its even lower operating ratios for 1961-64, provide evidence of increasing economies of scale. As discussed above, however, these lower operating ratios appear to be associated with the type of aircraft operated (DC-3, DC-4, or Electra) rather than with the size of operations. Note that throughout these years PSA's fleet never exceeded six aircraft. In fact, PSA never operated more than four DC-3's at one time (from August 1952 to November 1955), and four was the maximum number of DC-4's in its fleet (from June 1957 to December 1959).[21] Would anyone arguing that domestic airlines experience significant economies of scale be content to set the top limit of such economies during this period at the output of six aircraft?[22]

The survival over significant time periods of Mercer Enterprises and California Central Airlines (with total revenues of $128,000 and $177,000 for Mercer in 1964 and 1965, and from $1 to $2 million for CCA during 1950-54) provides additional evidence that important economies of scale can be achieved by small carriers. The fleets of these and other intrastate carriers were miniscule in comparison with those of the trunk carriers during the same time periods (see Appendix 5 of this book). Yet, it was possible for some of these small intrastate carriers to be profitable with fares per mile much lower than those of the certificated carriers.

Overall, the evidence provided by the intrastate carriers relative to the certificated carriers seems to be consistent with decreasing rather than increasing economies of scale. In any case, it is certainly inconsistent with the hypothesis that there were significant economies of scale in U.S. domestic airline operations through the mid-1960's over those attainable with, say, five aircraft of a given type.[23]

[21] PSA Company Records, and the records of the FAA, Western Region (see Appendix 5 of this book).

[22] Caves quotes several executives of trunk carriers regarding the minimum number of an aircraft type that can be "successfully used" or "efficiently maintained" by a carrier. Their estimates ranged from five to six units of a large jet aircraft, to seven or eight for a medium size jet, to ten for a turboprop aircraft. Caves, *Air Transport and Its Regulators*, pp. 91 and 317. Note that these estimates pertain to a single aircraft type within an airline operating several types of aircraft.

[23] Other studies have found increasing economies of scale between small and medium sized U.S. domestic certificated carriers, but little or no difference between medium and large carriers (if anything, they reported slightly decreasing economies of scale for the largest carriers). See H. D. Koontz, "Economic and

If this is indeed true, it becomes obvious that the CAB's control of entry has been very important to the existing certificated carriers. Without such entry control the experience of the California intrastate carriers implies that many more carriers would now be operating within the U.S. and that many other carriers would have operated at various times over a large number of small, simple route structures (see chapter 2). This, of course, would have increased the rivalry that the "grandfather" carriers would have otherwise experienced after 1938. There is little question that nonregulated airlines would not have evolved into a natural monopoly because of economies of scale. Quite the contrary, a prediction of fragmentation seems to be more reasonable than one of concentration.

Conclusion

This chapter shows that it has been possible for some airlines to survive and operate profitably within California under relatively low fares. Indeed, the fact of survival is persuasive evidence of the viability of such fares. PSA was consistently the intrastate carrier with the lowest fares and it survived and prospered throughout the period studied; California Central did well for several years before succumbing to the effects of such actions as an independent fare increase, a costly aircraft lease, and a strike; Mercer was successful in providing a very limited service at low fares; and several carriers operated until having to terminate service because of noneconomic factors. In addition, the actions of United and Western in the early 1950's and, again, in 1962-65 show that they preferred to offer low-fare service rather than accept a declining traffic share in the major markets. Overall, four or more carriers have consistently operated in the Los Angeles–San Francisco and Los Angeles–San Diego markets, whereas three or four carriers have operated between San Diego and San Francisco. Clearly, fares per mile substantially below those resulting from the CAB's across-the-board fare increases have proved to be high enough to attract and support extensive airline service in the major California markets ever since 1949.

Managerial Factors Underlying Subsidy Needs of Domestic Trunk Line Air Carriers," *Journal of Air Law and Commerce* 18, no. 2 (Spring 1951), pp. 127–56; Wheatcroft, *The Economics of European Air Transport*, pp. 76–93, esp. pp. 78–81; and Caves, *Air Transport and Its Regulators*, pp. 55–61. The California intrastate carriers would be classified as small domestic carriers. The findings of this study, therefore, question even the differences between small and medium sized airlines found in the above studies. Koontz recognized this possibility in his early article and went on to hypothesize that "route, more than any other factor explains the profit or loss characteristics of domestic trunk carriers" (p. 149).

If only very large airlines had been able to survive while providing low-fare service, this would provide evidence that economies of scale exist in the airline industry. The fact is, however, that the smallest of airlines introduced low-fare service and that at least one of these managed to survive while achieving operating ratios and returns on stockholder equity comparable or superior to those of the much larger certificated carriers operating under substantially higher average fares per mile. This indicates that there are no significant economies of scale in domestic air transportation that cannot be achieved by a carrier operating four or five aircraft of a suitable type over a small route structure. It follows from this that without regulation the U.S. airline industry would probably consist of many small carriers rather than a few very large ones.

Resource Utilization

11

Introduction

How was it possible for Pacific Southwest Airlines (PSA), Mercer Enterprises, and some of the other intrastate carriers to achieve profits with low fares per mile when the certificated carriers required much higher fares per mile to earn profits from their interstate operations? There appears to be no one simple answer to this question, and it seems likely that many large and small differences in operating practices combined to enable the surviving intrastate carriers to operate at lower costs than the certificated carriers. Indeed, one would expect that the ability of an airline to achieve low average costs would have a particularly high survival characteristic in the California markets where fares were low and where entry and exit were unimpeded by government regulation.

On the other hand, it may be that operating conditions in the major California markets (and in similar high-density interstate markets) naturally yield average costs that are lower than those attainable in smaller markets, so that the certificated and intrastate carriers' costs were about the same in these markets while being substantially different on a system-wide basis. If this is correct, it follows that the almost universal application of the Civil Aeronautics Board's fare policies and increases to all markets, regardless of their cost characteristics, results in large profit potentials in California-type interstate markets, even greater profit potentials in high-density, long-haul markets, and, of course, only low profits or even losses in short-haul, low-density markets.

Actually, low-cost carrier operations and low-cost markets are not mutually exclusive, and both could have existed within California during the period under study. That is to say, the intrastate

196

carriers may have been lower cost operators than the certificated carriers, *and* the major California markets may have been served by all carriers at costs that were lower than those required to serve smaller markets. Information is not available with which to investigate the direct effects of market characteristics on airline costs. It is possible, however, to study differences in carrier operating practices to determine whether they were an important source of differences in operating costs. This chapter will be devoted first to examining differences in aircraft utilization, and then to examining differences in personnel productivity. Together, these two types of resources— aircraft (capital) and personnel (labor)—provide the major inputs purchased by airlines; therefore, they probably account for a substantial part of the cost differences attributable to carrier operating practices.

Aircraft Utilization

The following three measures indicate the overall intensity with which aircraft are utilized by airlines:

1. The average number of revenue hours per day that each aircraft is operated (a measure of airframe utilization).
2. The number of seats installed in each aircraft type for a given class of service (which indicates the extent to which the aircraft's interior is used).
3. The average passenger load factor (which measures the degree to which the installed seats are utilized).

If a carrier flies its aircraft more hours each day, installs more seats in a given aircraft type for some class of service, and sells a higher percentage of those seats on each flight than other carriers, then it clearly utilizes its aircraft resources more intensively than the other carriers. In the following three subsections, the certificated and the intrastate carriers will be compared with respect to these three measures.

Revenue Hours per Aircraft per Day. Table 11-1 presents much of the fragmentary information that is available regarding the average number of revenue hours per day that the intrastate carriers operated their aircraft. In addition, comparable data for the certificated trunk and local service carriers are also presented. These data show that in 1964 three of the intrastate carriers had much lower daily aircraft utilizations than PSA, the trunk carriers, or the local service carriers. Of these three, California Time (with 1.8 hours per aircraft per day) was a short-lived carrier that obviously failed to find a significant

Table 11-1

Average Number of Revenue Hours per Aircraft per Day
Certificated and California Intrastate Carriers
All Services, Selected Years 1952-1964

Year	Average Number of Revenue Hours per Aircraft per Day[a]						
	Total Certificated		California Intrastate				
	Trunk	Local Service	CCA	CTA	Mercer	PSA	TCA
1952	7.3	6.0[b]	5.4	–	–	8.0	–
1955	7.7[c]	6.0	n.a.	–	–	7.3	–
1958	7.5	6.5	–	–	–	6.6	–
1961	5.9	5.4	–	–	–	7.0	–
1964	6.5	5.5	–	1.8[d]	0.8[e]	8.7	2.1[f]

n.a.—not available.
[a]Calculated by dividing the number of aircraft days assigned to service into revenue aircraft hours flown.
[b]Scheduled service only.
[c]Excludes a small number of hours flown by Eastern with aircraft not assigned to its fleet. Also, excludes National's helicopter operation.
[d]California Time Airlines operated from September 19, 1964, through February 1, 1965. This figure applies to this entire period.
[e]Mercer Enterprises inaugurated scheduled service on or about April 18, 1964. This figure applies to its first full 12 months of operation from May 1964 through April 1965.
[f]Trans California Airlines terminated service on October 7, 1964. This figure applies to its operation from January 1 through October 7, 1964.

Sources: Air Transport Association of America, *Comparative Statement of Flight and Traffic Statistics* (12 Months Ending December 31, 1952 and 1955). ATA, *Quarterly Comparative Statement of Air Carriers' Aircraft Operating Statistics* (12 Months Ending December 31, 1958, 1961, and 1964). Federal Aviation Agency, Western Region, Monthly Air Carrier Aircraft and Engine Utilization, California Time Airlines, Mercer Enterprises, Pacific Southwest Airlines, and Trans California Airlines. California Central Airlines and Pacific Southwest Airlines, Company Records.

demand for service between San Jose/Oakland, Burbank and Palm Springs. Since Mercer operated scheduled service only on weekends, its 0.8 hour per aircraft per day is not surprising. Daily service would have increased its aircraft utilization (but not necessarily its passenger load factor). Trans California's low utilization rate of 2.1 hours per day was due to its leasing arrangement with California Airmotive, whereby it agreed to keep four to five aircraft maintained and operable so that they would be immediately available for sale should such an opportunity present itself.[1] Actually, two aircraft could have adequately covered its schedule pattern and would have brought its average aircraft utilization up to almost five hours per day.

In contrast to these cases of very low aircraft utilization, the two largest intrastate carriers—California Central and PSA—appear to have been able to achieve utilizations generally equal to or above those of the local service carriers and quite comparable to the averages for the trunk carriers. While PSA had a higher average daily utilization than the trunk carriers in three out of the five years given in Table 11-1, its 6.6 to 8.7 hours per aircraft per day always fell within the annual range of daily aircraft utilization by the individual trunk carriers.[2] Similarly, California Central's 5.4 hours per day in 1952 was close to the lowest individual trunk carrier's (TWA) daily utilization of 5.7 hours for that same year.[3] Since the trunk carriers' routes have always been longer than those of the intrastate carriers, their average stage lengths have been greater, and longer flights tend to increase average daily utilization (by decreasing relative ground time). The intrastate carriers, therefore, may be penalized somewhat by a system-wide comparison with trunk carriers. At the same time, the intrastate carriers' average stage lengths have been greater than those of the local service carriers, thereby improving their showing relative to that group.[4] Overall, it seems proper to conclude that, aside from identifiably unique situations, the intrastate carriers utilized their aircraft about as intensively as the trunk carriers, and did somewhat better in this respect than most local service carriers.

Number of Seats Installed per Aircraft. A different situation emerges with regard to the number of seats installed in each aircraft. First, the intrastate carriers operated very little of what might be classified as first-class service. Aside from Pacific Air Lines' (the intrastate carrier) service in 1946–47, all intrastate carrier aircraft were operated in essentially high-density configuration, whereas the certificated carriers operated a large number of aircraft in low-density, first-class configuration.[5] This alone served to increase the average number of seats installed in the intrastate carriers' aircraft

---

[1] Conversation with Mr. L. A. Mudgett, former President of Trans California Airlines, May 24, 1965.

[2] CAB, *Handbook of Airline Statistics* (June 1960 ed.), pp. 4–20; and (1967 ed.), p. 391.

[3] CAB, *Handbook of Airline Statistics* (June 1960 ed.), pp. 4–20.

[4] See chapter 1, page 11 of this book.

[5] See chapter 3 of this book.

compared to the average number of seats in similar aircraft operated by the certificated carriers.

Putting aside the effects of class of service on the average number of seats per aircraft, a direct comparison between coach-configured aircraft shows that significant differences existed in the seating configurations of the carrier groups. As can be seen from the data in Table 11-2, with the exceptions of California Central's DC-4, PSA's initial DC-4 configuration, and the L-049's, the intrastate carriers consistently installed more seats in their aircraft than the certificated carriers did in their coach versions of the same aircraft.[6]

The relatively short routes and flight stage lengths of the intrastate carriers may facilitate the installation of more seats in a given cabin area since passenger comfort and payload restrictions are less critical on such stage lengths than they are on the longer stage lengths over which the certificated carriers operate their aircraft outside of California. Both United and Western, however, assigned special aircraft to serve just the major California markets, and even these aircraft had seating configurations that were not as dense as those adopted by PSA. Western's DC-6B Thriftair aircraft contained 92 seats, compared to the 98 seats PSA installed in its DC-6B; and United's B-727-100 Jet Commuter aircraft had 113 seats, compared to the 122 in PSA's B-727-100's. These differences of 6.5 and 8 percent are not tremendously large, but they are similar to the other differences shown in Table 11-2, thereby indicating that the certificated carriers did not limit the number of coach seats because of their longer stage lengths.

Given the strict physical dimensions of the interior of any aircraft, and given the consistency with which the intrastate carriers installed more coach seats within each aircraft type, it is clear that these carriers did utilize the cabins of their coach-configured aircraft more intensively than did the certificated carriers. When the certificated carriers' first-class or mixed-class configured aircraft are included to provide fleet-wide comparisons, the intrastate carriers' relative cabin utilization becomes even more intensive than that of the CAB-regulated airlines.

Passenger Load Factors. The final measure of aircraft utilization to be considered is average annual load factor—the percentage of

---

[6] The certificated carriers were Pacific, Trans World, United, and Western. Although individual carriers have slightly different configurations for the same aircraft type and class of service, industry sources show that the configurations of these four carriers were representative of the other certificated carriers for these years.

Table 11-2

Coach Seating Configurations for Aircraft Operated within California
by Both the Certificated and the California Intrastate Carriers
1949–1965

Aircraft Type	Certificated Carrier	No. of Seats	California Intrastate Carrier	No. of Seats	Intrastate % of Certificated
DC-3	United	—[a]	CCA	28 & 32	—
	Western	—[a]	PSA	28 & 31	
	Pacific	—[a]	Others	28	
M-202	Pacific	40	CCA	44	110%
DC-4	TWA	62	CCA	60	97–111
	United	64 & 66	PSA	62 & 70	
	Western	66	Others	73	
L-049	TWA	80 & 81	Futura	81	100–101
			Paradise	81	
L-749	TWA	—[b]	TCA	98	—
DC-6B	United	79	PSA	98	103–124
	Western	87, 92, 95			
Electra	Western	94 & 96	PSA	98	102–104
B-727	United	113	PSA	122	108

[a]The certificated carriers did not operate their DC-3's in coach configuration within California. United and Western installed 21 first-class seats in their DC-3's, while Pacific installed 28 such seats.

[b]TWA did not operate its L-749's in coach configuration within California. Its maximum first-class seating configuration for L-749's was 55 seats.

Sources: Company records, general schedules, various publications, correspondence, and telephone inquiries. Seating configuration data were collected from these sources by this writer over a ten-year period beginning in 1957. CAB, *Airline Statistics Handbook* (Calendar Years 1946–52), n.d., p. 66. CAB, Docket No. 10321, Air Carrier Reports for March 31, 1959. FAA, Western Region, various documents and reports. Cal. PUC, *Intrastate Scheduled "Coach Class" Air Carriers*, Exhibit No. 1-C (submitted December 14, 1949), pp. 25–38, Cal. PUC Case No. 4994, *et al.*

total seats flown that were actually occupied by revenue passengers. Table 11-3 presents load-factor data for the three carrier groups from 1946 through 1965, and shows that the trunk carriers' first-

Table 11-3

Average Annual Passenger Load Factors
for the Certificated and California Intrastate Carriers
Scheduled Service, 1946-1965

Year	Passenger Load Factor (Percent)		Total Cert. Local Service[a]	Total Intrastate[b]
	Certificated Trunk			
	First Class	Coach		
1946	78.8%	—	37.9%	n.a.
1947	65.7	—	29.8	n.a.
1948	58.5	72.9%[c]	27.1	—
1949	58.7	70.2	28.2	66.9
1950	61.2	74.2	31.5	73.9
1951	68.9	74.5	37.4	69.0
1952	65.3	75.6	37.5	65.9
1953	62.2	72.8	38.6	67.1
1954	61.2	68.2	42.2	69.2
1955	62.3	67.6	45.2	72.2
1956	62.4	67.3	45.8	75.7
1957	59.4	65.1	45.2	80.6
1958	58.9	61.7	45.7	72.4
1959	59.5	64.1	44.4	71.1
1960	56.1	63.3	41.9	71.1
1961	51.6	60.2	41.6	72.1
1962	46.6	57.6	42.3	75.3
1963	51.7	54.9	43.8	72.8
1964	49.9	57.8	46.4	74.9
1965	49.0	57.7	47.3	63.3

n.a.—not available.

[a]Some local service carriers operated small amounts of coach service in 1952-53 and from 1956 to early 1965. Their coach load factors were generally above their first-class load factors and, overall, equaled 51.3 percent. However, due to the limited quantity of coach service, the total local service load factor was no more than 0.3 percentage points above the first-class load factor in any one year.

[b]Partially estimated, includes all services.

[c]Coach service inaugurated November 4, 1948.

Sources: CAB, *Handbook of Airline Statistics*, pp. 50, 54, and 57. Calculated from data presented in Appendices 3 and 4 of this book.

class load factors ranged downward from 78.8 percent in 1946 and 68.9 percent in 1951, to a low of 46.6 percent in 1962. In comparison, their coach load factors ranged from 75.6 percent (1952) to

54.9 percent (1963) and were consistently 3 to 14 percentage points higher than those for their first-class service. Because the low average load factors for the local service carriers set them apart from the other two carrier groups, they will not be considered further in this section. It should be noted, however, that their low load factors are consistent with their large subsidy payments. If the local service carriers' subsidy payments were converted to passenger equivalents, their resulting passenger-plus-subsidy load factors would be much higher than their actual load factors.[7]

The most significant comparison is between the trunk carriers' coach load factors and the total load factors for the California intrastate carriers. From 1949 through 1953 (the end of the Korean War), the trunk carriers' coach load factors were generally above those of the intrastate carriers. Overall, during those five years the trunk carriers managed to fill 73.9 percent of their available coach seat miles, compared to the 69.8 percent the intrastate carriers filled (disregarding the denser seating configurations of the California carriers' aircraft).[8] In every year following 1953, however, the California intrastate carriers' average load factor exceeded that for the trunk carriers' coach service by amounts ranging from 1.0 percentage point in 1954 to 17.9 percentage points in 1963. From 1955 through 1964, the intrastate carriers' average annual load factor never fell below 70 percent and reached a high of 80.6 percent in 1957. Over the 12-year period from 1954 through 1965, their weighted mean load factor was 71.2 percent, compared to a 12-year average of only 59.1 percent for the trunk carriers' coach operations—a difference of 12.1 percentage points.[9]

As was discussed above in relation to cost differences, it may be that these large load-factor differences were due primarily to the differing characteristics of the markets served by the two carrier groups, or they may have been due in large part to different operating procedures resulting from management decisions and policies

[7] For example, during 1965 the local service carriers' 47.3 percent passenger load factor was obtained by carrying passengers paying a total of $203,423,000. Adding the $66,012,000 in subsidy payments to these passenger revenues yields an equivalent passenger-plus-subsidy load factor of about 62.7 percent. Calculated from data presented in CAB, *Handbook of Airline Statistics,* pp. 135 and 225.

[8] Calculated from data presented in CAB, *Handbook of Airline Statistics* (June 1960 ed.), p. 2; and in Appendices 3 and 4 of this book.

[9] Calculated from data presented in CAB, *Handbook of Airline Statistics* (1965 ed.), p. 132, and (1967 ed.), p. 132; and in Appendices 3 and 4 of this book.

that were quite independent of market characteristics. The best way to test which of these was the primary reason would be to compare the load factors of all turnaround flights operated by the certificated and intrastate carriers solely in the three major markets—that is, flights scheduled to serve mainly local traffic. Large differences in the load factors of such flights would imply that management decisions were primarily responsible for the carriers' performance, whereas inconsequential differences would indicate that market characteristics were the important factor. Unfortunately, such detailed information is not available. In fact, only system-wide load factor data are publicly available for the certificated carriers, and one of the intrastate carriers had a policy of not divulging information that would permit the direct calculation of even its system-wide load factors.[10] It is therefore necessary to rely upon indirect analyses to investigate the reasons for differences in overall coach load factors.

Several factors serve to indicate that different market characteristics were not the primary reason for the trunk carriers' lower coach load factors. First, prior to the widespread adoption of dual-configured jet aircraft in the early 1960's (see Tables 3–2 and 3–3 in chapter 3), the trunk carriers confined coach service to their high-density markets and provided only first-class service in relatively low-density markets. From 1954 through 1959, coach traffic accounted for 33 to 44 percent of total trunk RPM,[11] but even in this period the trunk carriers' coach load factors ranged from 1.0 to 15.5 percentage points under those of the intrastate carriers.

Second, as pointed out in chapters 2 and 6, the intrastate carriers also served several minor markets within California. Although the three major California markets did generate most of the traffic carried by the intrastate carriers as a group, it appears that the overall range of traffic densities for markets having coach service was greater for the intrastate carriers than for the trunk carriers. During the period studied, trunk carriers did not operate coach service in mar-

[10] It proved possible to calculate system load factors for this carrier through indirect methods.

[11] CAB, *Handbook of Airline Statistics*, p. 58. The extent to which domestic traffic is concentrated in a relatively few high-density markets is shown by origin and destination passenger data. For example, during 1961 the top 100 city-pair markets accounted for 41.1 percent of total certificated carrier O & D passengers, and the top 500 markets included 67.0 percent of such passengers. This is out of a total of 40,142 city pairs between which passengers were reported to have traveled that year. See CAB, *Handbook of Airline Statistics* (1962 ed.), p. 426.

kets as small as Burbank-Inyokern, Lake Tahoe-Oakland/San Jose, or Burbank-Brown Field, etc.

Finally, a comparison of system load factors for individual intrastate carriers shows that high average load factors were achieved in minor as well as in major markets. For example, Paradise achieved load factors of about 69 percent in its Lake Tahoe-Oakland/San Jose service during 1963 and early 1964, while Mercer Enterprises' load factor between Burbank and Brown Field was about 76 percent from April 1964 through 1965. In contrast, Trans California's average load factor was just 44 percent during its more than two years of service in 1962-64, even though it operated in the relatively major markets of Oakland-Burbank-Los Angeles-San Diego.[12] These performances are inconsistent with the hypothesis that high load factors result from serving high-density markets.

In contrast to the above findings, it seems reasonable to conclude that management decisions do play an important role in determining load factors. In the first place, high load factors could "easily" be achieved by the certificated carriers if all of their managements "simply" adopted the policy that flights would not be scheduled if they did not consistently operate at, say, a 70 percent load factor. Given various marketing (demand-increasing) activities that could be implemented, varieties of aircraft that could be utilized, levels of service quality that could be offered, and the relatively high marginal revenue resulting from the certificated carriers' fare level and structure, such a policy would probably not yield maximum profits, but it would increase average load factors. Another way to do this would be to lower the fare level. As fares decreased, greater numbers of passengers would be required on each flight in order to equate marginal revenues with marginal costs (other things held constant), and airline managers would be motivated to schedule flights to achieve higher load factors in order to maximize profits under the new fares. (Conversely, increases in fare levels would promote lower load factors.) Of course, the differences in fare levels for the certificated and intrastate carriers, described in chapter 5, are consistent with the observed differences in load factors between these carrier groups. Still another discretionary way to increase load factors would be to change the number of scheduled flights in accordance with daily, weekly, and seasonal (annual) fluctuations in traffic. Thus, fewer flights would be scheduled to depart at 3 A.M. than at 8 A.M. each day, fewer flights would be operated on Saturdays than on Fridays,

---

[12] Calculated from data presented in Appendices 3 and 4 of this book.

and fewer daily flights would be scheduled during February of any year than during the following August when traffic is at its seasonal peak.[13]

It happens that some data are available regarding traffic and schedule fluctuations in the three major California markets that support the hypothesis that management decisions did play a significant role in the intrastate carriers' achievement of relatively high load factors. PSA reported that Friday and Sunday each accounted for something over 21 percent of its total weekly traffic, with the other five days each accounting for between 10.5 and 13.0 percent.[14] Generally speaking, business travel predominates on Monday through Thursday, then on Friday and Sunday afternoons and evenings there is a large volume of weekend personal and pleasure travel which results in traffic peaks. Given such a predictable weekly traffic fluctuation, a concurrent fluctuation in schedules should yield a higher average load factor than if the same number of flights were distributed equally over the week so that 14.3 percent of total weekly flights were operated each day.

Table 11-4 gives the percentage of total weekly seats scheduled on Friday and Sunday (combined) in the three major California markets by the certificated and California intrastate carriers at various times from 1948 to 1965. This table shows that the certificated carriers' schedules were much less responsive to weekly traffic fluctuations than were those of the intrastate carriers. Indeed, it turns out that the median percentages of weekly seats operated by the certificated carriers on Friday and Sunday were 28.6 and 28.7 percent for both first-class and coach service in all three markets. This is the percentage that would be obtained if all flights were operated seven days a week—that is, 2/7 = 28.6 percent. In contrast, the intrastate carriers' Friday and Sunday median percentages were 35.8 percent for Los Angeles-San Francisco, 28.1 percent for Los Angeles-San Diego, and 31.2 percent for San Diego-San Francisco.

The intervals of the ranges for each series in Table 11-4 provide an even better idea of the relative scheduling flexibility of the two carrier groups. With two exceptions, the intervals for the certificated carriers are smaller than three percentage points, thereby indicating

[13] Seasonal traffic variations for the trunk carriers are given in CAB, *Air-Passenger Traffic Data Seasonally Adjusted Domestic Trunk Operations by Carrier and Class of Service, 1953-1964* (Washington, D.C.: CAB, December 1964).

[14] Conversation with Mr. H. N. Wood, Vice President-Sales, Pacific Southwest Airlines, May 13, 1965. Mr. Wood stated that this pattern had been in effect for a number of years.

Table 11-4

Percentage of Total Weekly Seats Scheduled on Friday and Sunday[a]
in the Three Major California Markets
by the Certificated and the California Intrastate Carriers
Selected Dates 1948-1965

	Percent of Total Weekly Seats Scheduled on Friday and Sunday[a]								
	LAX/BUR–SFO/OAK[b]			LAX/BUR/LGB/ONT–SAN			SAN–SFO/OAK/SJC		
Date	Certificated		Intra-	Certificated		Intra-	Certificated		Intra-
	First	Coach	state	First	Coach	state	First	Coach	state
8/ 1/48	28.7%	—	—	28.6%	—	—	28.6%	—	—
7/31/49	28.4	—	30.3%	24.4	—	29.6%	28.6	—	29.6%
3/ 1/51	28.7	30.8%	35.8	29.4	—	27.7	29.1	—	28.4
9/ 1/52	28.4	28.6	37.4	28.6	28.6%	29.7	28.6	28.6%	34.0
9/ 1/53	28.7	28.6	39.2	28.6	28.6	31.6	28.6	28.6	35.0
12/ 1/54	28.6	28.6	39.2	28.2	28.6	29.6	27.1	28.6	32.8
8/ 1/55	29.1	30.1	35.2	28.6	28.6	28.3	27.6	28.6	32.1
8/ 1/56	29.1	30.0	35.8	28.6	28.6	20.0	28.6	28.6	29.4
8/ 1/57	28.3	30.3	42.4	27.9	28.6	28.1	29.7	28.6	35.9
8/ 1/58	29.2	28.5	44.7	28.2	28.8	31.7	29.1	28.6	37.9
8/ 1/59	29.1	28.2	31.1	28.3	28.8	29.7	27.1	29.1	35.0
8/ 1/60	28.7	28.2	38.6	28.6	28.8	24.4	29.9	29.6	31.1
8/ 1/61	28.9	28.6	38.3	27.5	29.2	23.7	28.6	28.4	28.1
8/ 1/62	28.4	28.5	36.1	28.6	28.8	24.6	28.6	27.8	29.2
8/ 1/63	28.0	28.5	35.0	28.2	29.3	29.3	23.1	23.1	33.1
8/ 1/64	28.2	28.6	33.1	28.5	28.6	23.1	—	26.9	28.6
10/ 1/64	28.5	29.0	33.1	28.6	28.8	23.1	—	26.9	28.6
8/ 1/65	29.2	29.6	33.1	28.1	28.2	25.8	—	28.2	31.2
Median	28.7	28.6	35.8	28.6	28.6	28.1	28.6	28.6	31.2
Range	28.0– 29.2	28.2– 30.8	30.3– 44.7	27.5– 29.4	28.2– 29.3	20.0– 31.7	23.1– 29.9	23.1– 29.6	28.1– 37.9

[a]Flights scheduled to depart up to 2:30 A.M. on Saturday or Monday were considered to
have been Friday or Sunday flights.
[b]LAX/BUR/LGB/ONT–SFO/OAK/SJC.

Sources: Calculated from data presented in Appendices 15(A), 15(B), and 15(C) (total weekly
scheduled seats), and from data giving the number of seats scheduled to be operated
on Friday and Sunday obtained from the sources specified in these appendices.

only small changes in scheduling practices over these years.[15] In
comparison, the intervals for the intrastate carriers were 14.4, 11.7,

[15] The two exceptions are in the San Diego–San Francisco market. For the
period represented by 8/1/63, the very limited certificated carrier service (provided by Western) yielded Friday and Sunday percentages of 23.1 percent for
both classes of service (all provided in dual-configured Electras). Excluding the
percentages for this single date reduces the intervals for this market to 2.8 and
2.7 percentage points—within the three percentage-point interval of the other
city pairs.

and 9.8 percentage points. Obviously, the intrastate carriers varied their weekly schedules much more than the certificated carriers did.

Unlike the intrastate carriers' schedules for the two long-haul markets, a number of their Friday and Sunday percentages for the short-haul Los Angeles–San Diego market fell well below 28.6 percent. The lowest share was 20.0 percent (for 8/1/56), and the percentages for seven out of the last eleven dates were less than 28.6 percent. The low percentages for this market in these more recent years could have been due to a number of factors. First, the traffic pattern may have changed, reducing Friday and Sunday traffic. Such a reduction could have resulted from substantial improvements in freeways which might have encouraged automobile travel between these adjacent metropolitan areas. Second, personal and pleasure air travel may be relatively less important in this market, yielding a traffic low rather than a traffic peak on Fridays and Sundays. Third, it may be that PSA (the sole intrastate carrier in this market from 1957 through 1962) found itself short of aircraft and/or crews during these weekly peak periods and discovered that it was more profitable to concentrate its resources in the longer-haul markets. This could be particularly true of the period represented by 8/1/56, when PSA's total fleet consisted of only two DC-4's and when its Friday and Sunday percentage in this market fell to 20.0 percent.[16]

Regardless of whether the Friday and Sunday seat percentages were above or below 28.6 percent, the important fact is that the intrastate carriers did vary their schedules much more than the certificated carriers. This variability in the intrastate carriers' schedules implies a conscious effort by their managements to adjust output to correspond to the different demands existing during the week, and the system load factors given in Table 11-3 indicate that they were successful in this endeavor. In comparison, the certificated carriers tended to ignore weekly traffic fluctuations in the major California markets. To the extent their California practices represent their scheduling policies in interstate markets, their relatively low annual load factors are also consistent with their chosen operating procedures.[17]

[16] PSA's third DC-4 was not delivered until later that month. See U.S. Civil Aeronautics Administration, Western Region, Airplanes Utilized by Part 40 Operators, Pacific Southwest Airlines (dated August 31, 1956).

[17] Another test of the relationship between scheduling practices and load factors could be made by comparing the schedule variations of these two carrier groups in response to traffic surges resulting from holidays. A review of a limited number of schedules indicates that the intrastate carriers also scheduled relatively more extra holiday flights in the major California markets than did the certificated carriers.

It can be argued that PSA's (and the other intrastate carriers') traffic fluctuations differed significantly from those of the certificated carriers. The better-known certificated carriers may have attracted relatively more business travelers, whereas—due to their consistently lower fares—the intrastate carriers may have attracted more personal and pleasure travelers. Thus, the certificated carriers' traffic may have been more stable than that of the intrastate carriers. This explanation might apply to differences found in the 1950's, but with the introduction of Electra aircraft by PSA and the increasing demand for coach service for business travel, it would certainly not apply to the 1960's. Also, while there is no published data available, this writer knows from professional experience that the certificated carriers do experience weekly traffic peaks on Fridays and Sundays. Evidence of this can be found in their provisions for the "family plan" and "Discover America" promotional fares which generally suspend these promotional fares from Friday noon through Friday midnight or Saturday noon, and from Sunday noon through Monday noon—the same periods during which PSA experienced its traffic peaks.

Overall, the evidence is most consistent with the hypothesis that the intrastate carriers' relatively high load factors are primarily the result of conscious scheduling decisions by their managements, decisions that may well have been imposed by the requirements for survival under the low fares in effect since 1949. At the same time, the certificated carriers' less flexible scheduling practices and lower load factors may reflect the higher fares authorized by the CAB, and the emphasis on service quality by all such carriers in their attempts to obtain larger shares of total traffic when price rivalry is precluded by CAB regulation.

Summary. Taken together, the three parts of this section show that the intrastate carriers generally utilized their aircraft resources more intensively than the certificated carriers. This greater utilization appears not to have been the result of flying each aircraft more hours per day during the year. Rather, it resulted from the intrastate carriers generally installing more seats in each of their aircraft than the certificated carriers and then usually achieving higher load factors—that is, selling more seats on each flight. In addition, the offering of low-density, first-class service by the certificated carriers also served to decrease their overall aircraft utilization relative to the intrastate carriers.

Still another measure of aircraft utilization is the total number of years each aircraft is operated. It was pointed out in chapter 3 that the trunk carriers repeatedly purchased new aircraft to replace their existing aircraft, whereas, with the exception of PSA's Electras and B-727's, the intrastate carriers bought or leased used, obsolescent aircraft, most of which had been discarded by the trunk carriers. Thus, the intrastate carriers served to extend the productive lives of these aircraft, thereby increasing their overall utilization. This is another example of greater efficiency (increasing the output of a given resource) by the intrastate carriers. This efficiency was reflected in the low prices they paid for their used piston-powered aircraft which, in turn, served to lower their expenses.

The differences between the trunk and intrastate carriers in aircraft utilization appear to have been due more to differences in operating practices determined by management decisions than to differences in market characteristics (especially when the comparison is limited to coach-type operations). Both seat installation and fluctuations in weekly schedule patterns are directly controlled by management. In addition, the observed load factor differences are also consistent with the relative fare levels of these two carrier groups—that is, lower fares require larger passenger loads to equate marginal revenues with marginal costs and thus maximize profits. In California, management decisions determined both fare levels and scheduling practices, and those who made the correct decisions were rewarded with the survival of their companies.

Relative Output per Employee

Several measures of employee productivity are used in the airline industry. For example, the CAB publishes the following "crude measures" of productivity:

1. Overall available ton-miles per employee.
2. Overall revenue ton-miles per employee.
3. Total operating revenues (excluding subsidy) per employee.[18]

It is important to realize, however, that dividing some measure of total output by the total number of employees does not yield a measure of employee productivity. Rather, it indicates the amount of output per employee resulting from the *combined* use of all inputs. These inputs include those purchased by the airlines (such as labor, aircraft, airport facilities, and fuel), as well as those whose costs are not borne directly by the carriers (for example, the airway, air traffic control, and weather services provided by the federal gov-

[18] CAB, *Handbook of Airline Statistics*, p. 11. Caves, Koontz, and Wheatcroft all adopted available ton-miles as their basic measure of output for computing average costs (see footnote 23, chapter 10).

ernment). Even though output per employee does not indicate the absolute contribution of airline personnel to total output, it can be used to yield insights into relative employee productivity, providing comparisons are made between carriers or carrier groups whose proportions of labor to nonlabor inputs are roughly similar.

All airlines use the federal airways, lease airport facilities for their aircraft and traffic handling operations, and usually lease the land and buildings where they conduct their maintenance, sales, and administrative activities. These inputs, together with other supplies and services, are generally available to all carriers under equal or very similar terms, and the certificated and intrastate carriers appear to be comparable with regard to their use. This leaves aircraft as the most important nonlabor input by which the carrier groups might be differentiated. It turns out, however, that little difference seems to exist between the carrier groups in the use of this input relative to other capital inputs. For the years 1951 through 1965, the end-of-year book values of the trunk carriers' flight equipment plus spare parts and assemblies (at cost and before depreciation) comprised between 81.2 and 89.1 percent of the undepreciated book values of their total operating property and equipment (the higher percentages apply to the 1960's).[19] For the local service carriers, flight equipment plus spare parts and assemblies made up 78.3 to 89.4 percent of the total undepreciated book value of their operating property and equipment for these years.[20] Comparable data are not available for any of the intrastate carriers except for PSA from 1962 to 1965. During these four years, PSA's flight equipment, etc., accounted for 89.4 to 93.9 percent of the undepreciated book value of its total operating property.[21] Given a similarity in other nonlabor inputs, this apparent consistency in the dominance of aircraft over all real capital inputs means that if labor inputs are found to be roughly proportional to aircraft inputs it should be possible to use measures of output per employee to obtain fairly reliable estimates of relative labor productivity for these carrier groups.

An indication of the use of labor inputs relative to aircraft inputs may be obtained by dividing the total number of aircraft assigned to service for some period into the total number of employees for that

[19] Calculated from data presented in CAB, *Handbook of Airline Statistics* (1961 ed.), p. V-2, and (1967 ed.), p. 312. Total operating property includes flight equipment, spare parts and assemblies, ground property and equipment, and land. Construction work in progress was excluded from the above calculations.

[20] *Ibid.*, pp. V-5 and 315, respectively.

[21] PSA, *Annual Report*, 1963 and 1965.

period. The results of such a calculation for various years from 1949 through 1965 are presented in Table 11–5. The data in this table indicate that while California Central and PSA operated two-engine aircraft (through 1955), they utilized around 30 employees per aircraft (this estimate excludes the 48 employees per aircraft for PSA in 1951, on the assumption that it was inflated by employees engaged in fuel sale and flying school activities). This figure is about 25 percent lower than that of the local service carriers through 1961, the period when those carriers were mainly operating similar two-engine aircraft. PSA's adoption of DC-4's increased its number of employees per aircraft from around 30 to about 48—somewhat more than that of the local service carriers but just half the number for the trunk carriers for 1952–58, when those carriers produced about three-quarters of their total available seat-miles (ASM) in four-engine propeller aircraft that were mainly larger and faster than PSA's DC-4's. Following its adoption of Electras, PSA employed around 88 persons per aircraft, but this was still only about 90 percent of the number of employees per aircraft that the trunk carriers utilized during 1952–58, while operating aircraft that were slower than the Electra. The further increase in the trunk carriers' number of employees per aircraft in 1961, 1964, and 1965 shows that substantially larger numbers of employees were utilized to operate jet aircraft. Assuming the average speed and size of PSA's Electras in 1962–64 were roughly comparable to the average speed and size of the trunk carriers' diverse fleet during 1961 (when they produced 50 percent of their total ASM in jet aircraft, and 14 percent in turboprop aircraft), it appears that PSA utilized about 20 percent fewer employees per aircraft than the trunk carriers, while operating a similar "class" of aircraft.[22]

Overall, it is clear that the number of employees per aircraft is influenced by the size and speed of the aircraft operated. Given this, however, it seems that the intrastate carriers utilized around 25 percent fewer employees per aircraft than the certificated carriers for each class of aircraft. The law of diminishing returns, therefore, would lead one to predict somewhat greater average output per employee for the intrastate carriers. How much greater cannot be determined from these data, but if the differences in output per employee are much greater than the differences in number of employees per aircraft, it may still be reasonable to conclude that there are signifi-

---

[22] The percentages of total trunk carrier ASM produced in each class of aircraft were calculated from data presented in Jordan, *Economic Effects of Airline Regulation*, p. 546.

Table 11-5

Number of Employees per Aircraft Assigned to Service[a]
Total Trunk and Local Service Carriers, California Central Airlines
and Pacific Southwest Airlines, Selected Years 1949-1965

| Year | Number of Employees per Aircraft Assigned to Service[a] | | | |
| | Total | | | |
	Trunk[b]	Local Service	CCA	PSA
1949	77	39	—	—
1950	—	—	25[c]	—
1951	—	—	—	48
1952	93	41	—	—
1954	—	—	34	—
1955	96	40	—	29
1957	—	—	—	49
1958	98	44	—	—
1959	—	—	—	48
1961	108	41	—	—
1962	—	—	—	96
1963	—	—	—	85
1964	133	42	—	83
1965	143	46	—	85

[a]Calculated by dividing average number of aircraft assigned to service into the total number of employees. Employee data are for a brief period of time in each year, while data for the average number of aircraft pertain to the entire year.

[b]Domestic operations only.

[c]CCA's average number of aircraft assigned to service during 1950 was partially estimated.

Sources: Calculated from data presented in ATA, *Comparative Statement of Flight and Traffic Statistics* (12 Months Ending December 31, 1949, 1952, and 1955); ATA, *Quarterly Comparative Statement of Air Carriers' Aircraft Operating Statistics* (12 Months Ending December 31, 1958, 1961, 1964, and 1965); CAB, *Handbook of Airline Statistics* (June 1960 ed.), p. 21; and Appendices 5 and 17 of this book. Also, see Jordan, *Economic Effects of Airline Regulation*, pp. 548-49.

cant differences in relative labor productivity beyond the effects due to the use of different proportions of labor and nonlabor inputs. The following subsections show that this does seem to be the case.

ASM per Employee. The most general measures of physical output are available ton-miles and revenue ton-miles. Since it has not been possible to obtain such measures for the intrastate carriers, available seat-miles and revenue passenger-miles (RPM) are used here. Unfortunately, these more limited measures penalize the certificated carriers because a much larger portion of their total operations is involved in transporting cargo (freight, express, and mail). To compensate partially for this bias in favor of the intrastate carriers, an added output measure based on total operating revenues will also be used which, because of the differences in fare levels, is biased in favor of the certificated carriers.

It was possible to obtain employment information for only two years for CCA and for just eight years for PSA.[23] Appendix 17 of this book shows that CCA employed about 200 persons in both 1950 and 1954, while PSA's range from 1951 through 1965 was 115 to 740 employees. During the same period, the employment for Western (one of the smaller trunk carriers) ranged from 1,288 to 4,328 persons, while Pacific employed between 256 and 814 persons. At no time did PSA's employment equal Pacific's, even though by 1960 PSA's output was much larger than Pacific's.

Table 11-6 presents the average annual ASM per employee for the four carriers and the two certificated carrier groups for the 10 years from 1950 through 1965 for which CCA's or PSA's employment information is available. During these years, the total trunk carriers had much higher outputs per employee than the local service carriers as a group (increasing to almost twice the output per employee by 1965), whereas Western's outputs per employee were consistently higher than those for total trunk carriers, and Pacific's were higher than those for total local service carriers.[24] Over the 16-year period covered by the data, all of the certificated carriers' ASM per employee increased greatly, doubtless due in large part to the bigger and faster aircraft operated as the years progressed and, for the trunk carriers, to the increasing emphasis on high-density coach service.

The average annual ASM per employee for CCA in 1950 was almost equal to that for Pacific (both carriers operated DC-3's that year), although it was superior to that for total local service carriers. By 1954, when CCA was mainly operating Martin 202's, its output per employee was comparable to that for the total trunk carriers and was much superior to both Pacific and the total local service carriers.

[23] Paradise Airlines was the only other intrastate carrier for which employee information could be found. In March 1964 Paradise had 52 employees. See the transcript of the hearings before CAB Examiner S. Thomas Simon, Docket No. SE-462, March 20–April 7, 1964, vol. III, p. 264.

[24] Note that these rankings are similar to those that were found in chapter 10 to have existed for operating ratios.

Table 11-6

Average Annual Available Seat-Miles per Employee[a]
Total Trunk and Local Service Carriers, California Central Airlines
Western Air Lines, Pacific Air Lines, and Pacific Southwest Airlines
Selected Years 1950–1965

| Year | Average Annual Available Seat-Miles per Employee[a] | | | | | |
| | Trunk[b] | | Local Service | | California Intrastate | |
	Total	Western	Total	Pacific	CCA	PSA
1950	216,000	298,000[c]	152,000	190,000	184,000[d]	n.a.
1951	218,000	270,000[c]	161,000	168,000	n.a.	270,000[d]
1954	329,000	385,000	182,000	213,000	315,000[d]	n.a.
1955	341,000	408,000	179,000	220,000	–	499,000[d]
1957	368,000	410,000	193,000	274,000	–	617,000
1959	389,000	503,000	202,000	254,000	–	743,000
1962	499,000	726,000	257,000	310,000	–	970,000
1963	544,000	781,000	277,000	326,000	–	1,160,000
1964	567,000	774,000	298,000	315,000	–	1,290,000
1965	603,000	769,000	312,000	321,000	–	1,270,000

n.a.—not available.
[a]Calculated by dividing total number of employees into annual average scheduled available seat-miles. Employee data are for a brief period of time in each year, while the ASM data pertain to the entire year.
[b]Domestic operations only.
[c]Includes Inland Air Lines merged with Western on April 10, 1952.
[d]Based on data that are partially estimated.

Sources: Calculated from data presented in CAB, *Handbook of Airline Statistics* (June 1960 ed.), pp. 15, 20, and 38; (1967 ed.), pp. 46, 155, and 164; and Appendices 4 and 17 of this book.

The data for PSA show that even when operating DC-3's in 1951 and 1955, its ASM per employee were far superior to the local service carrier group and to Pacific. In fact, they were even 24 or 46 percent higher than those for the total trunk carriers and either equal to or 22 percent greater than Western's ASM per employee. Then, when it operated four-engine aircraft, PSA's average annual ASM per employee ranged from 34 to 67 percent higher than Western's and from 68 to 128 percent higher than the average for total trunk carriers. Finally, in 1965 PSA still managed to produce 111 percent more ASM per employee than the trunk carriers (and 65 percent more than Western), despite the fact that, whereas 80.6 percent of total trunk ASM were produced in jet aircraft, PSA did not introduce jets until April 1965 and produced only about a third of its ASM with such aircraft.[25]

RPM per Employee. A similar, but even more striking, difference is found when these carriers are compared on the basis of average annual RPM per employee (see Table 11-7). This measure is influenced by the generally superior load factors attained by the intrastate carriers,[26] and here there is no question about whether CCA was more like a local service carrier or a trunk carrier. In each of the two years for which employment data are available, CCA's average annual RPM per employee was much above that for the total local service carriers and even exceeded that for total trunk carriers by 4 percent. In fact, its figures for these two years were close to Western's relatively high outputs per employee.

PSA's achievements were even more impressive than CCA's. During every year for which information is available, its average annual RPM per employee exceeded that of the total trunk carriers and Western, not to mention the local service carriers and Pacific. In 1951 and 1955, while operating DC-3's (except for the last month and a half of 1955), PSA's outputs per employee were 19 and 60 percent higher, respectively, than Western's. During 1957 and 1959, while operating DC-4's, PSA's outputs per employee were 75 to 124 percent greater than that of both the total trunk carriers and Western. Then, in 1962-64, with an all-Electra fleet, PSA retained its 100 percent or more lead over Western while increasing its lead over the trunk carriers to 218 percent, despite the extensive operation of jet aircraft by these carriers. The large increase in PSA's personnel in 1965 (associated with the addition of five B-727-100's to its exist-

[25] See Table 3-2, chapter 3.

[26] Wheatcroft would question the use of this measure because he believes the difference between ASM and RPM merely reflects the load factor of each carrier, and "the load factor achieved on any route is to a very large extent determined by the volume of traffic which the route generates, and, therefore, the level of load ton-mile costs will be influenced considerably by the degree to which each of the airlines is certificated for large traffic flow routes." (Wheatcroft, *The Economics of European Air Transport*, pp. 80-81). The analysis of the previous section indicates, however, that management decisions regarding scheduling and equipment appear to be more important than traffic density in determining load factors. Thus, to limit employee productivity to the physical production of the service is to ignore an extremely important aspect of productivity in an industry which produces an instantaneously perishable good. After all, the employees of a carrier that manage to sell 75 percent of the available seat-miles produced by that carrier are certainly more productive than the employees of a carrier producing the same number of ASM per employee, but selling only 50 percent of the total.

Table 11-7

Average Annual Revenue Passenger-Miles per Employee[a]
Total Trunk and Local Service Carriers, California Central Airlines
Western Air Lines, Pacific Air Lines, and Pacific Southwest Airlines
Selected Years 1950–1965

Year	Average Annual Revenue Passenger-Miles per Employee[a]					
	Trunk[b]		Local Service		California Intrastate	
	Total	Western	Total	Pacific	CCA	PSA
1950	136,000	163,000[c]	48,000	87,000	142,000	n.a.
1951	152,000	175,000[c]	60,000	86,000	n.a.	208,000
1954	209,000	214,000	77,000	119,000	218,000[d]	n.a.
1955	218,000	241,000	81,000	122,000	–	386,000
1957	226,000	246,000	87,000	147,000	–	506,000
1959	239,000	303,000	90,000	136,000	–	529,000
1962	266,000	384,000	109,000	153,000	–	750,000
1963	293,000	422,000	121,000	167,000	–	897,000
1964	314,000	446,000	138,000	169,000	–	998,000
1965	333,000	431,000	147,000	170,000	–	804,000

n.a.–not available.

[a]Calculated by dividing total number of employees into annual average scheduled revenue passenger-miles. The employee data are for a brief period of time in each year, while the RPM data pertain to the entire year.

[b]Domestic operations only.

[c]Includes Inland Air Lines merged with Western on April 10, 1952.

[d]Based on data that are partially estimated.

Sources: Calculated from data presented in CAB, *Handbook of Airline Statistics* (June 1960 ed.), pp. 15, 20, and 38; (1967 ed.), pp. 47, 155, and 164; and Appendices 3 and 17 of this book.

ing six Electras) resulted in a drop in its output per employee, but its figure was still 87 percent larger than that of Western and 141 percent larger than that of the total trunk carriers.

There is just no question about it. Somehow, some way, PSA managed to achieve impressive levels of RPM per employee. Differences in the order of magnitude of 20 to 30 percent might properly be attributed to inaccuracies or noncomparability in the measures, or to differences in proportions of labor to nonlabor inputs. But consistent differences of from 75 to over 200 percent (since 1957) are just too large to be accounted for by these factors, especially when they were achieved while PSA operated DC-4's or Electras and the trunk carriers provided increasing amounts of jet service.

Revenues per Employee. Cargo has accounted for an increasing share of the certificated carriers' output since 1946. By 1965, 19.7 percent of the domestic trunk and 9.9 percent of the local service carriers' total revenue ton-miles were obtained from cargo.[27] Cargo ton-mile data are not available for the intrastate carriers, but they were prohibited from carrying mail or express, and it is known that they carried little freight during the period under study.[28] It is obvious, therefore, that cargo accounted for a very much smaller share of their total output. It follows that the certificated carriers' total employee figures are relatively larger than those of the intrastate carriers because of the additional employees required to handle cargo traffic. Data are not available that would permit the elimination of cargo employees from the certificated carriers' totals and, even if this adjustment could be made, the jointness of passenger and cargo output would make it impossible to obtain accurate calculations of ASM and RPM per noncargo-related employee. One way to compensate for this bias against the certificated carriers is to calculate average annual total operating revenues (from passenger, cargo, and other operations) per employee as an output measure. Of course, this measure is biased against CCA and PSA because their much lower average fares yield less revenue per unit of physical output. But, taken with the two previous measures, average annual operating revenues per employee should provide some useful insights into comparative airline productivity.

Table 11-8 shows that the average annual operating revenues per employee for CCA and PSA during 1950, 1951, and 1954 were quite similar to the total revenues (including subsidy) per employee for the total local service carriers.[29] Thus, during those early years, the

[27] Calculated from data presented in CAB, *Handbook of Airline Statistics*, pp. 132 and 135.

[28] See Appendices 16(C), 16(E), and 16(F) of this book for the total freight revenues of Paradise, Mercer, and PSA, respectively.

[29] In 1954, direct federal subsidy comprised 43 percent of all local service carriers' total operating revenues. (Calculated from data presented in CAB, *Handbook of Airline Statistics* [1961 ed.], p. IV-7.) The CAB chose to exclude subsidy payments from its "rough measure" of employee productivity based on operating revenues, but this distinction between sources of revenues does not seem relevant. Indeed, it implies that the value to society of subsidized airline service is less than the value of alternative goods that would have been produced by the resources expended on such airline service. One doubts that this is truly the position of the CAB. The inclusion of subsidy also seems appropriate because some of the local service carriers' personnel were occupied in subsidy negotiations with the CAB, with record keeping required for subsidy payments, etc.

Table 11-8

Average Annual Operating Revenues per Employee[a]
Total Trunk and Local Service Carriers, California Central Airlines
Western Air Lines, Pacific Air Lines, and Pacific Southwest Airlines
Selected Years 1950–1965

| Year | Average Annual Operating Revenues per Employee[a] | | | | | |
| | Trunk[b] | | Local Service | | California Intrastate | |
	Total	Western	Total	Pacific	CCA	PSA
1950	$ 9,100	$11,000[c]	$ 7,000	$ 8,600	$ 6,100[d]	n.a.
1951	9,800	10,700[c]	7,600	7,800	n.a.	$ 7,800[e]
1954	12,600	13,000	9,300	11,800	8,900[f]	n.a.
1955	12,900	14,600	8,800	11,000	–	13,800
1957	13,100	14,800	9,600	12,600	–	18,200
1959	15,300	19,900	10,700	13,400	–	21,700
1962	18,800	25,700	14,000	16,400	–	31,600
1963	19,700	26,200	14,700	17,300	–	37,600
1964	21,000	26,700	15,700	17,600	–	41,500
1965	22,200	26,100	16,300	18,000	–	32,500

n.a.–not available.
[a]Calculated by dividing total number of employees into total domestic operating revenues. The employee data are for a brief period of time in each year, while the total operating revenues pertain to the entire year.
[b]Domestic operations only.
[c]Includes Inland Air Lines, merged with Western on April 10, 1952.
[d]Based on revenues for the year ended March 31, 1951.
[e]Based on an estimate of total operating revenues of $930,000, calculated by applying average fares for 1951 (Appendix 7) to PSA's on-line O & D passenger traffic (Appendix 14).
[f]Based in part on estimated revenues of $103,000 for January 1-27, 1954.

Sources: Calculated from data presented in CAB, *Handbook of Airline Statistics* (June 1960 ed.), pp. 111, 116, and 134; (1967 ed.), pp. 93, 245, and 254; and in Appendices 7, 14(A), 14(B), 14(C), 16(A), 16(F), and 17 of this book.

intrastate carriers were able to obtain roughly the same revenues per employee with their low-fare, high-density coach service as the local service carriers were able to achieve with their high-fare, low-density, first-class service plus subsidies.

By 1955, when it benefited from the termination of rival service by CCA, PSA managed to earn total operating revenues per employee high enough to exceed those for total trunk carriers, total local service carriers, and Pacific, and to approach those for Western. With the adoption of DC-4's, PSA's operating revenues per employee for 1957 and 1959 increased to about 40 percent above those for the total trunk carriers and from 9 to 23 percent above Western's operating revenues per employee. PSA's introduction of Electras in late 1959 was associated with a further relative increase in revenues per employee until they were 98 percent higher than the total trunk carriers' and 55 percent higher than Western's (in 1964). Even in 1965, with a large increase in its number of employees and with its late adoption of jet aircraft, PSA still had a 46 percent advantage over the total trunk carriers and a 25 percent advantage over Western.[30]

Summary. Reviewing the percentage differences for all three measures, and recognizing the biases inherent in them, it seems proper to conclude that, while operating two-engine aircraft, the successful intrastate carriers essentially equaled the real output per employee of the total trunk carriers, fell somewhat below that of Western (who was always one of the highest trunk carriers in these measures), and consistently exceeded the output per employee of the total local service carriers and Pacific. Relative output changed radically once PSA obtained four-engine aircraft. From 1957 through 1965, its real output per employee generally exceeded that of the total trunk carriers by more than 100 percent and exceeded that of Western by over 60 percent. It appears that the intrastate carriers utilized about 25 percent less labor per aircraft for generally comparable classes of aircraft and, therefore, should have greater output per employee. But, even if the estimated differences in input proportions are correct, they still do not seem large enough to account for the really impressive differences found in relative outputs per employee. Other factors must account for an appreciable portion of these differences.

It may be argued that the large differences in output per employee were due to the intrastate carriers' purchasing maintenance and sales services from other firms rather than producing them

[30]The 1965 relationships appear to be temporary. In 1966 the total operating revenues per employee were $21,600 for total trunk carriers, $26,000 for Western, and $41,200 for PSA—that is, PSA's measure was 91 percent greater than the trunk carriers' and 58 percent above Western's. PSA's employment as of August 31, 1966 was approximately 950 persons. Calculated from data presented in CAB, *Handbook of Airline Statistics*, pp. 132, 155, 222, and 245; PSA, *Annual Report*, 1966; and E. F. Hutton, *Prospectus, Pacific Southwest Airlines* (October 26, 1966), p. 12.

within the company. The best available information for CCA indicates that its 1950 employee figure did include the maintenance, flight, and administrative personnel officially employed by its affiliated company, Airline Transport Carriers. There is no question, however, about its figure for 1954. The total employees of both CCA and ATC are combined in that figure. In the case of PSA, there is no possibility that total employment was understated because of the outside purchase of maintenance services. PSA consistently did its own maintenance at least as far back as early 1950.[31] If anything, PSA's fuel sale and flight training activities inflate its employment figures and thereby understate the output of ASM and RPM per employee. On the other hand, there are indications that both CCA and PSA relied heavily on travel agents for sales promotion, ticketing, etc. It is not known if their reliance was more extensive than that of the certificated carriers, but it is known from personal observation that during the early 1960's PSA maintained fewer sales offices than the trunk carriers in the three major metropolitan areas of California.

The above data indicate why PSA in particular managed to survive and prosper during the period studied, but they still do not explain why its output per employee was so far superior to that of the certificated carriers. The following is a list of some factors that pertain to this matter, but it is by no means complete:

1. PSA utilized its aircraft more intensively (as described in the previous section), which served to increase its output of ASM and RPM per unit of employee input.
2. PSA operated relatively few aircraft types, thereby reducing employment for crew and maintenance training, engineering, aircraft evaluation, etc. Also, until April 1965, there was only one brief period (in 1960-61) when PSA operated two different aircraft types at the same time (other than during brief transitional periods).[32]

[31] Civil Aeronautics Administration, Western Region, Non-Scheduled Air Carrier Inspection Report, Pacific Southwest Airlines (dated May 12, 1950), located in the files of the FAA, Western Region, Los Angeles.

[32] PSA operated only five different aircraft types through 1965. During the same period, most local service carriers flew only one or two aircraft types (mainly the DC-3), but individual trunk carriers generally operated well over five different types. Also, the trunk carriers invariably operated several different types concurrently. Overall, eight different aircraft types were operated by the California intrastate carriers between 1946 and 1965 compared with over 41 different types by the total trunk carriers. See Table 11-2, and Jordan, "Competition—A Two-Edged Sword in Improving Air Transportation Performance?" pp. 167-68.

3. PSA's pilots have always been paid for the number of scheduled miles flown, while certificated carrier pilots are paid for the amount of time flown.[33] PSA's pilots, therefore, have a significant monetary incentive to fly as fast as feasible (more miles per hour), which serves to increase output per crew member.

4. Whenever possible, PSA operated its flights under visual flight rules (VFR) rather than under instrument flight rules (IFR). In contrast, the certificated carriers operated all flights under IFR, in accordance with an industry agreement reached through the Air Transport Association. VFR operations serve to reduce flying time for each segment and thereby increase productivity. It should be noted, however, that since the FAA requires that all jet aircraft operate under IFR, PSA began to lose the advantage of VFR operations as of April 1965.

5. The specialization and resulting simplicity inherent in PSA's route and fare structures served to reduce personnel required to provide a given volume of reservation, ticketing, passenger and baggage handling, and accounting services, etc. These factors also decreased the training required for each employee.

6. The relative lack of regulatory proceedings and industry meetings reduced the need for personnel to conduct such matters, prepare reports, etc. (With the expansion of the PUC's regulatory powers in late 1965, PSA's regulatory activities and associated personnel requirements should be increasing.)

A thorough investigation of the reasons for PSA's greater output per employee is beyond the scope of this chapter. Indeed, it could well provide the basis for another major study. The crucial point to be made here is simply that the successful intrastate carriers were able to produce relatively more output per employee than the certificated carriers. In addition, as shown in the previous section, they also utilized their aircraft resources more intensively. The overall result of these and other unidentified factors was important differences in efficiency between these carrier groups.[34]

---

[33] The precedent for the certificated carriers' present method of paying pilots on the basis of time flown was established by Decision No. 83 of the National Labor Board (decided May 10, 1934). CAB, *Aeronautical Statutes and Related Material* (Washington, D.C., 1962), pp. 141–43. It is interesting to note that in the late 1920's and early 1930's, most airline pilots were paid on the basis of mileage flown.

[34] Those interested in investigating the reasons for differences in productivity and the resulting costs of the certificated and intrastate carriers will find the cost

Conclusion

The intrastate carriers' utilization of resources appears to have been substantially more effective than that of the certificated carriers. They demonstrated that it is feasible to achieve more intensive utilization of aircraft than has been attained by the trunk carriers, mainly by installing more seats in coach aircraft (and essentially ignoring low-density, first-class configurations) and by managing to fill a greater proportion of those seats with paying passengers. In addition, they increased the productivity of certain piston-powered aircraft by operating them after they were discarded by the certificated carriers. The intrastate carriers also demonstrated that it is possible to achieve substantially greater output per employee than that of the trunk (and local service) carriers. The ways that the intrastate carriers used to obtain relatively greater productivity appear to be manifold, and substantial changes in certificated carrier operations would be required for them to attain similar productivity. These changes would include major revisions in the route structures

---

theory presented in the following two articles to be useful: A. Alchian, "Costs and Outputs," published in M. Abramovitz, et al., *The Allocation of Economic Resources* (Stanford, Calif.: Stanford University Press, 1959), pp. 23–40. J. Hirshleifer, "The Firm's Cost Function: A Successful Reconstruction?" *Journal of Business* 35 (July 1962), pp. 235–55, esp. 241–43. Alchian hypothesizes that marginal costs are inversely related to the planned volume of output while being directly related to the rate of output, and that the total cost of any output schedule decreases with increases in the time interval between the present moment and the date of initial output. Hirshleifer expands Alchian's theory by hypothesizing that, given an aggregate rate of output, total costs will vary inversely with the width of output—that is, the fewer the flows (greater the width) within an overall output stream, the lower the total cost of that amount of output. Hirshleifer also gives several enlightening examples of the application of this new and more general cost theory to the airline, aircraft manufacturing, railroad, and trucking industries (see pp. 239–43 of his article).

It is my own opinion that, in addition to the management policies described in this chapter, the reasons for PSA's greater output per employee lie in its more specialized operation relative to that of the certificated carriers and in its use of price rivalry in addition to service-quality rivalry. PSA specialized in providing one class of service with a single aircraft type (at any point in time) over a homogeneous route structure (which it was free to modify at will). All of this served to increase its width of output. In addition, it was able to concentrate service in high-density markets having large volume characteristics (while, however, being restricted to relatively short-haul markets within the confines of California, thereby reducing the volume aspect of distance). The ability to use price rivalry enabled PSA to ignore high-cost innovations (which the certificated carriers adopted to achieve high service quality) and to delay adopting other technological innovations, thus reducing the cost of their adoption. See Jordan, *Economic Effects of Airline Regulation*, pp. 456–59, for an elaboration of these points in terms of the Alchian/Hirshleifer theory.

of the certificated carriers to give them simple structures similar to those of the intrastate carriers.[35] (Implicit in this would be a higher degree of specialization by each one of a greater number of carriers.) In addition, the rate of adoption of new aircraft types would be decreased, schedule patterns would be established to correspond more closely to predictable fluctuations in demand, methods of employee compensation changed, different aircraft operating procedures adopted, fewer classes of service offered, a reduction in the amount of regulatory and industry activities undertaken, etc. Increases in real output per employee of over 100 percent are difficult to comprehend, but the evidence provided by PSA's operations indicate they could be achieved, at least in markets comparable to the major California markets, and, if market characteristics are a relevant factor, even greater increases in average employee output could be realized by carriers specializing in serving the major transcontinental markets.

From the viewpoint of this study, a relevant question is: Did the more intensive utilization of aircraft and the relatively greater output per employee by the intrastate carriers stem in whole or in part from the less stringent regulation under which they operated until late 1965? The evidence at hand does not provide a categorical answer to this question. The more intensive aircraft utilization and greater output per employee, however, are consistent with the significantly lower per-mile fares that the intrastate carriers charged. Given these lower fares, it was crucially important for the intrastate carriers to minimize the costs of their operations in order to survive. Obvious ways to decrease average costs per passenger would be to increase the number of seats in each aircraft and to schedule aircraft so that a greater proportion of these seats were occupied. Another way would be to utilize labor inputs so that greater ASM, RPM, and revenues were obtained for each employee. These were actions that the intrastate carriers took, or, at least, that the viable intrastate carriers

[35] In a speech made in October 1969, Mr. F. D. Hall, president of Eastern Air Lines, proposed "that airlines be permitted by the Civil Aeronautics Board to swap routes to achieve greater efficiency. . . . He suggested that it might be appropriate for the major carriers to see if there were routes in their systems that may not be profitable to them but would, by fitting better into the routes of other carriers, provide both profitable operations and improved service to the public." (*Wall Street Journal*, Midwest Edition [October 3, 1969], p. 2.) The findings of this study support the assertion that this would improve airline efficiency. However, it is doubtful that limiting the exchange to a barter basis would maximize efficiency. Outright sale as well as swapping would probably yield even greater efficiency. Indeed, route sales to any proficient carrier might improve airline efficiency still more.

managed to take. Since the differences in passenger fares can be attributed more directly to differences in regulation, and since lower costs are required for survival under lower fares, the evidence on aircraft utilization and output per employee is consistent with the hypothesis that regulation, as practiced by the CAB, does have an adverse affect on efficiency in air transportation.

Conclusions

12

The Cartel Hypothesis

Comparing the certificated carriers' system-wide operations with the relatively nonregulated airline service within California from 1946 through 1965 shows that during this period Civil Aeronautics Board regulation served effectively to limit entry, transfer the assets of expiring carriers to other certificated carriers through merger or acquisition, reduce the number of carriers operating at any given time, and promote price discrimination. In addition, the coach fare levels authorized by the CAB were found to be substantially higher than the fare levels for comparable service within California. In fact, during late 1965 the coach fares in the major California markets were as much as 47 percent lower than what they would have been under CAB policies and authorizations.[1] Finally, the certificated trunk car-

---

[1] Throughout this study the relative levels of general fares in individual markets have been used to measure price differences. This fails to measure the effect of lower promotional fares on average revenues. Average yield (total annual passenger revenues divided by RPM) includes the effects of these discriminatory fares, but, unfortunately, such data are not available for individual markets, nor are they available on a system basis for all intrastate carriers. The available data for CCA and PSA, covering most of the years from 1949 through 1965, show that the combined average annual yields for these two major California carriers ranged from 3.20 to 4.13 cents per mile. This compares with average annual coach yields for the trunk carriers of 3.96 to 5.76 cents per mile for the same period, and 4.38 to 5.88 cents per mile for the local service carriers' coach yields from 1956 through 1965 (with the highs for all three carrier groups occurring in 1961–63). Thus, these two intrastate carriers' average yields were 20 to 30 percent lower than those of the certificated carriers. It is important to recognize, however, that these average yields were influenced by such things as the mix of markets having coach service (including the differences in the dis-

226

riers generally offered a higher quality of service than the California intrastate carriers. All of these effects are consistent with the hypothesis that CAB regulation made it possible for the certificated carriers to operate as a cartel, albeit an imperfect cartel.

On the other hand, the findings of this study are quite inconsistent with the implications of the consumer-protection hypothesis. This is not to say that no traveler has benefited from CAB regulation. Quite the contrary, those travelers who prefer high quality service relatively more than other goods, and those whose fares are paid by others are better off with CAB regulation and the resulting increased service quality. Also, travelers who qualify for the lowest of the certificated carriers' promotional fares may be better off than if these airlines were not regulated. It is difficult, however, to see how the majority of passengers have been benefited by being charged substantially higher general fares, by being discriminated against when they fail to qualify for promotional fares, and by being required to purchase higher quality service despite their demonstrated preferences for lower quality service if it is provided at significantly lower fares.

Obviously, the no-effect hypothesis also fails to explain the results of CAB regulation. This conclusion is particularly interesting because it is contrary to the findings of Stigler and Friedland that, through 1937, the state regulatory commissions appeared to have no measurable effect on the average level of electric utility rates and that price discrimination by utilities was the same with or without regulation.[2] It happens, however, that this apparent inconsistency can be resolved by comparing the nonregulated market structures of the electric utility and airline industries. Electric utilities are natural monopolies—that is, their economies of scale increase over a large range of output so that within (and somewhat beyond) that range the long-run average costs of a single utility will be lower than the average costs of two or more utilities together producing the same total amount of output. In this situation, minimum average costs can be achieved in a market only if one firm provides the output, thereby giving the existing utility a sufficient cost advantage to prevent the

tances associated with these markets), service-quality differences (such as the relative use of propeller and jet aircraft), different dates of fare increases, and availability and use of promotional fares. See CAB, *Handbook of Airline Statistics*, p. 112, for certificated carrier coach yields. CCA and PSA average annual yields calculated from data presented in Appendices 3, 16(A), and 16(F) of this book.

[2] Stigler and Friedland, "What Can Regulators Regulate? The Case of Electricity," pp. 8 and 9.

entrance of a potential rival. In contrast, the California intrastate carriers demonstrated that the airline industry is characterized by few, if any, economies of scale beyond those achievable with four or five aircraft. In medium- or large-sized city pairs, therefore, the non-regulated airline market structure would at least be that of an oligopoly with existing firms operating under an ever-present threat of new entry should profits exceed the market rate of return. If the primary result of industry regulation is to facilitate the organization of a cartel to obtain monopoly power, it follows that regulation of electric utility prices should be "ineffective," since such firms already have monopoly power. Since, however, airlines are not natural monopolies, the organization of a cartel should yield substantial economic effects of the kinds found to have been associated with the CAB's regulation of the certificated carriers. Thus, the economic performance of both the regulated airlines and the regulated electric utilities are consistent with the implications of the cartel hypothesis, once the effects of their different nonregulated market structures are taken into account.

Stigler and Friedland asserted that "there are two basic purposes of public regulation of prices: the curtailment of the exercise of monopoly power, and the elimination of certain forms of price discrimination."[3] Neither their findings nor the findings of this study are consistent with that assertion (which is simply another expression of the consumer-protection hypothesis). Indeed, the conclusions of both studies are consistent with the producer-protection hypothesis.

Imperfections

With the CAB's assistance, the certificated carriers have been able to solve many of the problems associated with establishing an effective cartel. They have reached agreements on pricing, entry and exit, and on a number of promotional and sales activities. In addition, low-cost methods of detecting and punishing violations of agreements have been established through the CAB and the Air Traffic Conference of the Air Transport Association of America.[4] In two

[3] *Ibid.*, p. 4.

[4] Kleiger describes a number of agreements made by the certificated carriers with respect to travel agents, advertising and other promotional activities, special sales facilities for large customers, Joint Military Ticket Offices, entertaining of postal employees, and baggage handling. She also describes how the airlines detect and punish violations of their agreements through the Air Traffic Conference and examines the role played by the CAB in these activities. See Kleiger, *Maximization of Industry Profits: The Case of United States Air Transportation*, pp. 115–38.

very important areas, however, the CAB's regulation has failed to facilitate the resolution of important cartel problems. First, an explicit allocation of industry output and profit among the regulated airlines has not been achieved. Second, and associated with this, airline rivalry on the basis of service quality has not been controlled.

Industry output and profit could be allocated explicitly among the certificated carriers if only one carrier were allowed to operate in each market. Also, such an allocation could be achieved wherever two or more carriers were authorized to serve individual markets if schedule quotas were assigned and if profits were pooled and then shared by the carriers on the basis of some accepted formula. The CAB, however, has chosen to authorize multicarrier service in most important domestic markets served by trunk carriers, thereby largely eliminating the first method of output and profit allocation for these carriers, and, with the exception of the Mutual Aid Strike Pact, profit pooling has not been practiced by the certificated carriers.[5]

Dewey demonstrates that all cartels are wasteful in the short run if they assign output quotas to members in such a way that marginal costs are not equalized among all firms.[6] Output quotas are not explicitly assigned by the CAB, but there is an implicit assignment of output *potential* through route awards. Existing studies show that the CAB does not give primary consideration to the relative marginal costs of carriers when new route authorizations are made—that is, other factors are given more weight than whether the addition of a route to carrier A's system would result in lower marginal costs of operation than if the route were awarded to carrier B.[7] Therefore, to the extent new route authorizations fail to equalize and minimize marginal costs among the certificated carriers, they are wasteful of resources. Dewey goes on to show that, in the long run, cartels in which output quotas are assigned but profits are not pooled are more wasteful of resources than are cartels where profits are pooled. In the former case the production of fixed quotas will lead to the construc-

---

[5] See Caves, *Air Transport and Its Regulators*, pp. 185–86. Also, CAB, *Handbook of Airline Statistics*, p. 470. Possible agreements regarding schedule quotas may eventually result from the Board's permission for the airlines to discuss the allocation of schedules to reduce congestion at major airports. The CAB is aware of this possibility and has imposed conditions "to preclude any unnecessary or anti-competitive activities by the carriers. . . ." See CAB Press Releases Nos. 68-81 (July 26, 1968) and 68-138 (December 5, 1968). Also, see CAB Order No. 68-12-11 (adopted December 3, 1968).

[6] Dewey, *Monopoly in Economics and Law*, p. 16.

[7] For example, see Richmond, *Regulation and Competition in Air Transportation*, pp. 191–236.

tion of plants that are smaller than optimum, while in the latter situation the lowest cost firms would produce all of the desired output in optimum-sized plants, thereby maximizing industry profits which could then be shared by all. The lack of profit pooling by the certificated carriers clearly places them among this more wasteful type of cartel.

The widespread authorization of multicarrier service in medium and large markets (served mainly by the trunk carriers) has made actual output allocation indeterminate in these markets. This, combined with the limited control of airline service quality (but complete control of prices), appears to increase the inefficiency of the regulated airlines beyond that envisioned by Dewey for cartels in general. First, there is the costly rivalry among the certificated carriers to obtain CAB authorizations to serve markets already served by other carriers (while each carrier endeavors to protect its own routes from incursions by rival carriers). Then, once authorized to serve a market with one or more other airlines, each carrier seeks to obtain larger shares of total market traffic (and, it is hoped, profits) by improving the quality of its service relative to that of the other carriers. Each carrier is motivated to purchase more of the newest aircraft, increase schedule frequencies, improve passenger service, and increase sales promotion on "competitive" routes until the marginal costs of such acts equal the expected marginal revenues, given the prevailing fare level and structure. All of this serves to increase the costs of airline production.

The above effects have been facilitated by the CAB's establishment in 1960 of a "fair" rate of return on investment of about 10.5 percent after taxes.[8] So long as this "fair" rate of return allows the regulated airlines to earn a return greater than the market rate, it encourages the purchase of aircraft (comprising almost 90 percent of total airline operating equipment) and other capital inputs.[9] In addition, if the industry's actual return happens to exceed even the "fair" rate specified by the CAB, purchasing new aircraft increases a carrier's investment base and increases operating costs, both of which reduce its rate of return toward the level approved by the Board. The primary motivation of service-quality rivalry, together with a higher-than-market "fair" rate of return on investment, serve to encourage excess capacity in the airline industry.[10]

[8] *General Passenger Fare Investigation*, 32 CAB 291 (1960). Also, see Caves, *Air Transport and Its Regulators*, pp. 391–402.

[9] See chapter 11, p. 211.

[10] A particularly outstanding example of excess capacity in the airline industry occurred in the early 1960's following the widespread adoption of

The load factor data for the certificated trunk carriers (see Table 11-3) indicates that except for times of national emergency the industry's excess capacity is chronic, and it seems likely to persist for the foreseeable future. In late 1967 the Air Transport Association estimated that the trunk carriers plus Pan American World Airways would spend approximately $8.8 billion for new aircraft during the *five* years from 1967 through 1971—that is, 33 percent more than the amount spent in the previous *ten* years.[11] Even after allowing for inflation and possible exaggeration, the expansion indicated by this figure, considered in relation to the load factors of the 1960's, yields a prediction of continuing excess capacity for the trunk carriers through the mid-1970's.[12]

---

turbine-powered aircraft and the substantial fare increases of those years. The trunk carriers' first-class load factor fell from 59.5 percent in 1959 to 46.6 percent in 1962, and their coach load factor fell from 64.1 percent in 1959 to 54.9 percent in 1963. These load factor decreases were commonly attributed to the great additional capacity provided by the new turbine-powered aircraft. The rapid retirement (and scrapping), however, of the DC-7's, L-1049's, and L-1649's (while older and smaller piston-powered aircraft were retained in service) demonstrated that the large-scale purchase of those late-model piston-powered aircraft in the mid-1950's was the cause of the excess capacity during the early 1960's. The turbine-powered aircraft were so much more efficient than the last of the piston-powered aircraft that average costs were reduced by grounding the relatively new DC-7's and L-1049's as soon as turbine-powered aircraft were available to replace them. The California intrastate carriers did not adopt the last of the piston-powered aircraft, and they did not experience the excess capacity problem of that period. Their load factors increased from 71.1 percent in 1959 to 75.3 percent in 1962 and 74.9 percent in 1964 (see Table 11-3 of this book for the above load factor data). Brief reviews of the development of excess capacity by the U.S. railroad industry during the late nineteenth and early twentieth centuries are given in G. W. Hilton, "Consistency of the Interstate Commerce Act," *Journal of Law and Economics* 9 (October 1966), p. 110; and in C. D. Stone, "ICC: Some Reminiscences on the Future of American Transportation," *New Individualist Review* 2, no. 4 (April 1963), pp. 5–8 and 12–13.

[11] ATA, *Major U.S. Airlines, 1967–1971 Financial Projections and Requirements*, Slide 19.

[12] For a prediction of increased capacity for 1970–73 see CAB, *Impact of New Large Jets on the Air Transportation System, 1970–1973* (Washington, D.C., November 1969), Appendix A-3. One way to reduce excess capacity has been proposed by Nathan S. Simat, president of Simat, Helliesen & Eichner, transportation consultants. "He recommends overcapacity be dealt with by establishing a government-backed purchasing company that would control the supply of transports to domestic airlines. Airline desire for additional aircraft would be constrained by bidding for the limited supply . . . ." (*Aviation Week and Space Technology* 91, no. 17 [October 27, 1969], p. 29.) Assuming this company operates without making major mistakes, it might well solve the overcapacity problem resulting from the CAB's regulation, and it would probably reduce the sales of the aircraft manufacturers. It seems likely, however, that price rivalry for aircraft by the carriers would transfer a large portion of their

Clearly, while the entry of new carriers into the interstate airline industry has been limited by CAB regulation, this same regulation has increased rather than reduced the influx of aircraft and other resources. In other words, the certificated carriers have purchased more aircraft and employed more people than a much larger number of nonregulated airlines would have purchased and employed to produce the same quantity of output.[13] All of this has served to increase average costs so that despite their relatively higher average revenues the certificated carriers have been unable to achieve the profits available from a more perfect cartel. Although airline profits have not been maximized, CAB regulation has had the effect of decreasing the risk of the certificated carriers' owners by limiting the means of exit from the industry to merger with or acquisition by another such carrier. Certificates of public convenience and necessity have provided a guarantee to stockholders that their equity would not be completely wiped out by adverse developments and resulting bankruptcy. Probably a somewhat similar reduction of risk has also been enjoyed by the managements of certificated carriers. In total, the certificated carriers' universal acceptance of regulation indicates that regulation is thought to be beneficial to the airlines—that is, they feel that even an imperfect cartel is preferable to an open and nonregulated airline market structure.

Although the certificated carriers have been unable to maximize industry profits under CAB regulation, aircraft manufacturers, airline employees, and other suppliers of airline resources appear to have benefited from the existence of incomplete regulation. For example, the demand for new aircraft has been substantially increased by the lack of output and profit pooling and the resulting service-quality rivalry. It is possible that without regulation the lower fares associated with price rivalry could have increased the amount of air transportation demanded and, despite the more intensive utilization of aircraft, a greater volume (but fewer varieties) of new aircraft might have been purchased. The lower production costs associated with such a revised output pattern might also have yielded larger profits to manufacturers than what they actually received. If, however, the airlines were to be regulated, and if such regulation were to cartelize the industry, then a more perfect cartel (one that eliminated service-quality rivalry) would have resulted in greater profits to the

cartel profits to this monopoly. In addition, there would be the problem of selecting the appropriate mix of aircraft from the available types. Obviously, a carrier's operating efficiency (and the size of its bids) would be influenced by the suitability of the available aircraft for operations over its routes.

[13] This conclusion is supported by the differences in the intensity of aircraft utilization and the output per employee reported in chapter 11.

airlines with fewer purchases of new aircraft. Thus, the imperfect airline cartel does seem to have benefited aircraft manufacturers more than if the airlines had been organized as a perfect cartel. Actually, it is difficult to imagine how the Civil Aeronautics Act of 1938 and the Federal Aviation Act of 1958 could have been written and interpreted to promote more effectively the interests of airline suppliers.

Most writers on the subject of airline regulation refer to the rivalry among the certificated carriers as evidence that there is some degree of competition within the regulated industry.[14] However, the evidence obtained by comparing the certificated carriers with the California intrastate carriers shows that the "competition" among the certificated carriers is not the form found in some intermediate market structure (such as oligopoly or monopolistic competition) lying between monopoly and competition. Rather, it is the form of competition (rivalry) that exists among the members of a cartel (monopoly) who, while making price and other agreements designed to benefit all members of the industry, have failed to allocate explicitly these benefits among themselves. In this case, each member has sought to obtain larger shares of the cartel benefits through service-quality rivalry in the market and procedural rivalry in regulatory activities. As a result, outsiders have been benefited, costs increased, and total industry benefits decreased from what could have been achieved with a more perfect cartel.

Market Structures within California

If the market structure of the certificated carriers is that of an imperfect cartel, how might the airline market structure within California be classified? This section will propose classifications based on

---

[14] Caves characterizes this form of competition as oligopoly: "Chapter 9 presented the evidence that the Board has placed much of its faith in direct point-to-point competition to insure the quality of air service. It has justified this faith by the belief that oligopoly, rather than monopoly, will yield the traveler the best service at the existing fares and promote the choice of air travel in preference to other means." (*Air Transport and Its Regulators*, pp. 250–51.)

Richmond specifies the extremes without naming the intermediate form: "It is clear that both competition and direct regulation can, in the appropriate circumstances, be substituted one for the other, as mechanisms for seeking to serve the public good in the economic phases of the air transportation industry. The difficult problem, and that which is yet unresolved, is the determination of the optimum blend of these two mechanisms. Whether the current blend is viable is not yet clear. . . . What is clear is that some blend is superior to the exclusive use of one or the other mechanism, i.e., a single monopoly carrier for the nation, or alternatively, unrestricted competition." (*Regulation and Competition in Air Transportation*, pp. 256–57.)

numbers of firms and pricing practices. There may be some question about the appropriateness of the classifications, but the essential point is that the California airline market structure during most of the period studied can not be termed a cartel.

The demand for common carrier air transportation throughout the United States (including California) has been fragmented among many individuals, firms, and public organizations, with no one comprising an appreciable portion of total demand. Changes in the air transportation market structure within California have therefore depended on changes in the organization of the suppliers of airline service, and several such changes have occurred since World War II. Actually, most of the minor California markets were served by only one carrier so that the structure in those markets was monopolistic. It was in the major California markets that the market structures changed and the following classifications pertain to them.

Prior to 1949, the certificated carriers were essentially the only suppliers in the major California markets (ignoring the unknown, but apparently minimal, impact of Pacific Air Lines in 1946-47). The structure of these markets, therefore, was that of an imperfect cartel. During 1949 and into mid-1950, the entry of the California intrastate carriers changed this structure to an imperfect cartel with a large oligopolistic "fringe," which accounted for about 35 percent of all passengers.[15] A further change in structure occurred in May 1950, when the CAB authorized the certificated carriers to match the fares and services of California Central, PSA, and Western Air Lines of California. From then until early 1955 the structure was an oligopoly consisting of four to five carriers in each major market (three, if the certificated carriers are considered to act together through the CAB's regulation). Fares were increased by all carriers in early 1951 with the aid of the leadership provided by the CAB. But this apparent collusion was short-lived. CCA's independent fare increase in June 1952 was not followed by the certificated carriers until early 1953, and PSA delayed its brief adoption of the increase to early 1954. In the meantime, CCA introduced a lower fare for DC-3 service, and, of course, PSA reduced its fares independently in April 1954 (see Appendix 7 of this book). The existence of promotional fares during these years indicates that the intrastate carriers' general fares were above marginal costs at that time.

The market structure from early 1955 to early 1962 reverted to an imperfect cartel with a small, one or two carrier, fringe. With CCA's bankruptcy and California Coastal's eventual demise, the

[15] Market share calculated from data presented in Appendix 14 of this book.

intrastate carriers' threat to the certificated carriers receded to relative insignificance. From 1955 through 1958, the intrastate carriers flew only 10.8 to 15.3 percent of total on-line O & D passengers in the Los Angeles–San Francisco and Los Angeles–San Diego markets, and even as late as 1959, PSA accounted for just 15.4 and 17.8 percent of total traffic in these two markets. The intrastate carriers' shares of total San Diego–San Francisco traffic were around 55 percent during these years, but this was the smallest of the three major markets and the two larger city pairs really determined the structure for the three combined markets.[16]

Given the apparent weakness of the intrastate carriers during those years, why did not the certificated carriers endeavor to drive them out of business through price rivalry? Aside from the difficulty of obtaining CAB approval for fare decreases, one possible reason is that to do so would have decreased the certificated carriers' short-term profits. In the Los Angeles–San Diego market, the intrastate carriers' fare was only 10 cents lower than that of the certificated carriers, but they still managed to attract 10 to 15 percent of the total traffic essentially on the basis of their service offering. This fact and the findings of the multiple regression analyses in chapter 9 indicate that it was by no means certain that the certificated carriers would have captured a substantial portion of the intrastate carriers' traffic in the other two markets merely by matching their lower fares. Even if it is assumed, however, that by adopting coach fares equal to the intrastate carriers' fares the certificated carriers could have forced their intrastate competitors to terminate service in all three markets, and if the unlikely assumption is also made that such lower coach fares would not have diverted additional passengers from first-class to coach service, adopting equal fares would have increased the certificated carriers' total revenues by no more than $280,000 in 1955, by about $930,000 in 1956 and 1957, and by up to $1,850,000 in 1958 and 1959. This comes to $1.50 to $5.60 per added passenger for the extra 190,000 to 350,000 passengers the certificated carriers might have gained by such action.[17] Since it seems unlikely that this marginal revenue would have equaled the marginal cost of carrying these passengers, the certificated carriers' profits would have been decreased. Even greater losses would have

---

[16] *Ibid.*

[17] Calculated from data presented in Appendices 6(B), 7, and 14 of this book. Since these low fares were already offered by the intrastate carriers, their adoption by the certificated carriers would probably not have increased the total amount of air service demanded in these markets.

been sustained had it been necessary to undercut the intrastate carriers' fares in order to drive them out of business.

Even if the certificated carriers had managed to remove all intrastate carriers by predatory pricing, with open entry in the California markets, what was to keep new intrastate carriers from reappearing if fares were increased after the demise of the earlier carriers?[18] Besides, CCA had gone bankrupt in 1955 and California Coastal terminated service in 1957. Surely during these years the certificated carriers could properly expect that even PSA would soon disappear without their having to adopt predatory pricing. It seems that, given their imperfect knowledge of the intrastate carriers' actual traffic volumes and future potential, the certificated carriers acted rationally in the late 1950's when they ignored the lower fares of California Coastal and PSA.

The situation changed radically in 1960. PSA's adoption of Electras increased its share of the Los Angeles–San Francisco market from 15.4 percent in 1959 to 27.6 percent in 1960, 32.0 percent in 1961, and 43.5 percent in 1962, with similar increases in the Los Angeles–San Diego and San Diego–San Francisco markets (17.8 to 37.5 percent, and 57.9 to 79.3 percent, respectively).[19] Had the certificated carriers been able to capture all of that traffic by equaling PSA's fares (and, also, the quality of its Electra service), their gain in total revenues for 1960 would have been about $5,200,000, increasing to $7,200,000 in 1961—$8.47 and $10.12 per added passenger.[20] Given these large increases in total revenues and revenues per added passenger, it is understandable why Western introduced its Thriftair service on June 1, 1962, and why United inaugurated Jet Commuter service in September 1964. By mid-1962 the structure for these major markets had reverted to being a noncollusive oligopoly and remained that way through 1965.

Changes in Traffic Rankings

In 1948, when the three major California markets had only first-class air service provided by the certificated carriers under CAB-

[18] For an analysis of the disadvantages of predatory pricing by large firms and evidence that it may not be such a common practice as it is often asserted to be, see J. S. McGee, "Predatory Price Cutting: The Standard Oil (N.J.) Case," *The Journal of Law and Economics* 1 (October 1958), pp. 137–69.

[19] Calculated from data presented in Appendix 14 of this book.

[20] Calculated from data presented in Appendices 6(B), 7, and 14 of this book.

authorized fares, they ranked approximately second, thirty-first, and eighty-fourth in size among all U.S. markets, based on true O & D passenger volumes.[21] In 1965, the combined on-line O & D passenger volumes for the certificated and intrastate carriers ranked Los Angeles/Burbank/Long Beach–San Francisco/Oakland first by over one million passengers (3,023,341 compared to 1,985,680 for second-place Boston–New York/Newark), the Los Angeles/Burbank/ Long Beach–San Diego market had increased from the thirty-first to the ninth largest market in the U.S., and the San Diego–San Francisco/Oakland market had leaped from eighty-fourth to twenty-third place.[22]

Many things happened in California during those years that would effect these changes in rankings. For example, relatively greater shifts in the demand curves for airline service resulted from above-average increases in population and per capita incomes, from more rapid economic development (yielding demand increases), and from the extensive construction of multilane highways connecting major cities (serving to decrease demand). In addition, it has been shown that substantial reductions in airline prices occurred in these markets relative to the price changes experienced in similar interstate markets where fares were regulated by the CAB (compare the 1950 first-class and 1965 coach prices per mile given in Table 7–2). No information is available regarding the different price elasticities of demand existing in these markets during these years, so it is impossible to estimate the extent to which the more rapid traffic increases in each of the three major California markets were due to the existence of relatively lower prices. Basic economic theory and a review of a large amount of material pertaining to this period lead me to believe that lower prices were a very important reason for the relatively greater growth of traffic in these three markets. A similar opinion was expressed by Western in 1950.[23] Unfortunately, no more than this informed conjecture can be presented on this matter.

---

[21] CAB, *Airline Traffic Survey* (March and September 1948). Los Angeles/ Burbank–San Francisco/Oakland ranked third during March and second during September 1948 among all domestic markets. The rankings for Los Angeles/ Burbank–San Diego were thirty-fourth and twenty-ninth for these two survey periods. San Diego–San Francisco/Oakland ranked eighty-fourth during both periods.

[22] These rankings for 1965 were obtained by comparing the total on-line O & D passenger volumes given in Appendix 14 with those published in: CAB, *Competition Among the Domestic Air Carriers* (1965).

[23] See the quotation on pp. 78 and 79, chapter 5.

238 AIRLINE REGULATION IN AMERICA

Social Costs

The bankruptcies and repeated exits from the ranks of the intrastate carriers might be cited as undesirable consequences of the lack of effective regulation within California. Clearly, there were wealth transfers from the owners (and some creditors) of the unsuccessful intrastate carriers to their passengers and to those who were able to purchase these carriers' aircraft and other real assets at low prices. In addition, as a result of their competition, the intrastate carriers managed to bring about wealth transfers from the certificated carriers to themselves as well as to air travelers who would have flown at the higher fares of the certificated carriers but opted for the lower-priced service of the intrastate carriers once it became available. In both cases, however, these wealth transfers did not impose costs on society in general, since the loss of one person or firm was offset by the gain by another member of society. What alternatives or opportunities, if any, did society in general forego (what economic costs were incurred) because of the activities of the unsuccessful intrastate carriers?

The major real assets of airlines are their aircraft. Were aircraft and associated resources used inefficiently by the intrastate carriers, or were such resources destroyed or otherwise lost to society whenever an unsuccessful intrastate carrier terminated service? The answer to both questions is no. First, until PSA began purchasing Electras in 1959 the intrastate carriers operated only used aircraft that had already been produced for other purposes and customers. Actually, the intrastate carriers probably served to prolong the productive lives of most of these used aircraft, and the evidence in chapter 11 shows that they utilized them, as well as the new Electras and B-727's, more intensively than the certificated carriers utilized their aircraft. Second, when California Central went bankrupt its aircraft were not destroyed. Rather they were sold to Allegheny Airlines and Southwest Airways (Pacific Air Lines), and they continued to provide service (albeit, subsidized service) over the routes of those carriers. Similarly, when Futura went bankrupt its two leased L-049's were repossessed by their owners and shortly reappeared on Paradise Airlines' routes. The aircraft that Western Air Lines of California leased from Western Air Lines were merely transferred from WALC's service to Western's new coach service on the day following WALC's demise. The nonscheduled airlines that operated scheduled service within California during 1949 also transferred their aircraft to other uses when they decided to terminate service within California. From society's point of view, the major losses resulting from the operations

CONCLUSIONS 239

of intrastate carriers appear to be those associated with the crash of California Arrow's DC-3 in December 1949, and the crash of the L-049 of Paradise in March 1964. As shown in Table 3-4, however, the intrastate carriers have not been the only U.S. airlines to destroy lives and aircraft unintentionally through crashes.

On the other hand, the CAB's entry and exit control and the lack of bankruptcies among the certificated carriers does not mean that regulation has prevented losses from being imposed on society. For example, what was the cost to society of the final round of the four-engine, piston-powered aircraft development? This study indicates that few if any of these aircraft would have been operated domestically without the existing regulatory environment. However, large numbers of DC-7's and late-model Constellations were produced and operated in 1953–58, only to become obsolete (with many being scrapped) after the extensive introduction of jet aircraft in 1959. Contrast this with the role of the intrastate carriers in prolonging the useful lives of aircraft by operating them in low-fare service. In addition, what is the cost to society of operating large numbers of aircraft at annual average load factors of 60 percent or less (with fewer seats installed) when, as shown by the intrastate carriers, load factors between 70 and 75 percent can be regularly achieved? At least with regard to increasing output per unit of aircraft resource, the intrastate carriers appear to have decreased the transportation costs borne by society compared with those resulting from the operations of the CAB-regulated airlines.

Another possible cost to society is the value of the foregone service over various routes pending the completion of route award proceedings by the CAB to decide which certificated carrier(s) should be awarded rights to operate over those routes. For example, on March 20, 1964, the CAB announced its intention to institute an investigation of the possible need for single-carrier service between the Pacific Northwest and the Southwest.[24] The order officially beginning the investigation was issued on August 13, 1964, and it gave the following reasons for such a case:

These two large sections of the country constitute the one remaining major service area lacking single-carrier service. . . .

At the present time, a large amount of Pacific Northwest–Southwest traffic is compelled to use circuitous routings to reach its destination. For example, the (true) O & D traffic moving between the major hubs . . . for the calendar year 1962 was 460,000 passengers, or in excess of 630 O & D passengers per day in each direction. . . . Although the California circuity in the Dallas–Portland and Dallas–Seattle markets is 27 and 31 percent, respec-

[24] CAB Press Release No. 64-31 (March 20, 1964).

tively, the availability of coach services and the time savings of the existing circuitous connecting service via California remains more advantageous to the traveler than first-class service only via the limited existing interchange operations or the more time consuming two-carrier connecting service at Denver. For example, California connections provide a fare savings of $18.20 and an elapsed travel time 3½ hours shorter.[25]

The traffic volume for calendar year 1962 indicates that direct single-carrier service would have existed in these large markets prior to 1964 had there been no regulation. Certainly a number of carriers demonstrated their interest in these markets by applying for permission to perform such service prior to and at the time the case was instituted. A delay of three years, however, was to occur between the time the CAB formally recognized the need for such service and the issuance of its first decision in the case on April 11, 1967.[26] An additional 2½ years were required before the *Reopened Pacific Northwest–Southwest Service Investigation* was terminated on October 31, 1969.[27] It seems reasonable to ask whether such lengthy route investigations serve to withhold valuable benefits (for example, direct service) from society which would otherwise have been provided sooner had regulation not existed.[28] Costs due to regulation may also be imposed on society when certificated carriers are delayed or prohibited from terminating service over routes where losses are being incurred—that is, where the value of the service as measured by its use under regulated prices is less than the market value of the factors of production required to produce the service. In this regard, recall the rapidity with which the intrastate carriers

[25] CAB Order No. E-21186 (adopted August 13, 1964), pp. 1 and 2.

[26] CAB Order No. E-24970 (adopted April 11, 1967). Petitions for reconsideration were denied by the CAB in Order No. E-25266 (adopted June 7, 1967). Extensive single-carrier service was authorized by the Board in its decision.

[27] CAB Order No. 69-10-163 (adopted October 31, 1969). The last certificate to be amended by this case was issued in Order No. 70-2-102 (adopted February 24, 1970), and the motion from another airline to postpone the effective date of that certificate was dismissed by Order No. 70-3-6 (adopted March 2, 1970). Overall, six years elapsed between the Board's first and last public pronouncements regarding this investigation.

[28] A similar delay in service occurred within California immediately after the PUC received authority to control airline entry. As described in chapter 6, PSA's attempt to inaugurate low-fare service between Los Angeles and San Jose was suspended by the PUC from October 12, 1965, to May 18, 1966, while it conducted an investigation regarding the desirability of this new service. See Cal. PUC Decisions Nos. 69764 (dated October 7, 1965) and 70657 (dated May 3, 1966).

terminated service in some of the minor California markets (see chapter 6).

The surviving intrastate carriers demonstrated an ability to operate more efficiently than the certificated carriers. It is not known how much of their greater efficiency was due to a lack of regulation and how much, if any, resulted from comparative advantages possessed by their employees or due to the locations of their operations bases, etc. It is clear, however, that the intrastate carriers were not equally efficient and that greater efficiency was rewarded with survival. Without question, none of the intrastate carriers would have been allowed to operate had the CAB controlled entry within California. Expanding this to the national scene, one might ask: How many potential carriers, able to equal or surpass the efficiency of the certificated carriers, have been prevented from demonstrating this in interstate markets? To the extent that this has occurred, the cost of air transportation to society has been increased, both because this more efficient service was not made available, and because those resources that could have produced it were required to work in activities where they were less productive.

Finally, an additional cost to society resulting from regulation is the lost output of the highly trained and talented individuals who devote their working lives to carrying out regulatory activities for the CAB, the airlines, and other interested parties. If, indeed, the primary result of CAB regulation has been to increase the wealth of airline owners, employees, and suppliers through the creation of an imperfect cartel, and if a viable and more efficient airline industry could exist without regulation, then the hard work of these individuals in maintaining and operating the cartel increases social costs by the value of the output they would have produced in other, nonregulatory activities. Some very limited idea of the social costs incurred by regulatory work per se is given by the following statements from two presidents of certificated trunk carriers:

> The hours of management and personnel used by the regulators to ponder how things might be done overlooks a necessity to get things done. This represents a wasteful emphasis on the precise establishment of past facts rather than an awareness of events shaping the future. Rule-making has lengthened, deepened, and inevitably created a rigidity, where all involved can too easily be the prisoners of their procedures.[29]

* * * * *

[29] M. A. MacIntyre, *Competitive Private Enterprise Under Government Regulation* (The Charles C. Moskowitz Lectures, No. 3; New York: School of Commerce, Accounts and Finance, New York University, 1964, p. 47). Mr. MacIntyre resigned as president of Eastern Air Lines shortly before presenting this lecture.

242   AIRLINE REGULATION IN AMERICA

During the last Hawaii case, extensive hearings, beginning in October 1959, were held in Honolulu. . . . The transcript of these hearings contains 8,749 pages, accompanied by several thousand more pages of Exhibits. There are 573 pages in the transcript of oral arguments presented to the CAB by counsel for the 18 airline parties and 53 civic parties who participated in the case. The Briefs and Pleadings filed by these counsel fill a large, long library shelf.

Huge amounts of money, time and effort were expended during the proceedings by the federal, state and local governments who participated, by the chambers of commerce and other interested civic groups, and by the airline applicants. One airline alone, which the CAB characterized as the least qualified of all the applicants, admitted to having spent over three-quarters of a million dollars on the case.[30]

Those who argue for airline regulation as being socially desirable might consider the above factors in their analysis. It is not clear that the kind of "cutthroat competition" that existed within California results in higher costs to society than the CAB's regulation.

Predictions

The findings of this study provide the basis for deducing what would happen should the regulatory powers of the CAB be reduced to the level possessed by the PUC prior to September 1965. Naturally, there would be a period of major adjustment, and given the acceptance of sunk costs, the trunk carriers could well have some initial advantages over new airlines attempting to provide scheduled passenger service. The existing supplemental, all-cargo, intrastate, and even the local service carriers, however, would doubtless provide substantial competition for the trunk carriers' passenger service, and there is every reason to expect that new airlines would eventually be organized to provide other competitive services. It is safe to predict that the market structures for major interstate city pairs would quickly change from an imperfect cartel to an oligopoly with some degree of price rivalry, that there would be substantial decreases in general fares and a reduction in the number of promotional fares, and that service quality would be decreased in these markets. The law of diminishing marginal returns would insure that service would not be limited to major markets. Small- and medium-sized markets

[30] Remarks made by Western Air Lines President Terrell C. Drinkwater at a news conference in Honolulu, Hawaii, on February 23, 1966, as printed in: *Western Air Lines Flight Times* 15, no. 2 (February 1966), pp. 1 and 3. Note: No route authorizations were made in the case referred to by Mr. Drinkwater. The subsequent *Transpacific Route Investigation* (Domestic Phase), Docket No. 16242, was finally decided in Order No. 69-7-105 (adopted July 21, 1969).

would be served, but by only one or two carriers, and they too would have lower fares and a reduced quality of service. For some of the smallest markets, direct subsidies would be required for service to be provided, just as is now the case for most markets served by the local service carriers. The comparative advantages of each carrier would determine where it would provide service. There would probably be more specialization by each of a larger number of carriers (more homogeneous routes and fewer types and numbers of aircraft at any given time). Efficiency would be increased, the rate of adoption of innovations decreased, and, overall, the cost of air transportation substantially reduced.

Of course, there is no reason to expect the CAB's powers ever to be reduced so drastically. Quite the contrary, it is much more likely that its power will someday be increased to control service quality, thereby making regulation more complete and correcting the deficiencies of the airline cartel. The implications to be drawn, therefore, from the California intrastate carriers' performance under the PUC's limited control are "academic" in terms of the certificated carriers, except that they do provide estimates of the economic effects of CAB regulation. Since, however, the PUC's power over the intrastate carriers was increased in 1965 to a level comparable with the CAB's power over the certificated carriers, the findings of this study might well prove useful in predicting how the California intrastate carriers will develop within their new regulatory environment. Fundamental to such a prediction is the extent to which the PUC actually implements the authority given it by Assembly Bill 413.[31] On the one hand, should the PUC approve all applications for entry by any carrier having an FAA commercial operator certificate and allow such carriers to operate in the California markets of their choice, if it continues to approve automatically all fare decreases and the initial tariffs of new carriers, and if it decides not to implement its extensive control over service quality, then there is little reason to expect any significant changes in the development of air transportation within California due to this increased regulatory power. If, on the other hand, the PUC effectively implements its new power in a manner similar to that adopted by the CAB, it seems reasonable to expect that the intrastate carriers will evolve in a manner similar to the evolution of the certificated carriers.

Should the PUC limit entry into California markets, one can predict that the existing intrastate carriers will endeavor to reach

---

[31] See Jordan, *Economic Effects of Airline Regulation*, pp. 36–39 for a review of the provisions of Assembly Bill 413.

agreements among themselves designed to increase their wealth and other benefits—that is, they will endeavor to form a cartel with the assistance and within the structure of the PUC's regulation. The next step would be to make agreements (implicit or explicit) with the certificated carriers operating within California that would be beneficial to all parties. These two steps would change the market structure in the major markets from the oligopoly of 1965 to a duopoly (comprised of two cartels), followed eventually by a "merger" into a single cartel, imperfect though it might be. If this is achieved, it is predicted that general fares will eventually increase above those viable in an open-market oligopoly, discriminatory fares will reappear, and, perhaps, service-quality rivalry will become dominant, with associated increases in aircraft investment, schedule frequencies, etc. The problems resulting from having to deal with two regulatory commissions will probably complicate cooperation between the two carrier groups, and it would be undesirable for them if a significant degree of rivalry develops between the CAB and the PUC (unless, of course, the rivalry happens to be over who can help the airlines the most).

The key factor in the above does appear to be entry control. Once airline entry within California is effectively closed by PUC regulation, all else becomes possible. It will be interesting to observe the development of the PUC's regulation of California air transportation during the next two or three decades. The study of the PUC's implementation of its expanded power during this period should provide additional evidence regarding the economic effects of airline regulation.

Bibliography

Books and Pamphlets

Air California. *Annual Report*. Santa Ana, Calif.: 1967–1968.

Air Transport Association of America. *Major U.S. Airlines, 1967–1971 Financial Projections and Requirements*. Washington: 1967. (Presentation to the CAB by the ATA, November 28, 1967.)

Alchian, Armen A., and William R. Allen. *University Economics*. 2d ed. Belmont, Calif.: Wadsworth Publishing Co., Inc., 1967.

Bernstein, Marver H. *Regulating Business by Independent Commission*. Princeton, N.J.: Princeton University Press, 1955.

Caves, Richard E. *Air Transport and Its Regulators*. Cambridge, Mass.: Harvard University Press, 1962.

Cherington, Paul W. *Airline Price Policy: A Study of Domestic Airline Passenger Fares*. Boston: Division of Research, Graduate School of Business Administration, Harvard University, 1958.

Dewey, Donald. *Monopoly in Economics and Law*. Chicago: Rand McNally & Co., 1959.

Gill, Frederick W., and Gilbert L. Bates. *Airline Competition*. Boston: Division of Research, Graduate School of Business Administration, Harvard University, 1949.

Hutton, E. F. & Company. *Prospectus, Pacific Southwest Airlines*. Los Angeles: February 13, 1963; October 24, 1963; March 29, 1966; and October 26, 1966.

Jordan, William A. *Economic Effects of Airline Regulation*. Unpublished doctoral dissertation, University of California, Los Angeles, 1968.

Keyes, Lucile S. *Federal Control of Entry into Air Transportation*. Cambridge, Mass.: Harvard University Press, 1951.

Kleiger, Linda J. *Maximization of Industry Profits: The Case of United States Air Transportation.* Unpublished doctoral dissertation, University of California, Los Angeles, 1967.

Kolko, Gabriel. *Railroads and Regulation, 1877-1916.* Princeton, N.J.: Princeton University Press, 1965.

MacIntyre, Malcolm A. *Competitive Private Enterprise Under Government Regulation.* The Charles C. Moskowitz Lectures, No. 3. New York: School of Commerce, Accounts and Finance, New York University, 1964.

Pacific Southwest Airlines. *Annual Report.* San Diego: 1963-1966.

——————. *Listing Application to New York Stock Exchange.* A-22453. San Diego: April 19, 1965.

Rand McNally & Company. *Cosmopolitan World Atlas.* Chicago: 1962.

Richmond, Samuel B. *Regulation and Competition in Air Transportation.* New York: Columbia University Press, 1961.

Stigler, George J. *The Theory of Price.* 3d ed. New York: The Macmillan Co., 1966.

United Air Lines. *General Schedule.* Elk Grove Township, Ill.: 1964.

Western Air Lines. Research Department. *Chronological Listings of Important Events in Western's History.* Los Angeles: Revised September 8, 1965.

Wheatcroft, Stephen. *Air Transport Policy.* London: Michael Joseph, 1964.

——————. *The Economics of European Air Transport.* Cambridge, Mass.: Harvard University Press, 1956.

Articles and Periodicals

Air Transport Association of America. *Comparative Statement of Flight and Traffic Statistics* (12 Months Ending December 31, 1947-1956).

——————. *Comparative Statement of Number of Employees and Average Annual Salaries by Account Classification* (December 31, 1949-1950).

——————. *Quarterly Comparative Statement of Air Carriers' Aircraft Operating Statistics* (12 Months Ending December 31, 1957-1965).

Air Travel, News Supplement of *Official Airline Guide,* 18-23 (1962-1967).

Alchian, Armen A. "Costs and Outputs." In *The Allocation of Economic Resources,* by Moses Abramovitz, *et al.* Stanford, Calif.: Stanford University Press, 1959, pp. 23-40.

American Aviation, 27 (May 1964), p. 40.

American Aviation Air Traffic Guide, 2-4 (1946-1948).

American Aviation Daily (December 14, 1948), p. n.a. (typewritten copy); (March 17, 1949), p. n.a. (typewritten copy); (March 28, 1949), p. n.a. (typewritten copy); (November 29, 1949), p. 132; (January 14, 1958), p. 98.

American Aviation Traffic Guide, 2 (1946).

Anderson, Charles E. "The Martinliner." *American Aviation Historical Society Journal*, 7 (Summer 1962), pp. 120-25.

Averch, Harvey and Leland L. Johnson. "Behaviour of the Firm Under Regulatory Constraint." *American Economic Review*, 52 (December 1962), pp. 1052-69.

Aviation Week, 54 (January 1, 1951), p. 62.

Aviation Week and Space Technology, 79-91 (1963-1969).

Brecher, Edward M. "Air Travel *Can* be Inexpensive." *Consumer Reports* (June 1950), pp. 270-75.

California Central Airline Guide (effective September 3, 1952; February 1, 1953; April 26, 1953; August 25, 1953; April 1, 1955; and January 4, 1956).

"California Central Flying Martinliners." *The Martin Star* (September 1951), pp. 4-6.

Christian, George L. "Cal Central Likes its 2-0-2 Fleet." *Aviation Week*, 56 (February 11, 1952), pp. 44 and 46.

Collins, James H. "The Plane With the Candy-Stripe Tail." *Sales Management* (September 1, 1952), pp. 105-9.

Drinkwater, Terrell C. "Remarks Made at a News Conference in Honolulu, Hawaii, on February 23, 1966." *Western Air Lines Flight Times*, 15 (February 1966), pp. 1 and 3.

Hilton, George W. "Consistency of the Interstate Commerce Act." *Journal of Law and Economics*, 9 (October 1966), pp. 87-114.

_____. Review of *Railroads and Regulation, 1877-1916* by Gabriel Kolko. *American Economic Review*, 56 (March 1966), pp. 271-73.

Hirshleifer, Jack. "The Firm's Cost Function: A Successful Reconstruction?" *Journal of Business*, 35 (July 1962), pp. 235-55.

"Inside Story of California Central Airways." *American Aviation*, 16 (August 4, 1952), pp. 23-24.

"Jet Traffic Climbs 35% Above Piston Aircraft." (Mohawk Airlines) *Air Chief*, 13 (November-December 1965), p. 3.

Jordan, William A. "Competition—A Two-Edged Sword in Improving Air Transportation Performance?" In John de S. Coutinho (Chm.). *Transportation: A Service*. Sesquicentennial Forum on Transportation Engineering. New York: New York Academy of

248

BIBLIOGRAPHY

Sciences, 1967, pp. 153–68. (Originally available as American Society of Mechanical Engineers' Publication No. 67-TRAN-29, August 1967.)
Koontz, Harold D. "Economic and Managerial Factors Underlying Subsidy Needs of Domestic Trunk Line Air Carriers." *Journal of Air Law and Commerce*, 18 (Spring 1951), pp. 127–56.
Levine, Michael E. "Is Regulation Necessary? California Air Transportation and National Regulatory Policy." *Yale Law Journal*, 74 (July 1965), pp. 1416–47.
Los Angeles Times (March 5, 1946) Part I, p. 7; (October 22, 1946) Part II, p. 6; (October 23, 1949) Part I, p. 38; (December 9, 1949) Part I, p. 1; (November 5, 1952) Part II, p. 2; and (August 28, 1962) p. n.a. (Obtained from the clipping files in the library of this newspaper.)
McGee, John S. "Predatory Price Cutting: The Standard Oil (N.J.) Case." *Journal of Law and Economics*, 1 (October 1958), pp. 137–69.
"Martinliners Set West Coast Aircoach Pace." Reprinted from *The Martin Star* (February 1962), p. n.a.
Official Airline Guide, North American Edition, 5-22 (1948–1966).
Pacific Southwest Airlines. *Flight Schedule* (1949–1956, 1960 and 1965–1966).
_____. *Press Releases* (April 1965).
"Price War." *Fortnight* (June 23, 1950), p. 20.
Rottenberg, Simon. "The Baseball Players' Labor Market." *Journal of Political Economy*, 64 (June 1956), pp. 242–58.
San Diego Evening Tribune (November 11, 1959), p. A-2; and (May 11, 1961), p. A-3. (Obtained from the clipping files in the library of this newspaper.)
San Diego Union (July 28, 1955), p. A-26; (September 22, 1957), p. B-5; (December 5, 1959), p. A-10; and (August 31, 1965), p. A-19. (Obtained from the clipping files in the library of this newspaper.)
"Scramble for LA–SF Traffic Intensifies." *Aviation Week and Space Technology*, 81 (September 14, 1964), pp. 43 and 47.
Self, Thomas M. "CCA Air Coach." *Aviation Week*, 54 (January 15, 1951), pp. 58–63.
Stigler, George J. "The Economist and the State." *American Economic Review*, 55 (March 1965), pp. 1–18.
_____, and Claire Friedland. "What Can Regulators Regulate? The Case of Electricity." *Journal of Law and Economics*, 5 (October 1962), pp. 1–16.

Stone, Christopher D. "ICC: Some Reminiscences on the Future of American Transportation." *New Individualist Review*, 2 (April 1963), pp. 3-15.

Taylor, Joseph W. "Cheap Flying." *Wall Street Journal*, Pacific Coast Edition (December 6, 1949), pp. 1 and 3.

Taylor, Marvel M. "Economic Regulation of Intrastate Air Carriers in California." *California Law Review*, 41 (Fall 1953), pp. 454-82.

United Air Lines. "Traffic Information Bulletin No. 17" (April 28, 1950).

Wall Street Journal, Pacific Coast Edition (January 16, 1967), p. 7; Midwest Edition (October 3, 1969), p. 2.

Watkins, Harold D. "Non-Regulated Operation Benefits PSA." *Aviation Week and Space Technology*, 79 (July 1, 1963), pp. 48 and 49.

_____. "PSA Business Traffic Proportion Grows." *Aviation Week and Space Technology*, 79 (July 8, 1963), p. 37.

Government Publications

California. Legislature. *Statutes and Amendments to the Codes, 1965 Chapters*, compiled by George W. Murphy, Legislative Counsel. Sacramento: California Office of State Printing, 1965.

California. Public Utilities Commission. *Annual Report*, 1964-1967 Fiscal Years. Sacramento: California Office of State Printing, 1964-1967.

_____. *Decisions of the Public Utilities Commission*, 49-63. Sacramento: California State Printing Office, 1949-1964.

_____. *Public Utilities Code and Related Constitutional Provisions*. Sacramento: California State Printing Office, 1965.

_____. Transportation Division, Passenger Section. *Intrastate Passengers of Scheduled Air Carriers*. Report No. 1511 (Quarters Ended March 31, June 30, September 30, and December 31, 1962-1965). San Francisco: 1964-1967 (mimeographed).

U.S. Civil Aeronautics Board. *Aeronautical Statutes and Related Material*, Revised June 1, 1954, and July 1, 1963. Washington: Government Printing Office, 1954 and 1963.

_____. *Air Carrier Analytical Charts and Summaries*, VII-4 (December 31, 1965). Washington: Government Printing Office.

_____. *Air Carrier Financial Statistics*, XIII-4 and XIV-4 (December 31, 1965 and 1966). Washington: Government Printing Office.

—————————. *Air Carrier Traffic Statistics*, XI-2, 5, 6, & 12, XII-12, XIII-12, and XIV-12 (December 1965–December 1968). Washington: Government Printing Office.

—————————. *Air-Passenger Traffic Data Seasonally Adjusted Domestic Trunk Operations by Carrier and Class of Service, 1953–1964.* Washington: December 1964.

—————————. *Airline Statistics Handbook* (Calendar Years 1946–1952). Washington: n.d. (Published for internal CAB distribution in late 1953 or early 1954.)

—————————. *Analysis of Domestic Fare Structure and Historical Fare Data.* Washington: April 21, 1966 (mimeographed).

—————————. *Annual Report*, 1941–1965. Washington: Government Printing Office, 1941–1965.

—————————. *Book of Official C.A.B. Airline Route Maps and Airport to Airport Mileages.* 10th ed. Washington: Air Transport Association of America, 1964.

—————————. *Civil Aeronautics Board Reports*, 12–37. Washington: Government Printing Office, 1951–1962.

—————————. *Competition Among Domestic Air Carriers, 1955–1965.* Washington: Air Transport Association of America, 1956–1966.

—————————. *Domestic Origin-Destination Survey of Airline Passenger Traffic, 1946–1965.* Washington: Air Transport Association of America, 1947–1966. (Title varies; published by the Government Printing Office prior to September 1950.)

—————————. *Handbook of Airline Statistics.* June 1960, 1961, 1962, 1963, 1965, and 1967 eds. Washington: Government Printing Office, 1960–1968.

—————————. *Impact of New Large Jets on the Air Transportation System, 1970–1973.* Washington: November 1969.

—————————. "Paradise Airlines, Inc., Lockheed Constellation, L-049, N 86504 near Zephyr Cove, Nevada, March 1, 1964." *Aircraft Accident Report*, SA-378, File No. 1-0002. Washington: July 15, 1965.

—————————. *Resume of U.S. Carrier Accidents (Calendar Year 1950).* Washington: August 1951.

—————————. *A Statistical Review and Briefs of U.S. Air Carrier Accidents*, Calendar Years 1949–1965. Washington: 1950–1966 (title varies).

—————————. *Traffic, Fares, and Competition, Los Angeles–San Francisco Air Travel Corridor*, Staff Research Rpt. No. 4. Washington: August 1965.

_____. M. Mikolajczyk. *Seasonal Adjustment of Domestic Trunk Air-Passenger Traffic Data: 1951-1961* (Preliminary), Staff Research Rpt. No. 3. Washington: February 1963.

U.S. Department of Commerce. Office of Business Economics. *Business Statistics.* 1967 ed. Washington: Government Printing Office, 1967.

U.S. Federal Aviation Agency. *Direct Operating Costs and Other Performance Characteristics of Transport Aircraft in Airline Service, Calendar Year 1964.* Washington: September 1965.

U.S. General Services Administration. Office of the Federal Register. National Archives and Records Service. *Code of Federal Regulations,* Title 14, Chapters I and II (Revised as of January 1, 1965). Washington: Government Printing Office, 1965.

U.S. Interstate Commerce Commission. *Annual Report,* 1948, 1957, and 1967. Washington: Government Printing Office, 1948, 1957 and 1967.

U.S. National Transportation Safety Board. *Annual Review of U.S. Air Carrier Accidents,* Calendar Years 1966 and 1967. Washington: 1967 and 1968.

_____. *A Preliminary Analysis of Aircraft Accident Data, U.S. Civil Aviation, 1968.* Washington: 1969.

Other Government Materials

California. Public Utilities Commission. *Decisions:* Nos. 43932, 45624, 48429, 48563, 54918, 56358, 56419, 56849, 57990, 58488, 59066, 59328, 61102, 61224, 61225, 63315, 63814, 64865, 65589, 67077, 69764, 70657, 71310, 71393, 71490, 71871, and 73487. San Francisco: 1950-1967 (mimeographed, and in *Decisions of the Public Utilities Commission*).

_____. *Fare Authorizations:* Nos. 20-12-58 (August 2, 1947), 20-12-121 (March 20, 1951), and 20-12-146 (April 29, 1952). San Francisco: (mimeographed).

_____. *General Orders:* Nos. 105, 105-A, 120, and 120-A. San Francisco: 1957, 1959, and 1964.

_____. Charles J. Astrue. *Intrastate Scheduled "Coach Class" Air Carriers.* Exhibits Nos. 1-C, 2-C, and 5-C, Case No. 4994, *et al.* San Francisco: 1949 and 1950 (mimeographed).

_____. Examiner Richard D. Gravelle. "Proposed Report." Application No. 47843, *et al.* San Francisco: February 28, 1966 (mimeographed).

California. Senate. *Senate Bill No. 1624*, introduced by Senator Hatfield, April 26, 1949, referred to Committee on Public Utilities. Sacramento: Legislative document, 1949.

U.S. Civil Aeronautics Board, *Economic Regulations*: Nos. ER-223 (August 16, 1957) and ER-338 (September 27, 1961). (Mimeographed and in 22 F.R. 6756 and 26 F.R. 9310.)

───────. *Order Serials*: Nos. 2164, E-3419, E-3612, E-4339, E-4835, E-5033, E-6493, E-6609, E-6686, E-7333, E-7377, E-7448, E-7627, E-7894, E-8108, E-8782, E-8904, E-12987, E-14593, E-14978, E-16068, E-16205, E-17885, E-18706, E-19313, E-19655, E-19963, E-20801, E-20821, E-21186, E-21505, E-22387, E-22958, E-23147, E-23818, E-23819, E-23958, E-24970, E-25266, E-25626, E-26625, E-26626, E-26967, 68-12-11, 69-7-105, 69-10-163, 70-2-102, and 70-3-6. Washington: 1943–1969 (mimeographed).

───────. "Petition for Enforcement." *Paradise Airlines, Inc., Respondent, Enforcement Proceeding*, Docket 14766. Washington: September 23, 1963 (mimeographed).

───────. *Press Releases*: Nos. 49-77, 49-95, 50-56, 51-10, 51-95, 58-5, 60-10, 60-13, 64-31, 64-62, 66-13, 66-19, 66-29, 66-34, 66-58, 66-103, 66-111, 68-69, 68-81, 68-138, and 69-3. Washington: 1949–1969.

───────. *Procedural Regulation*: No. PR-104. Washington: January 19, 1968 (mimeographed).

───────. *Report on Meetings Between the Civil Aeronautics Board and the Domestic Trunkline Carriers on Domestic Passenger Fares.* Washington: 1969 (mimeographed).

───────. Transcript of the Hearings before CAB Hearing Examiner S. Thomas Simon in: *N. E. Halaby, Administrator, Federal Aviation Agency, Complainant vs. Paradise Airlines, Inc., Respondent*, Docket No. SE-462, March 20–April 7, 1964. Washington: 1964 (mimeographed).

───────. Bureau of Accounts and Statistics, Research and Statistics Division. *Record of Computation of Route Miles Operated.* Washington: n.d. (unpublished worksheets).

───────. *Route Miles—Local Service.* Washington: n.d. (unpublished worksheets).

───────. *Route Miles—Trunk.* Washington: n.d. (unpublished worksheets).

───────. Office of the Secretary, Schedules and Records Unit. *Suspensions and Points Authorized (Exclusive and Combination).* Washington: n.d. (unpublished worksheets).

U.S. Department of Defense. Department of the Navy. Contract No. N123 (60530)7988A. Los Angeles: U.S. Navy Purchasing Office, July 1, 1956, as modified September 17, 1956 (mimeographed and typewritten).

U.S. Department of Defense. Department of the Air Force. Head-quarters, Military Air Transport Service. Negotiated Contracts Nos. 11(626)-733 (effective 5 October 1965) and 11(626)-735 (effective 4 January 1966). Scott AFB, Ill.: MAMPC, 1965 and 1966 (mimeographed and typewritten).

Documents Submitted in CAB or PUC Proceedings

California Central Airlines. "Application for Certificate of Public Convenience and Necessity," *In the Matter of the Application of California Central Airlines For authority to engage in air transportation under Section 401. . .*, CAB Docket No. 4482. Burbank, Calif.: May 19, 1950 (mimeographed).

_____. "Complaint," *California Central Airlines, a corporation, Complainant, vs. United Air Lines, Inc., a corporation, and Western Air Lines, Inc., a corporation, Defendants*, Calif. PUC Case No. 5397. Burbank, Calif.: July 22, 1952 (mimeographed).

El Dorado County. "Exhibits in Response to Information Requests," *Service to Lake Tahoe, California Investigation*, CAB Docket No. 16312. Lake Tahoe, Calif.: November 15, 1965 (mimeographed).

Pacific Southwest Airlines. "Answer of Pacific Southwest Airlines, Inc. (formerly Friedkin Aeronautics, Inc.)," *In the Matter of the Formal Complaint of Western Air Lines, Inc. Against Pacific Southwest Air Lines, Inc.*, CAB Docket No. 14075. San Diego: November 9, 1962 (mimeographed).

Paradise Airlines. "Motion for Order Disclaiming Jurisdiction, or in the alternative, Application for Exemption Order. . . ," *Paradise Airlines, Inc. Enforcement Proceeding*, CAB Docket No. 14766. Oakland, Calif.: October 26, 1963 (mimeographed).

San Jose, City of. "Exhibits," *Service to Lake Tahoe, California Investigation*, CAB Docket No. 16312. San Jose, Calif.: n.d. (mimeographed).

United Air Lines. "Chronology of United's First-Class Fare Level, 1938 to Date," Cal. PUC Application No. 39775. Chicago: March 12, 1958 (mimeographed).

Western Air Lines. "Application of Western Air Lines, Inc. for Exemption," *In the matter of the application of Western Air Lines, Inc. . . . for an exemption from Section 403(b) of the Act insofar*

as the provisions thereof would prevent Western from complying with a reparation order of the Public Utilities Commission of the State of California, CAB Docket No. 5599. Los Angeles: June 4, 1952 (mimeographed).

——————. "Complaint," *In the Matter of the Complaint of Western Air Lines, Inc. with respect to rules, fares and charges proposed by United Air Lines, Inc., applicable to Air Coach service . . .*, CAB Docket No. 4430. Los Angeles: April 18, 1950 (mimeographed).

——————. "Complaint and Request for Investigation and Enforcement," *In the matter of the complaint and request of Western Air Lines, Inc. for investigation of the fares, . . . and practices of California Central Airlines . . .*, CAB Docket No. 5660. Los Angeles: July 18, 1952 (mimeographed).

——————. "Formal Complaint," *In the Matter of the Formal Complaint of Western Air Lines, Inc. against Friedkin Aeronautics, Inc. d/b/a Pacific Southwest Airlines*, CAB Docket No. 14075. Los Angeles: October 9, 1962 (mimeographed).

——————. "Memorandum on Behalf of Western Air Lines, Inc. to Accompany Special Intrastate Air Coach Tariff for Service between Los Angeles and San Francisco–Oakland Filed with the Civil Aeronautics Board on March 27, 1950." Los Angeles: (mimeographed).

Tariffs Filed with the CAB or PUC

California Public Utilities Commission (California Railroad Commission to 1946), 1943–1966:
California Central Airlines, Cal. P.U.C. No. 1.
California Coastal Airlines, Cal. P.U.C. No. 1.
Mercer Enterprises, Cal. P.U.C. No. 1.
Pacific Air Lines (intrastate carrier), C.R.C. Nos. 1 and 2.
Pacific Air Lines (local service carrier), Cal. P.U.C. Nos. 2-5, 7, & 13.
Pacific Southwest Airlines, C.P.U.C. No. 1.
Paradise Airlines, Cal. P.U.C. Nos. 2-5.
Rogers, S. J., Agent, Cal. P.U.C. No. 1.
Southwest Airways, C.R.C. No. 1, and Cal. P.U.C. Nos. 2, 10, & 11.
Trans California Airlines, Cal. P.U.C. No. 1.
United Air Lines, C.R.C. Nos. 12 & 13, and Cal. P.U.C. Nos. 15, 16, 20, 22, 23, 25, & 28-30.

Western Air Lines, C.R.C. No. 1, and Cal. P.U.C. Nos. 2-4, 19-21, 23-28, & 30.

Western Air Lines of California, Cal. P.U.C. No. 1.

U.S. Civil Aeronautics Board, 1945-1966:

Redfern, M. F., Agent, Air Traffic Conference of America, C.A.B. Nos. 7, 15, 18, & 31 (C.A.B. Nos. 18 & 31 later filed by C. C. Hubbard and by J. B. Walker).

Squires, C. C., General Manager, Airline Tariff Publishers, Inc., C.A.B. No. 90.

Walker, J. B., Agent, Air Traffic Conference of America, C.A.B. No. 44 (later filed by C. C. Squires).

Weeks, W. A., Director of Tariffs, Eastern Air Lines, C.A.B. Nos. 83 & 160.

Government Files

California. Public Utilities Commission. Official files for the following applications: Nos. 39172, 39775, 39776, 39807, 40490, 40536, 41101, 41445, 41983, 42253, 42417, 42461, 42750, 43675, 44104, 44118, 44239, 44618, 45071, 45122, 47828, 47843, 48157, 48989, and 49001. San Francisco: PUC, 1957-1966.

_____. Official files for the following cases: 4994, 5271, 5397, 5450, 5867, 7668, and 7777. San Francisco: PUC, 1949-1964.

U.S. District Court. Northern District of California. Legal documents and company records of Paradise Airlines located in the files of the Court Clerk for Case No. 43394, *Peerless Insurance Co. vs. Paradise Airlines*. San Francisco.

U.S. District Court. Southern District of California. Legal documents and company records located in the files of the Court Clerk for the following proceedings in bankruptcy:

No. 45350-PH, Pacific Air Lines, October 16, 1947;
No. 59560-PH, Airline Transport Carriers, January 27, 1954;
No. 59561-PH, California Central Airlines, January 27, 1954;
No. 147405-WB, Futura Airlines, October 30, 1962.

Los Angeles.

U.S. Federal Aviation Agency. Western Region. Documents, reports, summaries, letters, orders, and other materials concerning Airline Transport Carriers, Western Air Lines, and the intrastate carriers listed in Appendix 1 for the years 1946-1966. Los Angeles.

Appendices

Appendix No. 1

CALIFORNIA INTRASTATE CARRIERS PROVIDING SCHEDULED SERVICE[a]
1946-1965

| Carriers | Date of | | Cities Receiving Service[b] |
	Entry	Merger or Exit	
Blatz Airlines[c]	7/ 5/63	12/26/63	BUR TNS 7/ 5/63 - 9/25/63 TVL 9/26/63 - 12/26/63
California Arrow[d]	5/23/49	12/ 7/49	BUR, OAK, SAC FAT 8/15/49 - 9/18/49
California Central Airlines[e]	1/ 2/49	2/14/55	BUR, SFO SAN 5/ 5/49 - 2/14/55 SAC 6/17/49 - 9/23/49 OAK 11/11/49 - 2/14/55 LAX 11/20/50 - 2/14/55 IYK 2/26/51 - 7/30/53 EDW 8/ 1/51 - 1/14/52
California Coastal Airlines, dba California Central Airlines[f]	3/15/55	8/ 9/57	BUR, OAK SFO 4/ 1/55 - 2/17/57 SAN 5/12/55 - 10/31/56 LAX 1/ 4/56 - 2/ 3/57
California Pacific Airlines[g]	1/21/50	2/10/50	BUR, OAK
California Skycoach[h]	4/26/49	5/na/49	BUR, OAK, SFO
California Time Airlines[i]	9/19/64	2/ 1/65	BUR, PSP, SJC OAK 11/ 1/64 - 1/12/65
Channel Airways	5/27/49	8/17/49	LGB, SFO
Futura Airlines[j]	6/15/62	9/19/62	LAX, TVL BFL, FAT, OAK, SAC 6/15/62 - 7/19/62 VNY 8/31/62 - 9/19/62
Mercer Enterprises[k]	4/18/64	-	BRF, BUR, LAX

258

| Carriers | Date of | | Cities Receiving Service[b] |
	Entry	Merger or Exit	
Pacific Air Lines[1]	3/ 6/46	6/ 3/47	BUR, SAC SFO 6/ 1/46 – 6/ 3/47 FAT 10/22/46 – 6/ 3/47 MOD 10/22/46 – 11/30*46 SCK 10/22/46 – 1/31*47

Pacific Southwest Airlines[m]	5/ 6/49	–	BUR, SAN
			OAK 5/ 6/49 – 3/31*54,
			     10/ 7/60 – 3/23/61,
			      1/ 5/65 – present
			SFO 7/20/51 – present
			LGB 10/ 1/53 – 6/16/54
			LAX 8/15/58 – present
			SJC 10/ 8/65 – 10/11/65

Paradise Airlines[n]	5/14/62	3/ 4/64	OAK, SJC, TVL
Robin Airways[o]	3/16/49	9/12/49	BUR, OAK
Trans California Airlines	8/15/62	10/ 7/64	BUR, OAK LAX 12/14/62 – 10/ 7/64 SAN 1/ 4/63 – 6/14/64
Western Air Lines of California[p]	8/19/49	5/31/50	BUR, OAK, SFO

[*]Estimated from monthly traffic and/or operating statistics, or from other sources in which the precise date was not specified.

na -- not available.

[a]This appendix lists those California intrastate carriers providing scheduled, common carrier service with DC-3 or larger aircraft during any period from 1946 through 1965.

[b]The following is a listing of the city codes used in this appendix:

BFL	Bakersfield	IYK	Inyokern
BRF	Brown Field (S. San Diego)	LAX	Los Angeles
BUR	Burbank (N. Los Angeles)	LGB	Long Beach
EDW	Edwards AFB	MOD	Modesto
FAT	Fresno	OAK	Oakland

PSP   Palm Springs   SJC   San Jose
SAC   Sacramento   TNS   Truckee-Tahoe (North Shore)
SAN   San Diego   TVL   Lake Tahoe (South Shore)
SCK   Stockton   VNY   Van Nuys (NW. Los Angeles)
SFO   San Francisco

If no dates are specified after a city it means that service was provided there throughout the carrier's existence so that the dates of entry and exit apply.

cBlatz operated as a large irregular/supplemental carrier from May 14, 1947 until October 23, 1962. In 1964 and 1965 it conducted contract operations as a private carrier.

dCalifornia Arrow's California PUC tariff was filed under the name of Arrow Airways, Inc., a large irregular carrier. In addition, its equipment was leased from Arrow Airways. The CAB suspended Arrow Airway's letter of registration on February 15, 1951 [12 CAB 405, 414 (1951)]. However, California Arrow's intrastate operations appear to have been terminated when one of its two DC-3's crashed near Vallejo, California on December 7, 1949 causing the deaths of the three crew members and six passengers on board.

eCalifornia Central was owned by the two majority stockholders and senior officers of Airline Transport Carriers, a large irregular carrier. Equipment and crews were leased from ATC. CCA and ATC were both adjudicated bankrupt on January 25, 1955 and their operating assets sold jointly as a single unit on February 14, 1955.

fCalifornia Coastal was organized by the original owners of California Central Airlines. Shortly after the operating assets of that latter company were sold in bankruptcy, service was inaugurated by California Coastal doing business as California Central Airlines. The date of entry adopted in this study is the original effective date of California Coastal's PUC tariff. However, it appears that service may actually have been inaugurated two or three weeks earlier, and that it may have been suspended between midnight, March 15 and March 18, 1955. California Coastal was also operated in close association with a reorganized Airline Transport Carriers. When California Coastal terminated operations, it appears that its remaining personnel and operating assets were merely transferred to ATC and were utilized by that company until it too terminated operations several years later.

gThe manager of California Pacific was Mr. D. W. Mercer, the present owner of Mercer Enterprises (see below). Mr. Mercer stated that California Pacific's operations were terminated when it was learned that United Air Lines planned to inaugurate coach service between Burbank and Oakland.

Appendix No. 1 (continued)

[h]California Skycoach had the same management as Trans American Airways, a large irregular carrier. The precise dates of California Skycoach's operation are not known.

[i]Following its service termination, California Time took part in a PUC proceeding concerning service between San Jose and Los Angeles. On October 20, 1965 it withdrew from that proceeding and filed an amendment to its application, No. 47843 (originally filed August 25, 1965). Also, during this period California Time participated in the CAB's Service to Lake Tahoe, California Investigation, Docket 16312, et al., but its applications in this case were dismissed by CAB Order No. E-22958 (adopted December 2, 1965).

[j]Adjudicated bankrupt on December 4, 1962.

[k]Operations limited to scheduled flights on Saturday and Sunday.

[l]Pacific Air Lines should not be confused with the CAB certificated local service carrier that adopted this name in 1958. From 1946 to 1958 the present Pacific Air Lines operated under the name of Southwest Airways. There is conflicting information regarding Pacific's date of entry. Service may not have been inaugurated until April 4, 1946. Pacific's termination of service on June 3, 1947 was followed by an involuntary bankruptcy proceeding in which it was adjudicated bankrupt on December 4, 1947. Schedules for a "Pacific Airways" were published in the October and November 1947 editions of the American Aviation Air Traffic Guide announcing Burbank, Fresno, Sacramento and San Francisco service. However, no evidence could be found indicating that this service was actually operated.

[m]Originally operated as a department of the Friedkin School of Aeronautics.

[n]Paradise's FAA commercial operator certificate was initially issued on December 7, 1962, but its original PUC tariff was effective on May 14, 1962 and airport records show that substantial operations began in May 1962. Thus, the earlier of the two dates appears to be the actual date of entry. Paradise's commercial operator certificate was suspended by the FAA three days after one of its Lockheed L-049 aircraft crashed near Lake Tahoe on March 1, 1964, with the loss of 85 lives. However, its last scheduled flight was operated on the day following the crash.

[o]In addition to operating as Robin Airways within California, the same organization performed interstate, nonscheduled service as Robin Airlines from April 1, 1949 to April 18, 1952.

[p]Western Air Lines of California leased aircraft, crews, reservations service, airport passenger facilities, accounting service, etc., from Western Air Lines. On November 15, 1950, 5½ months after WALC

terminated service, the CAB issued Order No. E-4835 requiring the
carriers to cease and desist from this relationship.

Sources:

California Public Utilities Commission:
   C. J. Astrue, Intrastate Scheduled "Coach Class" Air Carriers,
      Exhibit No. 1-C (submitted Dec. 15, 1949), pp. 4, 25-41,
      and Exhibit No. 5-C (submitted Feb. 10, 1950), p. 5, Case
      No. 4994, et al.
   Examiner R. D. Gravelle, "Proposed Report," Application No.
      47843, et al. (dated Feb. 28, 1966), p. 16 (mimeographed).
   Exhibit No. 6 (submitted Mar. 27, 1951), Case No. 5271.
   Decision No. 56419 (dated Mar. 26, 1958), p. 4 (mimeographed).
   Pacific Air Lines, tariffs: C.R.C. No. 1 (dated Apr. 4, 1946),
      and C.R.C. No. 2 (dated June 17, 1946).
   Pacific Southwest Airlines, Exhibit No. 4 (submitted Jan. 5,
      1967), Application No. 48989.
   Paradise Airlines, tariff: Cal. PUC No. 2 (originally effective
      May 14, 1962).
   Transportation Division, Passenger Section, Intrastate Passengers
      of Scheduled Air Carriers by Types of Carriers, No. 1511.13
      (Quarter Ended Sept. 30, 1965), fn 3.

U.S. Civil Aeronautics Board, Orders Nos. E-4835 (adopted Nov. 15,
   1950), E-6493 (adopted June 6, 1952), E-14978 (adopted Mar. 2,
   1960), E-22387 (adopted June 30, 1965), and E-22958 (adopted
   Dec. 2, 1965).

U.S. District Court, Southern District of California -- legal docu-
   ments and company records in the files of the Court Clerk for the
   following proceedings in bankruptcy:
   No. 45350-PH (filed Oct. 16, 1947), Pacific Air Lines.
   No. 59560-PH (filed Jan. 27, 1954), Airline Transport Carriers.
   No. 59561-PH (filed Jan. 27, 1954), California Central Airlines.
   No. 147405-WB (filed Oct. 30, 1962), Futura Airlines.

U.S. Federal Aviation Agency, Western Region:
   Air Carrier and Commercial Operator Data Report, Blatz Airlines
      (July & Dec. 1963).
   C.A.R. 42/45 Status Report, Blatz Airlines (Sept. 1962 & June
      1963), and Futura Airlines (Sept. 1962).
   Emergency Order of Suspension, Case No. WE-64-OC-02, Paradise
      Airlines (issued Mar. 4, 1964).
   Operations Specifications, Mercer Enterprises (May 18, 1964), and
      Trans California Airlines (Sept. 14, Dec. 14, and Dec. 31,
      1962).

Appendix No. 1 (continued)

Systemworthiness Inspection Report, Paradise Airlines (June 17, 1963).

Airport Records:
City of Long Beach, Dept. of Aeronautics.
City of Los Angeles, Dept. of Airports.
Port of Oakland, Oakland Metropolitan International Airport.
Port of San Diego, Lindbergh Field.
San Francisco Public Utilities Commission, Airport Department, San Francisco International Airport.

Company records of Pacific Southwest Airlines and Western Air Lines.

Conversations with Mr. D. W. Mercer, former manager of California Pacific Airlines and president of Mercer Enterprises (Oct. 13, 1965 & Dec. 22, 1965); Mr. L. A. Mudgett, former president of Trans California Airlines (May 24, 1965); and Mrs. C. C. Sherman, former secretary-treasurer of California Central, California Coastal, and Airline Transport Carriers (Dec. 15, 1965).

American Aviation Air Traffic Guide, Vols. 2-4, (June 1946), p. 90; (Dec. 1946), p. 177; (Feb. 1947), p. 167; (Oct. 1947), p. 199; and (Nov. 1947), p. 199.

American Aviation Daily (Mar. 17, 1949), p. n.a.

The Los Angeles Times, (Mar. 5, 1946), Part I, p. 7; (Oct. 22, 1946), Part II, p. 6; and (Nov. 5, 1952), Part II, p. 2.

REVENUE PASSENGER ORIGINATIONS[a] AND AVERAGE ON-LINE TRIP LENGTH[b]
CALIFORNIA INTRASTATE CARRIERS
SCHEDULED SERVICE,[c] 1946-1965

Year	Calif. Central[d] Calif. Coastal[e] Trans Calif.[f]	Number of Passenger Originations[a]			Average Trip Length[b] (St. Miles)
		Pacific Southwest	All Others	Total	
1946	-	-	n.a.[g]	n.a.	n.a.
1947	-	-	n.a.	n.a.	n.a.
1948	-	-	-	-	-
1949	77,881	15,011	93,743[h]	186,635*	330*
1950	82,541	45,372	56,800[i]	184,713*	332*
1951	127,131	75,995	-	203,126	320
1952	169,111	92,484	-	261,595	316
1953	125,800*	115,028	-	240,828*	327*
1954	135,200*	102,124	-	237,324*	338*
1955	59,000[j]	129,316	-	188,316*	339*
1956	54,000*	190,571	-	244,571*	335*
1957	8,000*	260,658	-	268,658*	334*
1958	-	295,878	-	295,878	331
1959	-	355,082	-	355,082	327
1960	-	621,280	-	621,280	328
1961	-	713,064	-	713,064	328
1962	11,276	1,032,514[k]	15,000[l]	1,058,790*	325*
1963	90,344	1,305,058[k]	63,000[m]	1,458,402*	320*
1964	80,523	1,532,243[k]	21,000[n]	1,633,766*	324*
1965	-	1,863,088[k]	8,300[o]	1,871,388*	318*

n.a. -- not available.

*Partially estimated.

[a] Unduplicated count of passengers originating journeys on the system of each carrier with the return portion of a round trip reported separately as an initial origination.

[b] Average length in statute miles of a passenger trip over the routes of a single carrier. Calculated by dividing revenue passenger originations into revenue passenger miles.

Appendix No. 2 (continued)

[c]Includes a small amount of nonscheduled traffic commingled and reported with scheduled operations.

[d]January 2, 1949 through February 14, 1955.

[e]March 15, 1955 through August 9, 1957.

[f]August 15, 1962 through October 7, 1964.

[g]San Francisco International Airport records show that Pacific Air Lines originated and terminated 1,072 passengers in August 1946, and 1,338 passengers in September 1946.

[h]California Arrow = 13,000*;   California Skycoach = 1,000*; Channel Airways = 1,200*;   Robin Airways = 28,605;   WALC = 49,938.

[i]California Pacific = 700*;   WALC = 56,100*.

[j]California Central = 14,000*;   California Coastal = 45,000*.

[k]PUC traffic reports state that PSA's on-line O & D passenger traffic totals for 1962-1965 were 398 to 6,479 passengers below the system passenger totals obtained from PSA and given here. [Compare these data with those given in Appendices Nos. 14(A), 14(B) and 14(C).]

[l]Futura = 6,000*;   Paradise = 9,000*.

[m]Blatz [not available, but El Dorado County (Lake Tahoe) Airport reported 295 enplaned and deplaned passengers for "Other Air Carriers" during October-December 1963 -- these may have flown on Blatz]; Paradise = 63,000*.

[n]California Time (not available, but Oakland Metropolitan International Airport records show 381 inbound and outbound passengers for this carrier during November and December 1964);   Mercer = 6,000*;   Paradise = 15,000*.

[o]California Time (not available);   Mercer = 8,300*.

Sources:

   California Public Utilities Commission:
      Astrue, Intrastate Scheduled "Coach Class" Air Carriers, Ex. No.
         1-C, pp. 16, 25-48, and Ex. No. 5-C, pp. 2 and 5, Case No.
         4994, et al.
      Mercer Enterprises, Application No. 48157 (filed Dec. 28, 1965),
         pp. 2-3.

265

Appendix No. 2 (continued)

Transportation Division, Passenger Section, Intrastate Passengers of Scheduled Air Carriers, No. 1511 (Quarters Ended Mar. 31, June 30, Sept. 30, and December 31, 1962-1965).

U.S. Civil Aeronautics Board, Service to Lake Tahoe, California Investigation, Docket No. 16312, et al.:
    Exhibits of El Dorado County, Calif., in Response to Information Request (dated Nov. 15, 1965), No. TAH-9, pp. 1 and 2.
    Exhibits of the City of San Jose, Calif. (n.d.), No. 1, p. 1.

U.S. District Court, Northern District of Calif., files of the Court Clerk for Case No. 43394, Peerless Insurance Co. vs. Paradise Airlines:
    Paradise Airlines, Weekly Station Reports for Lake Tahoe, Oakland and San Jose (July 22, 1963- Mar. 3, 1964).
    _____, letters to the San Jose Airport Manager (various dates).

U.S. District Court, Southern District of Calif., files of the Court Clerk for the following proceedings in bankruptcy:
    No. 59561-PH (filed Jan. 27, 1954), Calif. Central Airlines:
        History, Development and Analysis of California Central Airlines (n.d.), Appendices Nos. A-I through A-IV; Sections Nos. II-A and II-B; and certain unnumbered tables.
        Unpublished worksheets, reports and memoranda (various dates).
    No. 147405-WB (filed Oct. 30, 1962), Futura Airlines,
        Unpublished reports and memoranda.

Airport Records:
    City of Los Angeles, Dept. of Airports.
    Port of Oakland, Oakland Metropolitan International Airport.
    San Francisco Public Utilities Commission, Airport Dept.,
        San Francisco International Airport.

Company records of Pacific Southwest Airlines and Western Air Lines.

REVENUE PASSENGER-MILES[a] BY CARRIER
CALIFORNIA INTRASTATE CARRIERS
SCHEDULED SERVICE, 1946-1965

Year	Calif. Central[b] Calif. Coastal[c] Trans Calif.[d]	Pacific Southwest	All Others	Total
1946	-	-	n.a.	n.a.
1947	-	-	n.a.	n.a.
1948	-	-	-	-
1949	25,698	5,163	30,721[e]	61,582*
1950	27,461	15,026	18,910[f]	61,397*
1951	40,036	24,978	-	65,014
1952	52,820	29,817	-	82,637
1953	40,470*	38,215	-	78,685*
1954	44,950*	35,311	-	80,261*
1955	19,500[g]	44,426	-	63,926*
1956	17,820*	64,209	-	82,029*
1957	2,610*	87,023	-	89,633*
1958	-	97,924	-	97,924
1959	-	116,271	-	116,271
1960	-	204,018	-	204,018
1961	-	234,073	-	234,073
1962	3,676	337,378	3,420[h]	344,474*
1963	31,066	426,040	10,200[i]	467,306*
1964	27,513	498,767	3,230[j]	529,510*
1965	-	594,740	1,150[k]	595,890*

n.a. -- not available.

*Partially estimated.

[a]These revenue passenger-mile (RPM) figures are based upon CAB airport-to-airport mileages in order to make them comparable with the corresponding data for the certificated carriers. Since most of the intrastate carriers used airport-to-airport mileages that differed slightly from those adopted by the CAB, the figures in this appendix are somewhat different from the RPM figures calculated by the various intrastate carriers.

[b]January 2, 1949 through February 14, 1955.

[c]March 15, 1955 through August 9, 1957.

[d]August 15, 1962 through October 7, 1964.

[e]California Arrow = 3,990(000)*; California Skycoach = 330(000)*; Channel Airways = 430(000)*; Robin Airways = 9,325(000); WALC = 16,646(000).

[f]California Pacific = 230(000)*; WALC = 18,680(000)*.

[g]California Central = 4,650(000)*; California Coastal = 14,850(000)*.

[h]Futura = 2,100(000)*; Paradise = 1,320(000)*.

[i]Blatz (not available); Paradise = 10,200(000)*.

[j]California Time (not available); Mercer = 830(000)*; Paradise = 2,400(000)*.

[k]California Time (not available); Mercer = 1,150(000)*.

Sources:
    On-line origin and destination passenger data obtained from the sources listed in Appendix No. 2, multiplied by the appropriate airport-to-airport distances either given in Appendix No. 13 or derived from the sources specified in that appendix. PSA's data for 1962-1965 were calculated by its Controller utilizing PSA's confidential on-line O & D passenger records and the appropriate distances given in Appendix No. 13. [H. E. Swantz, letters to this author (Dec. 2, 1965 and Feb. 10, 1967).]

Appendix No. 4

AVAILABLE SEAT-MILES[a] BY CARRIER
CALIFORNIA INTRASTATE CARRIERS
SCHEDULED SERVICE, 1946-1965

	Available Seat-Miles[a] (000)			
Year	Calif. Central[b] Calif. Coastal[c] Trans Calif.[d]	Pacific Southwest	All Others	Total
1946	–	–	n.a.	n.a.
1947	–	–	n.a.	n.a.
1948	–	–	–	–
1949	35,090[*]	9,270[*]	47,630[e]	91,990[*]
1950	35,780[*]	23,630	23,650[f]	83,060
1951	56,790[**]	37,390[*]	–	94,180[**]
1952	80,150[*]	45,180[*]	–	125,330[*]
1953	60,670[*]	56,530[*]	–	117,200[*]
1954	64,890	51,030[*]	–	115,920[*]
1955	30,760[g]	57,770	–	88,530
1956	26,210[*]	82,210[*]	–	108,420[*]
1957	5,100[*]	106,130	–	111,230
1958	–	135,250	–	135,250
1959	–	163,530[*]	–	163,530[*]
1960	–	286,950	–	286,950
1961	–	324,650	–	324,650[*]
1962	8,050[**]	436,450	12,900[h]	457,400[*]
1963	76,000[*]	551,150	14,800[i]	641,950[*]
1964	57,000	645,240[k]	4,600[j]	706,840[**]
1965	–	940,000[k]	1,500[l]	941,500

n.a. -- not available.

[*]Partially estimated.

[**]Substantial estimates.

[a]These available seat-mile (ASM) figures are based upon CAB airport-to-airport mileages in order to make them comparable with the corresponding data for the certificated carriers. Since most of the intrastate carriers used airport-to-airport mileages that differed slightly from those adopted by the CAB, the figures in this appendix are somewhat different from the ASM figures calculated by the various intrastate carriers.

Appendix No. 4 (continued)

^{b}January 2, 1949 through February 14, 1955.

^{c}March 15, 1955 through August 9, 1957.

^{d}August 15, 1962 through October 7, 1964.

^{e}California Arrow = 8,280(000)*; California Skycoach = 610(000)**;
Channel Airways = 1,150(000)*; Robin Airways = 16,470(000)*; Western
Air Lines of California = 21,120(000).

^{f}California Pacific = 364(000)**; Western Air Lines of California
= 23,286(000).

^{g}California Central = 7,650(000)*; Calif. Coastal = 23,110(000)*.

^{h}Futura = 9,800(000)**; Paradise = 3,100(000)*.

^{i}Blatz (not available); Paradise = 14,800(000)**.

^{j}California Time (not available); Mercer = 1,100(000)*; Paradise = 3,500(000)**.

^{k}This figure was derived from PSA's published schedules for 1965
with an allowance made for extra sections operated during holiday
periods. Therefore, it primarily reflects ASM scheduled rather than
actually operated. Another calculation, based in part on FAA flight-
time data, indicates that this figure may be as much as 1.4 percent
under PSA's actual ASM due to substitution of B-727's for Electras on
schedules during May–July. However, it is believed that the reported
figure is the most accurate estimate available.

^{l}California Time (not available); Mercer = 1,500(000)*.

Sources: Little information is available directly specifying the available seat-miles (ASM) produced by the California intrastate carriers.
As indicated, most of the ASM figures were calculated from data that
were partially estimated, and some entailed substantial estimates.
However, these estimates were made with a great deal of care and were
cross-checked where possible so that the resulting figures are
believed to be fairly accurate.

California Public Utilities Commission:
    Astrue, Intrastate Scheduled "Coach Class" Air Carriers, Ex. No.
    1-C, pp. 25–41, and Ex. No. 5-C, p. 5, Case No. 4994, et al.
    Calif. Central Airlines, Ex. No. 18 (submitted Mar. 27, 1951),
    p. 8, Case No. 5271.
    Mercer Enterprises, Application No. 48157 (filed Dec. 28, 1965),
    p. 3.

270

Transportation Division, Passenger Section, Ex. No. 5 (submitted
Sept. 21, 1960), Application No. 42253.
_____, Intrastate Passengers of Scheduled Air Carriers by Types of
Carriers, No. 1511 (Quarters Ended Mar. 31, June 30, Sept. 30,
and Dec. 31, 1962-1965).

U.S. Civil Aeronautics Board, Calif. Central Airlines, "Application
for Certificate of Public Convenience and Necessity," Docket No.
4482 (filed May 9, 1950), Ex. B.

U.S. District Court, Northern District of Calif., files of the Court
Clerk for Case No. 43394, Peerless Insurance Co. vs. Paradise
Airlines:
    Paradise Airlines, Weekly Station Reports for Lake Tahoe, Oakland
      and San Jose (July 22, 1963 - Mar. 3, 1964).
    _____, letters to the San Jose Airport Manager (various dates).

U.S. District Court, Southern District of Calif., files of the Court
Clerk for the following proceedings in bankruptcy:
    No. 59561-PH, California Central Airlines:
      History, Development and Analysis of California Central Airlines
        (n.d.), Appendices Nos. A-II, A-III and A-IV.
      Ex. B of an unknown document pertaining to BUR-IYK service.
      Calif. Central Airlines and Airline Transport Carriers,
        Combined Aircraft Utilization (1952 & Three Quarters of 1953).
      Report of Debtors in Possession (May 5, Oct. 8 & Nov. 23, 1954).
      Press Release (Jan. 2, 1952), p. 2.
      Sales Letter No. 4 (Nov. 20, 1950).
      Operational Statistics (n.d.).
      Various worksheets and reports (n.d.).
    No. 147405-WB, Futura Airlines:
      Loading Schedule, FAL Form No. 13 (n.d.).
      Sales Activity Report (week ending July 20, 1962).
      Weekly Passenger Report (June 29 - July 18, 1962).

U.S. Federal Aviation Agency, Western Region:
    Airplanes Utilized by C.A.R. Part 40 Operators:
      California Central Airlines (June 30, 1954 - May 29, 1957).
      Pacific Southwest Airlines (June 30, 1954 - June 25, 1957).
    Aircraft Specifications-Aircraft Identification, PSA (June
      28, 1950 - Nov. 19, 1952).
    Letters from PSA amending Operations Specifications (Dec. 3, 1959 -
      June 10, 1965).
    Monthly Air Carrier Aircraft and Engine Utilization, Trans
      California Airlines (Aug. 1962 - Oct. 1964).

Airport Records:
    City of Los Angeles, Dept. of Airports.
    Port of Oakland, Oakland Metropolitan International Airport.

Appendix No. 4 (continued)

Company records of Pacific Southwest Airlines and Western Air Lines.

Pacific Southwest Airlines, Press Releases (Apr. n.d. and 19, 1965).

Airline Schedules:
California Central (Coastal) Airline Guide (Apr. 1, 1955 and
    Jan. 4, 1956).
Pacific Southwest Airlines, Flight Schedule (various dates,
    1949-1956 and 1965).
Official Airline Guide, North American Edition, Vols. 11-12, (Jan.
    1955), p. 506, (Feb. 1955), p. 508, (May 1955), p. 535, (June
    1955), p. 519, (July 1955), p. 526, (Aug. 1955), p. C 490,
    (Dec. 1955), p. C 508, (Jan. 1956), p. C 539, (June 1956),
    p. C 554, (July 1956), p. C 567.

American Aviation, Vol. 16, No. 5 (Aug. 4, 1952), p. 24.

The Los Angeles Times (Aug. 28, 1962), page number n.a.

Appendices Nos. 1, 3 and 13 of this book.

Appendix No. 5

AVERAGE NUMBER OF AIRCRAFT ASSIGNED TO SERVICE[a] BY AIRCRAFT TYPE
TOTAL CALIFORNIA INTRASTATE CARRIERS' ROUTES
ALL SERVICES, 1946-1965

Year	Average Number of Aircraft[a]								
	2-Engine Piston			4-Engine Piston			Turbo-prop	Turbo-jet/fan	Total
	CCA[b] CCA[c]	PSA[d]	All Others	CCA[b] TCA[e]	PSA[d]	All Others	PSA[d]	PSA[d]	
1946	-	-	n.a.	-	-	-	-	-	n.a.
1947	-	-	n.a.	-	-	-	-	-	n.a.
1948	-	-	-	-	-	-	-	-	-
1949	4.1**	0.9	1.7[f]	-*	-	1.2[g]	-	-	7.9**
1950	7.0	2.0	0.1[h]	0.7*	-	0.8[i]	-	-	10.6
1951	5.4*	2.3	-	1.1*	-	-	-	-	8.8*
1952	6.2	3.2	-	-[j]	-	-	-	-	9.4
1953	6.7	4.0	-	-[j]	-	-	-	-	10.7
1954	6.9	4.0	-	-	-	-	-	-	10.9
1955	2.4[k]	3.7	-	-	0.3	-	-	-	6.4
1956	1.7	0.1	-	-	2.3	-	-	-	4.1
1957	1.2	-	-	-	3.5	-	-	-	4.7
1958	-	-	-	-	4.0	-	-	-	4.0
1959	-	-	-	-	4.0	-	0.3	-	4.3
1960	-	-	-	-	0.4[l]	-	3.0	-	3.4
1961	-	-	-	-	0.4	-	3.7	-	4.1
1962	-	-	1.3[m]	0.7	-	0.5[n]	4.7	-	7.2*
1963	-	-	3.4[o]	4.0	-	1.3[p]	5.6	-	14.3*
1964	-	-	1.7[q]	3.2	-	0.3[p]	6.0	-	11.2
1965	-	-	2.1[r]	-	-	-	6.0	2.7	10.8

n.a. -- not available.

* Partially estimated.

** Substantial estimates.

[a] All aircraft owned, leased or rented in the possession of each carrier and available for service on its routes or undergoing maintenance. Calculated by dividing the number of aircraft days assigned to service by 365 or 366 (for 1948, 1952, 1956, 1960 and 1964) days.

[b]California Central Airlines, January 2, 1949 through February 14, 1955 -- 2-engine piston: DC-3, L-12 & L-18; 4-engine piston: DC-4 & L-049.

[c]California Coastal Airlines, dba California Central Airlines, March 15, 1955 through August 9, 1957 -- DC-2, DC-3 & C-46.

[d]Pacific Southwest Airlines -- 2-engine piston: DC-3; 4-engine piston: DC-4 & DC-6B; turboprop: Electra; turbofan: B-727-100.

[e]Trans California Airlines, August 15, 1962 through October 7, 1964 -- L-749.

[f]California Arrow = 1.1 DC-3; California Skycoach = 0.1** DC-3; Channel Airways = 0.5 DC-3.

[g]Robin Airways = 0.5 DC-4; WALC = 0.7 DC-4 (these aircraft were probably also counted as part of Western Air Lines' fleet).

[h]California Pacific = 0.1* DC-3.

[i]WALC -- DC-4 (see note g above).

[j]Airline Transport Carriers and California Central Airlines operated one L-049 jointly from July 17, 1952 through July 3, 1953. CCA accounted for only 4.4 percent of this aircraft's total revenue mileage in 1952, and 3.7 percent in 1953. Therefore, it is excluded from this summary.

[k]California Central = 0.8; California Coastal = 1.6.

[l]PSA owned three DC-4's throughout 1960 (they were sold on or about January 24, 1961). However, utilization of these aircraft totaled only 571 hours in 1960 compared with an average of 2,532 hours per aircraft in 1959. Therefore, these aircraft have been counted as only 0.2 aircraft for 1960.

[m]Paradise Airlines -- DC-3.

[n]Futura Airlines -- L-049.

[o]Blatz = 1.4** DC-3; Paradise = 2.0 DC-3.

[p]Paradise Airlines -- L-049.

[q]California Time = 0.3 M-202; Mercer = 1.1 DC-2 and DC-3; Paradise = 0.3 DC-3.

[r]California Time = 0.1 M-202; Mercer = 2.0 DC-3.

Appendix No. 5 (continued)

Sources:

California Public Utilities Commission, Astrue, Intrastate Scheduled "Coach Class" Air Carriers, Ex. No. 1-C, pp. 25-30, 34-40, and Ex. No. 5-C, p. 5, Case No. 4994, et al.

U.S. District Court, Southern District of Calif., files of the Court Clerk for proceedings in bankruptcy Nos. 59560-PH, Airline Transport Carriers, and 59561-PH, California Central Airlines:
  Reporter's Transcript of Hearing on Order to Show Cause, Debtors vs. Harold F. Brown, et al.; Pretrial Hearing on Objections to Claims of Pacific Airmotive Corp.; and Continued First Meeting of Creditors, on Feb. 15 & 16, 1955, p. 42.
California Central Airlines and Airline Transport Carriers, Combined Aircraft Utilization (1952 & Three Quarters of 1953).

U.S. Federal Aviation Agency, Western Region:
  Air Carrier and Commercial Operator Data Report, Paradise Airlines (June 1963 - Mar. 1964).
  Airplanes Utilized by C.A.R. Part 40 Operators:
    Calif. Central/Coastal Airlines (May 30, 1954 - May 29, 1957).
    Pacific Southwest Airlines (Sept. 15, 1955 - June 25, 1957).
  Application for Certificate to Operate as Irregular Air Carrier or Commercial Operator, Calif. Central/Coastal Airlines (Jan. 12, 1950 - May 31, 1956).
  C.A.R. 42/45 Status Report, Futura Airlines (Sept. 1962).
  Draft Permit to Use USAF Bases Within the Continental United States, Calif. Central Airlines (July 31, 1951).
  Letters from K. G. Friedkin, PSA (Dec. 3, 1959 - May 15, 1963).
  Memoranda regarding: Blatz Airlines (May 29, 1963), Calif. Central Airlines (Sept. 12, 1949), & PSA (May 6, 1949 & Sept. 22, 1955).
  Monthly Air Carrier Aircraft and Engine Utilization:
    Calif. Time Airlines (Sept. 1964 - Feb. 1965), Mercer Enterprises (Apr. 1964 - Sept. 1965), PSA (Jan. 1961 - Sept. 1965), and Trans Calif. Airlines (Aug. 1962 - Oct. 1964).
  Non-Scheduled Air Carrier Inspection Report, Calif. Central Airlines (Feb. 16, 1950 - May 13, 1954).
  Operations Specifications, PSA (Nov. 30, 1949 - Aug. 29, 1952).
  Systemworthiness Inspection Report, Paradise Airlines (June 17, 1963), pp. 27-28.

Company records of Pacific Southwest Airlines.

C. E. Anderson, "The Martinliner," American Aviation Historical Society Journal, Vol. 7, No. 2 (Summer 1962), pp. 120-125.

The Los Angeles Times (Oct. 23, 1949), Part 1, p. 38.

The San Diego Evening Tribune (Nov. 11, 1959), p. A-2.

Appendix No. 6(A)

CERTIFICATED CARRIERS'[a] ONE-WAY, FIRST-CLASS PASSENGER FARES
BETWEEN LOS ANGELES/BURBANK, SAN DIEGO, AND SAN FRANCISCO/OAKLAND
1946-1965[b]

Effective Date[c]	Car-rier[d]	One-Way, First-Class Fares					
		LAX/BUR-SFO/OAK[e]		LAX/BUR-SAN[e]		SAN-SFO/OAK[f]	
		Prop.	Jet	Prop.	Jet	Prop.	Jet
1946							
As of Jan. 1[g]		$15.15	–	$ 5.55	–	$20.70	–
1947							
Apr. 1		16.70	–	6.15	–	22.80	–
Sept. 5[h]		17.40	–	5.60	–	23.00	–
Dec. 12		19.15	–	6.15	–	25.30	–
1948							
Sept. 1[i]		21.05	–	6.75	–	27.80	–
1949							
Feb. 1	WAL[j]	20.00	–	6.40	–	26.40	–
Oct. 15	WAL[j]	21.05	–	6.75	–	27.80	–
1952							
Apr. 30	WAL	22.05	–	7.75	–	28.80	–
May 3	UAL	"	–	"	–	"	–
1958							
July 7		23.95	–	9.10	–	31.00	–
1959							
Mar. 1[k]		"	–	"	–	"	–
Oct. 31[l]	UAL	"	$25.95	"	–	"	–
1960							
June 1[m]	WAL	"	"	"	–	"	–
Oct. 10[n]	UAL	"	"	"	$10.10	"	$33.00
1961							
Jan. 9		25.55	27.55	10.35	11.35[o]	32.80	34.80[o]
Dec. 1	UAL	"	"	"	"	Canceled[p]	"
1962							
Mar. 20		26.35	28.45	10.70	11.75[o]	33.80[q]	35.90[o]
Aug. 1	UAL	Canceled[p]	"	Canceled[p]	"	–	"

276

Effective Date[c]	Car-rier[d]	One-Way, First-Class Fares					
		LAX/BUR-SFO/OAK[e]		LAX/BUR-SAN[e]		SAN-SFO/OAK[f]	
		Prop.	Jet	Prop.	Jet	Prop.	Jet
1963							
Apr. 28	UAL	–	$28.45	–	$11.75	–	Canceled
June 1	WAL	Canceled[p]	"	$10.70	"	$33.80	–
1964							
Mar. 1	WAL	–	"	Canceled[p]	"	"	–
Apr. 26	WAL	–	"	–	"	Canceled[p]	–
1965							
As of	UAL	–	28.45	–	11.75	–	–
Dec. 31	WAL	–	28.45	–	11.75	–	–

[a]United Air Lines and Western Air Lines.

[b]United and Western inaugurated service at Los Angeles International Airport on December 9, 1946. United terminated all service to Burbank on April 29, 1961, and Western did likewise on September 29, 1962. Neither carrier ever operated jet aircraft at Burbank. Western did not serve Oakland until September 3, 1946, and jet service was not available at Oakland until introduced by United on June 7, 1963. No single-plane jet service was operated between San Diego and Oakland during this period.

[c]For existing service, the effective date of each fare is that specified in a tariff filed with the California PUC. For new service, the date service actually was inaugurated has been adopted as the relevant effective date. For terminating service, the day following the last day of operations is given as being the date most comparable with a tariff cancelation date.

[d]Unless specified to the contrary, the effective date and associated fares apply to both United and Western.

[e]Fares available on nonstop service.

[f]Fares available on single-plane, limited-stop service.

[g]These fares were originally adopted on August 20, 1945.

[h]The expansion of service at Los Angeles International Airport at the expense of the Lockheed Air Terminal in Burbank caused a change in the airport-to-airport distances upon which fares were constructed. As indicated by these fare changes, the Los Angeles/Burbank-San Francisco/

Oakland mileage basis was increased while the Los Angeles/Burbank-San Diego mileage basis was decreased.

[i]In addition to this 10 percent one-way fare increase, a five percent, round-trip discount was introduced for first-class service.

[j]Western introduced a "no-meal" tariff which gave a five percent discount on all fares. This tariff was canceled effective October 15, 1949.

[k]Five percent, round-trip discount canceled.

[l]Date United inaugurated jet service. Actually, Trans World Airlines was the first carrier to operate jet service between Los Angeles and San Francisco. It did so on June 1, 1959 at the same fare subsequently adopted by United. [See Official Airline Guide, North American Edition, Vol. 15, No. 9 (June 1959), pp. C 325-328.]

[m]Date Western inaugurated jet service.

[n]United inaugurated jet service to San Diego on September 13, 1960. However, its jet surcharge for intrastate service did not become effective until October 10, 1960, so that propeller fares were applicable to jet service during the intervening period.

[o]United Air Lines only.

[p]Propeller first-class service was terminated on this date. However, this fare was retained in the tariff since it was the "base" fare for the construction of other fares.

[q]Western Air Lines only.

Sources: See the consolidated listing following Appendix No. 6(C).

CERTIFICATED CARRIERS'[a] ONE-WAY, DAY-COACH PASSENGER FARES
BETWEEN LOS ANGELES/BURBANK, SAN DIEGO, AND SAN FRANCISCO/OAKLAND
1946-1965[b]

Effective Date[c]	Carrier[d]	One-Way, Day-Coach Fares					
		LAX/BUR-SFO/OAK[e]		LAX/BUR-SAN[e]		SAN-SFO/OAK[f]	
		Prop.	Jet	Prop.	Jet	Prop.	Jet
1949							
Oct. 16[g]	WAL	$14.10	-	-	-	-	-
1950							
May 14	UAL	9.95	-	-	-	-	-
June 1	WAL	"	-	-	-	-	-
1951							
Mar. 1		11.70	-	-	-	-	-
Dec. 10	WAL	"	-	$ 5.55	-	$17.25	-
1952							
Feb. 1	UAL	"	-	"	-	"	-
Nov. 1	UAL	"	-	Canceled	-	Canceled	-
1953							
Feb. 1		13.50	-	5.55[h]	-	19.05[h]	-
1954							
Apr. 25	UAL	"	-	5.55	-	19.05	-
1958							
July 7		15.05	-	6.50	-	20.85	-
1959							
Oct. 31	UAL	"	$17.05	"	-	"	-
1960							
June 1	WAL	"	"	"	-	"	-
Oct. 10[i]	UAL	"	"	"	$ 7.50	"	$22.85
1961							
Jan. 9		16.45	18.45	8.00	9.00[j]	22.40	24.40[j]
1962							
Mar. 20		16.95	19.05	8.25	9.30[j]	23.10	25.20[j]
Apr. 7		"	23.70	"	10.90[j]	"	29.25[j]
Oct. 28	UAL	Canceled	"	"	"	Canceled	"

Effective Date[c]	Carrier[d]	One-Way, Day-Coach Fares					
		LAX/BUR-SFO/OAK[e]		LAX/BUR-SAN[e]		SAN-SFO/OAK[f]	
		Prop.	Jet	Prop.	Jet	Prop.	Jet
1963							
Jan. 1	WAL	$16.95	$23.70	$ 8.25	–	$19.85	–
Apr. 28	UAL	–	"	"	$10.90	–	Canceled
June 1	WAL	16.95	"	"	"	19.85	–
Aug. 1	WAL	13.50[k]	"	"	"	"	–
1964							
Oct. 10	UAL	–	14.50	"	"	–	–
1965							
July 1	WAL	Canceled	23.70	"	"	19.85	–
July 21	UAL	–	14.50	6.35	8.00	–	–
Aug. 1	WAL	–	23.70	8.00	"	19.85	–
Dec. 12	WAL	–	"	"	"	17.78	–
As of	UAL	–	14.50	6.35	8.00	–	–
Dec. 31	WAL	–	23.70	8.00	8.00	17.78	–

[a]United Air Lines and Western Air Lines.

[b]See footnote b, Appendix No. 6(A).

[c]See footnote c, Appendix No. 6(A).

[d]See footnote d, Appendix No. 6(A).

[e]Fares available on nonstop service.

[f]Fares available on single-plane, limited-stop service.

[g]This first certificated carrier fare was for night-coach service. All other fares given in this appendix are for day-coach service.

[h]Western Air Lines only.

[i]See footnote n, Appendix No. 6(A).

[j]United Air Lines only.

[k]Available between Los Angeles and San Francisco only. Western's Los Angeles-Oakland propeller coach fare remained $16.95 until such service was terminated in this market effective June 10, 1964.

Sources: See the consolidated listing following Appendix No. 6(C).

CERTIFICATED CARRIERS'[a] OTHER ONE-WAY PASSENGER FARES
BETWEEN LOS ANGELES/BURBANK, SAN DIEGO, AND SAN FRANCISCO/OAKLAND
1946-1965

I. United's Mainliner-300 (DC-6) First-Class Service Charge

	LAX/BUR-SFO/OAK[c]		LAX/BUR-SAN[d]	
Effective Date[b]	Service Charge	Total One-Way Fare	Service Charge	Total One-Way Fare
1947				
Aug. 1	$ 1.50	$18.90	-	-
Dec. 12	1.65	20.80	-	-
1948				
July 21	"	"	$ 1.10	$ 7.25
Sept. 1	"	22.70	"	7.85
Sept. 22	Canceled	-	Canceled	-

II. Thriftair and Jet Commuter Fares

		One-Way Fares			
Effective Date[b]	Western's Prop. Thriftair LAX/BUR-SFO/OAK[e]		Jet Commuter[f]		
		Carrier[g]	LAX-SFO/OAK	LAX-SAN	SAN-SFO/OAK
1962					
June 1	$12.95		-	-	-
1963					
Feb. 25	11.43		-	-	-
1964					
Sept. 27	"	UAL	$14.50	-	-
1965					
April 1	Canceled		13.50	-	-
June 4	-	UAL	"	$ 6.35	$19.85
As of		UAL	13.50	6.35	19.85
Dec. 31	-	WAL	13.50	-	-

Appendix No. 6(C) (continued)

III. United's Jet One-Class and Standard Class Fares

Effective Date[b]	One-Way Fares			
	One-Class LAX-SFO/OAK[g]	Standard Class		
		LAX-SFO/OAK	LAX-SAN	SAN-SFO/OAK
1963 Sept. 9	$26.00	-	-	-
1964 Aug. 9	"	$26.00	-	-
1965 Jan. 10	"	"	$11.30	-
Sept. 1	Canceled	"	"	-
As of Dec. 31	-	26.00	11.30	-

[a]United Air Lines and Western Air Lines.

[b]See footnote c, Appendix No. 6(A).

[c]No DC-6 service was operated at Oakland during this period. On November 12, 1947 all DC-6's were grounded because of inflight fires. DC-6 service was reintroduced between Los Angeles and San Francisco on April 16, 1948. Burbank-San Francisco DC-6 service was operated from June 1 to July 31, 1948 only.

[d]Los Angeles-San Diego only.

[e]Burbank-San Francisco Thriftair service operated June 1 - September 29, 1962. Los Angeles-Oakland service operated June 10, 1964 - March 31, 1965.

[f]United inaugurated jet commuter service on the following dates: Los Angeles-San Francisco, September 27, 1964; Los Angeles-Oakland, January 10, 1965; Los Angeles-San Diego and San Diego-San Francisco, June 4, 1965; San Diego-Oakland, October 31, 1965. Western inaugurated this service between Los Angeles and San Francisco/Oakland on April 1, 1965.

[g]Los Angeles-Oakland service operated April 1 - August 8, 1964.

Sources: See the consolidated listing on the following page.

282

Sources for Appendices Nos. 6(A), 6(B) and 6(C):

The following tariffs filed with the California Public Utilities Commission (or the California Railroad Commission) by United Air Lines and Western Air Lines:

United Air Lines,

C.R.C. No. 12,	originally effective	July	15, 1943.
" " 13,	" "	Mar.	1, 1947.
Cal. P.U.C. No. 15,	" "	Sept.	14, 1949.
" " " 16,	" "	Apr.	29, 1950.
" " " 20,	" "	July	31, 1959.
" " " 23,	" "	Sept.	27, 1964.
" " " 25,	" "	Nov.	1, 1964.

Western Air Lines,

C.R.C. No. 1,	originally effective	June	20, 1945.
Cal. P.U.C. No. 2,	" "	June	1, 1947.
" " " 3,	" "	Oct.	15, 1949.
" " " 19,	" "	July	31, 1959.
" " " 20,	" "	May	23, 1960.
" " " 21,	" "	Jan.	9, 1961.
" " " 23,	" "	Dec.	1, 1961.
" " " 24,	" "	Mar.	20, 1962.
" " " 25,	" "	Apr.	24, 1962.
" " " 26,	" "	June	1, 1962.

Official Airline Guide, North American Edition (and its predecessor publications, the American Aviation Traffic Guide, and the American Aviation Air Traffic Guide), Vols. 2-22 (various dates, 1946-1965).

United Air Lines, "Traffic Information Bulletin No. 17," Apr. 28, 1950.

Western Air Lines, Research Dept., Chronological Listings of Important Events in Western's History (Rev. Sept. 8, 1965), Parts I and II.

50 Cal. PUC 563 (1951).
62 Cal. PUC 553 (1964).

Cal. PUC, Fare Authorization No. 20-12-58 (dated Aug. 2, 1947).

CALIFORNIA INTRASTATE CARRIERS'[a] ONE-WAY PASSENGER FARES
BETWEEN LOS ANGELES/BURBANK, SAN DIEGO, AND SAN FRANCISCO/OAKLAND
1946-1965

Effective Date[b]	One-Way Fares[c]					
	LAX/BUR-SFO/OAK Pacific		LAX/BUR-SAN		SAN-SFO/OAK	
	CCA TCA	PSA WALC	CCA TCA	PSA	CCA TCA	PSA
1946						
June 17	$ 15.15^d	-	-	-	-	-
1947						
June 4	Canceled^d	-	-	-	-	-
1949						
Jan. 2	9.99^e	-	-	-	-	-
May 5	"	-	$ 5.55^e	-	$ 15.54^e	-
May 6	"	$ 9.99^f	"	$ 5.65	"	$ 15.64
May 23	"	9.95	"	"	"	15.60
Aug. 19	"	9.95^g	"	"	"	"
1950						
June 1	"	Canceled^g	"	"	"	"
1951						
Mar. 1	11.70	9.95	"	"	"	"
Mar. 28	"	11.70	"	5.55	"	17.25
May 20	"	"	"	"	17.25	"
1952						
June 15	13.50	"	"	"	19.05	"
1953						
Aug. 25	11.70^h & 13.50	"	"	"	"	"
Nov. 14	"	"	"	"	17.25^h & 19.05	"
1954						
Jan. 15	"	13.50	"	"	"	19.05
Mar. 24	"	11.70^i & 13.50	"	"	"	"
Apr. 8	"	9.99	"	5.45	"	15.44

284

Effective Date[b]	LAX/BUR-SFO/OAK Pacific CCA TCA	LAX/BUR-SFO/OAK PSA WALC	LAX/BUR-SAN CCA TCA	LAX/BUR-SAN PSA	SAN-SFO/OAK CCA TCA	SAN-SFO/OAK PSA
1955						
Feb. 15	Canceled	$ 9.99	Canceled	$ 5.45	Canceled	$ 15.44
Mar. 15	$ 11.70[j]	"	-	"	-	"
May 12	"	"	$ 5.55[k]	"	$ 17.10[k]	"
June 2	"	"	"	"	15.39[l] & 17.10	"
July 6	9.99[m] & 11.70	"	"	"	"	"
1956						
Jan. 4	"[n]	"	"	"	15.39[o]	"
Nov. 1	"	"	Canceled	"	Canceled	"
1957						
Feb. 4-18	9.99[p]	"	-	"	-	"
Aug. 10	Canceled	"	-	"	-	"
1958						
Apr. 14	-	11.81	-	"	-	17.26
1960						
Oct. 7	-	11.81[q] & 13.50	-	"	-	17.26[q] & 18.95
Dec. 12	-	13.50[r]	-	6.35	-	19.85[s]
1962						
Aug. 15	10.99[t]	"	-	"	-	"
1963						
Jan. 4	"	"	5.40[u]	"	16.39[u]	"
1964						
June 14	"	"	Canceled[u]	"	Canceled[u]	"
Oct. 8	Canceled	"	-	"	-	"
1965						
Jan. 5	-	11.43[v] & 13.50	-	"	-	17.78[v] & 19.85
Apr. 20 (Prop.)-	11.43[w]	-	"	-	17.78[w]	
(Jet) -	13.50	-	"	-	19.85	
As of (Prop.)-	11.43	-	6.35	-	17.78	
Dec. 31 (Jet) -	13.50	-	6.35	-	19.85	

^aLimited to intrastate carriers operating for nine months or more.

^bSee footnote c, Appendix No. 6(A).

^cExcept for the jet fares introduced by Pacific Southwest Airlines on April 20, 1965, all fares listed in this appendix are for services operated with propeller aircraft. See Appendix No. 1 for the dates that each of the indicated intrastate carriers served these various cities.

^dPacific Air Lines' fare.

^eThe fares in this column from this entry to that for February 15, 1955 are those of California Central Airlines.

^fExcept for that specified for Western Air Lines of California, the fares in this column are those of Pacific Southwest Airlines.

^gWestern Air Lines of California's fare. PSA's fare remained unchanged during this period.

^hCalifornia Central Airlines introduced a special tourist-class fare for DC-3 service in this market. The higher fare that had been effective since June 15, 1952 was retained for service provided with M-202 aircraft.

ⁱThe $11.70 fare was applicable to all travel on Monday through Thursday, thereby limiting the $13.50 fare to Friday through Sunday.

^jThe fares in this column from this entry to that for August 10, 1957 are those of California Coastal Airlines dba California Central.

^kThe fares in this column from this entry to that for November 1, 1956 are those of California Coastal Airlines dba California Central.

^lThe $15.39 fare applied to San Diego-San Francisco service only. The San Diego-Oakland fare remained $17.10.

^mThe $9.99 fare applied to Burbank-San Francisco service only. The Burbank-Oakland and Los Angeles-San Francisco/Oakland fares remained $11.70.

ⁿThe Burbank-Oakland fare was lowered to $9.99. This left only the Los Angeles-San Francisco/Oakland fares at $11.70.

^oThe San Diego-Oakland fare was reduced to equal the San Diego-San Francisco fare, i.e., $15.39.

^pCalifornia Coastal Airlines terminated service to Los Angeles around February 3, 1957 thereby canceling its $11.70 Los Angeles-San Francisco/Oakland fares.

qPacific Southwest Airlines resumed service at Oakland with a Los Angeles-Oakland fare of $13.50 compared with the $11.81 Los Angeles-San Francisco fare. By combining local fares, the San Diego-Oakland fare was $18.95 compared with $17.76 for the San Diego-San Francisco fare.

rPacific Southwest Airlines increased its Los Angeles/Burbank-San Francisco fares to equal the $13.50 Los Angeles-Oakland fare established two months earlier.

sThe equalization of the Los Angeles-San Francisco and Los Angeles-Oakland fares resulted in a similar equalization of the fares for San Diego-San Francisco and San Diego-Oakland.

tThe fares in this column from this entry to that for October 8, 1964 are those of Trans California Airlines.

uTrans California Airlines' fare.

vPacific Southwest Airlines resumed service once again at Oakland with a Los Angeles-Oakland fare of $11.43 compared with $13.50 for Los Angeles/Burbank-San Francisco. By combining local fares, the San Diego-Oakland fare was $17.78 compared with $19.85 for San Diego-San Francisco.

wIntroduction of a propeller/jet fare differential. This differential was established 11 days after PSA inaugurated jet service. Combining these fares with the Los Angeles/Burbank-San Diego fare yields the indicated propeller/jet fare differential for San Diego-San Francisco/Oakland.

Sources:

The following tariffs filed with the California Public Utilities Commission (or the California Railroad Commission) by the specified intrastate carriers:
    California Central Airlines, Cal. P.U.C. No. 1, originally
        effective Jan. 1, 1949.
    California Coastal Airlines, Cal. P.U.C. No. 1, originally
        effective Mar. 15, 1955.
    Pacific Air Lines, C.R.C. No. 2, originally effective June 17, 1946.
    Pacific Southwest Airlines, Cal. P.U.C. No. 1, originally
        effective May 3, 1949.
    Trans California Airlines, Cal. P.U.C. No. 1, originally
        effective Aug. 15, 1962.
    Western Air Lines of California, Cal. P.U.C. No. 1, originally
        effective Aug. 19, 1949.

50 Cal. PUC 563 (1951).

Appendix No. 1 of this book.

CERTIFICATED CARRIERS'[a] ONE-WAY, FIRST-CLASS PASSENGER FARES
BETWEEN BOSTON, NEW YORK/NEWARK, AND WASHINGTON, D.C.
1946-1965[b]

Effective Date[c]	Carrier[d]	One-Way, First-Class Fares					
		BOS-NYC/EWR[e]		BOS-DCA[f]		NYC/EWR-DCA[e]	
		Prop.	Jet	Prop.	Jet	Prop.	Jet
1946 As of Jan. 1		$ 8.35	–	$18.40	–	$10.05	–
1947							
Apr. 1		9.20	–	20.25	–	11.10	–
Oct. 5		"	–	20.30	–	"	–
Dec. 12		10.10	–	22.35	–	12.20	–
1948							
Mar. 1		"	–	22.30	–	"	–
Sept. 1[g]	AAL	11.15	–	24.55	–	13.40	–
Oct. 15[h]	EAL	"	–	"	–	"	–
1952							
Apr. 16	AAL	12.15	–	25.55	–	14.40	–
Apr. 27	EAL	"	–	"	–	"	–
1958							
Feb. 10		13.65	–	27.60	–	16.00	–
Oct. 20[i]		"	–	"	–	"	–
1960							
July 1		15.00	–	29.30	–	17.40	–
1962							
Feb. 1		15.45	$16.50[j]	30.20	–	17.95	–
Nov. 19	EAL	"	"	"	$32.30[k]	"	–
1964							
Mar. 1	EAL	"	"	"	"	"	$20.05[k]
1965							
Jan. 15	EAL	17.20	18.20	31.20	33.20	19.60	21.60[k]
May 23	AAL	15.45	–	30.20	–	17.95	20.05[k]
June 5	EAL	17.20	18.20	"	32.30	19.60	21.60
Oct. 31	EAL	Canceled[l]	"	"	"	"	Canceled[l]
Nov. 1	AAL	15.45	17.55[k]	"	–	17.95	20.05
As of	AAL	15.45	17.55	30.20	–	17.95	20.05
Dec. 31	EAL	–	18.20	30.20	32.30	19.60	–

Appendix No. 8(A) (continued)

[a]American Airlines and Eastern Air Lines. These two carriers have traditionally carried the majority of traffic in these markets.

[b]American and Eastern operated between these cities with propeller aircraft throughout this period, except that Eastern terminated its conventional (non-shuttle) propeller service between Boston and New York/ Newark on October 30, 1965. Jet operations were not allowed at Washington until the Dulles International Airport was opened on November 19, 1962. Over-all, little jet service was provided in all three markets until jet aircraft were allowed to use Washington National Airport beginning April 24, 1966, i.e., after the period covered by this study.

[c]For existing service, the effective date of each fare is that specified in a tariff filed with the Civil Aeronautics Board. For new service, the date service actually was inaugurated has been adopted as the relevant effective date. For terminating service, the day following the last day of operations is given as being the date most comparable with a tariff cancelation date.

[d]Unless specified to the contrary, the effective date and associated fares apply to both American and Eastern.

[e]Fares available on nonstop service.

[f]Fares available on single-plane, nonstop and/or one-stop service.

[g]In addition to this 10 percent one-way fare increase, a five percent, round-trip discount was introduced for first-class service.

[h]See Cherington, Airline Price Policy, pp. 87-91, for a summary of the circumstances surrounding the adoption of the third 10 percent, across-the-board fare increase. This summary indicates why Eastern and some other carriers were slow to adopt this increase.

[i]Five-percent, round-trip discount canceled.

[j]Eastern Air Lines inaugurated jet service on this date.

[k]Date of jet service inauguration.

[l]Service terminated, however, these fares were still filed in Eastern's tariff as of December 31, 1965.

Sources: See the consolidated listing following Appendix No. 8(C).

CERTIFICATED CARRIERS'[a] ONE-WAY, DAY-COACH PASSENGER FARES
BETWEEN BOSTON, NEW YORK/NEWARK, AND WASHINGTON, D.C.
1946-1965[b]

Effective Date[c]	Carrier[d]	One-Way, Day-Coach Fares					
		BOS-NYC/EWR[e]		BOS-DCA[f]		NYC/EWR-DCA[e]	
		Prop.	Jet	Prop.	Jet	Prop.	Jet
1953							
Dec. 9	EAL	$ 9.40	-	$19.50	-	$11.10	-
Dec. 13	AAL	"	-	"	-	"	-
1958							
Feb. 10		10.80	-	21.30	-	12.55	-
1959							
June 1	EAL	11.80	-	22.30	-	13.55	-
July 24	AAL	"	-	"	-	"	-
1960							
July 1		13.10	-	23.90	-	14.90	-
1961							
Aug. 20	EAL	"	-	23.85	-	"	-
1962							
Feb. 1	AAL	13.50	-	24.65	-	15.35	-
" "	EAL	"	$14.55	24.60	-	"	-
Nov. 19	EAL	"	"	"	$26.60[g]	"	-
1964							
Mar. 1	EAL	"	"	"	"	"	$16.40[g]
1965							
Jan. 15	EAL	15.40	16.40	25.90	27.80	17.10	18.10
Mar. 12	EAL	15.20	"	"	"	"	"
May 23	AAL	13.50	-	24.65	-	15.35	16.40[g]
June 5	EAL	15.20	16.40	24.60	26.60	17.10	18.10
Oct. 31	EAL	Canceled[h]	"	"	"	"	Canceled[h]
Nov. 1	AAL	13.50	15.60[g]	24.65	-	15.35	16.40
As of	AAL	13.50	15.60	24.65	-	15.35	16.40
Dec. 31	EAL	-	16.40	24.60	26.60	17.10	-

Appendix No. 8(B) (continued)

[a]American Airlines and Eastern Air Lines. These two carriers have traditionally carried the majority of traffic in these markets.

[b]See footnote b, Appendix No. 8(A).

[c]See footnote c, Appendix No. 8(A).

[d]Unless specified to the contrary, the effective date and associated fares apply to both American and Eastern.

[e]Fares available on nonstop service.

[f]Fares available on single-plane, nonstop and/or one-stop service.

[g]Date of jet service inauguration.

[h]Service terminated, however, these fares were still filed in Eastern's tariff as of December 31, 1965.

Sources: See the consolidated listing following Appendix No. 8(C).

CERTIFICATED CARRIERS'[a] ONE-WAY, AIR-SHUTTLE PASSENGER FARES
BETWEEN BOSTON, NEW YORK/NEWARK AND WASHINGTON, D.C.
1961-1965

Effective Date[c]	Eastern's One-Way, Air-Shuttle Fares[h]					
	BOS-NYC/EWR		BOS-DCA		NYC/EWR-DCA	
	Regular	Off-Peak	Regular	Off-Peak	Regular	Off-Peak
1961						
Apr. 30[d]	$10.91	-	-	-	$12.73	-
Dec. 2	11.82	-	-	-	13.64	-
1962						
Feb. 1	"	-	$24.55	-	"	-
Aug. 30	12.73	-	"	-	14.55	-
Nov. 16	12.38	-	23.81	-	14.29	-
Dec. 21	"	$ 9.52[e]	"	$20.95[e]	"	$11.43[e]
1963						
June 1	"	Canceled	"	"	"	Canceled
June 10	"	11.43[e]	"	"	"	-
1964						
Jan. 8	13.33	"[f]	"	"[f]	15.24	-
Oct. 1	"	"	24.76[g]	Canceled[h]	"	-
1965						
Jan. 15	15.24	13.33[f]	26.67[i]	-[j]	17.14	-
Apr. 25	"	"	Canceled[k]	-	"	-
As of						
Dec. 31	15.24	13.33[f]	-	-	17.14	-

[a]Eastern Air Lines is the only carrier that has offered Air-Shuttle type service between these cities.

[b]For nonstop service with propeller aircraft only. Jet aircraft were not utilized in Air-Shuttle service until the Washington National Airport was opened to jet operations on April 24, 1966.

[c]For existing service, the effective date of each fare is that specified in a tariff filed with the Civil Aeronautics Board. For new service, the date service actually was inaugurated has been adopted as the relevant effective date. For terminating service, the day following the last day of operations is given as being the date most comparable to a tariff cancelation date.

^dDate of service inauguration.

^eApplicable to travel on flights scheduled to depart between the hours of:
   10:01 a.m. - 2:59 p.m., and 7:59 p.m. - midnight on Monday through Friday.
   12:01 a.m. Saturday through 2:59 p.m. Sunday.

^fApplicable to travel on flights scheduled to depart between the hours of:
   10:45 a.m. - 2:45 p.m. on Monday through Thursday.
   12:01 a.m. - midnight on Saturday.

^gAir-Shuttle service between Boston and Washington replaced with Executive Shuttle service. The fare for this new service was 95¢ higher than the Air-Shuttle fare. The Air-Shuttle fare remained in effect, but required a change of planes at New York/Newark in order to be utilized.

^hThere was no off-peak Executive Shuttle fare. Eastern's off-peak Air-Shuttle fare remained in effect, but required a change of planes at New York/Newark in order to be utilized.

ⁱExecutive Shuttle fare, the regular Air-Shuttle fare applicable via connecting service at New York/Newark was increased to $25.71.

^jThe off-peak Air-Shuttle fare applicable via connecting service at New York/Newark was increased to $22.86.

^kExecutive Shuttle service was terminated on April 24, 1965. Note that at this time the propeller coach fare was $25.90, 77¢ lower than the Executive Shuttle fare and only 19¢ higher than the fare for the connecting Air-Shuttle service.

Sources: See the consolidated listing on the following page.

Appendix No. 8 (continued)

Sources for Appendices Nos. 8(A), 8(B) and 8(C):

The following tariffs filed with the Civil Aeronautics Board by:
M. F. Redfern, Agent, Air Traffic Conference of America,
Local and Joint Passenger Fares Tariff:
 No. PF-2, C.A.B. No. 7, originally effective Nov. 15, 1945.
 " PF-3, " " 15, " " Mar. 1, 1948.
 " PF-4, " " 18, " " Sept. 1, 1949.
 " C -3, " " 31, " " June 15, 1952.
 (Note: C. C. Hubbard became the issuing agent of tariffs Nos.
 PF-4 and C-3, effective June 24, 1952. J. B. Walker became
 the issuing agent of these tariffs effective Feb. 1, 1954.)
J. B. Walker, Agent, Air Traffic Conference of America, Local and
 Joint Passenger Fares Tariff, No. PF-5, C.A.B. No. 44, origi-
 nally effective Apr. 28, 1957. (Note: C. C. Squires became
 the issuing agent of this tariff effective July 19, 1959.
 Airline Tariff Publishers replaced the Air Traffic Conference
 of America as the issuing organization on Mar. 3, 1965. C. C.
 Squires was the first General Manager of this firm.)
W. A. Weeks, Director of Tariffs, Eastern Air Lines,
 Local Air-Shuttle Tariff, C.A.B. No. 83, originally effective
 Apr. 16, 1961.
 Local "Executive Shuttle" Tariff, C.A.B. No. 160, originally
 effective Oct. 1, 1964.

CAB, Handbook of Airline Statistics (1967 ed.), p. 448.

Cherington, Airline Price Policy, pp. 87-98 and 432-435.

Aviation Week and Space Technology, Vol. 84, No. 18 (May 2, 1966),
 p. 50.

Official Airline Guide, North American Edition (and its predecessor
publication, the American Aviation Traffic Guide), Vols. 2-22
(various dates).

Appendix No. 9(A)

CERTIFICATED CARRIERS'[a] ONE-WAY, FIRST-CLASS PASSENGER FARES
BETWEEN INYOKERN-LOS ANGELES/BURBANK, LAKE TAHOE-SAN FRANCISCO/OAKLAND,
LAKE TAHOE-SAN JOSE, LOS ANGELES/BURBANK-SAN JOSE AND SAN DIEGO-SAN JOSE
1946-1965

Effective Date[b]	Pacific's One-Way, Propeller First-Class Fares				
	IYK-LAX/BUR[c]	TVL-SFO/OAK[d]	TVL-SJC[e]	LAX/BUR-SJC[f]	SAN-SJC
1947					
Mar. 1	-	-	-	$14.50	-
Apr. 1	-	-	-	15.00[g]	-
June 1	-	-	-	15.45[g]	-
Sept. 5	-	-	-	16.15[h]	-
Dec. 12	-	-	-	17.75	-
1951					
Mar. 11[i]	-	-	-	19.50	-
1953					
Aug. 3	$5.00	-	-	"	-
1954					
July 8	5.75	-	-	"	-
Sept. 6	"	-	-	20.50	-
1956					
Oct. 1	6.75	-	-	"	-
1958					
July 7	"	-	-	21.85	-
1960					
Dec. 1	Canceled	-	-	"	-
1961					
Jan. 9	-	-	-	23.40	-
1962					
Apr. 24	10.40	-	-	"	-
1963					
Jan. 19	10.40	-	-	23.40	$30.25
July 14	10.75	-	-	"[j]	31.20
Oct. 27	"	$16.50	$18.50	"	"
1965 As of					
Dec. 31	10.75	16.50	18.50	23.40	31.20

Appendix No. 9(A) (continued)

^aPacific Air Lines (named Southwest Airways prior to March 6, 1958) was the only certificated carrier providing service in these markets.

^bSee footnote c, Appendix No. 6(A).

^cStarting August 3, 1953, Pacific provided service in this market (under Navy contract) for persons traveling on official government business. On October 1, 1956 the southern terminal of this route was moved from Burbank to the Los Angeles International Airport. The CAB granted Pacific a temporary exemption to provide common carrier service so long as the Navy had no objections [CAB Order No. E-14593 (adopted October 29, 1959)], and Pacific filed a tariff with the PUC to provide such service effective May 8, 1960. On December 1, 1960 the Navy contract was transferred to Avalon Air Transport and Pacific terminated all service, but in 1962 the CAB authorized Pacific to operate subsidized common carrier service in this market [35 CAB 50 (1962)] and Pacific inaugurated such service on April 24, 1962, whereupon the Navy terminated its contract with Avalon.

^dNo single-plane service was operated by Pacific between Lake Tahoe and Oakland during this period.

^eDuring the indicated period Pacific's service in this market consisted essentially of an eastbound flight operated on Sundays and holidays only. However, a daily westbound flight was also operated from August 1 through September 7, 1964.

^fService between Burbank and San Jose was provided from September 1, 1948 through March 31, 1949, and from March 7, 1955 through December 31, 1965.

^gPacific's two fare increases of April 1 and June 1, 1947 resulted in a combined increase of 6.6 percent compared with the 10 percent increase that the trunk carriers adopted on April 1, 1947.

^hThis corresponds to the fare changes resulting from the expansion of service at Los Angeles International Airport at the expense of the Lockheed Air Terminal at Burbank [see footnote h, Appendix No. 6(A)].

ⁱPacific did not adopt the 10 percent across-the-board fare increase authorized by the CAB effective September 1, 1948, until March 11, 1951. However, on March 15, 1949 it introduced the five percent round-trip discount that was part of the September 1, 1948 fare change.

^jPacific intentionally omitted Los Angeles/Burbank-San Jose (and two other city pairs) when increasing its other fares by three percent on this date. It stated that this was done pending the completion of an economic study of this market.

Sources: See the consolidated listing following Appendix No. 9(B).

296

CERTIFICATED CARRIERS'[a] ONE-WAY, COACH AND OTHER PASSENGER FARES
BETWEEN LOS ANGELES/BURBANK-SAN JOSE AND SAN DIEGO-SAN JOSE
1946-1965

Effective Date[b]	Pacific's One-Way, Propeller Coach and Other Fares	
	LAX/BUR-SJC[c]	SAN-SJC
1956 July 20	$13.50	−
1958 July 7	14.40	−
1961 Jan. 9	15.80	−
1962 Sept. 1	"	$22.40
1963 Jan. 18	"	Canceled[d]
1964 Apr. 26	Canceled	−
1965 Oct. 31	15.50	−
As of Dec. 31	15.50	−

[a]See footnote a, Appendix No. 9(A). Pacific did not operate coach service to Inyokern or Lake Tahoe during this period.

[b]See footnote c, Appendix No. 6(A).

[c]Coach service from July 20, 1956 to April 26, 1964. Commutair service inaugurated October 31, 1965 with propeller aircraft. Effective May 21, 1966 Pacific filed a propeller/jet fare differential for this service. The propeller fare was kept at $15.50 while the jet fare was $2.00 lower, i.e., $13.50. Jet service was inaugurated on August 22, 1966.

[d]Even though no service was being offered at the time, the San Diego-San Jose coach fare was increased to $23.10 on July 14, 1963.

Sources: See the consolidated listing on the following page.

Appendix No. 9 (continued)

Sources for Appendices Nos. 9(A) and 9(B):

The following tariffs filed with the California Public Utilities
Commission (or the California Railroad Commission) by Pacific Air
Lines (or Southwest Airways Company):
Southwest Airways,
    C.R.C. No. 1,   originally effective Nov. 22, 1946.
    Cal. P.U.C. No. 2,   "   "   June   6, 1947.
    "   "   " 10,   "   "   Sept. 18, 1953.
    "   "   " 11,   "   "   July 20, 1956.
Pacific Air Lines,
    Cal. P.U.C. No. 2, originally effective Jan.   1, 1960.
    "   "   "   3,   "   "   July   7, 1958.
    "   "   "   4,   "   "   July   7, 1958.
    "   "   "   5,   "   "   Aug. 24, 1959.
    "   "   "   7,   "   "   Aug. 24, 1959.
    "   "   " 13,   "   "   Oct. 31, 1965.

U.S. Civil Aeronautics Board, Order No. E-14593 (adopted Oct. 29,
1959).

U.S. Department of Defense, Department of the Navy, Contract No. N123
(60530)7988A, dated 1 July 1956, as modified 17 Sept. 1956.

Official Airline Guide, North American Edition (and its predecessor
publications, the American Aviation Traffic Guide, and the American
Aviation Air Traffic Guide), Vols. 3-22 (various dates, 1947-1965).

Pacific Airlines:
    CAB General Schedule No. 2, revised effective Apr. 24, 1962.
    Company records.

35 CAB 50 (1962).

Appendix No. 10

CALIFORNIA INTRASTATE CARRIERS'[a] ONE-WAY PASSENGER FARES
BETWEEN BURBANK-INYOKERN, BURBANK-EDWARDS AFB, EDWARDS AFB-INYOKERN,
LAKE TAHOE-OAKLAND, LAKE TAHOE-SAN JOSE, LOS ANGELES-SAN JOSE, AND
SAN DIEGO-SAN JOSE
1946-1965

Effective Date[b]	One-Way Propeller Fares						
	California Central			Paradise		PSA	
	BUR-IYK[c]	BUR-EDW	EDW-IYK	TVL-OAK	TVL-SJC	LAX-SJC	SAN-SJC
1951							
Feb. 26	$ 7.00	–	–	–	–	–	–
Aug. 1	"	$ 5.00	$ 4.00	–	–	–	–
1952							
Jan. 15	"	Canceled	Canceled	–	–	–	–
July 10	8.00	–	–	–	–	–	–
1953							
July 31	Canceled	–	–	–	–	–	–
1962							
May 14	–	–	–	$10.45[d]	–	–	–
Nov. 1	–	–	–	"	$10.45[d]	–	–
1964							
Mar. 4	–	–	–	Canceled	Canceled	–	–
1965							
Oct. 8	–	–	–	–	–	$11.43	$17.78
Oct. 12	–	–	–	–	–	Canceled[e]	Canceled[e]

[a]Limited to intrastate carriers operating for nine months or more.

[b]See footnote c, Appendix No. 6(A).

[c]The Navy Department guaranteed payment to California Central for
ten passengers per one-way flight, i.e., 40 passengers per weekday.

[d]Paradise's round-trip fare in this market was $19.20, i.e., 9.1
percent less than two one-way fares.

[e]PUC Decision No. 69764 (dated October 7, 1965) ordered the suspension of this service effective October 12, 1965. PUC Decision No. 70657
(dated May 3, 1966) gave PSA authority to operate between San Jose and
Los Angeles (and on to San Diego). PSA reinaugurated its service on May
18, 1966 utilizing Electra aircraft at the original $11.43 Los Angeles-

San Jose fare. Jet service was inaugurated in this market on October 17, 1966 under a $13.50 fare. San Diego-San Jose fares were not published in 1966, but could be constructed by combining the appropriate San Jose-Los Angeles fare and the $6.35 Los Angeles-San Diego fare.

Sources:

The following tariffs filed with the California Public Utilities Commission by the specified intrastate carriers:
California Central Airlines, Cal. P.U.C. No. 1, originally effective Jan. 1, 1949.
Paradise Airlines,
    Cal. P.U.C. No. 2, originally effective May   14, 1962.
    "   "   " 3,   "   "   Oct.   3, 1962.
    "   "   " 4,   "   "   May   9, 1963.
    "   "   " 5,   "   "   Sept. 13, 1963.
Pacific Southwest Airlines, C.P.U.C. No. 1, originally effective May 3, 1949.

Cal. PUC Decisions Nos. 69764 (dated Oct. 7, 1965) and 70657 (dated May 3, 1966).

American Aviation, Vol. 16, No. 5 (Aug. 4, 1952), p. 24.

PSA, Flight Schedule, Oct. 17, 1966.

Appendix No. 7 of this book.

CERTIFICATED CARRIERS'[a] ONE-WAY, FIRST-CLASS AND COACH PASSENGER FARES
BETWEEN LONG BEACH-SAN DIEGO, LONG BEACH-SAN FRANCISCO/OAKLAND, AND
ONTARIO-SAN FRANCISCO
1946-1965

Effective Date[b]	Carrier[c]	One-Way Propeller Fares[d]					
		LGB-SFO/OAK[e]		LGB-SAN[f]		ONT-SFO[g]	
		First-Class	Coach	First-Class	Coach	First-Class	Coach
1946							
As of							
Jan. 1[h]	WAL	$16.55	-	$ 4.15	-	-	-
Aug. 1	UAL	"	-	"	-	-	-
1947							
Apr. 1 [i]		18.25	-	4.60	-	-	-
Sept. 5[i]	WAL	18.95	-	4.80	-	-	-
Dec. 12		20.85	-	5.30	-	-	-
1948							
July 1	UAL	21.65[j]	-	"	-	-	-
July 8	WAL	"[j]	-	"	-	-	-
Sept. 1[k]		23.55	-	5.85	-	-	-
1949							
Feb. 1	WAL[l]	22.35	-	5.55	-	-	-
Oct. 15	WAL[l]	23.55	-	5.85	-	-	-
1950							
Apr. 20	WAL	22.05[m]	-	"	-	-	-
June 1	UAL	"	-	"	-	-	-
1951							
Dec. 10	WAL	"	$12.45	"	$ 4.80	-	-
1952							
Feb. 1	UAL	"	"	"	"	-	-
Mar. 9	UAL	"	Canceled	"	Canceled	-	-
Apr. 30	WAL	23.05	12.45	6.85	4.80	-	-
May 3	UAL	"	-	"	-	-	-
1953							
Feb. 1	WAL	"	14.25	"	4.80	-	-
1958							
July 7		25.00	15.85[n]	8.05	6.00[n]	-	-
1959							
Mar. 1		"[o]	"	"[o]	"	-	-

Effective Date[b]	Carrier[c]	One-Way Propeller Fares[d]					
		LGB-SFO/OAK[e]		LGB-SAN[f]		ONT-SFO[g]	
		First-Class	Coach	First-Class	Coach	First-Class	Coach
1961							
Jan. 9		$26.65	$17.25[h]	$ 9.40	$ 7.15[h]	-	-
1962							
Mar. 20		27.45	17.80[h]	9.70	7.40[h]	-	-
June 1	PAC	26.65	17.25	-	-	-	-
Aug. 1	UAL	27.45	-	Canceled	-	-	-
Sept. 30	WAL	"	17.80	9.70	7.40	$27.45	$17.80
Oct. 28	UAL	Canceled	-	-	-	-	-
1963							
July 14	PAC	27.45	17.80	-	-	-	-
1964							
Mar. 1	PAC	"	Canceled	-	-	-	-
Apr. 26	WAL	Canceled	17.80	Canceled	7.40	Canceled	17.80
June 12	WAL	-	14.10	-	"	-	"
Oct. 25	PAC	27.45	-	9.70	-	-	-
1965							
As of	PAC	27.45	-	9.70	-	-	-
Dec. 31	WAL	-	14.10	-	7.40	-	17.80

[a] Pacific Air Lines, United Air Lines and Western Air Lines.

[b] See footnote c, Appendix No. 6(A).

[c] Unless specified to the contrary, the effective date and associated fares apply to both United and Western. Information pertaining to Pacific is specifically noted in this column.

[d] Jet service was not operated in these markets during this period.

[e] Fares available on single-plane, limited-stop or nonstop service. United suspended single-plane service in this market during 1961 and the first four months of 1962.

[f] Fares available on nonstop service.

[g] Western inaugurated the first single-plane service between Ontario and San Francisco on September 30, 1962, after receiving the CAB's authorization to operate nonstop service in this market [35 CAB 50 (1962)].

[h] These fares were originally adopted on August 20, 1945.

Appendix No. 11 (continued)

^{i}See footnote h, Appendix No. 9(A).

^{j}This fare increase was independent of any CAB authorized across-the-board fare increase (see footnote m, below).

^{k}See footnote i, Appendix No. 6(A).

^{l}See footnote j, Appendix No. 6(A).

^{m}This decrease eliminated the "airport change" fare increase of September 5, 1947, and the independent fare increase of July 1-8, 1948. The application of the second and third 10 percent across-the-board fare increases to the April 1, 1947 fare yields this $22.05 fare.

^{n}Western Air Lines only.

^{o}Five percent, round-trip discount canceled.

Sources:

The following tariffs filed with the California Public Utilities Commission (or the California Railroad Commission) by:
Pacific Air Lines,
Cal. P.U.C. No. 5, originally effective Aug. 24, 1959.
" " " 7, " " Aug. 24, 1959.
United Air Lines,
C.R.C. No. 12, originally effective July 15, 1943.
" " 13, " " Mar. 1, 1947.
Cal. P.U.C. No. 15, " " Sept. 14, 1949.
" " " 16, " " Apr. 29, 1950.
" " " 20, " " July 31, 1959.
" " " 25, " " Nov. 1, 1964.
Western Air Lines,
C.R.C. No. 1, originally effective June 20, 1945.
Cal. P.U.C. No. 2, " " June 1, 1947.
" " " 3, " " Oct. 15, 1949.
" " " 19, " " July 31, 1959.
" " " 20, " " Jan. 9, 1961.
" " " 23, " " Dec. 1, 1961.
" " " 24, " " Mar. 20, 1962.
" " " 25, " " Apr. 24, 1962.

Official Airline Guide, North American Edition (and its predecessor publications, the American Aviation Traffic Guide, and the American Aviation Air Traffic Guide), Vols. 2-22 (various dates, 1946-1965).

35 CAB 50 (1962).

Appendix No. 12

CALIFORNIA INTRASTATE CARRIERS'[a] ONE-WAY PASSENGER FARES
BETWEEN LONG BEACH-SAN DIEGO, LONG BEACH-SAN FRANCISCO/OAKLAND,
AND BURBANK/LOS ANGELES-BROWN FIELD
1946-1965

Effective Date[b]	One-Way Propeller Fares		Mercer BUR/LAX-BRF[c]
	Pacific Southwest		
	LGB-SFO/OAK	LGB-SAN	
1953			
Oct. 1	$13.95	$ 4.80	-
1954			
Jan. 15	14.25	"	-
Apr. 8	12.72[d]	4.54	-
June 17	Canceled	Canceled	-
1964			
Apr. 18	-	-	$ 7.14
1965			
As of Dec. 31	-	-	7.14

[a]Limited to intrastate carriers operating for nine months or more.

[b]See footnote c, Appendix No. 6(A).

[c]The great majority of Mercer's operations was between Burbank
and Brown Field with relatively little through Los Angeles.

[d]Long Beach-San Francisco only, Oakland service was suspended
around April 2, 1954.

Sources:

    The following tariffs filed with the California Public Utilities
    Commission by:
        Mercer Enterprises, Cal. P.U.C. No. 1, originally effective
            Sept. 21, 1965.
        Pacific Southwest Airlines, Cal. P.U.C. No. 1, originally
            effective May 3, 1949.

    Conversation with Mr. D. W. Mercer, Dec. 22, 1966.

    Appendix No. 1 of this book.

NONSTOP DISTANCES[a] BETWEEN VARIOUS CALIFORNIA AIRPORTS
AND BETWEEN THE AIRPORTS OF BALTIMORE, BOSTON,
NEWARK, NEW YORK, AND WASHINGTON, D.C.

A. California Airports

And		BUR	EDW	IYK	LGB	LAX	OAK	SAC	SAN	SJC	SFO
					Nonstop Distance[a] Between						
Brown Field[b]	BRF	139*	-	-	-	127*	-	-	-	-	-
Burbank	BUR		60*	105	29	18	326	346	123	296	327
Edwards AFB	EDW			54*	-	-	-	-	-	-	-
Inyokern	IYK				-	122	-	-	-	-	-
Lake Tahoe[c]	TVL				-	350	145	85	-	149	157
Long Beach	LGB					17	354*	-	94	-	355
Los Angeles	LAX						339	361	109	309	340
Oakland	OAK							67	448	30	12
Ontario	ONT							-	-	-	362
Sacramento	SAC								-	-	79
San Diego	SAN									-	449
San Jose	SJC										32

B. Baltimore, Boston, Newark, New York, and Washington, D.C.

And		BOS	EWR	JFK	LGA	DIA[d]	DCA[e]
				Nonstop Distance[a] Between			
Baltimore	BAL	369	170	184	185	-	-
Boston	BOS		199	186	184	413	399
Newark	EWR			-	-	212	200
New York J. F. Kennedy	JFK				-	228	213
La Guardia	LGA					-	215

Appendix No. 13 (continued)

*Estimated by direct measurement from maps.

aStatute miles measured along a straight line connecting the two airports.

bSouth San Diego.

cSouth Shore.

dWashington Dulles International Airport.

eWashington National Airport.

Sources:

U.S. Civil Aeronautics Board, Book of Official C.A.B. Airline Route Maps and Airport to Airport Mileages, 10th ed., Washington, Air Transport Association of America, 1964, pp. 67, 92, 99, 100, 103 116.

Pacific Air Lines, Flight Control Department.

Rand McNally, Road Atlas, A supplement to the 93rd Edition of the Commercial Atlas and Market Guide, Chicago, Illinois, 1962, pp. 12-17.

_____, Cosmopolitan World Atlas, Chicago, Illinois, 1962, p. 82.

ON-LINE ORIGIN AND DESTINATION PASSENGER TRAFFIC BETWEEN
LOS ANGELES/BURBANK/LONG BEACH/ONTARIO & SAN FRANCISCO/OAKLAND/SAN JOSE
BY CARRIER, 1946-1965

| Year | Carriers | Number of On-Line Origin and Destination Passengers[a] | | LAX/BUR/LGB-SJC, and ONT-SFO/OAK[c] | Total All Carriers |
| | | LAX/BUR/LGB[b]-SFO/OAK | | | |
		Certificated	Intrastate		
1946	UAL	160,000[**]	-	-	
	WAL	224,000[**]	-	-	
	Others[d]	52,000[**]	n.a.	-	
	Total	436,000	n.a.	-	436,000[**]
1947	UAL	206,000[**]	-	-	
	WAL	165,000[**]	-	-	
	Others[d]	40,000[**]	n.a.	900[**]	
	Total	411,000	n.a.	900	411,900[**]
1948	UAL	194,000[**]	-	-	
	WAL	106,000[**]	-	-	
	Others[e]	34,000[**]	-	1,100[**]	
	Total	334,000	-	1,100	335,100[**]
1949	UAL-CCA	184,000[**]	70,776	-	
	WAL-PSA	90,000[**]	7,187	-	
	Others[f]	15,000[**]	92,400[f]	1,800[**]	
	Total	289,000	170,363	1,800	461,163[**]
1950	UAL-CCA	235,000[**]	66,488	-	
	WAL-PSA	162,000[**]	20,566	800[**]	
	Others[g]	9,000[**]	56,800[g]	2,000[**]	
	Total	406,000	143,854	2,800	552,654[**]
1951	UAL-CCA	n.a.	87,106	-	
	WAL-PSA	n.a.	27,652	n.a.	
	Others[e]	n.a.	-	n.a.	
	Total	n.a.	114,758	n.a.	n.a.
1952	UAL-CCA	335,000[**]	116,525	-	
	WAL-PSA	221,000[**]	35,857	1,800[**]	
	Others[e]	21,000[**]	-	1,800[**]	
	Total	577,000	152,382	3,600	732,982[**]

| Year | Carriers | Number of On-Line Origin and Destination Passengers[a] | | | |
| | | LAX/BUR/LGB[b]-SFO/OAK | | LAX/BUR/LGB-SJC, and | Total |
		Certificated	Intrastate	ONT-SFO/OAK[c]	All Carriers
1953	UAL-CCA	312,000**	85,459	-	
	WAL-PSA	217,000**	45,879	2,500**	
	Others[e]	25,000**	-	2,800**	
	Total	554,000	131,338	5,300	690,638**
1954	UAL-CCA	456,000**	96,404*	-	
	WAL-PSA	216,000**	45,146	2,300**	
	Others[e]	30,000**	-	6,100**	
	Total	702,000	141,550*	8,400	851,950**
1955	UAL-CCA	506,900*	45,000[h]	-	
	WAL-PSA	310,500*	60,470	4,900*	
	Others[e]	43,000*	-	8,500*	
	Total	860,400	105,470*	13,400	979,270*
1956	UAL-CCA	598,000*	42,000**	-	
	WAL-PSA	209,000*	100,167	2,000*	
	Others[e]	50,000	-	21,100*	
	Total	857,000*	142,167*	23,100	1,022,267*
1957	UAL-CCA	562,900*	8,000*	-	
	WAL-PSA	355,400*	143,605	2,600*	
	Others[e]	54,800*	-	28,600*	
	Total	973,100	151,605*	31,200	1,155,905*
1958	UAL	687,000*	-	-	
	WAL-PSA	217,000*	167,177	1,200*	
	Others[e]	65,000*	-	34,200*	
	Total	969,000*	167,177	35,400	1,171,577**
1959	UAL	647,660	-	-	
	WAL-PSA	335,640	205,156	1,750	
	Others[e]	88,780	-	50,610	
	Total	1,072,080	205,156	52,360	1,329,596
1960	UAL	628,620	-	-	
	WAL-PSA	278,320	403,377	990	
	Others[e]	91,230	-	58,900	
	Total	998,170	403,377	59,890	1,461,437

Appendix No. 14(A) (continued)

Year	Carriers	Number of On-Line Origin and Destination Passengers[a]			
		LAX/BUR/LGB[b]-SFO/OAK		LAX/BUR/LGB-SJC, and ONT-SFO/OAK[c]	Total
		Certificated	Intrastate		All Carriers
1961	UAL	677,380	-	-	
	WAL-PSA	223,770	488,561	440	
	Others[i]	83,020	-	53,870	
	Total	984,170	488,561	54,310	1,527,041
1962	UAL-TCA	494,520	11,276	-	
	WAL-PSA	314,580	731,787	5,740	
	Others[i]	76,650	-	72,770	
	Total	885,750	743,063	78,510	1,707,323
1963	UAL-TCA	394,530	80,613	-	
	WAL-PSA	561,270	942,632	48,580	
	Others[i]	93,640	-	64,810	
	Total	1,049,440	1,023,245	113,390	2,186,075
1964	UAL-TCA	412,650	74,289	-	
	WAL-PSA	816,350	1,098,279	69,240	
	Others[i]	115,910	-	61,260	
	Total	1,344,910	1,172,568	130,500	2,647,978
1965	UAL	984,750	-	-	
	WAL-PSA	571,830	1,292,581	89,330	
	Others[i]	174,180	-	61,246[j]	
	Total	1,730,760	1,292,581	150,576	3,173,917

n.a. -- not available.

*Partially estimated. For an explanation of the extent to which data were partially or substantially estimated, see Jordan, Economic Effects of Airline Regulation, pp. 629-632, 635-638, 642-643 & 647-648.

**Substantially estimated.

[a]One-way passengers. Round-trip, circle-trip and open-jaw passengers are counted as two one-way passengers. On-line O & D passenger data show where passengers originate and terminate their journeys on individual carriers. Thus, a San Diego-San Francisco true O & D passenger who flew United from San Diego to Los Angeles and then connected with Western to fly on to San Francisco would be counted as an on-line O & D passenger in both the San Diego-Los Angeles and the Los Angeles-San Francisco markets. Such connecting passengers are combined with single-carrier "local" passengers in each market to obtain total on-line O & D traffic for the market. Only on-line O & D passenger data are

309

available for the California intrastate carriers since these carriers
did not record the itineraries of connecting passengers.

[b]The CAB reported Long Beach O & D passenger data separately from
Los Angeles/Burbank from 1946 through 1961. During the various survey
periods for those years Long Beach accounted for between 0.3 to 3.5
percent of the total true O & D passengers reported as flying between
LAX/BUR/LGB and SFO/OAK on certificated carriers.

[c]Western was the only carrier providing single-carrier service for
ONT-SFO/OAK, while, with one exception, Pacific (listed with "other"
carriers) was the only carrier providing such service for LAX/BUR/LGB-
SJC (see footnote i, below).

[d]Certificated carriers: Pacific Air Lines (Southwest Airways),
Trans World Airlines (accounting for over 95 percent of these passen-
gers), and "unknown." California intrastate carriers: Pacific Air
Lines.

[e]American Airlines, Pacific Air Lines (Southwest Airways), Trans
World Airlines (usually accounting for over 90 percent of these passengers), and "unknown."

[f]Certificated carriers: see footnote e, above. California intrastate carriers: California Arrow = 11,700*; California Skycoach =
1,000*; Channel Airways = 1,200*; Robin Airways = 28,605; WALC =
49,938.

[g]Certificated carriers: see footnote e, above. California intrastate carriers: California Pacific = 700*; WALC = 56,100*.

[h]California Central = 10,000**; California Coastal = 35,000**.

[i]American Airlines, Delta Air Lines, National Airlines (all requiring routings via points in Arizona, Texas or points east thereof),
Pacific Air Lines, Trans World Airlines (usually accounting for over
90 percent of these passengers), and "unknown."

[j]Includes 1,976 passengers flying on PSA between Los Angeles and
San Jose from October 8, through October 11, 1965.

Sources: See the consolidated listing following Appendix No. 14(C).

Appendix No. 14(B)

ON-LINE ORIGIN AND DESTINATION PASSENGER TRAFFIC
BETWEEN LOS ANGELES/BURBANK/LONG BEACH/ONTARIO AND SAN DIEGO
BY CARRIER, 1946-1965

		Number of On-Line Origin and Destination Passengers[a]		
Year	Carriers	LAX/BUR/LGB[b]/ONT[c]-SAN		Total
		Certificated	Intrastate	All Carriers
1946	UAL	37,000**	-	
	WAL	52,000**	-	
	Others[d]	28,000**	-	
	Total	117,000	-	117,000**
1947	UAL	35,000**	-	
	WAL	30,000**	-	
	Others[d]	24,000**	-	
	Total	89,000	-	89,000**
1948	UAL	26,000**	-	
	WAL	32,000**	-	
	Others[d]	12,000**	-	
	Total	70,000	-	70,000**
1949	UAL-CCA	34,000**	1,565	
	WAL-PSA	27,000**	2,126	
	Others[d]	17,000**	-	
	Total	78,000	3,691	81,691**
1950	UAL-CCA	26,000**	5,402	
	WAL-PSA	25,000**	8,639	
	Others[d]	16,000**	-	
	Total	67,000	14,041	81,041**
1951	UAL-CCA	n.a.	11,052	
	WAL-PSA	n.a.	17,655	
	Others[d]	n.a.	-	
	Total	n.a.	28,707	n.a.
1952	UAL-CCA	60,000**	19,380	
	WAL-PSA	52,000**	22,485	
	Others[e]	49,000**	-	
	Total	161,000	41,865	202,865**
1953	UAL-CCA	81,000**	15,584	
	WAL-PSA	37,000**	24,293	
	Others[e]	33,000**	-	
	Total	151,000	39,877	190,877**

311

| Year | Carriers | Number of On-Line Origin and Destination Passengers[a] | | Total |
| | | LAX/BUR/LGB[b]/ONT[c]-SAN | | |
		Certificated	Intrastate	All Carriers
1954	UAL-CCA	102,000**	15,732*	
	WAL-PSA	35,000**	16,028	
	Others[e]	25,000	-	
	Total	162,000**	25,760*	187,760**
1955	UAL-CCA	102,200*	6,200[f]	
	WAL-PSA	48,100*	19,353	
	Others[e]	25,200*	-	
	Total	175,500	25,553*	201,053*
1956	UAL-CCA	138,000*	5,000**	
	WAL-PSA	40,000*	28,217	
	Others[e]	34,000	-	
	Total	212,000*	33,217*	245,217**
1957	UAL	155,200*	-	
	WAL-PSA	60,200	38,562	
	Others[e]	37,800*	-	
	Total	253,200	38,562	291,762*
1958	UAL	162,000*	-	
	WAL-PSA	34,000*	45,813	
	Others[e]	57,000*	-	
	Total	253,000*	45,813	298,813**
1959	UAL	168,720	-	
	WAL-PSA	50,410	59,006	
	Others[e]	53,540	-	
	Total	272,670	59,006	331,676
1960	UAL	178,660	-	
	WAL-PSA	41,000	87,589	
	Others[e]	55,530	-	
	Total	275,190	87,589	362,779
1961	UAL	165,210	-	
	WAL-PSA	32,280	92,779	
	Others[g]	50,770	-	
	Total	248,260	92,779	341,039
1962	UAL	121,330	-	
	WAL-PSA	38,600	127,676	
	Others[h]	52,540	-	
	Total	212,470	127,676	340,146

Year	Carriers	Number of On-Line Origin and Destination Passengers[a] LAX/BUR/LGB[b]/ONT[c]-SAN		Total
		Certificated	Intrastate	All Carriers
1963	UAL-TCA	139,100	1,834	
	WAL-PSA	51,330	162,275	
	Others[h]	59,840	–	
	Total	250,270	164,109	414,379
1964	UAL-TCA	139,480	1,367	
	WAL-PSA	68,530	198,332	
	Others[i]	84,500	6,000	
	Total	292,510	205,699	498,209
1965	UAL	177,070	–	
	WAL-PSA	70,530	282,247	
	Others[i]	99,950	8,300	
	Total	347,550	290,547	638,097

n.a. -- not available.

[*]Partially estimated [see the corresponding footnote to Appendix No. 14(A)].

[**]Substantially estimated.

[a]See footnote a, Appendix No. 14(A).

[b]See footnote b, Appendix No. 14(A). During the various survey periods for 1946 through 1961, Long Beach accounted for between 0.8 and 14.3 percent of the total true O & D passengers reported as flying between LAX/BUR/LGB and SAN.

[c]The reported volume of traffic between Ontario and San Diego was less than 100 on-line O & D passengers annually except for 1964 and 1965 when 1,340 and 650 passengers, respectively, flew between this pair of points.

[d]American Airlines.

[e]American Airlines and Bonanza Air Lines.

[f]California Central = 1,700**; California Coastal = 4,500**.

[g]American Airlines, Bonanza Air Lines, Delta Airlines, National Airlines, and "unknown."

Appendix No. 14(B) (continued)

[h]American Airlines, Bonanza Air Lines, Delta Airlines, National Airlines, Pacific Air Lines, and "unknown."

[i]Certificated carriers: see footnote h, above. California intrastate carriers: Mercer Enterprises.

Sources: See the consolidated listing following Appendix No. 14(C).

Appendix No. 14(C)

ON-LINE ORIGIN AND DESTINATION PASSENGER TRAFFIC
BETWEEN SAN DIEGO AND SAN FRANCISCO/OAKLAND/SAN JOSE
BY CARRIER, 1946-1965

| Year | Carriers | Number of On-Line Origin and Destination Passengers[a] | | Total |
| | | SAN-SFO/OAK/SJC[b] | | All Carriers |
		Certificated	Intrastate	
1946	UAL	16,000[**]	-	
	WAL	21,000[**]	-	
	Total	37,000	-	37,000[**]
1947	UAL	19,000[**]	-	
	WAL	13,000[**]	-	
	Total	32,000	-	32,000[**]
1948	UAL	13,000[**]	-	
	WAL	9,000[**]	-	
	Total	22,000	-	22,000[**]
1949	UAL-CCA	9,000[**]	4,526	
	WAL-PSA	10,000[**]	5,698	
	Total	19,000	10,224	29,224[**]
1950	UAL-CCA	11,000[**]	10,617	
	WAL-PSA	8,000[**]	16,167	
	Total	19,000	26,784	45,784[*]
1951	UAL-CCA	n.a.	18,350	
	WAL-PSA	n.a.	30,688	
	Total	n.a.	49,038	n.a.
1952	UAL-CCA	18,000[**]	21,414	
	WAL-PSA	23,000[**]	34,142	
	Total	41,000	55,556	96,556[*]
1953	UAL-CCA	21,000[**]	17,474	
	WAL-PSA	14,000[**]	44,856	
	Total	35,000	62,330	97,330[*]
1954	UAL-CCA	32,000[**]	22,619[*]	
	WAL-PSA	11,000[**]	40,950[*]	
	Total	43,000	63,569	106,569[*]
1955	UAL-CCA	35,900[*]	7,800[c]	
	WAL-PSA	25,100[*]	49,493[*]	
	Total	61,000	57,293[*]	118,293[*]

315

Year	Carriers	Number of On-Line Origin and Destination Passengers[a] SAN-SFO/OAK/SJC[b]		Total
		Certificated	Intrastate	All Carriers
1956	UAL-CCA	42,000*	7,000**	
	WAL-PSA	12,000*	62,187	
	Total	54,000*	69,187*	123,187*
1957	UAL	46,000*	-	
	WAL-PSA	12,300*	78,491	
	Total	58,300*	78,491	136,791*
1958	UAL	56,000*	-	
	WAL-PSA	4,000*	82,888	
	Total	60,000*	82,888	142,888*
1959	UAL	56,120	-	
	WAL-PSA	9,950	90,920	
	Others[d]	50	-	
	Total	66,120	90,920	157,040
1960	UAL	50,120	-	
	WAL-PSA	4,690	130,314	
	Others[d]	60	-	
	Total	54,870	130,314	185,184
1961	UAL	52,820	-	
	WAL-PSA	4,740	131,724	
	Others[d]	190	-	
	Total	57,750	131,724	189,474
1962	UAL	30,380	-	
	WAL-PSA	13,100	170,506	
	Others[e]	980	-	
	Total	44,460	170,506	214,966
1963	UAL-TCA	17,200	7,897	
	WAL-PSA	34,340	199,753	
	Others[e]	1,060	-	
	Total	52,600	207,650	260,250
1964	UAL-TCA	16,140	4,867	
	WAL-PSA	40,530	234,824	
	Others[e]	1,130	-	
	Total	57,800	239,691	297,491

| Year | Carriers | Number of On-Line Origin and Destination Passengers[a] SAN-SFO/OAK/SJC[b] | | Total |
		Certificated	Intrastate	All Carriers
1965	UAL	51,150	–	
	WAL-PSA	27,520	279,805	
	Others[e]	800	–	
	Total	79,470	279,805	359,275

n.a. -- not available.

*Partially estimated [see the corresponding footnote to Appendix No. 14(A)].

**Substantially estimated.

[a]See footnote a, Appendix No. 14(A).

[b]Single-carrier service was not available between San Diego and San Jose until Pacific Air Lines inaugurated service at San Diego on July 1, 1962, and single-plane service was not operated until January 19, 1963. The following numbers of on-line O & D passengers were reported to have flown Pacific in this market: 1962 = 300, 1963 = 470, 1964 = 450, 1965 = 250.

[c]California Central = 2,300**; California Coastal = 5,500**.

[d]American Airlines (requiring routings via points in Arizona or points east thereof) and "unknown."

[e]American Airlines, Delta Air Lines, National Airlines (all requiring routings via points in Arizona, Texas or points east thereof), Pacific Air Lines, and "unknown."

Sources: See the consolidated listing on the following page.

Appendix No. 14 (continued)

Sources for Appendices Nos. 14(A), 14(B) and 14(C):

California Public Utilities Commission:
Astrue, Intrastate Scheduled "Coach Class" Air Carriers, Ex. No.
1-C, pp. 16, 25-41, and Ex. No. 5-C, pp. 2 & 5, Case No. 4994,
et al.
Mercer Enterprises, Application No. 48157 (filed Dec. 28, 1965),
pp. 2-3.
Pacific Southwest Airlines, Ex. No. 5 (submitted Jan. 5, 1967),
Application No. 48989.
Transportation Division, Passenger Section, Intrastate Passengers
of Scheduled Air Carriers by Types of Carriers, No. 1511 (Quarters Ended Mar. 31, June 30, Sept. 30, and Dec. 31, 1962-1965).

U.S. Civil Aeronautics Board:
Competition Among Domestic Air Carriers, Washington, Air Transport
Association of America, 1955-1965 (Mar. 1-14 and Sept. 17-30
surveys for 1955-1958, annual surveys for 1959-1965).
Domestic Origin-Destination Survey of Air Passenger Traffic (and
its predecessor publications), Washington, Air Transport Association of America, 1946-1965 [Mar. and Sept. surveys from Sept.
1946 through Mar. 1952 (1951 surveys not published), Sept. 16-
30, 1952 survey, Mar. 1-14 and Sept. 17-30 surveys for 1953-
1958, annual surveys for 1959-1965].
Handbook of Airline Statistics (1967 ed.), pp. 509-510.

U.S. District Court, Southern District of Calif., files of the Court
Clerk for Bankruptcy No. 59561-PH, California Central Airlines:
History, Development and Analysis of California Central Airlines
(n.d.), Appendices Nos. A-I through A-IV; Sections Nos. II-A
and II-B; and various unnumbered tables.
Unpublished worksheets, reports and memoranda (various dates).

Airport Records:
City of Los Angeles, Department of Airports.
Port of Oakland, Oakland Metropolitan International Airport.
San Francisco Public Utilities Commission, Airport Department,
San Francisco International Airport.

Company records of Pacific Southwest Airlines and Western Air Lines.

Official Airline Guide, North American Edition, Vol. 18, No. 9
(June 1962), p. C 273.

Appendix No. 9(A) of this book.

NUMBER OF SEATS PER WEEK SCHEDULED ON NONSTOP FLIGHTS BETWEEN
LOS ANGELES/BURBANK/LONG BEACH/ONTARIO & SAN FRANCISCO/OAKLAND/SAN JOSE
BY AIRCRAFT TYPE, CARRIER GROUP[a], AND CLASS OF SERVICE
SELECTED DATES 1948-1965

| Date | Aircraft Type | Number of Scheduled Seats Per Week | | | |
| | | Certificated[b] | | Intrastate | Total All |
		First	Coach	Coach[c]	Carriers
8/ 1/48	DC-3	5,250	–	–	5,250
	DC-4	5,544	–	–	5,544
	DC-6, L-049	2,156	–	–	2,156
	Total	12,950	–	–	12,950
7/31/49	DC-3	1,470	–	3,640	5,110
	Cv-240	4,960	–	–	4,960
	DC-4	2,420	–	2,190	4,610
	DC-6, L-049	5,286	–	–	5,286
	Total	14,136	–	5,830	19,966
3/ 1/51	DC-3	–	–	2,559	2,559
	Cv-240	3,760	–	–	3,760
	DC-4	–	8,580	924	9,504
	DC-6, L-049/749	6,638	–	–	6,638
	Total	10,398	8,580	3,483	22,461
9/ 1/52[d]	DC-3	–	–	1,710	1,710
	M-202	–	–	4,004	4,004
	Cv-240	3,920	–	–	3,920
	DC-4	–	9,240	–	9,240
	DC-6, L-049/749	4,450	–	–	4,450
	DC-6B	3,248	–	–	3,248
	Total	11,618	9,240	5,714	26,572
9/ 1/53[e]	DC-3	–	–	3,375	3,375
	M-202	–	–	2,552	2,552
	Cv-240/340	4,044	–	–	4,044
	DC-4	–	11,466	–	11,466
	DC-6, L-049/749	2,100	567	–	2,667
	DC-6B	6,580	–	–	6,580
	Total	12,724	12,033	5,927	30,684
12/ 1/54[f]	DC-3	–	–	2,601	2,601
	M-202	–	–	2,379	2,379
	Cv-340	1,848	–	–	1,848
	DC-4	–	10,164	–	10,164
	DC-6, L-049/749	2,100	3,185	–	5,285
	DC-6B, L-1049	10,506	–	–	10,506
	Total	14,454	13,349	4,980	32,783

| Date | Aircraft Type | Number of Scheduled Seats Per Week | | | |
| | | Certificated[b] | | Intrastate | Total All |
		First	Coach	Coach[c]	Carriers
8/ 1/55	DC-3	–	–	3,513	3,513
	Cv-340	2,288	–	–	2,288
	DC-4	–	11,880	–	11,880
	DC-6, L-049/749	4,000	2,401	–	6,401
	DC-6B, L-1049	9,404	910	–	10,314
	Total	15,692	15,191	3,513	34,396
8/ 1/56	DC-3	–	–	1,792	1,792
	M-202	360	760	–	1,120
	Cv-340	1,144	–	–	1,144
	DC-4	–	11,656	3,100	14,756
	DC-6, L-049	2,050	2,835	–	4,885
	DC-6B/7, L-1049	15,274	1,722	–	16,996
	Total	18,828	16,973	4,892	40,693
8/ 1/57	DC-3	–	–	608[h]	608
	M-202	–	1,680	–	1,680
	DC-4	–	4,608	4,800	9,408
	DC-6, L-049/749	5,150	6,720	–	11,870
	DC-6B/7	11,594	9,288	–	20,882
	Total	16,744	22,296	5,408	44,448
8/ 1/58	M-202	920	960	–	1,880
	DC-4	–	–	5,320	5,320
	DC-6, L-049	950	13,600	–	14,550
	DC-6B/7, L-1049/1649	16,014	11,602	–	27,616
	Total	17,884	26,162	5,320	49,366
8/ 1/59	M-202	320	520	–	840
	F-27	1,360	240	–	1,600
	DC-4	–	–	6,300	6,300
	DC-6, L-049	4,300	13,905	–	18,205
	DC-6B/7, L-1049G	11,943	10,983	–	22,926
	Electra	2,772	–	–	2,772
	Four-Engine Jet	966	1,365	–	2,331
	Total	21,661	27,013	6,300	54,974
8/ 1/60	M-202/404[h]	1,176	546	–	1,722
	F-27	840	280	–	1,120
	DC-6, L-049	1,700	13,986	–	15,686
	DC-6B/7, L-1649	8,581	8,820	–	17,401
	Electra	2,772	–	11,172	13,944
	Four-Engine Jet	4,582	7,925	–	12,507
	Total	19,651	31,557	11,172	62,380

Date	Aircraft Type	Certificated[b] First	Certificated[b] Coach	Intrastate Coach[c]	Total All Carriers
8/ 1/61	M-202/404[h]	1,134	–	–	1,134
	F-27	1,320	–	–	1,320
	DC-6, L-049	–	4,581	–	4,581
	DC-6B/7	3,712	2,408	–	6,120
	Electra	2,100	8,988	14,602	25,690
	Four-Engine Jet	9,172	20,349	–	29,521
	Total	17,438	36,326	14,602	68,366
8/ 1/62	M-202/404[h]	440	1,100	–	1,540
	F-27	–	480	–	480
	DC-6B/7, L-1049G	–	16,394	–	16,394
	Electra	676	5,348	21,168	27,192
	Four-Engine Jet	9,734	27,483	–	37,217
	Total	10,850	50,805	21,168	82,823
8/ 1/63[i]	M-202/404[h]	308	748	–	1,056
	F-27	200	560	–	760
	L-749	–	–	4,508	4,508
	DC-6B, L-1049G	–	15,470	–	15,470
	Electra	660	8,964	27,440	37,064
	Four-Engine Jet	11,520	35,741	–	47,261
	Total	12,688	61,483	31,948	106,119
8/ 1/64	M-404	44	–	–	44
	F-27	2,440	–	–	2,440
	L-749	–	–	4,116	4,116
	DC-6B	–	23,181	–	23,181
	Electra	–	7,050	35,280	42,330
	B-727-100	–	1,932	–	1,932
	Four-Engine Jet	7,124	33,219	–	40,343
	Total	9,608	65,382	39,396	114,386
10/ 1/64	F-27	1,960	–	–	1,960
	L-749	–	–	4,116[j]	4,116
	DC-6B	–	24,472	–	24,472
	Electra	–	7,708	35,280	42,988
	B-727-100	–	15,108	–	15,108
	Four-Engine Jet	7,528	28,467	–	35,995
	Total	9,488	75,755	39,396	124,639
8/ 1/65[1]	M-404	528	–	–	528
	F-27	1,400	–	–	1,400
	Electra	–	6,392	33,516	39,908
	B-727-100	292	28,462	26,840	55,594
	Four-Engine Jet	7,934	50,242	–	58,176
	Total	10,154	85,096	60,356	155,606

[a]Detailed information regarding the number of seats scheduled by each carrier in individual aircraft types is given in Jordan, Economic Effects of Airline Regulation, pp. 651-667.

[b]Pacific Air Lines, Trans World Airlines, United Air Lines, and Western Air Lines.

[c]California Arrow, California Central/Coastal Airlines, Channel Airways, Pacific Southwest Airlines, Robin Airways, and Trans California Airlines (see Appendix No. 1 for dates of service).

[d]California Central's schedule effective September 3, 1952.

[e]United's schedule effective September 8, 1953.

[f]United's schedule effective December 12, 1954.

[g]California Coastal terminated service on August 9, 1957.

[h]From January 1960 to January 1964, Pacific operated both M-202 and M-404 aircraft without differentiating between them in its published schedules. By 1961 the majority of Pacific's Martin fleet was comprised of M-404's.

[i]United's schedule effective August 5, 1963.

[j]Trans California terminated service on October 7, 1964.

[k]PSA's schedule effective August 6, 1965.

Sources: See the consolidated listing following Appendix No. 15(C).

Appendix No. 15(B)

NUMBER OF SEATS PER WEEK SCHEDULED ON NONSTOP FLIGHTS BETWEEN
LOS ANGELES/BURBANK/LONG BEACH/ONTARIO & SAN DIEGO
BY AIRCRAFT TYPE, CARRIER GROUP[a], AND CLASS OF SERVICE
SELECTED DATES 1948-1965

| Date | Aircraft Type | Number of Scheduled Seats Per Week | | | |
| | | Certificated[b] | | Intrastate | Total All |
		First	Coach	Coach[c]	Carriers
8/ 1/48	DC-3	2,940	-	-	2,940
	DC-4	924	-	-	924
	DC-6	1,456	-	-	1,456
	Total	5,320	-	-	5,320
7/31/49	DC-3	1,764	-	1,512	3,276
	Cv-240	1,680	-	-	1,680
	DC-6	2,548	-	-	2,548
	Total	5,992	-	1,512	7,504
3/ 1/51	DC-3	1,848	-	2,109	3,957
	Cv-240	2,800	-	-	2,800
	DC-4	-	-	858	858
	DC-6	2,912	-	-	2,912
	Total	7,560	-	2,967	10,527
9/ 1/52[d]	DC-3	1,764	-	1,710	3,474
	M-202	-	-	1,936	1,936
	Cv-240	2,240	-	-	2,240
	DC-4	-	1,848	-	1,848
	DC-6	3,724	-	-	3,724
	DC-6B	812	-	-	812
	Total	8,540	1,848	3,646	14,034
9/ 1/53[e]	DC-3	882	-	2,759	3,641
	M-202	-	-	1,936	1,936
	Cv-240/340	4,144	-	-	4,144
	DC-4	-	924	-	924
	DC-6	5,558	-	-	5,558
	DC-6B	812	-	-	812
	Total	11,396	924	4,695	17,015
12/ 1/54[f]	DC-3	294	-	1,911	2,205
	M-202	-	-	1,320	1,320
	Cv-240/340	3,584	-	-	3,584
	DC-4	-	2,772	-	2,772
	DC-6	3,724	2,814	-	6,538
	DC-6B	2,406	-	-	2,406
	Total	10,008	5,586	3,231	18,825

323

Date	Aircraft Type	Number of Scheduled Seats Per Week			
		Certificated[b]		Intrastate	Total All
		First	Coach	Coach[c]	Carriers
8/ 1/55	DC-3	–	–	2,770	2,770
	Cv-240/340	3,584	–	–	3,584
	DC-4	–	2,772	–	2,772
	DC-6	4,046	3,668	–	7,714
	DC-6B	2,464	–	–	2,464
	Total	10,094	6,440	2,770	19,304
8/ 1/56	DC-3	294	–	448	742
	Cv-240/340	4,760	–	–	4,760
	DC-4	–	1,820	2,356	4,176
	DC-6	2,646	5,376	–	8,022
	DC-6B	2,870	406	–	3,276
	Total	10,570	7,602	2,804	20,976
8/ 1/57	Cv-240/340	4,672	560	–	5,232
	DC-4	–	896	3,648	4,544
	DC-6	3,646	4,368	–	8,014
	DC-6B/7	3,218	406	–	3,624
	Total	11,536	6,230	3,648	21,414
8/ 1/58	Cv-340	2,376	–	–	2,376
	DC-4	–	–	4,200	4,200
	DC-6	2,618	6,304	–	8,922
	DC-6B/7	6,520	2,163	–	8,683
	Total	11,514	8,467	4,200	24,181
8/ 1/59	Cv-340	2,156	–	–	2,156
	DC-4	–	–	5,180	5,180
	DC-6	3,190	5,120	–	8,310
	DC-6B/7	3,780	9,912	–	13,692
	Total	9,126	15,032	5,180	29,338
8/ 1/60	Cv-340	1,232	–	–	1,232
	DC-6	2,212	9,208	–	11,420
	DC-6B/7	3,584	6,076	–	9,660
	Electra	924	–	8,036	8,960
	Total	7,952	15,284	8,036	31,272
8/ 1/61	Cv-340	1,760	–	–	1,760
	DC-6	–	7,856	–	7,856
	DC-7	812	4,242	–	5,054
	Electra	1,176	5,026	9,506	15,708
	Four-Engine Jet	2,100	3,934	–	6,034
	Total	5,848	21,058	9,506	36,412

Appendix No. 15(B) (continued)

| Date | Aircraft Type | Number of Scheduled Seats Per Week | | | |
| | | Certificated[b] | | Intrastate | Total All |
		First	Coach	Coach[c]	Carriers
8/ 1/62	DC-6	–	3,206	–	3,206
	DC-6B/7	224	8,733	–	8,957
	Electra	364	4,652	11,956	16,972
	Four-Engine Jet	2,548	4,844	–	7,392
	Total	3,136	21,435	11,956	36,527
8/ 1/63[g]	DC-6, L-749	–	8,442	1,764	10,206
	DC-7	448	518	–	966
	Electra	680	4,424	11,956	17,060
	Four-Engine Jet	2,926	7,434	–	10,360
	Total	4,054	20,818	13,720	38,592
8/ 1/64	DC-3	–	–	192	192
	DC-6	–	6,160	–	6,160
	Electra	–	8,554	12,740	21,294
	Four-Engine Jet	4,828	11,335	–	16,163
	Total	4,828	26,049	12,932	43,809
10/ 1/64	DC-3	–	–	192	192
	DC-6	–	5,390	–	5,390
	Electra	–	9,024	12,740	21,764
	Four-Engine Jet	4,830	11,319	–	16,149
	Total	4,830	25,733	12,932	43,495
8/ 1/65[h]	DC-3	–	–	192	192
	F-27	616	–	–	616
	DC-6	–	2,898	–	2,898
	Electra	–	5,076	10,976	16,052
	B-727-100	–	6,328	10,614	16,942
	Four-Engine Jet	5,738	18,381	–	24,119
	Total	6,354	32,683	21,782	60,819

[a]See footnote a, Appendix No. 15(A).

[b]American Airlines, Delta Air Lines, National Airlines, Pacific Air Lines, United Air Lines and Western Air Lines.

[c]California Central/Coastal Airlines, Mercer Enterprises, Pacific Southwest Airlines, Trans California Airlines (see Appendix No. 1 for dates of service).

d, e, f, g, h[See footnotes d, e, f, i and k, respectively, Appendix No. 15(A).

Sources: See the consolidated listing following Appendix No. 15(C).

NUMBER OF SEATS PER WEEK SCHEDULED ON SINGLE-PLANE SERVICE[a]
BETWEEN SAN DIEGO & SAN FRANCISCO/OAKLAND/SAN JOSE
BY AIRCRAFT TYPE, CARRIER GROUP[b], AND CLASS OF SERVICE
SELECTED DATES 1948-1965

Date	Aircraft Type	Number of Scheduled Seats Per Week			
		Certificated[c]		Intrastate	Total All
		First	Coach	Coach[d]	Carriers
8/ 1/48	DC-3	1,029	–	–	1,029
	Total	1,029	–	–	1,029
7/31/49	DC-3	294	–	1,512	1,806
	Cv-240	1,680	–	–	1,680
	Total	1,974	–	1,512	3,486
3/ 1/51	DC-3	–	–	2,139	2,139
	Cv-240	2,200	–	–	2,200
	DC-4	–	–	858	858
	Total	2,200	–	2,997	5,197
9/ 1/52[e]	DC-3	–	–	1,860	1,860
	M-202	–	–	2,024	2,024
	Cv-240	1,400	–	–	1,400
	DC-4	–	1,848	–	1,848
	DC-6	350	–	–	350
	DC-6B	812	–	–	812
	Total	2,562	1,848	3,884	8,294
9/ 1/53[f]	DC-3	–	–	2,914	2,914
	M-202	–	–	2,024	2,024
	Cv-240/340	1,484	–	–	1,484
	DC-4	–	924	–	924
	DC-6	350	–	–	350
	DC-6B	812	–	–	812
	Total	2,646	924	4,938	8,508
12/ 1/54[g]	DC-3	–	–	2,162	2,162
	M-202	–	–	1,408	1,408
	DC-4	–	2,772	–	2,772
	DC-6	350	–	–	350
	DC-6B	2,406	–	–	2,406
	Total	2,756	2,772	3,570	9,098
8/ 1/55	DC-3	–	–	3,109	3,109
	Cv-340	616	–	–	616
	DC-4	–	2,772	–	2,772
	DC-6	1,000	–	–	1,000
	DC-6B	2,058	–	–	2,058
	Total	3,674	2,772	3,109	9,555

Date	Aircraft Type	Number of Scheduled Seats Per Week			
		Certificated[c]		Intrastate	Total All
		First	Coach	Coach[d]	Carriers
8/ 1/56	DC-3	–	–	576	576
	Cv-340	308	–	–	308
	DC-4	–	1,820	2,604	4,424
	DC-6B	2,464	406	–	2,870
	Total	2,772	2,226	3,180	8,178
8/ 1/57	DC-4	–	448	4,096	4,544
	DC-6	1,000	504	–	1,504
	DC-6B	1,812	–	–	1,812
	Total	2,812	952	4,096	7,860
8/ 1/58	DC-4	–	–	4,620	4,620
	DC-6	300	1,008	–	1,308
	DC-6B	3,856	–	–	3,856
	Total	4,156	1,008	4,620	9,784
8/ 1/59	DC-4	–	–	5,600	5,600
	DC-6	1,500	1,440	–	2,940
	DC-6B	406	2,660	–	3,066
	Total	1,906	4,100	5,600	11,606
8/ 1/60	DC-6	650	3,888	–	4,538
	DC-6B	1,160	–	–	1,160
	Electra	462	–	8,820	9,282
	Total	2,272	3,888	8,820	14,980
8/ 1/61	DC-6	–	1,800	–	1,800
	DC-7	812	602	–	1,414
	Electra	–	2,016	11,172	13,188
	Four-Engine Jet	392	1,008	–	1,400
	Total	1,204	5,426	11,172	17,802
8/ 1/62	DC-7	–	1,806	–	1,806
	Electra	–	2,496	12,740	15,236
	Four-Engine Jet	392	1,008	–	1,400
	Total	392	5,310	12,740	18,442
8/ 1/63	L-749	–	–	1,764	1,764
	Electra	520	1,768	13,328	15,616
	Total	520	1,768	15,092	17,380
8/ 1/64	Electra	–	2,444	13,720	16,164
	Total	–	2,444	13,720	16,164
10/ 1/64	Electra	–	2,444	13,720	16,164
	Total	–	2,444	13,720	16,164

Date	Aircraft Type	Number of Scheduled Seats Per Week			
		Certificated[c]		Intrastate	Total All
		First	Coach	Coach[d]	Carriers
8/ 1/65[h] Electra		–	2,444	12,152	14,596
B-727-100		–	7,119	11,712	18,831
Total		–	9,563	23,864	33,427

[a]Includes seats provided on all first-class flights making two intermediate stops or less, and all coach flights making three intermediate stops or less.

[b]See footnote a, Appendix No. 15(A).

[c]United Air Lines and Western Air Lines.

[d]California Central/Coastal Airlines, Pacific Southwest Airlines, and Trans California Airlines (see Appendix No. 1 for dates of service).

[e]California Central's schedule effective September 3, 1952.

[f]United's schedule effective September 8, 1953.

[g]United's schedule effective December 12, 1954.

[h]PSA's schedule effective August 6, 1965.

Sources: See the consolidated listing on the following page.

Appendix No. 15 (continued)

Sources for Appendices Nos. 15(A), 15(B) and 15(C):

California Public Utilities Commission:
Astrue, _Intrastate Scheduled "Coach Class" Air Carriers_, Ex. No.
1-C, pp. 25-36, Case No. 4994, _et al._
California Central Airlines, Ex. Nos. 7 & 8 (submitted Mar. 27,
1951), Case No. 5271.
Mercer Enterprises, App. No. 48157 (filed Dec. 28, 1965), p. 2.
Trans California Airlines, Cal. P.U.C. Tariff No. 1 (originally
effective Aug. 15, 1962), p. 22.

U.S. Civil Aeronautics Board:
Docket No. 10321, air carrier reports giving seating configurations
effective Mar. 31, 1959.
Airline Statistics Handbook, Cal. Yrs. 1946-1952, (n.d.), pp. 64-66.
Handbook of Airline Statistics (1967 ed.), p. 492.

U.S. District Court, Southern District of Calif., files of the Court
Clerk for Bankruptcy No. 59561-PH, California Central Airlines,
unpublished worksheets, reports and memoranda (various dates).

U.S. Federal Aviation Agency, Western Region, Aircraft Specifications-
Aircraft Identification, for California Central Airlines, California Coastal Airlines, Pacific Southwest Airlines (various dates).

Official Airline Guide, North American Edition (and its predecessor
publication, the _American Aviation Air Traffic Guide_), Vols. 4-21
(various dates, including the months specified in the Appendices),
schedule pages for the indicated carriers.

Airline Schedules:
California Central Airline Guide (Sept. 3, 1952 & Aug. 25, 1953).
PSA, _Flight Schedule_ (Nov. 1950, June 1, 1952, June 5, 1953, June
24, 1955, July 11, 1956, July 19, 1957 & Aug. 6, 1965).
Trans California Airlines, _Company Schedule_ (n.d.).
United Air Lines, _General Schedule_ (June 1, 1964), 1st rev. p. 29.

American Aviation, Vol. 27, No. 12 (May 1964), p. 40.

Company records of PSA, United Air Lines and Western Air Lines.

Personal correspondence and telephone conversations with employees of
the following carriers: American, Delta, National, Pacific, Trans
World, and United (various dates 1957-1967).

Port of Oakland, Oakland Metropolitan International Airport, airport
records for California Central/Coastal Airlines (Aug. 1957), and
Trans California Airlines (Aug. 1962, Aug. 1964 and Oct. 1964).

Western Air Lines, _Chronological Listings of Important Events in
Western's History_ (Rev. Sept. 8, 1965), pp. VIII-1 to VIII-4.

Appendix No. 16(A)

SELECTED FINANCIAL DATA, OPERATING RATIO & RETURN ON STOCKHOLDER EQUITY
CALIFORNIA CENTRAL AIRLINES, FEBRUARY 1, 1949–DECEMBER 31, 1954

Item	2/1/49–3/31/49	Year Ended				4/1/53–12/31/53	1/28/54–12/31/54[d]
		3/31/50	3/31/51	3/31/52	3/31/53		
Total Operating Revenues	$102,477	$848,597	$1,175,549	$1,652,808	$2,113,473	$1,279,389	$1,734,920[e]
Total Operating Expenses	98,771	879,033	1,114,569	1,636,109	2,123,047	1,441,053	1,760,011[f]
Operating Profit (Loss)	3,706	(30,436)	60,980	16,699	(9,574)	(161,664)	(25,091)
Net Nonoperating Income (Expense)	0	10,102	2,234	3,815	(1,338)	35,889	(13,529)[g]
Net Income Before Taxes	3,706	(20,334)	63,214	20,514	(10,912)	(125,775)	(38,620)
Income Taxes	778	(778)	19,069	6,154	(3,274)	0	0
Profit (Loss) after Taxes	$ 2,928	$(19,556)	$ 44,145	$ 14,360	$ (7,638)	$ (125,775)	$ (38,620)
Stockholder Equity	n.a.	n.a.	n.a.	n.a.	n.a.	$ 10,232[c]	$ (114,584)[h]
Operating Ratio[a]	96.4 %	103.6 %	94.8 %	99.0 %	100.5 %	112.6 %	101.4 %
Return on Stockholder Equity[b]	n.a.	n.a.	n.a.	n.a.	n.a.	(1,129.2)%	—

Appendix No. 16(A) (continued)

n.a. -- not available.

[a]Total operating expenses divided by total operating revenues (times 100).

[b]Profit (Loss) after taxes divided by stockholder equity (times 100).

[c]As of August 31, 1953.

[d]Airline Transport Carriers and California Central Airlines combined statement. During this period, CCA accounted for 99.5 percent of total revenues generated by these two carriers. Therefore, these combined data provide a good estimate of CCA's revenues and expenses.

[e]Passenger revenues = $1,633,902; other revenues = $101,018.

[f]Breakdown of expenses: operations and maintenance = $1,005,414; passenger service = $116,502; selling and administration = $528,257; depreciation = $109,838.

[g]Nonoperating income = $14,301; nonoperating expense = $27,830.

[h]As of October 31, 1954.

Sources:

California Public Utilities Commission, California Central Airlines, Complaint (filed July 22, 1952), Ex. B, Case No. 5397.

U.S. District Court, Southern District of Calif., files of the Court Clerk for Bankruptcies Nos. 59560-PH, Airline Transport Carriers and 59561-PH, California Central Airlines:
Airline Transport Carriers and California Central Airlines Monthly Earned Revenue, Jan.-Aug. 1954, (n.d.).
Audit of California Central Airlines' Operations, Feb. 1, 1949-Dec. 31, 1954. Attached to Memorandum of Airline Transport Carriers, Inc., in Re Motion to Consolidate (filed with the Referee in Bankruptcy, May 28, 1955).
California Central Airlines and Airline Transport Carriers, Consolidated Statement of Profit and Loss (filed Jan. 25, 1955).
Proposed Modified Arrangement (filed Dec. 3, 1954), Ex. D.

Appendix No. 16(B)

SELECTED FINANCIAL DATA AND OPERATING RATIO
WESTERN AIR LINES OF CALIFORNIA, AUGUST 19, 1949-JANUARY 31, 1950

Item	Aug. 19, 1949-Jan. 31, 1950
Operating Revenues	
Passenger	$ 593,914
Excess Baggage	2,605
Total	596,519
Operating Expenses	
Charter Fees	556,466
Commissions	17,014
Advertising & Publicity	18,036
Timetables & Supplies	4,816
Ticketing & Resv. Service	15,062
Accounting Service	3,252
Miscellaneous	4,523
Total	619,169
Operating Profit (Loss)	(22,650)
Net Income	
Before Taxes	(22,650)
Provision for Taxes	150[a]
Profit (Loss) after Taxes	$ (22,800)
Operating Ratio[b]	103.8 %

[a]Tax on $560 operating profit for the period August 19-December 31, 1949.

[b]Total operating expenses divided by total operating revenues (times 100).

Source:

Western Air Lines of California, Inc., Statement of Profit and Loss for the Period August 19, 1949 to February 28, 1950. (Note: The data for Feb. 1950 were estimates. Therefore, they are excluded from this appendix.)

Appendix No. 16(C)

SELECTED FINANCIAL DATA, OPERATING RATIO & RETURN ON STOCKHOLDER EQUITY
PARADISE AIRLINES, APRIL 6, 1962–DECEMBER 31, 1963

Item	Apr. 6–Dec. 31, 1962	1963
Operating Revenues		
Passenger	n.a.	$ 582,647
Charter	n.a.	32,231
Freight & Other	n.a.	1,003
Total	$ 150,358	615,881
Operating Expenses		
Operations	91,078	329,969
Maintenance	15,415	84,022
Passenger Serv. & Limousine	1,701	14,990
Selling & Administration	13,314	189,343
Deprec., Amort. & Leasing	14,922	23,034
Total	136,430	641,358
Operating Profit (Loss)	13,928	(25,477)
Nonoperating Expenses		
Interest	4,567	10,729
Other	9,693	739
Net Income		
Before Taxes	(332)	(36,945)
Income Taxes	0	0
Profit (Loss) after Taxes	(332)	(36,945)
Stockholder Equity[a]	$ 11,399	$ (31,752)
Operating Ratio[b]	90.7 %	104.1 %
Return on Stockholder Equity[c]	(2.9)%	–

n.a. -- not available.

[a] As of December 31.

[b] Total operating expenses ÷ total operating revenues (times 100).

[c] Profit (Loss) after taxes ÷ stockholder equity (times 100).

Sources:

Paradise Airlines, Profit and Loss Statement, 1962 and 1963; and
Balance Sheet, Dec. 31, 1962 and 1963.

U.S. Federal Aviation Agency, Western Region, Systemworthiness
Inspection Report, Paradise Airlines (June 17, 1963), p. 26.

333

SELECTED FINANCIAL DATA AND OPERATING RATIO
TRANS CALIFORNIA AIRLINES, MAY 1, 1963-MARCH 31, 1964

Item	May 1, 1963-March 31, 1964
Operating Revenues (net)	$ 1,087,543
Operating Expenses	
Operations	625,192[a]
Maintenance	64,740
Passenger Service	8,329
Selling & Administration	367,142
Depreciation	449
Total	1,065,852[a]
Operating Profit	21,691[a]
Nonoperating Income (Rentals)	700
Net Income	
Before Taxes	22,391[a]
Provision for Taxes	n.a.
Profit (Loss) after Taxes	n.a.
Stockholder Equity[b]	$ (108,760)
Operating Ratio[c]	98.0 %

n.a. -- not available.

[a] Excludes aircraft leasing and overhaul charges of about $312,000 (3,120 a/c hours x $100 per hour). These charges were "waived" by the owners of TCA's aircraft in return for a $150,000 personal promissory note from TCA's president. Thus, $150,000 appears to approximate the actual market value of these excluded charges.

[b] As of March 31, 1964.

[c] Total operating expenses divided by net operating revenues (times 100). Adding $150,000 to operating expenses yields a ratio of 111.8%.

Sources:

    U.S. Federal Aviation Agency, Western Region:
      Monthly Air Carrier Aircraft and Engine Utilization, Trans Califor-
        nia Airlines (May 1963-Mar. 1964).
      L. A. Mudgett, President of TCA, Letter to the FAA (dated May 27,
        1964), Exhibits A and B.

    Conversation with Mr. L. A. Mudgett, May 24, 1965.

SELECTED FINANCIAL DATA, OPERATING RATIO & RETURN ON PROPRIETOR EQUITY
MERCER ENTERPRISES, 1964 & 1965

Item	1964	1965
Operating Revenues		
Passenger	$ 69,258	$ 65,906
Charter & Freight	58,467	66,274
Military Contract	0	44,991
Total	127,725	177,171
Operating Expenses		
Operations & Maintenance	60,377	108,025
Ground	2,524	7,901
Taxes	5,707	6,581
Administration & General	15,333[a]	16,144[a]
Depreciation	3,226	40,869
Total	87,167[a]	179,520[a]
Operating Profit (Loss)	40,558	(2,349)
Nonoperating Income/Expense		
Capital Gains	3,561	16,053
Miscellaneous Income	79	6,576
Interest Expense	6,199	7,938
Net Income		
Before Taxes	$ 37,999[b]	$ 12,342[b]
Proprietor Equity[c]	$ 35,980	$ 48,935
Operating Ratio[d]	77.6 %	108.1 %
Return on Proprietor Equity[e]	72.3 %	0.7 %

[a]Does not include any charge for the manager's (owner's) salary.

[b]As a sole proprietorship, taxes for this firm depend on the owner's personal tax status. Since information regarding Mr. Mercer's tax status was not available, after tax profits could not be determined.

[c]As of December 31.

[d]Total operating expenses (increased by $12,000 estimated salary of the owner/manager) divided by total operating revenues (times 100).

[e]Net income before taxes (reduced by $12,000 estimated salary of the owner/manager) divided by proprietor equity (times 100).

Source:

California Public Utilities Commission, Ex. No. 5 (submitted Aug. 9, 1966), Tables Nos. 1 & 3, Application No. 48157.

Appendix No. 16(F)

SELECTED FINANCIAL DATA, OPERATING RATIO & RETURN ON STOCKHOLDER EQUITY
PACIFIC SOUTHWEST AIRLINES, VARIOUS YEARS 1950-1965

Item	1950	1955	1956	1957	1958	1959
Operating Revenues						
Passenger	n.a.	n.a.	n.a.	$2,786,658	$3,516,452	$4,331,552
Freight	n.a.	n.a.	n.a.	5,492	5,809	7,717
Contract & Other Flight	n.a.	n.a.	n.a.	0	11,715	15,315
Other (principally fuel)	n.a.	n.a.	n.a.	334,104	395,945	421,409
Total	$505,988[d]	$1,587,697	$2,264,850	3,126,254	3,929,921	4,775,993
Operating Expenses						
Operations	n.a.	n.a.	n.a.	1,521,151	1,863,880	2,158,276
Maintenance	n.a.	n.a.	n.a.	494,034	530,007	633,897
Selling & Administration	n.a.	n.a.	n.a.	489,279	612,877	730,102
Obsolescence & Depreciation	n.a.	109,712	127,280	222,615	260,545	344,940[e]
Total	489,939[d]	1,523,385	2,144,385	2,727,079	3,267,309	3,867,215
Operating Profit	16,049[d]	64,312	120,465	399,175	662,612	908,778
Nonoperating Income/Expense						
Interest Income	n.a.	0	0	0	0	0
Interest Expense	n.a.	2,465	21,877	37,569	30,581	33,177
Capital Gain (after taxes)	n.a.	206,150	0	0	0	0
Net Income						
Before Taxes	n.a.	267,997	98,588	361,606	632,031	875,601
Reported Income Taxes	n.a.	24,000	40,000	165,000	310,000	419,700
Profit after Taxes	n.a.	$ 243,997	$ 58,588	$ 196,606	$ 322,031	$ 455,901
Stockholder Equity[a]	n.a.	n.a.	n.a.	$ 86,550	n.a.	$1,057,609
Operating Ratio[b]	96.8 %	95.9 %	94.7 %	87.2 %	83.1 %	81.0 %
Return on Stockholder Equity[c]	n.a.	n.a.	n.a.	227.2 %	n.a.	43.1 %

336

Appendix No. 16(F) (continued)

Item	1960	1961	1962	1963	1964	1965
Operating Revenues						
Passenger	$7,545,309	$ 9,657,650	$13,915,999	$17,451,572	$20,473,095	$22,947,457
Freight	27,848	45,522	54,721	68,528	95,215	329,869[i]
Contract & Other Flight	75,786	111,870	59,361	0	0	475,000[i]
Other (principally fuel)	481,540	485,251	174,834	332,348	205,062	262,935
Total	8,130,483	10,300,293	14,204,915	17,852,448	20,773,372	24,015,261
Operating Expenses						
Operations	3,473,418	3,938,057	4,511,600	5,488,512	6,191,146	8,830,496
Maintenance	1,717,798	1,957,978	2,282,141	2,727,471	3,349,171	3,722,766
Selling & Administration	1,361,630[f]	1,613,508	2,001,597	2,522,740[h]	2,890,463	3,344,322
Obsolescence & Deprec.	1,556,842[f]	1,663,573	1,991,841[g]	2,161,686[h]	2,396,653	3,707,600
Total	8,109,688	9,173,116	10,803,179	12,900,409	14,827,433	19,605,184
Operating Profit	20,795	1,127,177	3,401,736	4,952,039	5,945,939	4,410,077
Nonoperating Income/Expense						
Interest Income	0	0	0	74,029	123,459	35,415
Interest Expense	19,996	441,694	557,966	339,349	243,517	796,560
Capital Gain (after tax)	0	0	0	0	0	0
Net Income						
Before Taxes	799	685,483	2,843,770	4,686,719[h]	5,825,881	3,648,932
Reported Income Taxes	300	375,000	1,475,000[g]	2,435,000[h]	2,880,000	1,614,000
Profit after Taxes	$ 499	$ 310,483	$ 1,368,770	$ 2,251,719	$ 2,945,881	$ 2,034,932
Stockholder Equity[a]	n.a.	n.a.	$ 3,007,734	$ 7,429,810	$10,075,046	$11,504,770
Operating Ratio[b]	99.7 %	89.1 %	76.1 %	72.3 %	71.4 %	81.6 %
Return on Stock. Equity[c]	0.0 %	n.a.	45.5 %	30.3 %	29.2 %	17.7 %

337

n.a. -- not available.

[a]As of December 31.

[b]Total operating expenses divided by total operating revenues (times 100).

[c]Profit after taxes divided by stockholder equity (times 100).

[d]This figure appears to pertain to air transport service only.

[e]Includes $83,112 in leasing charges for Electra aircraft subsequently purchased.

[f]Includes $1,258,292 in leasing charges for Electra aircraft subsequently purchased.

[g]In 1962, PSA accounted for $100,000 in investment tax credits by reducing reported income taxes and increasing obsolescence and depreciation expenses by this amount. These adjustments have been eliminated in this appendix. It is believed that this improves the comparability of the 1962 data with that for 1964 and 1965, and with that of the published income statements of the certificated carriers.

[h]In 1963, PSA accounted for $55,000 in investment tax credits by reducing reported income taxes and increasing obsolescence and depreciation expenses by this amount. See footnote g, above.

[i]Estimated by allocating $804,469 of "Other flight revenue, principally training" between flight training revenues (see Prospectus, March 29, 1966, p. 10) and freight. This was done under the assumption that little or no other contract operations were conducted during 1965.

Sources:

California Public Utilities Commission:
PSA, Application No. 39172 (filed June 22, 1957), Ex. A, p. 1.
PSA, Ex. No. 3 (submitted Sept. 16, 1960), Application No. 42253. This exhibit consists of a report prepared by C. R. Considine, CPA. Ex. No. 2 of that report was used for this appendix.
K. G. Friedkin, President of PSA, letter to PUC (dated Mar. 19, 1951), Statement No. 1, contained in Ex. No. 20, Case No. 5271.

E. F. Hutton, Prospectus, Pacific Southwest Airlines (Feb. 13, 1963), pp. 3, 4, 24, 25 & 28; and (Mar. 29, 1966), p. 10.

PSA, Annual Report, 1963, 1964, 1965 and 1966.

PSA, Listing Application to New York Stock Exchange, A-22453 (Apr. 19, 1965), p. 11.

Appendix No. 17

TOTAL NUMBER OF EMPLOYEES FOR TOTAL TRUNK AND LOCAL SERVICE CARRIERS,
CALIFORNIA CENTRAL AIRLINES, WESTERN AIR LINES, PACIFIC AIR LINES
AND PACIFIC SOUTHWEST AIRLINES, 1949-1965

| Year | Total Number of Employees | | | | | |
| | Trunk[a] | | Local Service[a] | | California | Intrastate |
	Total	Western	Total	Pacific	CCA	PSA
1949	56,031	1,250[b]	3,209	274	n.a.	n.a.
1950	57,295	1,288[b]	3,941	256	194[c]	n.a.
1951	67,150	1,470[b]	4,804	305	n.a.	120[d]
1952	73,394	1,646	5,409	354	n.a.	n.a.
1953	77,893	1,811	5,860	334	n.a.	n.a.
1954	77,835	1,871	6,015	293	206[e]	n.a.
1955	87,901	2,129	6,622	386	–	115[f]
1956	99,310	2,336	7,584	425	–	n.a.
1957	108,210	2,793	8,567	476	–	172[g]
1958	107,857	2,558	9,308	577	–	n.a.
1959	117,755	2,956	11,437	691	–	220[h]
1960	118,189	2,733	12,470	742	–	n.a.
1961	120,005	2,784	13,479	658	–	n.a.
1962	119,787	3,065	14,760	736	–	450[i]
1963	124,174	3,461	15,414	693	–	475[j]
1964	132,734	4,041	16,221	761	–	500[k]
1965	147,036	4,328	17,826	814	–	740[l]

n.a. -- not available.

[a]Domestic operations only. From 1949 through 1955 these data represent an average of the number of persons employed at the beginning and end of the payroll period ending nearest December 15. For subsequent years these data represent the number of full- and part-time employees, permanent and temporary, during the pay period ended nearest December 15.

[b]Includes Inland Air Lines merged with Western on April 10, 1952.

[c]As of December 1950 or early January 1951.

[d]As of January 21 February 1, 1952.

[e]As of January 16-31, 1955. Includes all persons employed by Airline Transport Carriers as well as California Central Airlines.

[f]As of July 1955.

[g]As of September 1957.

339

[h]As of early December 1959.

[i]As of February 1963.

[j]As of October 1963.

[k]As of early December 1964.

[l]As of late August 1965. In April 1965, PSA employed 575 persons.

Sources:

U.S. Civil Aeronautics Board,
Handbook of Airline Statistics (1961 ed.), pp. III-26, III-31,
  & III-44; (1967 ed), pp. 87, 155 & 164.

U.S. District Court, Southern District of Calif., files of the Court
Clerk for Bankruptcies Nos. 59560-PH, Airline Transport Carriers,
and 59561-PH, California Central Airlines, "First Report and
Accounting of Trustee, Petition to Pay Expenses of Administration,
and Petition for Order that Estate Remain Open for Further Administration," (filed May 24, 1955).

U.S. Federal Aviation Agency, Western Region, "Special Inspection
of Pacific Southwest Airlines," (Jan. 21-Feb. 1, 1952).

Air Transport Association of America, Comparative Statement of Number
of Employees and Average Annual Salaries by Account Classification
(Dec. 31, 1949 and 1950).

Aviation Week, Vol. 54, No. 1 (Jan. 1, 1951), p. 62.

San Diego Union (July 28, 1955), p. A-26; (Sept. 22, 1957), p. B-5;
(Dec. 5, 1959), p. A-10; & (Aug. 31, 1965), p. A-19.

E. F. Hutton, Prospectus, Pacific Southwest Airlines (Feb. 13, 1963),
p. 11; & (Oct. 24, 1963), p. 10.

Pacific Southwest Airlines, Listing Application to New York Stock
Exchange, A-22453 (Apr. 19, 1965), p. 7.

Index

Accidents, fatal, 19, 21, 50-51, 179, 238-39. *See also* Safety
Agreements: and cartel problems, 6-7, 70, 72, 228; enforcement of, 9-10 n, 70, 155, 228; equipment interchange, 34 n; and increased PUC regulation, 243-44
Air California, 131 n
Aircraft: effects of CAB regulation on, 55-56, 224-25, 230-31 n, 232; inputs, 211-13, 220; pressurized, 38-40; productive lives of, 209-10, 223; proposed purchasing company for, 231-32 n; purchases of, encouraged, 230; and other capital inputs, 211; and output per employee, 220; turbine-powered, 40-44
—types: introduced, by carrier group, 53; efficient number of, 193 n; number operated, 221 n; and operating ratios, 186-91, 193
—utilization: differences in, 210; intensity of, 197-210, 221, 223; and social costs, 238-39
Airline regulation. *See* CAB regulation; PUC regulation; Regulation
Airlines. *See* Carriers
Airline Transport Carriers, 20-21, 81, 181-82
Airports: California airline, 27; number of, served, 25-26
Air-Shuttle fares. *See* Coach fares: Air-Shuttle
Air Taxi operators, 14 n
Air Traffic Conference, 70, 228
Air Transport Association, 43 n, 70, 222, 228, 231
Alchian, A. A., cost theory of, 222-223 n
Allegheny Airlines, 17 n, 20, 238

American Airlines, 104-106, 136
Available seat-miles: by carrier class, 39; defined, 29; per employee, 213-16; growth in, 29; percent of, by carrier class, 30-31; theoretical shortcomings of, 29-30 n
—produced in: coach service, 45-47; pressurized aircraft, 38-40; turbine-powered aircraft, 40-44

Bankruptcy: as means of exit, 18, 20-21, 23, 32; and social costs, 238; and uneconomic operations, 181-84
Bernstein, M. H., 5 n
Blatz Airlines, 22, 28, 131-32 n
Bonanza Air Lines, 17 n, 47, 69
Braniff Airways, 48

California Arrow, 19, 50-51, 239
California Central Airlines (CCA): and Airline Transport Carriers, 20-21, 81; bankruptcy and low fares, 181; CAB influence over, 80-81; and California Coastal Airlines, 20, 83; and economies of scale, 193; employees, number of, 214; employees per aircraft, number of, 212-13; entry of, 18, 78; exit of, 20, 181; fare increase of, 80-82; fares and traffic density of, 122, 132; inauguration of coach service of, 18, 28, 78, 131-32 n; income statements of, 183-84; investment rate of return of, 183; load factors of, 120; location of, operating base, 174; operating ratios of, 183-84; output per employee of, 214-20; passengers, on-line O & D, 119-20; pricing practices of, 118-22;